PHILOSOPHICAL EXPLORATIONS

Edited by George Kimball Plochmann

Spinoza on Nature

JAMES COLLINS

FOREWORD BY
GEORGE KIMBALL PLOCHMANN

SOUTHERN ILLINOIS UNIVERSITY PRESS

CARBONDALE AND EDWARDSVILLE

Library of Congress Cataloging in Publication Data

Collins, James Daniel.
  Spinoza on nature.

  (Philosophical explorations)
  Bibliography: p.
  Includes index.
  1. Spinoza, Benedictus de, 1632–1677.   2. Philosophy
of nature—History—17th century.   I. Title. II. Series.
B3999.N34C64   1984   113'. 092'4   83–20125
ISBN 0–8093–1160–7

Printed in the United States of America

Designed by The Bookworks, Inc./Frank O. Williams

87 86 85 84   4 3 2 1

To Elinor Collins
and
To Jean, Robert, and John Potter

Contents

Foreword

OF THE TWO MAJOR SYSTEMS of shorthand developed in English-speaking countries in the past century and a half, that inaugurated by Isaac Pitman attempts to represent in a line all the successive consonantal sounds of a word, leaving most of the vowels as a kind of afterthought, to be indicated by secondary dots and dashes. The Gregg system, on the other hand, commences a long word with both consonants and vowels quite fully indicated in a single complex flourish, often giving mere hints of the later syllables of the word. *Spinoza on Nature* makes brilliant use of the Gregg plan, for in this book we are afforded an analysis, painstaking and profound, of the great insight which is the starting point of Spinoza's philosophy, while the later materials of that philosophic system are made clear chiefly as they have direct relation to that insight. Spinoza's principle itself is compound: that God necessarily exists and is identical with the whole of nature, that God is conceived by us in two parallel ways, through thought and extension, and that these are expressed in modes. What Dr. Collins has accomplished not only is a masterly exposition of this triple conception traced through all of Spinoza's writings, but is also a serious consideration of the possible rightness of the principle and its implications in the generating of an entire system of philosophy. The most casual reader of that system knows that it includes theories of the living body, of knowledge, of the emotions both passive and active, of human blessedness, of man's religious nature and his hopes for a union with God, and finally of the formation of communities in which the practice of the virtues becomes more than a mere possibility.

For all practical purposes, the earliest generation of serious American studies of Spinoza commenced about fifty years ago with the publication of Richard McKeon's and Harry Austryn Wolfson's books, both excellent but very different from each other. The first of these sought to expound the unity of Spinoza's thought, while the second was erected on the premise that the *Ethics* could be traced to a hundred early and not always compatible sources, biblical, Aristotelian, medieval Hebraic and Arabic, and finally Cartesian, with consequent gaps and dislocations appearing here and there, even in the finished treatise. Subsequent studies of Spinoza have generally pursued one or the other line of approach, either taking Spinoza as a successful builder of a system or else asserting that he failed to blend all his opinions, borrowed or new, into a unity more than merely stylistic. The present book throws a great weight into the scales on the side of the conceptual unity, for its author not only finds coherence within each of the works, running from Spinoza's textbookish exposition of the philosophy of Descartes all the way to the unfinished *Tractatus Politicus,* but also points out that *between* all these books there is a consistency of treatment, the leading insight never having been forgotten or consciously abandoned by Spinoza, only clarified and reapplied.

The literature on each of the major philosophers in history is by now very large, so large that one man can scarcely be expected to conquer it all, and this is expecially true of the writings early and late, long and short, that have taken Spinoza as their subject. Dr. Collins's own contribution is unusual in its combining of a clearheaded critical faculty with a wholehearted willingness to give full due to the philosopher's solutions. Three, four, five, six possible meanings of leading terms are proposed, weighed, and assigned, and like numbers of tightly inferred conclusions are set forth following upon such interpretations. Many of these implications are new or at least not standard fare in the literature, and Spinoza emerges not as an eclectic or as a simple romantic, an intoxicated mystic, but as a highly independent thinker calling relentlessly upon his own powers of intuition, reason, and—occasionally—imagination to solve the most perplexing questions involving God, man, and society.

If you ask whether Professor Collins has dealt with all of Spinoza's philosophy, the answer is both no and yes; no because the avowed aim of this book is to examine Spinoza's novel (and heretical) view of God as nature; and yes because this is infused into everything else that Spinoza has to say in physics, physiology, psychology, spriptural exegesis and its social consequences, and political theory. The author scrutinizes the Latin and Dutch texts very closely, viewing them also in the light of modern debates and dialectical excursions. He shows how Spinoza strikes a delicate balance between man's relation to the infinite God, on the one hand, and man's relation to various finite modes, including other men and societies at large, on the other. It becomes clear toward the end of the book that in this system there can be no exclusively metaphysical problem, no exclusively epistemological problem, and no purely moral problem. The three kinds are fused; they are analytically different but not really diverging aspects of the same considerations of reality, knowledge, and action. For Spinoza to have created a philosophy of the whole which yet retains its articulations of parts was a signal contribution to the history of thought. And for a book written in our time to explicate fully, deliberately, and clearly this contribution is itself an important addition to the scholarly thinking of the late twentieth century.

George Kimball Plochmann

Southern Illinois University at Carbondale

Preface

FOR THE PURPOSE OF READY RECALL, we often associate a tag line with a philosopher's thought. In the case of Spinoza, the most common identifying phrase is "God or nature," to which is often added the formula "naturing nature and natured nature." These quotations are authentic enough, in the sense that they are drawn from Spinoza's own writings and are given some prominence by him. But the meaning they have for him is not immediately apparent from the words. "God or nature" seems to affirm a strict equivalence, an identification between the reality of God and that of nature. Yet this does not square readily with Spinoza's many warnings against equating God with every valid and important meaning of nature. Indeed, a major function of "naturing nature and natured nature" is to alert us to some distinctions that prevent any such outright equation. What we take initially to be easy category phrases turn out, upon reflection, to be carriers of a complicated line of reasoning concerning nature.

My aim in this book is to probe Spinoza's thoughts on nature, sorting out some chief meanings and showing their main systemic relationships. Nature is one of the master themes in his philosophy, permeating every corner and coloring every particular problem and conclusion. It is not possible to read very far into a passage without encountering either an explicit treatment of some aspect of the problem of nature or an implicit use of a facet of Spinoza's reflection thereon. There is a mutual relation, such that the master theme of nature supplies a broad frame of reference for treating regional issues, which in turn help to deepen and differentiate the doctrine on nature.

This reciprocity affects my own procedure. I give central attention to those texts that deal formally and fundamentally with the question of nature. Spinoza gradually builds up a working context of nature theory, which brings coherent unity to his handling of problems throughout the wide band of philosophizing. There is a definite limit in my choice of more particular arguments for analysis. I try to concentrate upon some problems where the impact of the Spinozan conception of nature is most strongly felt. And my interpretation of these places confines itself to a study of how the view of nature gets incorporated and better articulated in the specific course of reasoning. This governing intent leads to an emphasis upon certain conceptual and linguistic features which are visibly marked by Spinoza's persistent concern with nature theory.

Every general account of his philosophy seeks to elucidate the *Ethics,* and the present study is no exception to this rule. Chapters Five and Six offer a nature-reading of the *Ethics.* The task is postponed until that point, however, in order to understand the careful preparatory moves that Spinoza makes elsewhere. He presupposes our acquaintance with four basic developments, an appreciation of which enables us to approach the *Ethics* with better-informed minds. Chapter One examines those points in his negative and positive evaluation of Descartes and current authors of university textbooks that begin to demarcate his own position on nature. Chapters Two and Three study the *Short Treatise* from the standpoint of its radical transformation of the concepts of God and man, as they are submitted to the naturization process. What sea changes this same process introduces into logic, reconceived as the instrument for gaining speculative and practical knowledge of nature, is the burden of Chapter Four on Spinoza's *Emendation.*

Just as all the feeder roads lead into the *Ethics,* so do all the prolonging branch roads lead out from it. Chapter Seven traces the nature-regulated transforming of several primary religious ideas, as proposed in the *Theological-Political Treatise.* And Chapter Eight resets the *Political Treatise* in the main line of the community relationships found within all aspects of nature. In the concluding chapter, I attempt to thematize some persistent elements in the Spinozan conception of nature as here set forth.

Two matters of usage indicate two corresponding limits placed upon this present study. I use the term *Spinozan* to refer to Spinoza's own writings and thought, as herein interpreted. The word *Spinozistic* concerns subsequent philosophies that have been influenced, in one way or another, by Spinoza. Except incidentally, I do not enter into the intricate and fascinating story of the various Spinozistic and anti-Spinozistic philosophies. The second point is that I refrain from categorizing Spinoza's thought as a form of "naturalism." This term is not inaccurate, but it raises the question of what kind of naturalism is meant. I prefer to have the distinctively Spinozan meaning emerge gradually from an examination of the naturizing process, the argument of the *Ethics,* and the prolongation into religious and social spheres. Only at the end, then, does it become informative to speak about (if one cares to do so) Spinoza's naturalism.

The source text used here is *Spinoza Opera,* edited by Carl Gebhardt. It is at present the best available edition, from which I translate all quotations from Spinoza. The closer a translation remains to the original text, the more clearly it brings out Spinoza's unceasing concern with the problem of nature and with the principles and arguments needed for treating of nature in its manifold aspects. His theory of nature emerges only cumulatively from the contributions made by each of his writings examined in this study.

Finally, it gives me pleasure to acknowledge the aid given by several persons. Professor Marianne Childress, Chairman of the Department of Philosophy at Saint Louis University, kindly supported the preparation of the typescript. George Kimball Plochmann, Professor of Philosophy, Emeritus, Southern Illinois University at Carbondale, read the manuscript meticulously, made many useful suggestions, and wrote the helpful Foreword. Above all, I am indebted to my wife Yvonne Collins. At every stage of the work, she has given efficient and cheerful assistance. I am immeasurably grateful for her help and companionship throughout the years.

Saint Louis University   JAMES COLLINS
January 1984

Spinoza on Nature

CHAPTER ONE

Critique of Cartesian Nature

AT THE VERY OUTSET, it is well to notice Spinoza's own attitude toward writing. He established a close bond between his vocations as a personal teacher and as a writer. These two activities modified and supported each other, so that he did not feel comfortable unless there was an interplay between them. Spinoza was a man of the speaking word as well as of the book. Thereby, his Jewish heritage blended both with Aristotle's observation that a truly wise man communicates his thought by teaching and with the modern technology which makes a printed book out of a prepared manuscript. The oral, literate, and print media fused beneficially in his life's work.

A major reason why Spinoza settled with Collegiant groups of Dutch dissenters was their cultivation of wide-ranging questions and free discussions.[1] They provided a social milieu where he quietly developed his own thought. He could test it through their sharp queries in conversation and correspondence and could even begin to observe its repercussions among study groups in the wider world. Friendly pressure was exerted upon him to commit his arguments to writing. He discreetly circulated sections of his manuscripts among eager discussants, even when these sections were still tentative portions of some as yet unfinished treatise.

The serious reception of his views by Dutch intellectuals did more than encourage Spinoza's general inclination toward sustained written argumentation. It also specifically branded his written efforts with four marks. His writings showed: a sensitivity to other positions and the need to reinterpret or refute them; a thoroughly exploratory and revisionary approach toward his own work, whatever his tight format or close reasoning; a habit of working on several projects at once; and an openness to specific occasions of composition, such as he noticed in Maimonides and Descartes. Thus Spinoza became a philosophical writer of a distinctive breed. He used scholia and appendices to search out the crannies and

explain the springs of his opponents' positions; he always kept an eye
open for the systematic consequences elsewhere for any thesis he presently espoused; he often held back on publishing, out of intellectual
concerns as well as prudential ones; and he combined love for the eternal
with an intense awareness of a philosopher's responsibilities concerning
practical issues of his own time. Any characterization of Spinoza the
teacher and writer must bear all these aspects in mind and hence must be
unavoidably complex and tensional.

One such tension concerned the balance between the degree of privacy
required for maintaining Spinoza's own freedom and integrity of
philosophizing, and the degree of public statement required by the human
community at large and more particularly by the confusing conditions in
the Holland of his day. Some of that confusion arose at university centers
which were uncertain about how to reconcile the new philosophy of
Descartes with their traditional philosophical and theological sources.
Hence, during his years at Rijnsburg near Leiden University, Spinoza did
some tutoring of students in Cartesian thought—an extension of his discussions beyond the more congenial circle of his friends. At the insistence
of the latter, however, he published *Part I and II of René Descartes'
Principles of Philosophy, Demonstrated in a Geometrical Manner,* along
with the appended *Metaphysical Thoughts* (1663). This book gained him
the reputation of being a thorough student and independent appraiser of
Descartes and led in 1673 to an invitation to a professorship at Heidelberg
University. His refusal of this post was based partly on the conviction—
shared with Bacon and Descartes before him—that intellectual creativity
had fled the university centers. But it also stemmed from Spinoza's highly
developed sense of intellectual freedom, his awareness that the academic
and civil establishments would resist his developing views on nature and
God, politics and religion.

The present chapter examines *Descartes' Principles* and *Metaphysical
Thoughts* for what they tell us about Spinoza's early conception of nature.
Because of their largely expository stance toward Descartes and school
manuals, these writings provoke the preliminary question of whether they
convey *anything* about the Spinozan notion of nature. Once this matter is
affirmatively determined, we can then discover how much Spinoza reveals about his own position in the course of criticizing the Cartesian
teaching on nature. Although our procedure is therefore unavoidably
indirect, it serves to demarcate the Spinozan position and prepare for his
new philosophical way of thinking about nature.

1. Achieving Philosophical Distance

Spinoza aimed at bringing his writing projects eventually into publishable form. But the saving adverb *eventually* was intended to preserve his freedom of variation and revision, his judgment that a manuscript was not sufficiently reworked to give an accurate public expression to his current reflections and arguments on a specified topic. His sense of responsible authorship usually led him to leave some projects incomplete, to delay others until they attained the proper form or until circumstances favored their publication, and, in any case, to refrain from brashly rushing into print for its own sake. It is this attitude of self-critical development and controlled communication, rather than foolish bravado, which shines through his remark: "I do not presume that I have found the best philosophy; but I do know that I understand the true one."[2]

In the case of his *Descartes' Principles,* however, Spinoza did feel that his hand was being forced into premature publication. Of course, he recognized that his careful analysis of the leading thinker of the age would subsequently encourage a favorable reception of his own philosophy. But his recasting here of Descartes' *Principles of Philosophy* in a geometrical form did not sharply distinguish between exposition, criticism, and some degree of original Spinozan philosophizing. Spinoza included all three elements, conjoined in unequal measure, in his *Descartes' Principles.* The situation was only compounded by the fact that, both in this main work and in the Appendix of *Metaphysical Thoughts,* the key terms were being used sometimes in their school-manual and Cartesian senses and sometimes in an already distinctively Spinozan meaning which was not fully spelled out and justified. Indeed, in 1663, Spinoza was still very deeply engaged with his friends in basic doctrinal and methodological discussions which affected the written formulations of his own theory of nature.

Drastic steps had to be taken, therefore, to avoid confusion and to make *Descartes' Principles* a constructive phase of his own work. Hence, he arranged for a preface that would furnish interpretive guidance to readers not involved in his more intimate discussion circles. This preface was written by Dr. Lodewijk Meyer, physician, philosophical discussant and correspondent with Spinoza, and a prime mover for getting Spinoza to prepare his treatment of Descartes for publication. Under Spinoza's close supervision, Meyer distinguished carefully between Descartes' doctrine, Spinoza's reworking of Cartesian philosophy, and Spinoza's own position on a number of specific topics. Also (as a recently discovered letter from Spinoza to Meyer establishes), Spinoza wanted his friend to undertake a careful examination of the main text and its appendix in order to make the work as free as possible from theological entanglements. With Meyer's help, then, Spinoza did all he could toward keeping misunderstandings and misattributions at a minimum, once granted that the project itself was to be carried through to publication.[3]

Given these complications, cautious scholars have followed the policy of making only a confirmatory and supplementary use of *Descartes' Principles* and *Metaphysical Thoughts*. Texts are taken from these sources only when they agree with Spinoza's doctrine as elsewhere expressed, or when they clarify notions and schematic divisions coming under his criticism. This rule is safe enough to follow, but it is insufficient for catching additional shades of meaning in these writings. In line with the long tradition of philosophical commentaries, Spinoza intends not only to show his mastery *of* a major source but also to establish some creative distance *from* it through subdued criticisms and hints of new positions. How he achieves this liberating distance, in preparation for his own theory of nature, can be ascertained through direct study of the preface and (in the rest of this chapter) the body of the work itself.

Meyer's preface does prepare us for Spinoza's intimate yet independent reading of Descartes.[4] One unobtrusive point is that, although the work is formally a restructuring of Descartes' *Principles of Philosophy,* it also takes into account several Cartesian positions set forth in the *Discourse on Method,* the *Meditations on First Philosophy,* and the *Replies to Objections* raised against the *Meditations.* To know that Spinoza keeps this broader horizon in mind is important for my purpose, because some of Descartes' most explicit statements on the meanings and relations of nature are set forth in these other books. Commensurately, Spinoza's criticisms of the Cartesian theory of nature are intended to apply to that theory in its fuller exposition, not solely to its presentation in the particular work under comment.

Another consideration is the genetic order in which Spinoza worked out his reformulation of Cartesian thought. Because he lacked confidence in the intelligence and discretion of his student Casearius, Spinoza tutored him primarily in Part II and the beginning of Part III of Descartes' *Principles of Philosophy,* while merely sketching some metaphysical positions involved therein. The enthusiastic Meyer then urged Spinoza to flush out his tutorial notes on Part II, to complete his treatment of Part III, and, above all, to add his presentation of the metaphysical Part I. In the published *Descartes' Principles,* Spinoza did indeed treat Parts I and II at length, but left the third part incomplete and remained silent on Part IV.

This matter may seem to be only of bioliterary significance, until we attend to the content of the four parts of Descartes' book under discussion.

Part II of the *Principles of Philosophy* deals with the principles of material things, or with the bodily universe generally considered. The nature of matter or body is determined according to the Cartesian meaning of corporeal substance and extension, as governing the laws of nature and rules of motion in the one material universe. During his stay at Rijnsburg, Spinoza felt that he could deal most confidently in public forum with the philosophy of physical nature set forth in these general propositions. His task as commentator was to explicate them, indicate some particular points already shown by scientific advance to be untenable (such as the sixth law of impact), and add that some metaphysical aspects required fuller consideration elsewhere.

Among these underlying topics were the metaphysical meaning of substance and nature, God and causality, truth and mind-body union in man. Quite properly, Descartes had included them in Part I of his treatise. They also constituted the main problems currently being rethought by Spinoza in his discussion groups and exploratory manuscripts. Since he held some radically different views from Descartes on these complex questions and was still engaged in elaborating and unifying his own positions, Spinoza was understandably reluctant to treat in print the first part of the *Principles of Philosophy.* Hence Spinoza's actual commentary in Part I of *Descartes' Principles* contented itself with recasting Cartesian reasoning in the geometrical form used by Descartes himself at the end of his *Replies to Objections II.*[5] Yet even this move obliged Spinoza to reformulate and rearrange the definitions-postulates-axioms-theorems used in his geometrical presentation. These changes really amounted to a severe criticism and transformation of Cartesian foundations, but the full import of the modifications was left implicit. It would have exceeded the intent and bounds of *Descartes' Principles* to have explained the new philosophy fully and in accord with Spinoza's own order of proof.

Meyer was quick to anticipate three difficulties, however, which a Cartesian-trained reader might experience in studying Spinoza's reworking of Part I of *Principles of Philosophy:*

(a) On the methodological side, one might argue that Spinoza's employment of geometrical demonstration could lead only to establishing the truth of Cartesian metaphysics. In reply, Meyer noted that Spinoza's shift from the usual Cartesian analytic procedure to a synthetic one, his restating and reinterpreting of Cartesian axioms, and his independent judgment about what should be proved and how the proof should proceed prevented a simple equation between geometrical form and philosophical truth. This established a wedge of significant difference between the two philosophers. As a good commentator, Spinoza was exhibiting the consequential reasoning behind Descartes' *sententia* and *dogmata*, his stated convictions and firmly-held doctrines. But as for the truth of the matter, Spinoza was operating from *alia via* and *alia fundamenta*, from another way of reasoning and other foundations. In an independent treatise, Spinoza would use his own medium for convincing avid seekers of truth, certitude, and the peak of human cognition. Meyer predicted that the clear outcome would be the acceptance of a philosophy radically different from that of Descartes.

(b) People who were method-blind might be unable, however, to discern the difference between Spinoza the faithful expositor and Spinoza the philosophical innovator. Hence Meyer warned explicitly that his friend did *not* subscribe to the Cartesian meaning of will, freedom, and other aspects of an abstract faculty theory applied to man and God. He also singled out the phrase "this or that exceeds human grasp" as one expressive of Descartes' mind rather than of Spinoza's.[6] Taken together, these differences hinted that the Spinozan view of the relation of nature to man and God was by no means identical with the Cartesian and school-manual schemata being taught in the Dutch universities.

(c) This philosophical divergence about nature became especially prominent in the one issue that Meyer elaborated upon.

> Descartes only supposes, but does not prove, the human mind to be unconditionally thinking substance. Since on the contrary, our author [Spinoza] admits indeed that there is thinking substance in the nature of things, but yet denies that that [substance] constitutes the essence of the human mind, he holds rather that in the same way that extension is determined by no limits, thus also is thinking determined by no limits. Just as the human body is not extension unconditionally but only as determined in a certain mode through motion and rest in accord with the laws of extended nature [*secundum leges naturae extensae*], so also the mind or human soul [Dutch translation reads only: "the human soul"] is not thinking unconditionally but only as determined in a certain mode through ideas in accord with the laws of thinking nature [*secundum leges naturae cogitantis*]. This [mind or human soul] is necessarily concluded to be given, where the human body begins to exist.

This sample of Meyer's prose packed an entire metaphysic behind it, showing how wise Spinoza was to present his own position only indirectly in *Descartes' Principles*. Otherwise, he would have had to offer, besides an explanatory reconstruction of Descartes' opinions and reasonings, an argued presentation of his own thought on substance, on the need to use the human body as a guide in explaining the human mind, and on the relation between laws of nature and determined modes of thinking and extension. Within the context of a critical exposition, however, it was sufficient to arouse interest in the Spinozan meaning of the rather odd terms *natura extensa* and *natura cogitans*. Are they merely designations of the components in man, or do they have a much broader connotation reaching not only to laws of the physical universe but perhaps also, in some fashion, to God?

Meyer's preface also sets us to wondering why Spinoza did not follow the relatively smooth path of completing his comments on Part III, and perhaps moving into Part IV, of *Principles of Philosophy*. This really embodies two distinct questions. Why did he venture even a slight distance into Part III? And why did he nevertheless stop short of rounding off his account of the entire book? For replies, we must turn to Descartes' book itself and notice some broad structural relationships between the Cartesian and Spinozan approaches to nature.

In the last principle (64) of Part II of *Principles of Philosophy*, Descartes declares that geometrical figures, magnitudes, and motions are the only principles needed so that ''all-the-phenomena-of-nature'' (*omnia naturae phaenomena*) can be explained, and so that some of these phenomena can be given demonstrations.[7] Then at the outset of Part III he states the conditions required of a good general hypothesis, so that it can indeed give a reasonable explanation of the orderly genesis of the forms constituting all-the-phenomena-of-nature. This latter phrase is a technical expression covering the general look of things perceivable in the visible universe, including the prevailing appearances on the earth as well as in the heavens. With this claim about geometrical quantity and its comprehensive hypothesis for the material world, Descartes comes to the very limit of his general physics. In turn, Spinoza continues his reformulation just up to this same limit. Thus, he makes only a selective incursion into those early sections of Part III which stipulate the general conditions for an explanatory hypothesis involved in understanding all-the-phenomena-of-nature.

But in the main, Parts III and IV of *Principles of Philosophy* are occupied with particular Cartesian accounts of the solar system and the fixed stars and comets, of quicksilver and nitre and heat, of glass and magnets and tides. Such topics belong within special physics, where

Descartes relies heavily upon likely hypotheses, analogical reasoning, and moral certainty. Descartes admits that he has not determined his mind completely on these matters, partly because a thorough study would involve his theory of the mind-body union in man. In turn, Spinoza refrains from analyzing Cartesian special physics in *Descartes' Principles*. For these sections become particularized and descriptive on topics where Spinoza himself has not yet tested and revised the special hypotheses sufficiently to reach conclusions of his own. For him, such topics belong in that *philosophia naturalis* which he intended to include among the special parts of his own philosophy. His hope of developing that part was never to be realized, although he discussed a few of the issues in correspondence with scientists.

Four significant conclusions emerge from Spinoza's self-limitation. First, he keeps his fundamental theory of nature distinct from, and independent of, that "natural philosophy" which cooperates with scientific research on specialized problems of the world. Were it ever to be completed, such a *philosophia naturalis* would be destined for subordinate incorporation into his plenary system of philosophy. Second, his basic doctrine of nature must include some theory about all-the-phenomena-of-nature. It must show men how to view the latter comprehensively in terms of extension and thought. Third, the general theory of mind and body and the question about the nature and union of the human mind and human body can be, and must be, developed within Spinoza's general conception of nature. Enough about the nature of body and human body is philosophically demonstrable to help constitute the theory of man within the basic reasoning on nature, regardless of how many particular issues are postponed for "natural philosophy." And finally, Spinoza's primary account of nature must contain, as an essential component, a theory about the kinds of human knowing, the methods of developing human knowledge, and the ways of correcting human error. Otherwise, Spinoza could not lead minds toward his general view of nature. Neither could he justify his own interpretation of all-the-phenomena-of-nature and the role of hypotheses and experiments in the scientific study of nature--themes that loom large in Descartes and have a presence in the Dutch university fusion of Cartesian and school-manual versions of "natural philosophy."[8]

2. Cartesian Foundations under Probe

In reworking Descartes' principles, Spinoza does not hesitate to criticize his predecessor's teaching on the method of universal doubt and the Cogito, the idea of God and atheism, as well as some key metaphysical distinctions used by Descartes and the textbook writers. Descartes himself includes these matters within his metaphysics, as furnishing the root and soil from which his philosophy of nature takes its determinate shape. Hence any critical probing of these metaphysical roots by Spinoza cannot but affect the Cartesian philosophy of nature so centrally as to demand its radical revision. And this search for *alia fundamenta* is precisely what Spinoza arouses by introducing a whole cluster of concepts and language-forms about nature which require, for their understanding and coherent use, some new principle of interpretation of nature.

(a) *Universal doubt and the correlate Cogito.* Before clothing his thought in geometrical form, Spinoza begins *Descartes' Principles* with an important prolegomenon written in ordinary prose.[9] Its purpose is both to summarize the exposition of methodic doubt given in Descartes's own *Discourse on Method, Meditations,* and *Principles of Philosophy,* and to suggest an alternative way of philosophizing. Indeed, the need for another way grows out of Spinoza's objections to the claims of philosophical primacy made for the Cartesian method of doubt.

Descartes calls his methodic doubt "hyperbolical," both because its universal scope must be deliberately maintained by an act of will and because the supreme doubt requires an appeal to a deceiving God. But Spinoza regards the doubt as hyperbolical in a more downright sense, namely, because of its strained and ultimately unconvincing nature. He is disposed against any procedure which depends upon treating the human will as a distinct faculty and a supreme expression of mental freedom. Moreover, there is something artificial and unwarrantedly forced about that kind of doubt which would withdraw our existential assent from all beings in nature, including corporeal nature in common (*natura corporea in communi*) and its main properties. This would even involve calling into question mathematical propositions, our own body, and its affirmation of real sensible things. Spinoza is skeptical about whether this sweeping doubt can really be made by men, and made to hold on stronger grounds than acceptance of one's own body, the bodily world, and the total field of nature.

In the prolegomenon, Spinoza treats the Cartesian Cogito in tandem with Cartesian doubt. Objections against the method of doubt inexorably affect the Cogito, since the latter is the strict outcome of following the doubting operation to the point where it must halt at the evidence for our thinking existence (itself the source of the doubting activity). But if universal doubt is a strained exercise--as Spinoza contends--then there is something similarly artificial and attenuated about the Cogito itself. It is methodically denuded of its own human body, its natural surroundings, and its mathematical achievements. Spinoza's criticism centers here upon the Cogito considered precisely as the correlate of Cartesian doubt.

Too great a philosophical burden is placed by Descartes upon his correlate Cogito. It cannot recover the truth of its natural human condition directly, but only through the roundabout route of first proving the existence of a veracious, all-powerful God. This leads to the well known charge of circular reasoning, since Descartes appeals now to the Cogito's clear and distinct perceptions in proof of God, and now to the divine veracity as guarantor of human inference and memory. Spinoza remarks acidly that not everyone is convinced by Descartes' defense against a solipsistic, skeptical view of the Cogito and its inferential scope. The trouble lies in the theory of a correlate Cogito, which reduces its basis in reality too far to make any subsequent expansion of truth beyond its own pinpoint affirmation of itself. Hence Spinoza rejects the Cartesian *tam/quam* (as/as) principle that "whatever is perceived as clearly and distinctly as that [foundation of truth in the Cogito] is true." The Cartesian Cogito is too constricted and frail to support the project of a systematic recovery of the truth about God and nature, man and the sciences.

(b) *The idea of God and the "atheists."* Spinoza now sets about to remove traces of Descartes from the foundation of philosophical truth. Instead of being located in a Cogito generated by the method of universal doubt, it is found in the true idea of God. In *Descartes' Principles,* Spinoza does not present his full doctrine on the true idea of God (which would involve the metaphysical and methodological complexities of his own direct argumentation) but confines himself to its meaning as a clear and distinct concept which we possess.

Even in this limited sense, however, there are sufficient problems to consider, as the following passages testify.

> The pivot of the whole matter is about this sole point, namely, that we can form forth [*efformare*] such a concept of God which so disposes us that it is not equally easy for us to think him to be a deceiver as not to be one, but which forces us to affirm him to be supremely truthful. For where we have formed forth such an idea, that reason [the notion of a deceiving God] for doubting about mathematical truths is removed. For wherever we then turn the mind's focus so as to doubt about some one of those [truths], we hit upon nothing from which we ought not to conclude that that matter is most certain, just as occurs concerning our existence. . . . And provided that we have that [clear and distinct idea of God], howsoever we have acquired it, it will suffice, as is already shown, for removing all doubt. These points being

therefore premised, I respond to the difficulty advanced. We can be certain of no thing, not indeed as long as we are ignorant of God's existence (for of this matter I have not spoken), but as long as we do not have a clear and distinct idea of him. . . . And provided that we do have such an idea of God as I have abundantly shown, we will be able to doubt neither about his existence nor about any mathematical truth.[11]

This carefully nuanced argument deserves to be commented upon.

(i) Spinoza's reticences are as instructive as his overt statements in *Descartes' Principles*. He remains reserved here about two crucial relationships of our idea of God: that to God's existence, and that to man's mind. It will be left for other occasions to determine the relation between God's essence or powerful nature, his existence, and the manner in which the idea of God signifies them. And the precise way in which our mind comes to have, or share in, the idea of God must also be developed elsewhere.

(ii) Yet through use of the verb *efformare,* Spinoza already eliminates the notion that we are passive receptors of the true idea of God. For *efformare* means an active bringing forth, an expressive act of our mind as it forms an idea from and for itself, a process of clarifying and rendering distinct an idea of God emerging from the core dynamism of our mind.

(iii) The cognitive efficacy of the idea of an unconditionally truthful God is also stressed against both Cartesian methodic doubt and skepticism. As a human phenomenon, of course, doubting can occur and can generate the cloudy hypothesis of a deceiving God. But in the presence of the clear and distinct idea of God, such doubting cannot prevail to the point of shaking either our recognition that this is indeed a true idea or our assent to our own existence and to mathematical truths. Spinoza deliberately couples essential, existential, and mathematical objects of true assent. The Cartesian deceiver cannot paralyze our perception of the philosophical foundation in the true idea of God. In turn, the latter undercuts any evidentiary standing for radical skeptical suspension of human judgment and reasoning about God, man, and the universe.

(iv) We cannot overlook the qualifying phrase *not equally easy,* used to deny our indifferent facility for conceiving Spinoza's God as a deceiver or not. This phrase belongs in the same family of words as *greater or less difficulty* and *more or less perfect or good.*[12] They are either meaningless (if implying a comparison between infinite power and nothingness) or too obscure to justify their use in Cartesian axioms. They are relational terms and have their legitimate use only within some relation into which human judgments and valuations enter. In the present context, ''not equally easy" refers to a relation between our conceiving power and the figment of a deceiving God. Spinoza himself often uses such comparative terms as *greater, less, more,* and *insofar as,* but does so only within the relational context of his own metaphysics and ethics of nature. Hence such usage is not regulated directly and unconditionally by a quantifying logic of ease, difficulty, and degree, but comes only *after* such a logic has been reformed by his governing metaphysico-ethical context.

(v) In a subsequent discussion of how the essence of God involves God's necessary, infinite existence or eternity, Spinoza notes that such involvement clearly and distinctly sets off the idea of God from ideas of other things. When this is understood, "no one will be able to doubt whether he has some idea of God (which surely is the primary foundation of human beatitude)."[13] Here is the more ample sense in which the true idea of God is the *primum fundamentum,* the primary foundation of Spinoza's philosophy. By debilitating the method of doubt, it supplants the Cartesian correlate Cogito as the primal ground of metaphysics. It supplies the ultimate basis of certitude for: mathematical truths (which Galileo used to explain the material universe mechanically); our own existence (which Descartes made the cornerstone of his metaphysics of Cogito, God, and the world); and human beatitude (which all men, including moral philosophers, seek under one form or another). Thus Spinoza is indirectly preparing us for a philosophy which maintains an unshakeable nexus between the scientific, metaphysical, and ethical approaches to man. His conception of nature is intended precisely to knit these aims into a unified whole.

Yet a philosophical foundation in the idea of God would seem to be readily vulnerable to the flat assertion that one does not have such an idea. Spinoza was familiar with atheistic declarations and explorers' reports to this effect, as well as with Descartes' reply that the idea of God could be culturally overlaid and obscured but could not be expunged entirely from the human mind. Locke used the anthropological findings to suggest that the idea of God is not innate and is, in any case, open to a wide variation of meanings, some of them unrecognized by Europeans as signifying the divine.

In *Descartes' Principles* Spinoza proposes a somewhat different interpretation which refrains from bringing to bear his metaphysical meaning of our having the idea of God. He concentrates neither upon non-European peoples nor upon philosophical deniers of God's existence, but rather upon those who confess they have no idea of God, even though they claim to worship and love him. They are "atheists" in an accommodated and limited sense only, such as describes the attitude of some fideistic skeptics and nondoctrinaire freethinkers in seventeenth-century Europe.

Spinoza makes four observations on their state of mind. First, they deny having any *idea* of God, and hence it might be better to call them nonideational theists. That they accept the *reality* of God in some sense is conceded in their acts of worship and love. Whether they can worship and love God without having some sort of notion of him is a moot question, but obviously they are dissatisfied by any candidate-meanings with which they are already acquainted.

Second, when we probe into why they deny the idea of God, their replies usually boil down to saying that they can form *no image* of him in their brain (*nullam ejus imaginem in cerebro formare possunt*).[14] Spinoza, Descartes, and a host of other philosophers would concur in denying that we have any cerebral image of God, but would point out that this only sharpens the distinction between an image and an idea of him.

Third, however, the deniers in question may resist all efforts to clarify and refine even their religious meaning of God through the critical use of definitions and explanations of attributes. In this resistive sense, they place themselves beyond the pale of all philosophical inquiries about God and about how our natural reality is related to him. Their real problem may concern the relation of any philosophical idea of God to religious life and revelation, in which case they can be properly termed antiphilosophical theists. Spinoza postpones his examination of this position until his theologico-political work on philosophy and revealed religions.

But finally, Spinoza's humanism never permits him to make a complete break with atheists in any of the meanings offered above. For just as their words of denial cannot arrest the philosophical study of God, so they themselves cannot rightfully be treated ''like a new kind of animals, namely, as midway between men and brutes.'' They cannot be conveniently branded as savage Calibans, but are still human persons having a somehow reachable intelligence. For Spinoza they belong within the order of nature and mankind, which he will not allow to be absolutely fissured even over the question of God and philosophical foundations. The unity of nature holds precedence over any temptation to sanction a split between reasonable men and Caliban opponents.

(c) *Metaphysical distinctions and natural things.* Spinoza scholars rightly make a very guarded use of the short appendix on *Metaphysical Thoughts*. Divided into general and special metaphysics, it informs us about the Cartesian and mid-seventeenth-century Dutch textbook teach-

ing on basic metaphysical terminology, especially as used in the philosophy of God. Thus, it gives invaluable access to current usage of the key
terms which Spinoza himself had to employ in a reformed meaning, again
with special reference to that free-creationist and plurisubstantialist
theism he set about criticizing.

What we do not always recognize, however, is the corrective function
assigned to a reflection on nature, in respect to the chief points of friction.
Thus, in general metaphysics Spinoza's basic criticism of Heereboord and
the teaching establishment is that they are philosophers of mere words and
grammar, "for they judge things from names, but not names from
things."[15] They are concerned mainly with inculcating a memorative
logic and theological grammar. This is seen in their pervasive use of
diagrams and rules of memory for arranging the generic and specific
classes and definitions to which they relentlessly reduce all natural things,
and in terms of which they establish a relation to God.

In Spinoza's estimate, they are the contemporary nominalists in philosophy, becaue they seek to absorb natural realities into universal terms
or entities of reason (which he will later call, more precisely, entities of
imagination). A major feature of the Spinozan revolution is to recenter the
problem of nominalism, not around the recognition or nonrecognition of
universals but around the primacy or nonprimacy of natural things for our
philosophical thinking. When Spinoza remarks, "I am not accustomed to
dispute about names," he is not voicing a careless indifference to linguistic precision. Rather, he makes a deliberate return to the consideration of
things in nature and the regulation of our general defining and reasoning
by the structure and relations of things thus considered.

He makes this reordering toward the reality of nature decisive on two
cognate issues, namely, the distinction between the possible and the contingent, and the relation between the order of nature and God's decree.[16]

(a) The distinction between the possible and the contingent does not
signify some real being, but only a defective use of our understanding in
its study of things. "The possible" means that *we* know a thing's efficient
cause, but do not know whether this cause has been determined actually to
produce the thing. "The contingent" means that *we* consider a particular
thing solely in its own essence, while failing to relate it to its cause. The
only valid signification of these terms is the phenomenological one of
referring to a defective use of *our* perception. Such language does not
convey some additional meaning in the real order, as though the possible
and the contingent were real entities and foundations of our knowledge.

(b) Spinoza traces the above defective use of just-now-described understanding to our deeper failure to relate a natural thing to the integral order of nature, as well as to grasp the manner in which nature depends upon God. It is proper to distinguish really between the thing's existence and its essence. But this distinction does not permit us to divorce the actual cause of its existence from the entire order and series of causes in nature. Within the integral framework of the causal order in nature, a particular cause receives its necessary, actual determination. Since adequate knowledge of a thing includes a reference to the order and series of causes in nature, that knowledge must also involve an affirmation of the orderly causal determination of the particular cause upon which a natural thing depends for its actual existence. Such affirmation rules out any real possibility, distinct from the shortcoming of our own intelligence.

Similarly, the determinate structure of a particular natural thing's own essence does not license us to isolate the essence from its causal connections. Along with all its internal components, the thing enjoys reality only within the matrix of nature and its causal order. To attain an adequate knowledge of the thing's essence, we must view that essence contextually in its real causal connectives in nature. When we do know the essence in its constitutive relations with nature's eternal laws and necessitating causes, we have good grounds for assigning contingency to a defective apprehension of each thing's causal webbing in nature.

Spinoza allows no escape from this nature-matrix analysis of things and their components by appeal to the will and decree of God. Unlike the way in which Descartes views the theistic tradition, he regards the will and decree of God as being just as eternally necessary as God's understanding (if ''will,'' ''decree,'' and ''understanding'' are applied to God at all, for the sake of argument). From eternity, God necessarily wills and decrees the totality of nature with its laws and orderly series of causes. There is no real foundation in nature, described as thus originated and maintained, for the possible and the contingent. From the standpoint of a ''divine will and decree,'' the necessity to exist is not attenuated by distinguishing existence from essence. Whatever distinctions may be drawn, they do not alter the determinate necessity of all things in nature, together with every essential and existential principle in these things. ''Since nothing is more necessary, so that a thing may exist, than that God has decreed that it should exist, it follows that the necessity-of-existing [*necessitatem existendi*] was in all created things from the eternal.''[17] Thus, Spinoza finds a remedy for talk about possibility and contingency by communicating to our otherwise defective understanding some hint of his own teaching on the natural whole and its relation to God.

As the appendix on *Metaphysical Thoughts* moves ahead into special metaphysics, it draws even more heavily upon Spinoza's own theory of nature for a critical basis. Even though his theory cannot there be suitably argued and ordered through its own principles, some of its thought and language do manage to seep into the analysis. Especially concerning the topic of God's understanding and will, Spinoza frequently appeals to his conception of nature for a rectifying standard.

The later sections of *Metaphysical Thoughts* afford at least four striking texts in which this corrective process is observable:[18]

(i) Spinoza invokes his totalizing view of nature to tighten the comparison between the necessity of mathematical relations and that among all natural things. "For if men were to understand clearly the entire order of nature [*totum ordinem naturae*], they would discover that all things are just as necessary as all those matters which are treated in mathematics."

(ii) Lest the stringency of this necessity be relaxed by the Cartesian notion that, in principle, divine freedom can change mathematical truths and laws of nature, Spinoza consolidates the theological topics of divine knowledge and divine decree. "In short, if we attend to the analogy of the whole of nature [*ad analogiam totius naturae*], we can consider it [nature] as one being, and consequently there will be only one idea of God, or decree concerning natured nature," (*de natura naturata*). Reflection on the unity of produced nature enables us to discern the identity between the necessary idea and the divine decree about nature in its produced aspect. This imparts a unifying necessity to all the basic formulas and laws of nature.

(iii) Spinoza permits no escape from the seamless unity and necessity of nature through some divinely revealed additional decrees that might be beamed to us from a supernatural source discontinuous with nature's uniformly necessary, immanent laws. "Moreover, the laws of that [natured] nature are the decrees of God revealed by the natural light. . . . [To say that God acts beyond nature but not against it means that] God has many operational laws which he has not communicated to the human understanding, but which, if they had been communicated to the human understanding, would be just as natural [*aeque naturales*] as the other" operational laws. Hence *all* decrees and laws of divine activity share the same necessity and coherent pattern in the totality of generated nature. Like possibility and contingency, the supernatural signifies the limits of the human mind rather than another sort of reality somehow enjoying freedom from the necessity and unity of nature's laws.

(iv) Throughout this discussion, Spinoza treats man as one of the natural things and hence as subject to all the facets of his theory of nature. Man belongs wholly within, and not in any respect outside of, nature and its general requirements. There is no special crevice opened up even by the qualities of moral action and its language, for this would endanger the unity of produced nature. "The entire natured nature [*tota natura naturata*] is nothing but a unique being: whence it follows that man is a part of nature, which [part] ought to cohere with the rest." Our ought-language expresses the necessary relation of coherence between the human portion and the rest of nature. Hence moral obligation does not fracture the integral necessity of nature but, instead, finds its ground and meaning in the necessary whole of nature itself.

Neither the thought nor the language used here about nature would be entirely unfamiliar to Spinoza's contemporaries. Yet they would wonder about the technical insistency of his usage and his application of concepts on nature to so broad a set of philosophical and theological problems. They would likely surmise that his confident reinterpreting of Descartes and others arose from a quite distinctive outlook on nature, whether still in the making or already established. Thus the readers of *Descartes' Principles* and *Metaphysical Thoughts* could be expected to be somewhat curious and eager to study what Spinoza had to say in his own right. This attitude of receptive interest toward his other philosophical work was precisely what Spinoza hoped to arouse through his first published book. More specifically still, he hoped to predispose inquiring minds to attend carefully to the fresh view of nature which governed his entire critical and reconstructive philosophizing.

3. Cartesian Intimations of Nature

There are two extreme positions to avoid in formulating the relationship between Descartes and Spinoza, both in general and in regard to nature. The first may be called the geometrical-consequence view that Cartesian thought furnishes a group of definitions, axioms, and postulates that Spinoza merely explicates into an organized system of coherent theorems. That this is a simplistic account is shown historically by Spinoza's development of his main convictions prior to his detailed study of Descartes. The Jewish and Greek, Western medieval, and university textbook influences on Spinoza are basic and permanent. Moreover, analysis of *Descartes' Principles,* the *Ethics,* and other writings of Spinoza brings out the radical nature of his criticism of Descartes, which reaches not only to particular Cartesian doctrines but to their fundamental premises as well. There is an encounter here between two highly original minds, neither of which could content itself primarily with spelling out the implications of the other's principles.

Perhaps as a compensating overreaction, another extreme is often proposed: the total-rejection view of how Spinoza relates himself to Descartes. But though the Spinozan criticism cuts deeply, it never degenerates into an indiscriminate, wholesale repudiation of Descartes. Spinoza remains very much aware of what he owes his predecessor for so thoroughly introducing him to the problems, terminology, and leading positions of philosophy in their century. And the detailed argumentation of *Descartes' Principles* and *Metaphysical Thoughts* testifies that the influence went far beyond a preliminary orientation. To appreciate the reasoned relationship of concord and discord between these two philosophers, one must compare their positions in the broad perspective of the theory of nature. From this vantage point, I will examine three functions of Cartesian thought that markedly affect Spinoza's understanding of nature: anticipation, schematization, and systematization:

(a) *Descartes as anticipator.* A careful reader of Descartes would not be completely unprepared for Spinoza's philosophy. There are several hints and difficulties in the French thinker that could be reinterpreted in a manner that would dispose one to give a fair hearing to Spinoza.

The most obvious of these anticipations is the dispositive reference Descartes makes to "God or nature."[19] Although this usage may be pared down by a thousand qualifications, it refuses to die in the process. The phrase is found in numerous medieval sources and later textbooks which are unimpeachably theistic. They explain it in terms of the transcendent God's creation-and-conservation of the natural universe. Descartes himself accepts a causal explanation of this equivalence between God and nature as his manifesting handiwork. Moreover, the actual Cartesian word for *or (aut, ou)* can be taken as meaning, in certain contexts, a disjunction rather than an equivalence. Hence, the exegesis of "God or nature" depends upon what type of causality is established between God and the natural universe, and upon what sorts of contexts are legitimate for determining their relationship. It is through this crucial margin of further argumentation on cause and context that one opening can be made from Descartes to Spinoza. Change the doctrine on divine causality and contextual relationship with the universe, and one then transforms the sense of "God or nature."

Still another passageway develops out of the famous definition of substance given in *Principles of Philosophy:* "a thing which so exists that it needs no other thing for [its] existing."[20] Descartes is visibly dissatisfied with his own definition, because of the ambivalent implications is has for finite things. If they are dependent upon God for their act of existing, then this existential need prevents them from being real substances. But if they are indeed substances, then they exist independently of each other and of God. In order to avoid this alternative of substantial monism versus discrete substantialism, Descartes stipulates that the above definition applies, in an absolutely strict sense, to God alone. Finite things fulfill its meaning only relatively (insofar as mental and bodily substance are existentially independent of each other) and analogically (as being at least dependent upon continuous divine causality). They are relative substances or active existents; but they remain always caused and dependent on God, whose own substantiality is thus not univocally the same as theirs.

It is not difficult to grasp the reason for Descartes' uneasiness about uniting "substance" and "relative." From thence it is only a step to Spinoza's suggestion that "substance" should be construed more rigorously, with no escape hatch left for "relative" cases which destroy its stable meaning. Consequently, in Spinoza's reformed usage, "substance" is reserved for the essentially-existentially-noetically independent being of God, and must be denied to finite things which are dependent nonsubstances.

But Spinoza's criticism of plural finite substances does not blind him to one valuable aspect of the Cartesian approach. In his account of what we can know about the relation between finite things and God, Descartes consistently opposes any philosophical inferences based on final causes. He does so in the face of a longstanding and widespread appeal to design in the world as proof of God's existence and beneficence. His intent is not to weaken human thinking about God but to temper its evidential claims, so that the unsound ones will not infect the sound.

Cartesian antifinalism is both humanistic and theistic. The humanistic motif comes across plainly in the Fourth Meditation, when Descartes is brooding about the causes of error. He wants to show that many errors are of our own making, owing to incaution about the human situation. Even after assuring ourselves of the existence and infinite power of God, we fail to draw some consequences for our limited minds. We keep asking about the "why" and "how" of divine creative activity, although that activity escapes our reach in regard to so many things. Descartes concludes soberly, "It is not without rashness that I think myself competent to inquire into God's purposes."[21] If nothing else will break the habit of

seeking to plumb the divine aims, then epistemological modesty should
do so.

The theistic motivation is prominent in Descartes' replies during an
interview conducted by a Dutch student, Frans Burman. Although this
report was not available to Spinoza, he could have appreciated Descartes'
lively assault upon the anthropomorphic presuppositions behind seeking
out God's purposes in natural events. "We think of God as a sort of
superman, who thinks up such and such a scheme, and tries to realize it by
such-and-such means. This is clearly quite unworthy of God." Here,
Descartes anticipates the frequently expressed Spinozan criticism of imagining God to act like a man. Granted that Spinoza goes on to reject any
affirmation of understanding, will, and mystery in God, he nevertheless
finds a pointer in the arguments mounted by Descartes (and, before him,
by Maimonides) against using the finality principle in our philosophical
theory of God and the world.

A final instance of Descartes' parasceval function in the theory of
nature comes to light in his response to objections that he does not prove
the human soul's immortality. He maintains that his philosophical meditations do show sufficiently the immateriality of our mind and its intrinsic
independence of the body—leaving it for faith to take over from there in
making an affirmation of immortality. But what constitutes fertile ground
for reconsidering Descartes' entire view of the universe is his reluctance
to match the mind's destiny exactly with that of the body. The reason for
his refusal is that, whereas this or that human mind is itself a distinct
substance, this or that correlative human body is a modal collocation of a
single material substance. This strong imbalance between plural finite
thinking substances and the monism of extensive substance furnishes an
incentive for rethinking the entire problem of substance and modes in
nature. Spinoza's countersuggestion now becomes unavoidable. Perhaps
the modal analysis of bodies is paradigmatic for that of minds. In that
case, there is but one substance having all bodies and minds as its modes.

(b) *Schematization* of the meanings of nature is made by Descartes in
his early work *The World*, as well as in his mature *Meditations*.[22] In the
former place, he follows an overriding polemical intent of eliminating the
personified image of a goddess nature. Hence he restricts the proper
general meanings of nature to three: God; the formal factor in the visible
world; and the material factor therein. Since Descartes makes this division prior to his systematic elaboration of metaphysics, he is primarily
concerned with so distinguishing the formal and material senses of nature
from the divine that there remains no basis for intercalating a personified

fate or fortune. He identifies the formal meaning of nature with the mathematico-mechanical laws of Galilean motion and the material meaning with the extensive particles subject to such laws of motion. Since both the patterns of motion and the material particles are directly produced by the geometrizing, omnipotent God, their meanings remain mechanical and depend solely upon God's creative causality. This theory of nature is retained in Descartes' published works as a general governing schema, within which to fit any specific problems.

One need not be in possession of Spinoza's full account of nature to predict his likely response. Like Descartes, he demythologizes any talk about goddess nature by tracing back fortune and fate to some misguided human beliefs about divine causality and mechanical laws, freedom and contingency. But a genetic account of human convictions must be regulated, in turn, by a metaphysical theory of God and the universe. Thus Spinoza shifts the emphasis of general meanings of nature to the question of *how* God exerts his causal power and relates himself to the mechanically regulated universe. Clearly, some distinction must be kept between the three Cartesian general meanings for nature, but it must be counterbalanced by the problem of *unifying* these meanings within a truly comprehensive theory of nature in its wholeness. The themes of divine causality, unified nature, and the latter's internal differentiations are always correlatively treated by Spinoza.

Not unexpectedly, Descartes' own metaphysical account of the more particular meanings of nature involves his doctrine on mind and body. In the *Meditations,* "nature" may signify the human mind alone, the human body alone, the composite unity of the two as effected by God, the interworking of the entire physical world of bodies under divine governance, and our judgment about this or that particular nature or natural operation. These five meanings roughly foreshadow Spinoza's transition from *Ethics I* on God to *Ethics II* on the human mind and body (taken along with the discussion of knowledge and its variants, in *Emendation of the Understanding*). Spinoza broadens the scope of these meanings of nature by treating the human mind and body as instances of the more general topics of the idea of a body and that body itself.

Within this broader context of natural things, we can expect three consequences to follow in Spinoza's treatment: First, he will keep the body-mind relation in man always connected in principle with the more general relation of every bodily thing in the extended universe to the idea of that bodily thing; next, he will emphasize the composite union of man's mind and body rather than their supposed "aloneness," using the analysis of our body to guide much of his theory about the human mind and the union itself; lastly, he will conjoin a discussion about human judgment concerning natural things and laws with a practical account of human passions and power, as exemplified in the last three parts of *Ethics*. A student of the latter treatise is all the more appreciative of its distinctive look at nature after having read Descartes and pondered the differences.

(c) *Systematization.* The main question here concerns the relationship between the theory of nature and a systematically developed philosophy. Neither Descartes nor Spinoza is so parochial as to restrict every acquaintance with nature to that kind achieved in philosophy. They both perceive the need for a philosophy open enough and powerful enough to assimilate the views of nature provided by science and technology, society and religion. But where the two philosophers part company is over the position and function of the philosophical conception of nature itself.

Three differences become apparent in regard to the unity, necessity, and ethical import of that conception. First, Descartes distributes his teaching on nature between metaphysics (which yields the general meanings of nature in terms of God, the human mind and its body, and the existing world) and a philosophy of nature proper (which deals with the general laws of mechanical motion and the mechanistic analysis of particular phenomena). Spinoza too admits phases in the study of nature, but not in a manner that would displace its centrality everywhere in philosophy. For him, the study of nature is the comprehensive theme of philosophy as a whole, so that theories about God, man, and world are systematic specifications of the one underlying task of all philosophizing. Only within this unified inquiry into nature are differentiations rightly made between the several parts of philosophy and human learning.

Second, the Cartesian transition from metaphysics to the general and special theories of nature is not totally necessitated but retains an aspect of contingency. This is owing basically to the freedom accorded to the divine creative will, which can act or not act in producing the physical universe, and which can sovereignly choose between this or that set of general physical laws, essential natures, and truths constituting the actual universe and human knowledge thereof. From Spinoza's viewpoint, the consequences of this notion of God's creative freedom are disastrous for the continuity and necessity of philosophical inference. He does not quarrel with a regional study of the physical world by scientists and philosophers, but only with the peril to systematic reasoning caused by joining this study with an arbitrary creationism. Lest the necessary transitions in his theory of nature be weakened by such a conjunction, Spinoza is already radically rethinking both the divine productive activity and the several kinds of human cognition of bodily things and oneself.

The third point of contrast becomes visible only when we ask what systematic difference it makes that Descartes and Spinoza should clash over the unity and necessary articulations in nature and nature-theory. Spinoza replies that there is a serious practical difference observable in the quality of human knowing and acting conjoined. Cartesian philosophy breaks down at the two most critical transitions in the system: from God to the visible world, including man; and from man as object of metaphysical and physical analysis to man as moral agent. Descartes overstresses the split between passions, willfulness, and virtuous life. Hence he can supply no certainty on the internal means for assuring the wisdom, virtuous activity, and happiness which men seek and for the sake of which some men develop their philosophies. Spinoza's own vocation is thereby defined as a search after a philosophy that will not break apart at these two critical junctures, and that will hence give men the internal cognitive and moral power to reach a good measure of wisdom and beatitude in this life.

Precisely *how* his search proceeds and *why,* in his estimate, it finds a footing in the reconsideration of nature remains for subsequent chapters to determine. My study of his critique of Cartesian philosophy of nature suggests that this comparison is not the sole approach to Spinoza's reconstruction, but rather that it is *one* effective means used by him to educate people about his reasons for seeking a new foundation and ethical reorientation of philosophy. Indeed, there is a certain teasing and provocative quality in Spinoza's critical writings on Descartes and the textbook authors. He suggests counterpositions without working out his detailed arguments and relationships right there on the spot. In effect, we are being told to look elsewhere for the positive developments he was already making in accord with his own method and principles. We must therefore follow this hint by next examining Spinoza's earliest direct efforts at reforming philosophy by reforming the meanings of "nature": the *Short Treatise on God, Man, and His Well-Being* and the *Treatise on the Emendation of the Understanding.*

CHAPTER TWO

Naturizing the Theory of God

THIS CHAPTER AND THE NEXT ONE examine Spinoza's earliest work, the *Short Treatise on God, Man, and His Well-Being*. Following the main division suggested by this title, the present chapter dwells mainly on the problem of God, while Chapter Three will consider mainly the problem of man and his welfare. It is necessary to use the qualifying adverb *mainly,* since the whole drift of Spinoza's argument is that the questions of God and man cannot be completely separated from each other but are mutually related. Why and how they are coimplicatory is one of the major issues to be faced. In a preliminary way we can suppose that the two questions stand in some sort of mutual relationship, because of their joint inclusion within Spinoza's comprehensive view of nature. To treat of God within the philosophical context of nature means unavoidably to treat of the active source from which man and the rest of the world must come forth. And reciprocally, a philosophical analysis of man in terms of his dependencies, activities, and satisfactions in nature is bound to embrace his reference to God.

Like any other philosophy of God, the *Short Treatise* has to develop a position on some standard topics. They include: proofs that God is and what God is; the sense in which God is one, causal, and infinite; the names of God, his attributes and properties; the attempt to reach a true definition of God in terms of these other issues; and the guiding pattern of thought and discourse in connecting God with man and the visible universe. What saves Spinoza's treatment from being a mere duplication of previous theories of God, however, is his insistence upon relating every main phase of his argument to the continuing themes of nature and the human inquirer and desirer.

1. Cautionary Approach to the Short Treatise

General expositions of Spinoza's philosophy usually make a minor and fragmented use of the *Short Treatise*. Hence, it is necessary to examine some reasons for such a use before undertaking a more unified and accentuated analysis of the work than is customary. There are some persuasive grounds for downplaying and scattering its contributions, but under scrutiny these grounds reveal some further aspects which call for bringing the work within a steadier systematic focus. The obstacles that the *Short Treatise* furnishes are also instruments for better appreciating its achievements and, hence, for giving due attention to the latter, especially in a study of the Spinozan theory of nature.

(a) We can begin with the relatively late date of the manuscript's rediscovery and publication. In manuscript form, the *Short Treatise* was circulated among study circles during Spinoza's lifetime and perhaps for a while thereafter. But it was not printed in the 1677 edition of his *Posthumous Works*, even though references to it kept cropping up in letters and bibliographical notices for a century thereafter. An outline of the *Short Treatise* was published in 1852; a Dutch manuscript was found shortly thereafter and first published in 1862 by Johannes van Vloten (who also came into possession of a second, older Dutch manuscript while editing the first one); an unsatisfactory conflation of the two manuscripts was included in van Vloten and Land's edition of Spinoza's collected works (1883); and after considerable international criticism and translation, a critical text was finally presented in Carl Gebhardt's 1925 edition of Spinoza's works.

These matters can be regarded as being of merely bibliographical interest today, until the dates of rediscovery, publication, and critical editing are related to the general chronology of modern philosophy. Once the correlation is made, though, it reminds us that the view of Spinoza given by Bayle and the enlightenment, by Storm-and-Stress and Romanticism, by Hegel and the idealistic historians of philosophy is shaped without benefit of acquaintance with the *Short Treatise* (and without a critical text until a half-century ago). The historically recurring quarrels over Spinozism have lacked the moderating influence which a reading of this work could have exerted over enthusiasts and attackers alike. Any considerable use of the work has a revisionary effect upon our historical understanding of Spinoza's philosophy.

(b) Even after the *Short Treatise* became available in reliable editions, its use was retarded by the fact that the surviving text is in the Dutch language. This obstacle was lessened by the pioneer labor of German, French, and English translators, who usually added a genetic and analytic account of the work. It was widely agreed that one of the extant codices was copied from the other one; that both manuscripts depended upon a presumed Dutch source contemporary with Spinoza; and that this primary

Dutch version was itself a translation of an original text written in Latin (the primary Dutch translation having probably been commissioned by Spinoza's friend, Jarig Jelles, who was not at home with the Latin). Gebhardt further complicated the account by suggesting that Spinoza himself followed his custom of dictating some original materials in Dutch and then reworking them into the Latin text, from which the commissioned Dutch translation was made. In any case, the interlarding of Latin phrases and constructions within the extant Dutch *Short Treatise* has made scholars aware of the intimate use of the two languages in the making of that work, especially in the edited form in which it is presently known.

It would be shortsighted to disconnect these linguistic problems from a philosophical interpretation of Spinoza. For these problems caution us to attend closely to the Dutch equivalents for the key Latin terms and phrases from which Spinoza constructs most of his other writings. Much of his correspondence with study groups adapts to the two-language situation, namely, to the fact that the intimate discussing and criticizing of his thought often took place in Dutch intermixed with academic Latin terms and eventually communicated in Latin prose.

I will select two instances where the Dutch *Short Treatise* is fortunately helpful in capturing some nuances that might otherwise escape our notice.[1] The prime example is *Zelfstandigheid*, the term for *substantia* or *substance*. Whereas the Latin word directly signifies a supportive subject of inherence, the Dutch word emphasizes a positive and active sufficiency of "self-standingness." This enables Spinoza to specify directly that the sufficiency-unto-itself concerns both the order of being and that of knowing. When he comes to define modes, it is then done in contrast with such sufficiency. That the dependence of modes upon substance is not a relation of the inhering actualization of an underlying potential substrate follows from this sense of active self-sufficiency which Spinoza assigns to substance from the outset.

A second instance where he exploits the Dutch connotation is the family group of *Wezen*, *Wezentheid*, and *Wezentlykheid*. *Wezen* is the term for *ens* or "being." There are two other significations for *Wezen:* alternately with *Zyn*, it stands for *esse* or "being" in the intensive sense of "actual to-be"; and it is one designation for *essentia* or "essence." But *Wezentheid* is a more determinate term for *essentia* or "essence"; and *Wezentheid* sometimes is the term for *entitas* or "entity." *Wezentlykheid* stands for *existentia* or "existence" while *Bestaan* and *Existeeren* render *existere*, "to exist".

Spinoza takes full conceptual advantage of this Dutch lineage to illumine his use of the Latin terms. The permeating presence of *Wezen* enables him to link essence and existence closely together in any analysis of being. Further, the relation between *Wezentheid* and *Wezentlykheid* disposes one to perceive active being and essence at the heart of existence--a relationship of what we may call "effective essentiation" underlying all of Spinoza's arguments from the a priori requirements of adequately conceived essence to existence. Nor does he overlook the convergence of this entire Dutch grouping upon "actual to-be" and "to exist," since this strengthens the causal and actively self-expressive meaning of substance. These several incorporated meanings find concentrated expression in the phrase *Wezentlykheid van zelfstandigheid*. Thus in the *Ethics,* Spinoza packs considerable metaphysical and linguistic significance into his curt wording: *existentia substantiae* or "existence of substance."[2]

(c) Finally, the early composition and unfinished editing of the *Short Treatise* have rightly led scholars to be cautious in using it. The dating of its several components is approximately 1658–61, so that the composing of the *Short Treatise* probably overlaps that of the *Emendation of the Understanding* but precedes the remainder of Spinoza's writings. There are some discordances between these later writings and the *Short Treatise,* which even wavers internally about the propriety of calling the divine attributes of thought and extension "substances." Hence the accepted policy has been to make positive use of this work only insofar as it agrees with the *Ethics* and other later works, except for purposes of illustrating difficulties and developments in Spinoza's thought.

This is a safe rule to follow in general introductions to Spinoza, in purely analytic reconstructions of his system, and in some developmental sketches. But even while retaining the corrective comparisons with the *Ethics,* one must make a more thorough use of the *Short Treatise* in two kinds of studies: that which attempts a detailed account of the genesis of Spinoza's entire philosophy; and that which follows some major theme through the main phases of his thinking. Even in the latter approach, the degree of use of the *Short Treatise* will depend upon the relative prominence given there to the theme under investigation. The present work is a thematic study of nature, and as it happens that topic is developed both fundamentally and fulsomely throughout the *Short Treatise*. Hence, my use here of this work has to be correspondingly detailed. Careful examination of the *Short Treatise* shows how crucial the conception of nature is to its entire treatment of God, man, and human well-being; although it will take the subsequent chapters to establish that this same conception of nature is not a transient view but an enduring principle of Spinoza's entire philosophy.

The *Short Treatise* contains four distinct components: the main text of chapters, the notes, the two dialogues, and the two appendices. Roughly speaking, the main text and the notes are prior in composition to the dialogues and appendices. Spinoza never fully integrated these four components, thus leaving the work in an unfinished condition. He even left the task of the precise internal ordering of materials to his friends, who commissioned the Dutch translation and wanted something resembling the sequence of university manuals on God and man. Yet the very incompleteness of the project carries its own attraction, since it permits us to observe Spinoza's mind in genesis and thus modifies Hegel's complaint that "Spinoza is not aware of how he arrives at these individual determinations" of his basic definitions.[3] The *Short Treatise* does permit us to trace the growth of many Spinozan definitions and ideas, most notably that of nature itself.

Each of the above-mentioned components manifests some facet of Spinoza's intense experimentation in thought and expression. The main text resembles the chapters of straightforward definition and exposition found in school manuals and his own *Metaphysical Thoughts* and political writings. His self-criticism is that this form may perhaps achieve only superficial and arbitrary unity unless guided by some foundational principles and reasoning. Precisely what these guiding principles are in the *Short Treatise* is not sufficiently elaborated in the main tissue of chapters.

That is why Spinoza began the notes, which represent his intention not only of rewriting and improving upon the main body of his arguments, but also of clarifying particular passages. In the latter respect these notes foreshadow Spinoza's *Notes on the Theological-Political Treatise*, which refines some points and makes further remarks on controverted issues. From start to finish, Spinoza is his own most relentless critic and reformulator. He offers some important reconsiderations about his general theory of nature in the notes to the *Short Treatise*, just as he was to do later on in those notes started for his *Theological-Political Treatise* concerning nature's religious and political side.

As for the two dialogues, they are intelligently placed (probably by Spinoza's Amsterdam friends) in regard to the whole course of topics gathered in the *Short Treatise*. They function as a significant pause between the general proofs that God is and what he is and the more specialized treatment of his attributes, properties, and causality. In the first dialogue, Spinoza makes us mindful that the whole inquiry is conducted by men sharing in the drives to desire and love, to reason about and understand the infinite reality. And the other dialogue warns about the pitfalls in applying the language of cause-and-effect, whole-and-part, to our relationship with the infinite reality. Taken together, the dialogues invite us to relate the problem of nature and God with that of having some cognition and love of the infinite. But although Spinoza admired the Greek and Renaissance uses of dialogue in philosophy, he was also realistic enough to recognize that he himself lacked the literary skill to transform dialogues from a wooden device into a form that captivates our assent and consent. Hence the dialogue form never became his primary mode of philosophical communication.

The kind of marriage he sought between rigorous argument and compelling presentation is better adumbrated in the two appendices to the *Short Treatise*.[4] The first appendix is, in fact, a trial run for Spinoza's geometrical presentation in *Descartes' Philosophy* and the *Ethics* itself. It treats of what God is, through a set of axioms and propositions and a series of proofs which appeal to these axioms and propositions. There is a general corollary on nature, but formal definitions are lacking because Spinoza's theory of definition depends upon a more developed teaching on nature than the brief corollary provides (even retroactively).

In the second appendix he deals with the human soul by making a scanning run over the entire *Short Treatise*. The sweep is so broad, the arguments so thorny, and the conclusions about human immortality so tentative, that this section constitutes an indirect plea for the more clearly organized and gradual approach eventually achieved in the *Ethics*. But even in his earliest work, Spinoza manages to convey some telling points on our general theme. Problems concerning the human soul are bound up with one's position on God and nature; such problems must therefore be relocated within a nature-oriented theory of divine attributes, causal activity, and modal constitution of the world; this ontological matrix is itself indissolubly joined with the question of a method for obtaining clear knowledge; and even under the best methodological and ontological conditions, the problem of immortality will remain difficult to resolve in relation to individual human knowers and agents.

Thus, these appendices forewarn philosophical inquirers to provision themselves with such a conception of nature and a methodology for amending human cognition as will aid them in the pursuit after ethical power and the happy life. But as even the *Ethics* shows, there will always remain some obscure issues requiring various sorts of excursuses. Their dual purpose is to probe into recalcitrant human beliefs and thus to clarify and purify the hopes of mankind, measured by the reality of nature.

2. What We Do in Inquiring about God

Spinoza's *Short Treatise* makes an abrupt start. It plunges straightway into proofs that God is and then what he is, without paving the way with any introductory remarks. Some scholars have felt obliged to offer a conjectural beginning that might lessen the jolt, but to do so is a risky and perhaps misleading undertaking.

For one thing, Spinoza distinguished between introductory remarks for a particular work and a general introduction to his philosophy as a whole. Because he did not make a final redaction of the *Short Treatise*, it lacked the aid of some remarks leading the reader smoothly into the particular subjects under discussion. But during the years 1660–61, he was quite preoccupied with the need to furnish an introductory path to his whole philosophy. This need was satisfied by the opening pages of his *Emendation of the Understanding*, while the remainder of that work continued the task of preparing minds for the rest of his philosophizing. Hence, he permitted the *Theological-Political Treatise* and the *Ethics* to move at once into substantive issues without benefit of the usual introductory statements; for these latter works did suppose the basic introduction and methodological preparation given in the *Emendation*. An example of Spinoza's restricted kind of introduction came in the two opening chapters of the *Political Treatise*, where (because of its late composition) he was able to refer readers explicitly to the background already provided by his ethical and theological-political writings.

A full-scale introduction to the extant Dutch version of his *Short Treatise* would have been misleading, since the sections were never definitively arranged by Spinoza himself. Especially in the case of the first two chapters, dealing respectively with the *that* question and the *what* question about God, the actual arrangement reflected the order found in many current university manuals. Spinoza had no intention of canonizing this movement from God's existence to his essence, but instead sought to reform the entire order and significance of inferences concerning God.

Hence he confronts us at once with the compound issue of the-*that*-and-the-*what* of God.[5] After setting forth the a priori and a posteriori proof structures in this inquiry, he submits the complex whole to a twofold analysis. The first stage consists of a direct comparison among the proofs involved here, with the aim of determining the fundamental theme that

governs the reasoning. In the second stage, Spinoza steps back sufficiently to reflect upon the inquiring process as a whole, so as to identify
and render explicit its ultimate intellectual *intent*. Thus he is interested
respectively in (a) the main basis of proof, and (b) the fulfilling meaning
of our philosophical arguments about the-*that*-and-the-*what* of God.

(a) From the first or comparative viewpoint on the proofs, everything
pivots around understanding in a clear and distinct way that something
belongs to the infinite essence or nature of God. A priori proof that God is
rests upon identification of that "something" with infinite eternal existence. A posteriori proof that God is requires the presence in our mind of a
veridical idea about that existence. Spinoza accords the primacy to the a
priori way, since it expresses the effective order in which the divine
essential nature stands actively related both to God's own existence and to
our idea of that existence. Just as the divine nature or essence actively
sustains its own eternal existence, so is it (rather than the finite world and
our finite mind by themselves) the active source of our clear, distinct, and
hence objectively reliable idea about this existence as belonging to God.

Thus for Spinoza, the main basis of proof that God exists is the active
divine nature itself. The latter is both self-donative of its own act of
existing (*causa sui*) and also the intimate source of our truth-yielding idea
of eternal existence. Since this forces us back to an inquiry into God's
nature or what God is, the two questions of *what* and *that* are so related
that the former maintains an epistemological as well as an ontological
primacy.

(b) Spinoza stamps his own cachet upon the discussion, therefore, by
further asking about the fulfilling meaning of inferences about the nature
and existence of God. This is not a search after some contingent
psychological aim that may or may not be present in man, but rather after
the intent of the arguments themselves. The human inquirers about God
share in the argumentation and its intentional structure. Hence it may be
reflectively asked: What are we doing when we inquire about God, in
terms of what his being is and that it is? This is a metaquestion, but not one
that evacuates the specific forms of proof or that satisfies itself with
behavioral descriptions of mind. Rather, Spinoza is looking for some
further unifying meaning toward which the arguments about God point
and in which the human investigators discover the fuller sense of their
common search.

In the *Short Treatise*, Spinoza identifies this fulfilling intent through
use of two key phrases: *overweginge van de Natuur* and *die formelyk in
de Natuur is*, "consideration of nature" and "what formally is in na-

ture."[6] That is, the study of God turns out to be a major way of conducting
the study of nature; and the outcome of such inquiry turns out to be some
findings about what is really present in nature. I repeat the words "turns
out to be," without implying that Spinoza uses some sleight of hand or a
purely psychological description to establish his points. Rather, these
words signify that he pushes the second-level analysis of philosophy of
God toward a consequence which many philosophers either do not recognize or do not admit to follow validly from their own theories on God.
Spinoza has to labor at uncovering the ultimate intent of philosophical
inquiries about God.

In support of his position, Spinoza reinterprets the appeal to "our idea
of God" made in many current philosophies of God. This move is essential for naturizing the theory of God, since it brings any use of "our idea
of God" firmly within the ambit of the more inclusive theory of nature.

There are three interrelated texts in the *Short Treatise* that serve as
stages in showing the foundation, in theory of nature, for inferences
appealing to our idea of God.

> [i] We say he [God] is a being [*een wezen*] of which all, or infinite attributes
> are predicated, each of which attributes is itself infinitely perfect in its kind.
> . . . [ii] From all this follows then: that of nature all-in-all is predicated, and
> that therefore nature consists of infinite attributes, each of which is itself
> perfect in its kind. This agrees at once with the definition that one gives to
> God. . . . [iii]Corollary. Nature becomes known through itself, and not
> through any other thing. It consists of infinite attributes, each of them
> infinite and perfect in its kind. Existence belongs to that being [*wezen*], such
> that outside of itself there is no more being [*wezen*] or actual to-be [*zyn*].
> And therefore it [nature] agrees exactly with the being [*het wezen*] of the
> alone glorious and blessed God.[7]

Each of these passages brings Spinoza closer to manifesting the ultimate
aim of the philosophy of God, namely, its incorporation within the study
of nature and its corrective regulation by that aim.

[i] Among the philosophers and theologians within his study range,
Spinoza finds at least a minimal consensus on the meaning of God. Hence
in the first text he proposes a working content of our idea of God, a
designation of what God is, sufficiently definite to make some comparison with a general meaning for nature. Discourse about God concerns
itself with the presence of essential being or active reality. This affirmative presence is foundational for any comparisons or negations that
philosophers of God use to relate things in our world to him. At this initial
stage, Spinoza does not permit the basic sense of what God is to become

entangled in school disputes over the divine essence. It is commonly agreed that no limit can be placed upon the attributes pertaining to God's being. All or an infinite number of attributes are affirmed, and in such fashion that each one is unlimited in its own kind or line. Spinoza finds it important to identify this core meaning for what God is, so that controversies over the significance and relationship among candidate attributes will not obscure the ground of comparison between God and nature. That relationship is seen only when the minimal but firm view on God stands forth.

[ii] The second text has a retrospective ring to it. We may have made a separate study of the meaning of nature and done so without any explicit intent of comparing the result with a doctrine on God. But in summing up our findings and those of others, we have expressed the encompassing reality of nature itself as *alwezen* or "the all-being". In terms of attributes, this means that all-in-all is affirmed of nature, which is the actively pervasive being. A nuance is added now to the meaning of attributes, since they are that of which nature itself consists. We affirm them truly of nature only because nature actively presents them as constituting its own being. Moreover, nature comprises all or infinite attributes, each of which is unlimitedly perfect in its kind. But once we have explicated the meaning of nature this far (and have refrained from becoming distracted by particular controverted issues), we recognize its agreement with the working meaning of God given in the first text.

Spinoza makes two further refinements here. First, our grasp of the God/nature agreement rests upon the equivalence which holds "at once" in the reality under analysis. We come to recognize that the same actual being is signified now as God and now as nature. And next, Spinoza is not reluctant to refer to the "definition" given of God. In the degree that God's being is viewed in terms of nature, there is a basis for controlling our affirmations about God, dealing with specific difficulties and conflicts thus far avoided, and thereby showing that the meaning for God is a defensible definition.

[iii] The third text is called a corollary because it comes at the very end of the appendix in which Spinoza treats, in geometrical fashion, the topic of what God is. In the main body of propositions in this appendix, he treats the unicity of substance, both in terms of God's attributes and in terms of what exists in nature. The function of the corollary is to state explicitly that what holds good for the being of nature is precisely what holds good for God's being, thus eliminating any real distinction in their substantive reality.

The full corollary establishes four points intended to support this one-ness in substance between nature and God. First, Spinoza applies to nature his working definition of substance. Nature is not only in itself, but, most emphatically, is also that which is known through itself and not through something else. This is the anchor for denying causal production and noetic reference among plural substances. The one real substance is God or nature. Second, the meaning of the infinite divine essence is transferred to nature in respect to infinite attributes, making the point that nature's essence consists of these affirmed attributes and that each attribute enjoys infinite perfection in its own order. The phrase *infinite and perfect* suggests that the real basis of our perfection-talk lies in the unlimited expression of divine power through this or that kind of attribute.

The third point is that the essence-existence relationship must accord with nature's unique substantiality and infinity of attributes. Nature imparts existence to things without making them substantial existents apart from itself. Whatever beings do exist in the plural have their reality within all-enveloping nature and do not add more substantial being or essence to it. The common maxim: "More beings but not more being" holds quite precisely for the relation of things to the infinite existing substance, whether regarded as God or as nature.

Spinoza's fourth aim is to reiterate the exact agreement between nature itself and the divine being, on the grounds offered above. But he concludes with a salutation of "the alone glorious and blessed God." This phrase signifies that the sameness of God and nature is no denigration of the former, but only a penetration into what is holy and divine about nature. One hears the reverberation of mankind's religious traditions, especially the Bible and its Jewish commentators, interfused with the human search for blessedness. Spinoza is telling us that our religious and ethical valuation of God finds fulfillment in the unique actual being of nature. This lays the remote groundwork for his subsequent naturizing of man and his well-being.

Spinoza's theory of nature is not a pendant, therefore, but the very core of his interpretation of what transpires in treating of God. A consideration of nature must intervene to establish two primary conjunctions: between the *that* and the *what* of God, as well as between the divine being and our recognition of it as holy and blessed. Only through reflecting upon "what is formally in nature" can we truly understand the essential being of God as substance, which necessarily exists and maintains its infinite reality. And only the inclusiveness of the *all* of nature provides solid ground for our relationship to the eternal blessedness of God. We must now examine the Spinozan conception of nature more closely in itself, but without losing sight of its synthesizing function in the philosophical theories of God and man.

3. Incitements toward a Theory of Nature

Problems do not suddenly disappear when Spinoza reaches the position that conclusions made about God's existence and essence are actually conclusions about nature. Although this view gives some guidance to the inquiry, its high level of generality does not yet specify which aspects of a theory of God manifest precisely which traits of nature. To establish this closer relationship is to exhibit, in one major part of philosophy, the interpretive power of Spinoza's own theory of nature. But he does not move at once into the main internal structuring of nature, lest his presentation be exposed to the charge of being purely arbitrary and unresponsive to the genuine difficulties always plaguing mankind's study of God and nature.

In the *Short Treatise*, a prime function of the two dialogues and the subsequent review of topics found in textbook treatments of God is to pinpoint the difficulties which urge Spinoza onward toward a comprehensive theory of nature. The three principal inciters are: (a) his own minimal meaning of nature as thus far achieved; (b) theistic discussion of the causality and properties of God; and (c) the underlying search of men for a way of defining God that will be both true and satisfying on the questions raised.

(a) In showing the exact agreement between proofs of God and the study of nature, Spinoza is led to make a preliminary determination of the latter's meaning.[8] "Nature, which comes from no causes, and which we nevertheless rightly know that is, must necessarily be a perfect being, to which existence belongs." Alone fulfilling the meaning of substance as necessarily existent, nature is "the one, wholly unique, and total being." About this *alwezen* or "all-being," Spinoza concludes that "it is one eternal unity, infinite, omnipotent, and so forth, that is, that nature is infinite, and all is included within itself, and the denial of this we call the nought." These determinate descriptions of nature convey the radical proposal that every philosophy of God be reconstrued as part of an inquiry about nature and be correctively reinterpreted from the latter standpoint. The term *alwezen*, used as a synonym for the all-embracing reality of nature, is Spinoza's signature word for this strategy.

The provocative characterization of nature as the omnibeing elicits a flurry of theistic objections coming from our still wavering cognitive desire (which, in the first dialogue, has not yet been stabilized by reason and love). It interjects that nature is being treated as a whole, that "whole" is a second intention or universal idea, and that such an entity of thought cannot dictate what reality must be, nor can it deprive things of their substance. Our undisciplined desire for cognition also regards the correlative inclusion of all things in substantial nature as only a mental construct or *ens rationis*. Its acceptance as a real relational principle of containment would deprive God of his creativity and created things of their own substantial reality.

(b) These theistic misgivings about the soundness of the Spinozan *alwezen* are intensified when the causal power and properties of God are reviewed. There seems to be no ground left for the freedom, transcendence, and creative character of divine causality. And if God is reformulated in terms of nature, he cannot exercise personal providence and predetermining purposive care over things, especially over human agents. Conversely, the latter cannot be contained in divine nature and still be subject to defect, failure, and (in man's case) sin and loss or gain of the highest good. With the suppression of guiding wisdom and mercy, the religious bond between man and God is effectively broken and our hope for sharing in the blessed life shattered.

Throughout all this criticism drawn from conventional theistic thinking, Spinoza underscores the presence of the human factor. The problems do not solely concern nature and God by themselves but involve *human theories* concerning nature and God and *human consequences* drawn from such theories. These intellectual concerns of men inevitably get modified, along with the ways of conduct and hope correlated with speculations on nature and God. Thus even before coming to the latter half of the *Short Treatise* and the formal theory of man, Spinoza suggests that human self-understanding and moral values are already being affected by his naturizing of the theory of God. This prospect of altering our self-understanding and action only intensifies the incitements leading Spinoza toward his divisions of nature.

His examination of counterpositions extends to the doctrine on the names of God, who is regarded as being eternal and the cause of all things, omniscient and merciful, the highest good, and other designations of supremacy. Spinoza subjects these assertions initially to a sorting-out process. None of them are *attributes*, in the strict Spinozan sense of constituting the divine essence, so as to tell us what God is. Some of them ("eternal" and "the cause of all things") are indeed *properties* peculiar to

God, but still do not show what he is or what attributes belong to him. And still other divine names ("omniscient" and "merciful") characterize the *modes* in which God expresses himself but which, by that very fact, refer back to and depend upon what God is, without constituting either his attributive essence or properties. As for the trait of being the highest good, this either refers reiteratively to the divine property of being cause of all things or else derives from that confused *notion of man* and human will which silently underlies so much philosophizing about God.

Does Spinoza conclude, therefore, that what-God-is cannot be known in any way? His intent is not to reach this unrelieved negative conclusion but rather to bring out the impasse in previous philosophical efforts. Working backwards with the above distinctions, his point is that a corrected notion of man depends on a sound theory of modes, that the latter depends partly upon recognizing divine properties for what they can and cannot yield, and that both the modes and the properties are ultimately grasped and regulated through knowledge of divine attributes. Spinoza is provoking us to ask about the conditions, content, and limits of our understanding of these attributes and thus of what-God-is. His short answer is that this entire network of knowledge depends upon comprehending the divisions of nature. Once these divisions are established, there is a basis for removing both overclaims and underclaims about knowing God.

(c) Those who do apply the above names to God often couple them with the assertion that such predications cannot manifest the divine essence itself, and hence that "no true or rightful definition of God" can be given.[9] Spinoza would agree only that an ascription of properties, modes, and human relationships does not tell us what God is and thus does not give a definition of God. But he criticizes three arguments for maintaining, more strongly, that it is impossible in principle to give a true or right definition of God.

He treats two of these arguments curtly and almost casually, because Descartes had put them to rest and because they did not lead directly to Spinoza's own division of nature and theory of attributes. One argument is that the proper definition of a thing must be affirmative, but that we can know God only in a denying and not in an affirming way. We negate finitude and mutability of God, but the result is not a positive adequate knowledge of what he is in his essence. In reply, Spinoza merely refers readers to Descartes' *Replies to Objections*, which repeatedly distinguishes between having an adequate knowledge of God in the sense of a comprehensive grasp of his being, and having a clear and distinct understanding of the true and immutable nature signified by our idea of God. This amounts to a distinction between two bases of cognition: the complete idea of a being and the idea of a complete being. The latter knowledge is adequate in the sense of being sufficient for our having a true and proper definition of God.

Another objection states that God cannot be proved a priori, since he has no cause, but only from his effects or through probable reasoning. The latter routes would rule out any definitional knowledge through a causal principle or through essential certainty. Both Descartes and Spinoza regard God as cause-of-himself or *causa sui*, where "cause" refers to the actively efficacious divine essence as formally affirming its own existence, rather than to some efficient and external source of the divine reality. To know God as cause-of-himself is to attain apriority of definitional knowledge of him. Spinoza links our true knowledge of the divine essence with the primacy of his a priori proof of God's existence, so that the kind of probative knowledge used to establish the latter also suffices to remove the position that definition of what-God-is is impossible.

However, Spinoza reserves his most vigorous response for the argument that definition is made through genus and difference, whereas God cannot be regarded as being himself a genus or as functioning as a specific difference within any wider class. Spinoza picks his path carefully through this mine field laid for philosophers down the centuries.

First, he does not accept the argument as it stands, with its conclusion about God's indefinability. The notions of genus and specific difference are human artifacts, which do not impose rigid conditions upon reality or upon knowledge of the real source of the human mind. Next, Spinoza refuses to tinker with the terms of the objection, for instance by regarding being as a genus and infinite/finite as its specific difference. His refusal is not based upon an appeal to being as transcendental and nonunivocal, however, since for him the transcendental notions are also artificial and empty in themselves. Only an illusory definition could result from using such notions as the primary determinants of definitional knowledge of God. Finally, Spinoza rejects any combination of these countermoves that would so place God beyond all genera and species that one could only conclude that we can know what God is not, but not what he is. Eventually, this would open the floodgates to appeals to the unknown, arbitrary deity—appeals that are definitively excluded only by maintaining that we can have some true and correct, affirmative and definitional, knowledge of what God is.

Such critical reflections lead Spinoza to divorce the question of God's definability from the purely formal logic of genus and specific difference, and to realign that question with a logic based on his division of nature. The epistemic and emotive sense of liberation induced by this refounding act communicates itself in a strongly worded passage. Philosophers of God say *"that legitimate definition must consist of genus and difference. However, although all the logicians admit this, I do not know where they get this from. . . . Yet, considering we are free and not at all to be bound down to their assertions, hence in accordance with the true logic [de waare Logicam], we will furnish other rules of definition, namely, in accordance with the divisions that we make of nature."*[10] This text expresses Spinoza's reshaping of the theory of God by a nature-based philosophy, which involves a logic of definition regulated by the structure of nature.

He does not intend to eliminate generic and specific concepts entirely. They have a limited usefulness, but they cannot be given a dominant role in determining the rule of definition and the legitimacy of this or that proposed definition. The need to demote them to a very restricted scope in philosophy is vividly illustrated by their inability to cope with Spinoza's middle way of a true and proper, affirmative and yet not totally comprehensive understanding of what God is. To justify such knowledge, he challenges the actual educational practice of deciding philosophical issues on the basis of what is already laid down in logic manuals. The question about where logicians get their rules is not intended to raise an issue of historical provenance but to suggest that such rules are neither self-evident nor grounded in the reality of nature in such radical fashion as to govern all our metaphysical and ethical investigations.

Precisely because he does strive after such rooting in nature's ways of being, Spinoza feels emancipated from the dominant principles of an ungrounded logic. His ideal is not to engage in logicless rhapsodizing but to attain and employ "the true logic." This is characterized functionally by its molding of all basic concepts and rules in line with what holds or does not hold in nature. True logic is an alloreferential logic, one that is responsive to nature's structure and activity as set forth in the divisions of nature. Spinozan freedom is *from* an autonomous logic and *for* a logic that reflects the human mind's fundamental opening to natural being. Such openness salvages everything useful in the logic of genus and specific difference, without barring that knowledge of the divine essence which nature permits and wherein human beatitude consists.

4. The Surmodel of Nature

The naturizing of a theory of God and man requires recognition of their presence and interrelated activities within nature. For this purpose, Spinoza's main division of nature provides an overview and guides his study of the particular difficulties that arise.[11] This guiding overview constitutes his surmodel of nature or broadest context of interpretation. (See Figure 1.) Within the surmodel, one can then properly understand and develop the regional philosophical treatments concerning God, the world, and human action. Spinoza uses this surmodel and its major components as the basic referents for his own systematic reasoning, as well as for the criteria in criticizing and using the work of other philosophers.

As Spinoza actually employs it, this schema of nature is not a Procrus-

Division of Nature as a Whole

I. *Natura naturans* or *naturing nature*. God the immanent cause and sole substance, with distinctive properties and infinite eternal attributes. We know the essential being of two divine attributes:

                                                      God

               Thought   *Extension*

II. *Natura naturata* or *natured nature*. All modes as caused by God. We know that modal world which is produced under the attributes of Thought and Extension.

  1. *General natured nature*. Infinite eternal modes immediately produced by God. Those constituting our modal world are:

               Infinite Un-   *Motion-and-*
               derstanding   *Rest*

  2. *Corporeal natured nature as one individual whole*. Infinite mediate mode of our world, with all bodies varying in infinite ways but remaining the same individual whole:

                                          Pattern of the
                                        Whole Universe

  3. *Particular natured nature*. Finite modes or singular things within our modal world:

               Minds   *Bodies*
               (ideas of
               bodies)

tean bed but a very supple means for comprehending, amending, and interconnecting a wide range of themes. Thus one major function of the surmodel is topological: to interrelate the several components within Spinoza's unified theory of nature and to orient our study of them. It illuminates, for instance, the main topic of this chapter and the next one: the naturizing of the theory of God and the theory of man.

In the *Short Treatise* and subsequent writings, Spinoza follows the procedural rule of rethinking all problems about God in terms of *natura naturans*. This specifies more closely the equivalence between God and nature, since it does not signify an identification between God and nature as a whole but rather one precisely between God and naturing nature. Discussion of divine causality and substantiality, knowable attributes and properties, is thereby regulated by the manner in which such questions are treated in reference to naturing nature. The Spinozan theory of God neither isolates him from the world (since the necessary consequences for *natura naturata* must always be considered) nor identifies him simply with the world (since this would violate the distinction between nature as naturing and as natured). Similarly, the Spinozan theory of man always situates itself within the complex structure of being and meaning that holds for natured nature. Reference to this framework prevents the isolation of the human mind and human body from the pervasive conditions of mind-body relationships within corporeal nature as a whole. Even the ties between God and man are discreetly affirmed through the phrase *we know* which qualifies the theory of nature in both its naturing and natured phases.

The proximate issue that prodded Spinoza into setting forth his division of nature receives its own clarification here. There is no ironclad requirement that all valid definitions must consist of genus and difference. Within the Spinozan perspective of a true and liberating logic of nature, we must differentiate between a defining knowledge of naturing nature and one of natured nature. In the former case, it becomes a question of adapting the definitional rule to the meaning of attributes and their manner of becoming known. They constitute and manifest the essence of divine substance or naturing nature, which subsists through itself and makes itself known through itself. Since the attributes express this subsistent being and its own way of being known, they "need no genus, or anything whereby they become more understood or explained."[12] In the case of natured nature, however, man and other things *are* modes of the divine substance. Hence our better knowledge of them makes use of the theory of divine attributes. The latter can serve a purpose similar to that of a genus, in the sense of giving us a more comprehensive framework in *natura naturans* for understanding and explaining the modal or natured world.

5. Usage of "Nature"

The surmodel of nature cannot be used primarily in either a topographical or a deductive sense, although it contains aspects of each. It is not just a translucent map to be fitted over every topic of philosophic inquiry, since analysis of a specific topic invariably reveals complexities and relationships that require consideration now in one setting and now in another. The Spinozan surmodel suggests various ways of unfolding and relating these complications, so that it develops an art of thinking about nature rather than a mechanical categorizing of it. Furthermore, the surmodel is adaptable to our different human ways of thinking. To an imaginative mind it may appear as an image of reality, although the risk of error is large along this route. Where reasoning predominates, it serves to incite our analytic work and guide our acts of inference concerning nature, without supplanting these acts through an effortless cascade of deductions. Yet the surmodel of nature also conveys an ideal to our minds, one that we can sometimes grasp as an intuitive whole and enjoy as a satisfying actuality. Insofar as the naturizing of the theory of God involves our own cognitive and conative activities, it receives complementary support from the naturizing of the theory of man.

We can build a bridge from the one naturizing process to the other by considering, in more particular fashion, some of Spinoza's uses of "nature."

(i) Taken just by itself, the occurrence of the term *nature* is quite indefinite. It is little more than an invitation to search the context for an indication of this or that definite meaning intended by Spinoza. Sometimes, the qualifier is found easily within the very sentence or paragraph in which the queried term appears. But Spinoza often makes us look farther afield—say, to some other proposition or part of the *Short Treatise* or *Ethics*—for grasping either a single determining context or the many-level context within which to construe the meaning. And especially where more than one sense of "nature" may be in question, we are occasionally confronted by an ambiguity which the text does not totally remove. In such a situation, our best procedure is to distinguish the meaning or meanings found to be definitely intended from those others that may or may not also be implied. "Explicitation of the context" is the normal hermeneutical procedure in any study of Spinoza's teaching on nature; it encourages us to take a relational and plural look at the wording on an issue; and in inconclusive cases, it compels us to recognize the limits of the human mind reflecting on nature.

(ii) The phrase *the whole of nature* proves to be at once the most enlightening and the most troublesome usage.[13]

(a) Spinoza often uses the phrase explicitly in a broadly inclusive sense: *Natura tota, geheel [gheel] de Natuur*. It comes frequently in the possessive form, as emphasizing the orderly structure and scope of reality: "the order of the whole of nature and "a part of the whole of nature," *ordo totius Naturae* and *een deel van geheel de Natuur*.

(b) But as his argument flows along, Spinoza is likely to compress his language to: "nature" and "the order of nature," "in nature" and "outside of nature" (just the unaccompanied words *natura* and *ordo naturae, in de Natuur* and *buyten de Natuur*). In such cases, he may mean to include "the whole of" in his wording, but he leaves it implicit as far as the written text is concerned. One must then examine the wider context, the drift of the argument, and parallel passages in order to find the grounds for either including or excluding the additional words in one's interpretation of the text.

(c) The interpreting task becomes fraught with even more difficulties when it concerns the several components in the surmodel of nature. Of course, the totality of nature may signify quite unconditionally the full union of naturing and natured nature. But the exigencies of his argument frequently force Spinoza to restrict the connotation to the whole of naturing nature considered in itself, or else to the whole of natured nature distinctively intended. Even this restriction is often insufficient to specify the causal powers operative in the naturizing process. Spinoza must focus now upon the whole of naturing nature viewed through the attribute of thought, and now upon the whole of naturing nature viewed through the attribute of extension. Similarly, he must distinguish the whole of natured nature considered as modes in the line of thought from the whole of natured nature considered as modes in the line of extension. All the distinctive actualities of infinite and finite modal nature get their holistic meaning specified only in relation to these variously shaded senses of "the whole of nature." The interpretive discipline needed for discerning and synthesizing these relationships educates our minds in the Spinozan theme of the unity and interactivity of nature.

(d) Finally, reflection on this question performs an important corrective function. Spinoza's repeated criticism of the abstract logic of whole-and-parts requires some qualifications. He does not deny the usefulness of universal concepts of whole and part in resolving problems in mathematics and other abstract disciplines. But he does object against erecting these concepts into independent metaphysical principles which impose themselves upon our philosophical study of nature. His declaration of freedom from such imposition means that henceforth the philosophical meaning and use of whole-and-part will depend upon the constitution of nature, and not the converse. The theme of ''the whole of nature'' marks the rehabilitation of the concepts of wholes and parts as concrete meanings for nature in its several aspects and our several ways of considering these aspects. The concepts lose their autonomy and dictatorial force, only to gain valid use as ways of stating the immanent causation, articulation, and unity of nature.[14] Their valid employment comes in calling nature the *alwezen* (the whole of real being) and in the surmodel of the divisions or parts of nature.

(iii) There was a long Western lineage for variants of the doublet *natura naturans/natura naturata*, a lineage adverted to in Spinoza's remark (quoted in paragraph [b] below) that even the Thomists speak of God as *natura naturans*. (St. Thomas himself had remarked more cautiously that ''certain ones'' employed this terminology, thus establishing his own critical distance from it.) Much more to the point for Spinoza's adoption of this pairing, however, was its presence in the textbooks of Heereboord and other current authors studied at Leiden and elsewhere.[15] The school manuals employed it rather routinely, as one orthodox theistic way of stating the relationship between the creator of nature and his handiwork. If a word of warning was deemed necessary against regarding God as soul of the world or as nature's own activity, this admonition was intended to clarify the doublet rather than to rule out its use by theists. It was sufficiently uncontroversial to give Spinoza's usage a hearing, and sufficiently indeterminate to permit him to stamp his own uncompromised meaning thereon.

That distinctive meaning is built around a threefold consideration of the doublet itself and each of its members in turn.

(a) As far as the pair itself is concerned, Spinoza wants to use it to mark a distinction that never breaks up into a disruption of the unity of nature. The usage of *natura naturans/natura naturata* signifies most basically an active coupling or knitting together of all the components in nature. Hence it corresponds to the primary, most adequate sense of ''the whole of nature.'' Something would be lacking in the wholeness of nature were only one member of the relationship present. It is this active intrinsic componency that prevents a shredding of nature's integrity. The latter admits of differentiation but not of a one-sided rendering absolute of either the naturing or the natured principle.

With the couplet's aid, Spinoza can elucidate further the meaning of *alwezen* or "the all-being." He has already proposed that this designation belongs to God's essence and to that of nature as a whole. But the opportunity now arises for stating more precisely that the all-being comprises God's active being as it produces, orders, and unites with itself all the things and actions in the universe. One consequence for Spinoza is that the numinous quality of God the all-being belongs, in a philosophically controllable sense, to nature as a whole. Hence when he refers to *divine nature,* in its full and peak connotation, he is centering upon this totality of naturing and natured nature grasped in their complex unity. This will have some far-reaching implications for his thought on ethical fulfillment and religious aspiration.

(b) We can now study the two accounts of *natura naturans* given respectively in the *Short Treatise* and *Ethics I:*

> [1] By *Natura naturans* we understand a being that we clearly and distinctly conceive (through itself, and without having need of anything other than itself, like all the attributes (*Attributa*) which we have so far described), that is, God. Likewise the Thomists also have understood God by it, but their *Natura naturans* was a being (so they called it) beyond all substances. . . .
> [2] By *Natura naturans* we must understand that which is in itself and is conceived through itself, or those attributes of substance which express eternal and infinite essence, that is (*Proposition* 14, *Corollary* 1, and *Proposition* 17, *Corollary* 2), God, insofar as he is considered as free cause.[16]

These texts regard naturing nature as real being, rather than as a construct of reason or imagination. Moreover, it is real being in the sense of substance, not a modal reality. As substantial being, naturing nature enjoys a unique self-sufficiency that manifests itself in an active uncoerced expression of causal power.

In both passages, Spinoza unifies his position on the attributes of substance through the theme of naturing nature. This is an index of the fundamental importance of the theory of attributes in his philosophy. Just as the substantial character of naturing nature assures that the latter is conceived through itself, so does its synthesis of attributes assure its power of expressing the eternal and infinite essence. Naturing nature does not elude all knowledge and does not remain inactive or only dependently active. The attributes enable us to gain some essential knowledge of this infinite divine power.

These points can be further elucidated through a distinctive question posed by each text quoted above. Why does Spinoza bother to specify that, for Thomists, God or *natura naturans* is beyond all substances (text 1)? They sought to remove God from the category of substance, which would make him finite and submit him to the status of a support requiring further actuations. Spinoza does not regard substance as a categorial class, within which plural substances belong. Hence he does not regard the noncategorial meaning of being-in-itself as placing God beyond all substances. Rather, this is the meaning of God precisely as the unique substance, which is to say that self-subsistence is reserved for naturing nature. Self-subsistence assures that naturing nature is not an unknown mystery, but is conceived through itself, through the self-expression of its essence in the attributes. Knowledge of any divine attribute means knowledge of naturing nature in its eternal, infinite essence as God.

Then why does Spinoza add that, in this cognition, God is being considered as free cause (text 2)? To grasp God as substance is to do so through himself, through his own self-activity or self-determination and not through any modal determinant. This is to know him precisely as free cause. Now such a dynamic, sourcing apprehension of God is just what "naturing nature" signifies. A clear and distinct considering of God in his eternally active, free causation constitutes the primal meaning of nature as naturing being. It expresses God in terms of true understanding, and does so by making the divine causal essence manifest to the understanding through modally available attributes.

(c) One way to regard the theory of *natura naturata* is as a somewhat unfamiliar and transformative way of viewing familiar things. It leads us to recognize that things are not unrelated or drawn into only chance associations, but belong in a totality, a world order. Nothing is thereby dictated arbitrarily to our natural experiences and natural sciences. But their naturality receives further meaning and connectedness within the philosophical context of natured nature. Reference to this context is both ontic and epistemic: it affects both the being of natural things and the proper conception of them.

In the *Short Treatise*, Spinoza makes his own use of the school-manual and Cartesian distinction between general and particular, or special, philosophy of nature. A general theory of nature does treat of the widest traits of the universe which Galileo and Descartes formulated in terms of general laws of motion.

But Spinoza adds a threefold qualification. First, motion-and-rest must be correlated with a comprehensive meaning of modes of the understanding. This requirement is visited upon all instances of natural things under

conditions of motion-and-rest, such that these instances are strictly correlated with some proportionate modal "idea" in the line of the understanding. Second, motion-and-rest and understanding are not only *derived*
from God's causality but are *expressive of* distinctive divine attributes,
respectively, extension and thought. Thus the world of natured nature
never ceases to have a divine significance and to manifest it, in some
degree, through our reflective minds. Third, Spinoza interprets the division into general and particular nature as a philosophical theory about the
infinite and the finite modes of natured nature. The infinite and eternal
character of motion-and-rest and the understanding underlines their immediate relationship to the appropriate divine attributes of extension and
thought. Not only is this living relationship imparted to the finite order of
existing bodies and minds, but it is also incorporated into their adequate
meaning and truth. We must refer to that larger context in order to understand ourselves and other natural things better and to improve our active
life.

The terminology of "natured nature" serves several other purposes in
Spinozan philosophy. It signifies a thorough dependence upon naturing
nature, as well as a thorough determination by the latter's activity as free
cause. Yet the language also emphasizes a consonance between the naturing principle as infinitely powerful substance and the natured world as its
modal expression. Natured things are ordered and determined, but this
does not rule out causal activity on their part. Spinoza criticizes any view
of the world that underestimates the latter's rooting in, and energizing by,
the divine causal act. In distinguishing between divine substance and the
universe of infinite and finite modes, he avoids any position that would
place God and universe in competition or that would regard the universe
as a shadow realm, a degeneration of power, a region of second-rate
substantial beings.[17] Natural things are not quasi substances and passive
receptacles, but are proper modal centers for expressing, manifesting,
and uniting with God their sustaining nourisher.

We have seen that only in the union of the naturing and natured realities
themselves is the concrescent being of divine nature or the whole of
nature present. Hence it is only within this matrix that Spinoza can
develop the several strands and subpatterns in his theory of nature. The
fabric is now tough enough to permit a more particular study of finite
natured nature to occur, without tearing the latter away from the whole.
This is the condition required for a specific theory of man that comple-
ments and deepens, rather than violates, the now fundamentally naturized
theory of God.

CHAPTER THREE

Naturizing the Theory of Man

W̲ERE WE TO MAKE ONLY A HASTY SCAN of the chapter headings and contents of the later chapters of the *Short Treatise,* we might conclude that they do little more than reformulate current materials on the soul, body, and powers of man. But in fact, Spinoza used these common topics to naturize the philosophy of man just as radically as he had already done for the philosophy of God. He could not do otherwise. The momentum toward philosophical reconstruction generated in the first half of the *Short Treatise* could not be brought to a sudden halt with God, but was bound to continue onward into the rest of nature, especially man.

My present chapter raises four questions which are intended to bring Spinoza's reinterpretation of man into bolder relief. What functions does the theory of man perform within the total conception of nature? How is a differentiating approach taken to human cognition? What primary meanings of "things" establish man's total immanence in nature? And what reforms are needed in human talk about the laws and community of beings in nature? Although these questions are not exhaustive, they do give some measure of the depth and direction of Spinoza's early overhauling of the philosophy of man.

1. Functions of the Theory of Man

Spinoza usually recommends his philosophy on two grounds: comparative and intrinsic, and in both respects the relation between nature and man is crucial. Whatever his awareness and use of past traditions, he is most keenly concerned to establish the superiority of this thought by comparison with philosophies *currently* being held and taught. Descartes, especially, finds it difficult to develop a unified theory of man. The problem concerns not only his attempt to join two kinds of substance internally in human nature, but also his broader effort to bring human

reality into systematic focus. His early *Treatise on Man* is only a tailpiece
to his *The World, or Treatise on Light,* and does not get beyond a
physiological and perceptual analysis.[1] Within his mature system, man
receives only a scatter-shot, distributive handling. In the *Meditations,*
Descartes deals formally with the human composite but uses it as a
staging point for showing the existence of the material universe. His
Principles of Philosophy never quite arrives at a distinctive study of man;
the *Treatise on the Passions* is physiologically and psychologically
oriented; and his moral view of man must be patched together from
sections of his books and letters.

Spinoza's verdict is that a thoroughly unified teaching on man eludes
Descartes, not through accidental circumstances of his life and writing but
through a fundamental failure of his method and basis of synthesis.
Paradoxically, methodic doubt and the Cogito are too narrowly based on
some human operations to enable a complex and relationally inclusive
philosophy of man to be elaborated. Descartes was indeed on the right
trail in seeking to ground his concept of man (as more than the self or
Cogito) upon that of nature, but he lacked a sufficiently unifying and
generating notion of nature itself. Reforming the latter notion in response
to the reality of total nature must entail, on Spinoza's reading, a revision of
the philosophy of man. A major consequence of naturizing the theory of
God is, therefore, to furnish adequate means for focusing philosophical
argument and synthesis upon the theory of man.

But the latter is no mere passive beneficiary of the naturizing of God.
Rather, there are two intrinsic sorts of contribution which the theory of
man is called upon to make toward Spinoza's inclusive notion of nature.
Retrospectively, it helps render more explicit certain features of his view
of naturing nature itself. And prospectively, his study of man entails a
further determining of his meaning for natured nature. Taken together,
these functions remind us that the Spinozan conceptions of man and
nature do not meet as already fixed and complete doctrines. The one
about man grows within the context of a reflection on nature and, in doing
so, serves to modify and articulate the latter's own growth as a whole.

One retrospective point is simply that the *Short Treatise* propounds
Spinoza's *theory* about nature. He does not regard this theory as an
arbitrary or fictional construction, but rather as the philosophical truth
about nature. The latter, as it were, finds a voice in the statements on
nature which Spinoza makes in this work and refines in his other writings.
The meaning and truth of nature come to expression by means of what he
calls the true logic, the true philosophy containing our human reflections

on natural reality. Such a philosophy must eventually inquire into that active human principle in nature which does the reflecting and theorizing and logicizing. This inquiry can neither be suppressed forever nor dismissed as private psychologizing nor referred to some reflective source apart from nature. Man and his instruments of inquiry are: irrepressible expressions *of* nature's power, cognitive insights *into* nature's structure and activity, and operative centers *within* the natural totality.

Thus, the study of man provides Spinoza with an opportunity both for affirming the rootedness of philosophical anthropology in his general account of nature and for underlining man's essential contribution to a true understanding of nature.

Bearing this correlation in mind, we can now recognize the import of certain linguistic expressions occurring in Spinoza's presentation of the theory of naturing nature. He studs his text unobtrusively with the expression *wy zien,* "we see," and with such modal variants as that we "consider" and "compare," "conclude" and "know."[2] These phrases are not rhetorical flourishes aimed at gaining assent through the use of familiar first-person-plural discourse, as presuming or encouraging agreement to what all of us thoughtful persons hold. Nor are these modes of expression merely added contingently and extrinsically to the discussion, without essentially affecting the argument. Spinoza weaves them too closely into the web of his definitions, explanations of counterpositions, and norms of his own position to permit a rhetorical and extrinsic interpretation to suffice.

As his study of man proceeds, it has the retroactive effect of rendering explicit the epistemic factor already present in the theory of naturing nature. This latent epistemic component in the Spinozan doctrine on naturing nature is signified by the "we see" type of expressions, along with the requirement that this or that affirmation about God must arise from a clear, distinct, and adequate grasp of the issue. For a position to be truly established and incorporated into the theory of naturing nature or God, it must survive some cognitive tests of its reliability to manifest that naturing reality.

But does not the explicative role here of the study of man render the entire conception of naturing nature flatly anthropomorphic, aligning Spinoza with those who view God merely as man writ large? For now, I will restrict the denial of this consequence to grounds furnished by the *Short Treatise,* adding only that Spinoza elsewhere turns the objection back upon his opponents. When he defines naturing nature as that which we conceive clearly and distinctly through itself and without having need of anything other than itself, he thereby distinguishes God from the entirety of modal nature, including the human conceiver himself. What the latter conceives clearly and distinctly is that naturing nature is the sole substantial reality, and that all of natured nature has need of this reality in order *to be* modally and *to be known* truly. Far from reading his own reality into God, then, Spinozan man self-referentially includes himself with the whole of natured nature which is modal rather than substantial.

Precisely at this juncture, we can spy the other general function of the theory of man, namely, to develop in a forward-looking direction the meaning of natured nature. Spinoza cannot remain satisfied with just a global inclusion of man in modal nature. From the standpoint of modal nature itself, he must press on from its *being other* than naturing nature to *the way* in which it is a positive causal expression of the latter. More can be learned than the general point that modal nature is causally expressive of the sole and infinite substance under its infinite attributes. For the theory of man specifies more closely that we are concerned with modal nature as it comes within the range of reflective human experience. Because human reality is compositely extended and thinking, any further analysis of modal nature requires that the latter be considered as causally expressive of naturing nature under its known attributes of extension and thought.

Thus the basic facticity of man helps to shape Spinoza's view of natured nature as well as of the divine attributes. Whatever temporary and tactical concessions he makes to the Cartesian style of calling thought and extension substances, he ultimately rejects a strict substantial pluralism as being destructive of the unity of nature. "We clearly see that they [distinct plural substances] have no community at all together as thought and extension, of which we nevertheless consist."[3] The force of the adverb *nogtans* (*nevertheless*) is that man's self-experience is decisive for regarding thought and extension as attributes of the one only substance, and hence for structuring accordingly the humanly determinate view of natured nature. *Some* theory of natured nature is required because the sense in which we "consist of" thought and extension is not directly evident, but in any case *all* components in such a theory must submit to the humanly decisive requirement of being modal expressions of substance under the attributes of thought and extension.

Spinoza regards human facticity not as a brute unintelligible given but as a determinate reality, open to various sorts of cognition and able to guide his theory of natured nature (in cooperation with that of naturing nature). Such theory-guidance stems from two points of assurance about our own reality: (a) that it is finite, and (b) that it involves a union of modal expressions of thought and extension under conditions of this finitude.[4] These two footings enable Spinoza to develop a conception of natured nature that is at once faithful to man's self-comprehension and coherent with the naturing doctrine on God.

(a) The ordinary division of natural philosophy into general and particular, or special, was systematically misleading, because it led one to expect a doctrine about generic concepts and laws of motion and their specific consequences and individual instances. Hence, in the Spinozan approach to modal nature, both ''general'' and ''particular'' receive new significance. The generality is not inclusive of all nature but only of natured nature. It signifies natured nature taken as a whole, which is expressive of naturing nature under definite attributes thereof, and which enjoys a certain inclusive yet individual reality of its own. Under insistent pressure from man's awareness of his finitude, then, Spinoza interprets the general theory of natured nature as being a study of *infinite* modes, immediately and mediately referred to the causal power of divine substance. Under this same pressure, the particularized theory of natured nature becomes a study of the *finite* modes of divine substance. Thus the reformed doctrine on natured nature emphasizes both the distinction and the unifying bonds between infinite and finite modes.

(b) Our drive toward specifying *which* modes and *what* modal significations come within a humanly accessible view of natured nature reflects our previous distinction between knowing that God has infinite attributes and knowing the distinctive essential meaning of only certain attributes. Once more, the specification and assurance of access well up from what the finite human mode is and grasps about itself. In various degrees of lucidity and certainty, man perceives himself to be a union of powerfully expressive modes of thought and extension, operating under limiting conditions. Hence although natured nature embraces in principle all modal entities, the human philosophy about it focuses more definitely upon the infinite and finite modes of thought and extension.

The *Short Treatise* designates the understanding as the immediate, infinite, eternal mode of substance under the divine attribute of thought, and motion-and-rest as the immediate, infinite, eternal mode of substance under the divine attribute of extension.[5] The brevity of treatment of the infinite modes of natured nature does not prevent Spinoza from relating these modes not only to God or naturing nature but also to man as a complex unity of finite modes of natured nature.

Although science of nature properly examines motion-and-rest in detail, the latter is also intimately involved in the philosophical study of man's constitution and knowledge, his passions, and felicity. This bearing upon man gives a controlled if limited perspective on motion-and-rest and, conversely, furnishes a framework for analyzing human passions and felicific activity in connection with the whole of naturing and natured nature. The systematic broadening of the study of man is further reinforced by Spinoza's statement that the understanding consists of a clear and distinct, unchanging and satisfying comprehension of everything at all seasons. This view of the understanding as the infinite mode of thought provides man with an integrative actual standard of clear and distinct knowledge that is based on, and ordered toward, a grasp of nature as a whole. In the course of its naturization, then, the theory of man both gives and receives--all to the benefit of Spinoza's total concentration on nature.

2. Cognitive Paths within Nature

Spinoza's theory of the modes of knowing is often presented separately as though it were a purely epistemological topic, and as though the main problem were merely to compare his several accounts and reach a coherent theory of knowledge. The task of analysis, comparison, and unification must of course be carried through, yet not in any spirit of epistemological separatism. Such purism has to give way to the actual influence of his comprehensive conception of nature, internal to which the examination of human knowing is made, and is made to serve the larger purposes of his philosophy. Spinoza's contextualist intent stands forth so strikingly in the *Short Treatise* that it cannot be ignored. It bids us ask: (1) where the theme of our several modes of knowing belongs in the comprehensive study of nature; and (2) what its content is within that natural frame.

(1) Once the inquiry begins examining special nature or the realm of finite modes, there is a burgeoning of its possible scope. For distinctions must now be recognized between ''such and such a nature,'' between ''this nature and that nature.''[6] Spinoza warns against permitting the language of these distinctions to lead us either toward abstract conceptual definitions in terms of genus-and-species or toward an endless description of discrete individuals. The finite modes are particular existing things, indeed; but they are subject to some determinations already made in the theory of nature. Particular natures that can be positively distinguished and analyzed within a human knowledge of nature are those which actu-

ally express substance under the attributes of thought and extension. They are also those which come within the modal fields of infinite understanding and motion-and-rest.

Determinations of this kind do not block any road of investigation for Spinoza. They simply direct his attention toward problems reachable philosophically in the area of finite modes of nature. Although the chapter headings of Part Two of the *Short Treatise* announce a rather familiar approach to man in terms of his cognitive powers, passions, and aims, the actual inquiry is ordered by four further developments in the theory of finite modes of nature.

Given his present investigative resources, Spinoza first limits this theory to a study of man and the world of bodies (whatever other finite modalities exist apart from human experience). His second move is to approach the bodily world initially from the perspective of man's presence and relationships to it, leaving the further study of body to the natural sciences and subsequent work in philosophy of nature. Third, his account of man in the *Short Treatise* does not revolve primarily around the union of mind and body; important though that topic is here, it does not have the systematic centrality accorded it in the *Ethics*. Consequently, the fourth trait of the *Short Treatise* is its exploratory study of the human mind as far as it can be considered by itself. Spinoza carries this experiment as far as he can, thereby effectively establishing the limits of a mind-centered analysis and the need to place systematic emphasis upon the union of human mind and human body and the intercausation of man's composite nature and the rest of the bodily world, within a well-ordered analysis of nature.

(2) Within the framework of these methodic steps, Spinoza can now give his own significance to the age-old topic of the different kinds of human knowledge. There is a palmary difficulty in the very fact of this topic's recurrence in his philosophical anthropology. A first glance at the Spinozan surmodel of nature as a whole might suggest that, within finite modal nature, nothing more need be said than that the human mind is a particular case of being the idea or soul of a body—in this instance the idea of the human body. However, the human mind is not only so regarded because of our self-acquaintance, but also because of situating it within the general theory of naturing and natured nature. Hence, some specific grounds must be adduced from both self-acquaintance and the general theory of nature for "saying something more" about the human mind which will constitute a doctrine on the several ways of human knowing.

Skepticism provides a helpful goad, by constantly criticizing our efforts to know and blocking every route toward knowledge. It sets forth in scrupulous detail the human mind's attempt to reach demonstrative knowledge and certainty, the failure of each kind of effort, the retreat to opinion and private conviction, and the practical pressures nevertheless requiring firm decisions to be made. Spinoza makes preliminary use of the skeptical depiction of the human mind as being laden with prejudice and doubt, error and futility. Such a description justifies some internal analysis of the human mind, just as physics and physiology provoke a closer look at the human body. Spinoza's countercriticism of skepticism as a philosophical position and human attitude will be postponed until the next chapter.

Another compelling reason for doing more than supplying an unanalyzed block-definition of the human mind as the idea of the human body comes from the previous discussion of naturing nature in Part One of the *Short Treatise*. There, Spinoza has had to do more than remove the prejudice against counting extension as a divine attribute. His every chapter on the properties of God has required him to attack the inadequate beliefs and false opinions held by religious people and supported by the argumentation of theologians. In each instance, the errors about God and our relationship to him are traced back to defective notions on naturing and natured nature. In a corrected view, providence is, "with us, nothing other than the effort which we experience both in the whole of nature and in the particular things, tending to protect and preserve their own being."[7] Religious misconceptions about an all-providing transcendent God result from a failure to recognize this striving or conative trait of natured nature and of all particular modal things. A similar failure to understand the necessary, omnipresent causality of naturing nature underlies theological talk about how divine power overcomes the physical evil and confusion of nature, and how divine grace overcomes sin in man.

Thus, Spinoza cites both skeptical and theological discourse as witnesses to the presence of many unclarified images and misleading assertions within the human mind. Improvement of our knowledge and conduct depends, then, upon distinguishing among the several kinds of cognition involved in the actual complexity of our mind or idea of the human body. In the language of the *Short Treatise*, these components are neutrally called "conceptions" and "modes of which man consists," "different knowledges" and "manners of knowing" (*begrippen* and *wyzen uyt de welke de mensch bestaat, verscheide kennissen* and *manieren van kennen*).[8] Internal analysis leads to these ways of describing the complex constitution of the human mind as a finite mode of natured nature, considered under the attribute of thought.

Spinoza becomes more evaluative in specifying the four manners of knowing or modes of cognition.[9] They are: (a) opinion or belief based on hearsay; (b) opinion or belief based on one's limited and fluctuating experience; (c) true belief based on reasons that something must be as it is so demonstrated; and (d) clear knowledge based on seeing things themselves which are perceived and enjoyed in themselves. They all can be regarded as ways or manners of knowing, since they convey something about one's own body, about the physical world, or about one's state of mind.

The two types of opinion (*a* and *b*) are not intrinsically misleading and, indeed, bring home the value of an experiential grasp of existing realities. But they rely upon reports of other people or upon our own uncertain rules and experiences that cannot be generalized and hence that are subject to error. Opinion-grounded beliefs lack the critical controls to keep us from making false assertions about nature, including human nature. Hence, they differ from true belief and clear knowledge (*c* and *d*), which are not subject to error but are essentially generative of truth about nature. Here the difference lies between knowledge through a strong proof, based on reasons or true reason (*c*), and knowledge coming from direct acquaintance with a reality beheld and felt as truly present (*d*). True belief informs us that something must be in accord with our demonstrative reasoning *about* it, but it does not render this thing present in itself to our mind. That latter comprehension through a reality's own presence to our mind is reserved for clear knowledge. Inferential reason points in the correct direction, but the apex of clear knowledge comes through an act of the understanding, which includes an affective perception of the presented reality. In the *Ethics,* Spinoza refers to this culminating grasp as "intuitive knowledge" (*scientia intuitiva*), which term stresses both the true understanding and the intimate possession of the known reality.[10]

That reality about which we may opine, truly believe, and properly know is nature in its many naturing and natured aspects, including these cognitive acts of man. Spinoza's explicit distinction among the human manners of knowing serves a threefold function in his reflections on nature.

First, it helps to refine and render more determinate his theory of finite natured nature in its human realization. Whatever else is admitted into his view of man bears some relation to this distinction among cognitions and gets variously interpreted in correlation with them. Hence, Spinoza can say that our nature "consists of" these cognitive ways, which join in modalizing the human mind and affecting all aspects and meanings of our composite nature.

Second, these kinds of cognition are *intra*differentiations or active formations within nature. Spinoza does not set them apart from nature, as though they were outside observers of it. Neither does he regard them and the human mind as a wholly separate realm that would be in nature, indeed, but not subject to its otherwise pervasive causation and necessity. They retain their distinctive operations, which yet are entirely internal to nature and regulated by its necessary causation. Their distinctiveness is just as marked as that of particular modal nature as a whole, and of the human body whose idea or mind they serve to specify in the unity of man. Their inclusion within the whole of nature is just as thorough and unreserved as is that of natured nature, of which their entire reality is a partitive constituent. Distinctive functions without externalization and separation—this is the rule governing the cognitive phase of Spinoza's naturizing of the theory of man.

But a third consequence must be drawn with equal insistence. Every thew which binds the human mind and its cognitive modes to the rest of nature also expands the scope of our cognition to include, in one fashion or another, the rest of nature. The qualifying phrase *in one fashion or another* is necessary for several reasons. It prevents the false inference that we can entirely overcome our cognitive limitations so as to know every feature of nature comprehensively or in its entire being. Spinoza does not rescind the limits already specified concerning our knowledge of naturing nature and its infinite attributes, as well as the full range of natured nature. Yet he acknowledges that we entertain opinions and beliefs (however deficient and productive of error), true belief or inferences through reason, and understanding, of many aspects of nature. Although our cognitions are not of equal surety and worth, they do relate the human mind variously to nature in its complexities and unifications.

It is this variety, of course, which elicits philosophical reflection, criticism, and control over our modes of cognition and our discourse about nature. For gaining its original admission into the Spinozan theory of nature as a whole, every statement must submit to some kind of relating to the main ways of human knowing. What may be apt and sufficient in one modality may be found misleading in another cognitive context and hence subject to drastic criticism and reinterpretation. And when we in turn try to grasp Spinoza's theory of nature, we have to retrace this process. We educate ourselves into the discipline of considering every Spinozan proposition on nature in the perspective now of opinionative imagery, now of true belief or rational argument, and now of intuitive or presential understanding. Thus, for Spinoza to naturize the theory of man means, at the same stroke, to impose this comparative epistemological rule upon our reading of his every statement about nature in whole and in part.

3. Man among the Things in Nature

A primary aim of Spinoza's early theory of man is to sever the relation between philosophical anthropology and any total transcendence of nature. The more that gets known about what man is and seeks, the more grounds get uncovered for integrating his reality with the rest of nature, rather than for directing him ultimately beyond nature. Almost every particular chapter of the latter half of the *Short Treatise* contributes something toward this general aim. There is a superabundance of themes here that state their argument and also point toward future developments, somewhat in the manner of the opening section of a Dvořák symphony or a Bartók concerto. I will select two of these themes for present consideration, bearing in mind both that they cooperate toward establishing man's immanence in the broader whole of nature, and that they are discussed again in Spinoza's other writings. They concern the meaning and ramifications of the analogy of things and the manifestation of nature in man. The common function of these two themes is to show that everything known about man binds him closely to his natural context and does not encourage any breakaway, for whatever reasons that can be philosophically inspected.

(a) *Analogy of things as analogy within nature.* A reasonably attentive reading of Spinoza's Latin works shows that he makes an analogical use of the term *res* or "thing."[11] For instance, it can designate a mind or its components, a body or its components, a mind-body composite, and an individual agency of the minutest or the most embracing sort. This diversity of the term's real referents is not unusual among Spinoza's contemporaries, since writers of school-manuals included *res* among the transcendentals applicable to all beings, and since Descartes also gave it considerable latitude to cover beings and truths we can comprehend. But such usage poses special difficulties for Spinoza, who regards all the transcendentals as abstract conceptual impositions and the Cartesian conception of thing as permitting God's actions to elude the necessity of nature.

This is a case where the Dutch *Short Treatise* is helpful. It manifests

Spinoza's uneasiness, right from the start of his systematic reconstruction, with the whole problem of thinghood. He explores the Dutch-language difference between *ding* and *zaak* (comparable to the German *Ding* and *Sache*) for whatever aid it can provide. This distinction is never fully worked out or rigidly adhered to. Nevertheless, it does suggest that a complex set of meanings of "thing" is intended to be included in any fuller discussion of the problem, as formulated in the statement that "all things [*dingen*] that are in nature, are either things [*zaaken*] or actions [*werkingen*]."[12] Spinoza interprets this principle in accord with his divisions of nature.

Thing (1). The very broadest significance is that of *dingen,* as including all the real entities in nature. This is distinct from the entities of reason or imagination, which do not exist in nature apart from the products of our imagination. But otherwise, thing (1) is quite capacious, signifying all the beings that are in nature without yet employing the divisions of nature. Nevertheless, Spinoza's philosophy builds upon these divisions, and when they are drawn, they must generate further senses for "thing."

Thing (2). When "nature" refers to the immanent causal source of modal reality, that is, to naturing nature, then the *zaak* is none other than the divine sole substance. In the *Short Treatise,* Spinoza several times uses the plural form *zaaken* (things). He employs this usage in reference to the several divine attributes, and its significance is twofold. Sometimes, it indicates a development of his own position on these plural attributes, especially a clarification of the sense in which they may be called "substances." They can be so designated only in the sense that they refer the understanding toward the one divine substance, as signified by this or that irreducibly distinct attribution. Hence, the second reason for plural usage is clearly marked by Spinoza as being a corrective communication addressed to the Cartesians, who regard thought and extension as substantive things in their own right. This emendative use of the plural is clearly signaled in Spinoza's two parenthetical remarks: "Both the infinite extension and thought, together with other infinite attributes (or, according to *your* style, substances). . . . The attributes (or, as *others* call them, substances) are things [*zaaken*], or to speak better and more properly, is one being [*wezen*] subsisting through itself."[13] This self-subsisting being is God the unique substance, the *zaak* (thing [2]) of which naturing nature consists. This is the reformed sense in which nature or thing (2) comprises all aspects of divine causation that issue forth in natured nature.

Thing (3). When the key term *nature* is then specified to refer precisely to the immediate and mediate infinite outcome of God's causation, it signifies the infinite modes or things (*dingen*) in natured nature. They all are modes of the unique divine substance and, taken together, they give us a general view of natured nature as a whole.

In a clear effort to reform Cartesian usage, Spinoza adjusts the phrases "the thinking thing" and "the extended thing" to his division of nature.[14] Depending upon the context, these expressions can signify the divine substantial thing (2) itself, when it is called "the thinking substance" or "the extended substance." But in other settings, the "thinking thing" and the "extended thing" will name the immediate and mediate infinite modes or things (3) constituting natured nature, as considered under the divine attributes of thought and extension. In this latter usage, these words do not signify the Cartesian mind-substance and body-substance in man, but rather the infinite modal centers that actively unify and incorporate the finite modalities of thinking and extension. For Spinoza, the sphere of things (3) is that of the infinite modal universe, related by causal origin to thing (2) and by causal origination to finite beings in the fourth meaning of "thing." The connectedness among these orders of things rests on the actions or active workings (*werkingen*) proportionate to each order of things.

Thing (4). Both human experience of nature and his own philosophizing compel Spinoza to press onward from the general to the particular view of natured nature. Here the emphasis falls upon the particular things (*dingen*) that are present and active in natured nature. There are at least two urgent reasons for carrying the theory of thing to this degree of particularity. First, it enables Spinoza to explain concretely that the idea or soul of every thing rests upon there being an idea "of the particular things [*dingen*] that at each time come to exist, . . . of each particular thing [*ding*] which really comes to be."[15] It can be distinctively affirmed of particular things that they come into existence, without yet sharply distinguishing between a purely temporal and an eternal way of interpreting their existential becoming. Second, thing (4) does provide a clear contrast between a real being and a being of reason or imagination. To underscore that will belongs to the latter class, Spinoza refuses to include will among "things [*dingen*] that truly are in nature." Instead, "the will is no thing [*zaak*] in nature, but is only a fancy."[16] The particular things in nature, taken together, belong in the order of *ens reale*, rather than in the purely logical imaginary spheres.

Spinoza has now furnished the basis for grasping his dictum that the only things existing in nature (rather than just in the understanding) are substance and modes. This is equivalent to saying that reality consists respectively of thing (2) and things (3) and (4), or of naturing and natured nature.

Thing (5). Until this point, the tendency of the theory of thing has been toward ever-increasing particularization and multiplicity. But we have just noticed that a countermovement is already under way, when particular things are taken together as a boundary of real being. Further recapitulation occurs when we reflect that thing (4) is the realm of finite causal determinations of thing (3) within natured nature, and that the latter is, in its turn, the immediate and mediate expression of naturing nature or thing (2). To complete this reunification process, Spinoza affirms that substance and modes, naturing and natured nature, are dynamically joined as one thing (5). This is the integrative meaning of nature as a whole, a meaning that is presaged by the thing (1) view of all the beings that are in nature. Yet thing (5) is no mere echo but a meaning that only emerges in and through the differentiation of the several registers of "thing." Indeed, thing (5) expresses the synergic union of all these signified realities, considered precisely as the total active being or *natura tota*. That this brings out the comprehensive meaning of nature as the divine whole or all-being is made evident in Spinoza's affirmation about man and all modal realities. "All things [*dingen*] become united through nature, and united into one, namely, God. . . . All consist in one sole thing [*zaake*], which is God himself."[17] This sole thing (5) weaves into active individual form all the substantial reality and modal realities composing the meanings of "thing," together with their respective actions. And this not only comes about *in and through* nature but also yields the maximum signification *of* nature itself available in a human philosophy.

This differentiation of things in nature affects the systematic topics of analogy and immanence. Clearly, Spinoza's theory of thing is not univocal. On the contrary, it requires that the proper meaning of "thing" be distinctively specified whenever a precise use of that term becomes important in a text. The several meanings are not equivocal, since together they govern our various ways of treating the beings that are in nature. There is an analogy among these things, serving as a basis for the use of "thing" in Spinozan statements and arguments. And since this theory of thing rests on the division of nature, there is a strain of analogy present in nature as conceived by Spinoza: *analogia rei*, the analogy of things within nature.

There are lower and upper limits to this latter analogy.[18] The lower limit is seen in one of Spinoza's basic criticisms of Bacon—namely that he relies upon imagery in his own mind rather than upon the analogy of nature. Such philosophical tasks as tracing the sources of error or determining the range of philosophy and the forms of reality depend upon our apprehension of nature. One grasp of nature's reality supplies the only reliable surmodel to guide our reflection, the governing analogue for every specific investigation. But nature is the all-enveloping whole, not just a primary analogate that measures some other forms of reality.

At the upper limit, Spinoza rejects the language of the school-manualists and Descartes, when they maintain that some aspects of man and the world are present in the first cause "eminently but not formally." This would prevent the attribution of extension to God; it would invite unmitigated equivocation in our discourse about God in other respects; and it would provide justification for taking a skeptical position on human knowledge in general. Spinoza regards these consequences as fracturing the unity of nature, and hence, as a countermeasure, he treats analogical predications as differentiations made well within his conception of the whole of nature. In a word, all analogies *among* things remain analogies *within* nature. Thus, analogical reasoning that employs different senses of "thing" is founded upon his metaphysical logic of the senses of "nature."

This is the foundation of Spinoza's confidence that his theory of thing reinforces man's immanence in nature. Whether there be a movement of reflection from one to another meaning of thing or a movement of desire and love from one to another actuality among things, the entire development occurs within the whole that is nature. This whole still allows for paths of transcendence, but they concern the overcoming of limits in some particular condition of things, some enlargement of vision and power concerning things and actions within the analogy of nature. Such internal transcendence does not validate any effort to go beyond things as a whole: such an effort would abandon the being of nature, resulting in a fanciful and self-deceptive removal from reality. For man to develop his insight and activity in a real way means to unite himself increasingly with the totality of things, not to cut himself off from the inclusive life of nature. Thus Spinoza's interpretation of every form of transcendence and immanence conforms with his general principle that "outside of nature, which is infinite, no more being is or can be."[19]

(b) *The manifesting of nature in man.* In terms of the theory of thing, the second part of the *Short Treatise* deals mainly with one sort of thing (4), namely, man as a complex and interrelated natural reality. Throughout the individual chapters devoted to the analysis of man runs the common theme that nature manifests itself in him and in his primary constituents and actions. This theme is specified through analyses of the problems of man's body, feeling, and understanding. In each instance, Spinoza argues that our human drive is not to use nature as a springboard toward something else but to improve our recognition and appreciation of nature's presence and power. That presence-and-power of nature discloses itself as being the fulfillment as well as the foundation of human activity.

If we can judge by the frequency with which he reaffirms it, Spinoza's chief interest lies in the general principle underlying his particular studies of man. With only slight variations fitted to the context, he repeats the principle that God in his attributes, or naturing nature, "is a being subsisting through itself and therefore, through itself, makes itself known and reveals itself. . . . Nature becomes known through itself, and not through any other thing."[20] Everywhere in the *Short Treatise,* the emphasis is upon total nature's *manifestation through itself,* whether it be how God or naturing nature imparts knowledge of itself, or else how it arouses us to an understanding and appreciation of the whole of nature united actively in the all-being. Just as there is no being that exists apart from nature, so is there no means of grasping the true meaning of being apart from nature's own showing of itself, as well as no other genuine realization for us than union with this whole of nature.

To characterize man's direct response to his situation, Spinoza next gives special prominence to the thesis "that there is a body in nature."[21] What is surprising is not the content of this thesis, but rather its position in the whole discussion of man and the manner of its proof. Spinoza places the problem of body within the chapter on our happiness in order to stress its ethical import against those who would treat it solely as a theoretical issue in epistemology and cosmology. The question of human happiness concerns the whole man, a real composite of soul and body; and it concerns the way to gain active mastery over the passions of the soul which are aroused by changes in the body. Such an approach to human happiness would not be serious and accurate, were bodily factors excluded or declared ultimately unreal. And since Spinoza upholds a certain proportioning between *our* body and *our* soul, he is doubly obligated to associate our search for happiness with the reality of our body in a real bodily world.

The path of proof is distinctively Spinozan. One can draw upon previous proofs that God is and what God is. Naturing nature exists, and among its infinite attributes is to be counted extension. The world known by understanding and our experience includes the modal reality of body, under the attribute of extension. What exists through divine causation is natured nature, including the infinite mode of motion-and-rest and the extended bodily world in its plural finite formations.

Spinoza emphasizes the existential as well as the necessary causal connection between extended bodies and naturing nature with its attribute of extension. His intent is twofold. The existentiality on the part of naturing as well as natured nature obviates that sort of analogy which would attribute extension only eminently and causally to God, not as formally belonging to his own being. And the necessary causation removes the Cartesian need to appeal to divine veracity as guarantor of our belief in an existing bodily world and our own bodies. Spinoza's theory of the relation between naturing and natured nature makes it unnecessary to follow the Cartesian route of radical doubt, probable belief in the bodily world, and an appeal to God's veracity when his causation of extended natured nature would be otherwise questionable. This same theory also blocks any interpretation of the human search for God as a fracturing of nature's immanent wholeness. There are neither existential nor causal grounds for pitting a relationship with God against this immanence.

Spinoza assigns a remarkably complex role in this discussion to *gevoel*, which is "perceptive feeling" and "feelingful perception" alike. Through the theme of feeling, his theory of the grades of cognition contributes to the problem of human immanence in nature. Feeling cements the lowest with the highest sort of cognition. It begins to function at that phase of the theory of thing (4) where we can speak not only of plural finite bodies in general but also of *us*, of *our* human body and soul (or idea of that body) in interchange with other bodies. "And this change in us, arises from other bodies which work upon us, and cannot be without that the soul, which then constantly changes, becomes aware of this change. And this change is properly that which we call feeling [*gevoel*]."[22] Feeling changes us, in the sense of directing our awareness first toward the extended world of other bodies, and only thereafter to our own bodily self thus affected. Through this orientation, feelingful perception opens one's human experience toward other individual extended existents, indeed in principle toward the entire existing reality of the extended thing (3).

Spinoza returns to the analysis when he explains why human understanding is dissatisfied with the necessary verities of reason. Since man has tested this perceptive experience, so replete with feeling, he must continue to seek an existential and individual relationship with self-imparting nature, a cognition that incorporates the sure truths of reason within an experiential apprehension of the whole reality of nature. Consequently, Spinoza is careful to state that clear knowledge of total nature comes to be in us, "not through conviction of reason but through a feeling, and enjoying of the thing itself."[23] The decisive phrase *door een gevoelen, en genieten van de zaake zelve* is richly laden. The apex of our cognition reaffirms perceptive feeling, with its openness to the whole scale of meanings for "thing," as well as its bent toward the thing itself in its individual existential act. And hence, such knowledge must essentially include a praxic and affective aspect, an active striving which enables us to enter into an enjoying relationship with the breadth of things in nature. Man's immanence in nature is reaffirmed, not abandoned, in this affective-cognitive-praxic satisfaction.

From this perspective, we can see the grounds of Spinoza's paradoxical remarks about the understanding as being both passive and active. It is passive, not within a framework of abstraction or of Cartesian perception apart from the will's assent, but in a peculiarly Spinozan sense.

> [1] Man as being a part of the whole of nature, on which he depends, by which he is also ruled, cannot do anything by himself toward his wholeness and well-being.
> [2] The understanding is a pure passion, that is, a perception, in the soul, of the essence and existence of things [*zaaken*]; so that it is never we who affirm or deny something of the thing [*zaak*], but it is the thing [*zaak*] itself that affirms or denies, in us, something of itself.[24]

These passages are closely related in their expression of man's condition and of the way to improve his lot.

At first glance, we might think that text [1] conveys a pessimistic, or at least a quietistic, counsel. Nature's determination weighs heavily upon man and reaches thoroughly into his springs of action. But the simple words *by himself* effectively qualify the nature-and-man relationship. If he denies or forgets this relationship, then he is indeed doomed to futility in seeking his own integrity and welfare. But if he acknowledges how he really stands within nature and thereby abandons an artificial isolation and autonomy, then he has taken the essential step toward achieving felicity. It comes only from recognizing and following the consequences of his being a part of natured nature, in whose active striving for closer union with naturing nature he can then intimately participate. The chapter within which this text appears is entitled "Usefulness of the Foregoing" analysis of God and man. Spinoza briskly invites us to reflect and act upon the uses or praxic consequences of his theory of man acting consciously as an integral portion of the whole of nature.

A quick reading of text [2] might convince us, however, that the practical implication is still one of passivity rather than activity, at least as far as our cognition is concerned. Yet, here again, the operative word "we" signifies a conventional, uncritical approach to reality solely in terms of images and definitions of our own making. This leads to a blockage of the corrective work of the understanding and its positive response to actuality.

The self-reforming "we" must learn to see, feel, and enjoy the things of nature as they affirm themselves within human understanding. The latter has to remove any roadblocks of imagery and definition, insofar as they would substitute themselves for the expansive grasp of naturing-natured nature in its active totality. Such a grasp unites this or that finite human understanding to the infinite understanding, to the latter's comprehension of the extended world of motion-and-rest, and to their joint causal origin in God or naturing nature. All these factors have to manifest themselves and resonate within our cognition if we are to arrive at understanding in the active sense.

Without fear of misinterpretation, then, Spinoza can now bring out the more positive implications of these two texts. Thus text [1] is supplemented by the affirmation that "we depend in such a way on that which is the most perfect of all, that we also are as a part of the whole, that is of him; and, so to say, bring to it also our share toward elaboration of so many aptly ordered and perfect works as are dependent thereon."[25] What counts most is the way we construe our dependent being as parts of the whole of nature. The phrase *in such a way* reminds us about the opening afforded us to take an active practical attitude toward our partitive relation to the whole of nature. Spinoza encourages us to take active advantage of making our own contribution toward the totality of natural reality, through shaping our relationships with its parts. He inserts the qualifying words *so to say,* not in order to weaken or fictionalize our contribution but to keep it within the context of dependence on the primal power of naturing nature and the whole order of nature.

Text [2] already stresses the active interiorizing of natural objects. There is a qualitative transformation of our understanding when it does achieve an attentive grasp of, and feel for, the essential and existential being of natural things. The term *thing* is repeated in this text as a reminder of the many senses in which we can become one with vivifying natural realities. Spinoza finds it advisable, however, to elucidate the sense in which such unions enable us to grow more conscious of the essence and truth of the things involved.

> In order to grasp this better, it may be helpfully remarked that the understanding (although the word sounds otherwise) is a clean or pure passion, that is, that our soul becomes changed in the very way that she gets other modes of thinking which she previously did not have. When now someone, because the whole object has formed in him, gets similar shapes or modes of

thinking, it is thus clear that that one obtains an entirely other feeling of the shape [*gevoel van de gestalte*] or quality of the object than an other [thinker] who has not had so many causes.[26]

This text synthesizes a number of points about our knowledge of nature.

Spinoza exhibits his usual linguistic sensitivity, since the word *understanding* has an active ring about it. This active signification would be easily justified if the question concerned only the infinite mode of understanding, which is supremely active knowing. But Spinoza's direct concern here is with understanding in its human condition, in its presence in our soul. As distinguished from the opinions, images, and theories we construct, our understanding is attentively open to the objective essence, interpreting the real structure and act of things in nature. It is not mindlessly passive, as though it were a mirror or printout of the world. But it undergoes the process of growth in perception or awareness, thus constantly improving its true knowledge.

This sort of passion is clean and pure, both because its development leads to some improved modes of thinking and because its aim is precisely to become active through obtaining truth about natural actualities. Spinoza expresses this becoming active, on the part of a finite form of understanding, as an act of becoming more truly conscious of the patterned shape or gestalt of the entire object, and hence more fully affirmative of its essential and existential act. He calls this activity an improved feeling for the object as a whole, a sharpened awareness of its qualitative individuality and relationships.

Taking thing (5) in its most comprehensive sense, the act of understanding seeks ultimate active union with the whole of nature grasped as the naturing-natured reality. As for the exact way in which the action of many causes upon the knower is converted from being an effect in us to being an awareness of our own power in nature, Spinoza makes us wait for the account to be given in the latter portion of the reworked *Ethics*. In any case, he is already insistent that our increase of understanding and feeling, awareness and activity, joins us all the closer to nature in an immanent union. To break away from this wholeness would bring impurity to man, regardless of one's exalted notion of a transnatural object.

4. Anticipations on Religion, Law, and Community

As the *Short Treatise* heads toward culmination in the doctrine on man's well-being, it becomes more programmatic and less doctrinally worked out. Spinoza is setting forth for himself a comprehensive list of agenda whose shape can be stated in manifesto form, but which will require the detailed reasoning in his subsequent writings to establish through philosophical argumentation. Nevertheless, his general aim is outlined clearly enough in the *Short Treatise,* especially his projected reform of human convictions about religion, law, and community as measured against his now-firm view of nature.

(a) When he treats of nature in its general divisions and in its specific forms, Spinoza criticizes some *religious* views of nature. Fideistic skeptics base their disparagement of human reason and philosophical argument upon man's being engulfed in nature. The latter is declared untrustworthy on two counts. Considered in a general way, nature is confused; and considered in its human manifestation, nature is weak. The fideistic conclusion is that man cannot guide his life by the supposed order and resources of nature but must, instead, rely exclusively on supernatural faith.

Spinoza's response foreshadows the kind of criticism advanced in the nineteenth century by Feuerbach and Marx. He regards the attribution of confusion and weakness to nature as a matter of language, which has beclouded those who speak in this fashion. Such ways of characterizing nature must be traced to the human speakers, not only for the origin of the talk itself but also for the basis of the assertions. Skeptical religious talk about nature reveals something about the condition of the talkers but not about nature in its general consideration. The confusion and weakness in question do not truly characterize nature as a whole, which signifies divine order and power present in both the naturing causal source and the natured modal consequence. Even the particular modal nature of man is not confused and weak in its essential being and activity. Only when men fail to clarify their opinions and rectify their passions do they believe confusedly and become weak victims of circumstance. Spinoza calls men in this frame of mind "weak souls."[27] These *zwakke ziele* then project their unhappy condition upon nature itself as a whole. They depreciate it in favor of some extranatural phantoms, to which they give a religious response at the expense of loyalty to nature.

But Spinoza does not advocate abandonment of men caught up in their own confused beliefs and weaknesses. On the contrary, the main practical task he envisages for his philosophy is to study the predicament of human servitude and offer the means for surpassing it, that is, for understanding and enjoying the powerful order of nature. This includes a careful study of Jewish and Christian religious beliefs about God and man, since they convey some masked truths about nature as naturing and natured. In Chapter Seven of the present work, Spinoza's nature-governed exegesis of religion will be examined in the final form taken in his later writings, incorporating the start already made in the *Short Treatise*. Some main problems will be to determine (within the framework of his developed theory of causality) the philosophical meaning of religious regeneration and beatitude.

In the *Short Treatise* itself, Spinoza anticipates some of his procedures and reinterpretations of religion. Procedurally, he proposes a massive conceptual translation project for finding the philosophical meanings conveyed by religious language. Three prominent instances are to translate religious talk about sin, law, and grace into their respective themes in the philosophical conception of nature: sway of passions, rational knowledge about good and bad, and liberating active power. As for actual reinterpretations, Spinoza's rethinking of the passage from a passive to an active view of our understanding guides his account of religious regeneration. He liberally appropriates the religious vocabulary of "conversion," "rebirth," and "eternal life." They express our coming to recognize the active staying power of understanding as it harmonizes with nature's other activities. Spinoza's conviction is that the highest act of human cognition yields a feelingful enjoyment of God or naturing nature, along with an understanding thereof. This legitimates his own use of emotive expressions, which signify in principle a philosophical reworking of religious attitudes.

It is in this transforming spirit that the *Short Treatise* freely uses religious language, especially that of the Bible. We saw that Spinoza hails "the being of the alone glorious and blessed God," without any fear that such a phrase may overpass his general account of nature. Correlatively, he exclaims about ourselves as parts of nature: "We are truly servants, yes, slaves of God."[28] The religious act consists in binding together the sense of these two expressions. When we ascribe all originative activity to God, love him in his being and throughout all nature, and offer ourselves to him, then we achieve "both the true service of God [*godsdienst*, "religion"] and our eternal welfare and happiness." Human integrity and happiness are simultaneously realized, not destroyed, through leading a life of service to God.

These religiously expressed affirmations incorporate Spinoza's personal religious formation and study. They also look ahead to his further philosophical reformulations to be made in the light of how God and man are united in the whole of nature. The promise of a thoroughly philosophical overhauling of religious beliefs underlies the Spinozan counsel to anyone seeking eternal happiness. "So long as he is a part of nature, then he must follow the laws of nature, the [doing of] which is the service of God [*godsdienst,* "religion"]. And so long as he does such, he is in his well-being," and need not search elsewhere for beatitude.[29] Clearly, such advice supposes one's familiarity with the relationship between God and a part of nature, as well as its practical consequences for man as a part of nature seeking fulfillment.

(b) Consequently, the *Short Treatise* forewarns readers about the need to reconsider their concepts of law and community.[30] Spinoza shows special concern about *law* in two of its meanings: the laws laid down in a revealed religion and the laws of nature. He is already preparing us to interpret the former sense of law in terms of the latter. Those laws which believers accept as being commandments from God must eventually be submitted to rational analysis, based on philosophical notions of good and bad, the will of God and the will of man, freedom and finality. In turn, these ethical concepts have to be criticized and reconstructed from the standpoint of Spinoza's theory of nature. Only the latter can provide decisive grounds for determining the true significance of laws proposed within a religious context.

As for laws of nature, the *Short Treatise* raises more questions than it settles. This work does not come to close grips with the issue of relating scientific and philosophical concepts of the laws of nature. In principle, that relationship depends on Spinoza's theory of the types of cognition, with its account of the contributions of experience and imagination, reason and understanding. However, it remains for him to work out explicitly the meaning and limits of scientific laws of nature obtained through hypothesis and experiment, the need for rational philosophizing about laws of nature, and the integration reached through an understanding of nature in its primary divisions and wholeness.

Above all, Spinoza the moralist will have to reflect upon how God operates with respect to law-regulated nature, as well as how man conducts himself within it. Are laws of nature rules imposed from without by divine decree? Or do the laws of natured nature express the necessitation that governs naturing nature as well? Is man's destiny as a part of natured nature totally set by the latter's laws and, indeed, set in such manner as to render futile all talk about human power and liberation? And if moral liberation *is* operative, does it come about through man's opposition to the rest of natured nature, through his ineffable flight to a God existing beyond the laws and sphere of nature, or through an act of human integration with nature as a whole? This pile-up of fundamental questions symbolizes the many lines of inquiry that Spinoza can still be expected to pursue in other writings.

Serving as guiding clues to his future developments are a few remarks made toward the end of the *Short Treatise*. There Spinoza strategically connects the theme of nature-as-a-whole with that of *community*. Philosophically understood, laws of nature are the eternal laws of God which pervade the whole of nature and maintain its well-being. The laws of men seek to secure our own well-being. But they actually do so only insofar as they guide us toward acting as parts of the whole of nature and hence toward sharing in the well-being of nature as a whole. All effective laws thus converge upon the welfare of the totality of nature, which is the prevailing inclusive community of agents. This great community encompasses naturing and natured nature, operating together as the law-structured actuous thing (5), the actively unified whole of nature.

All discussion of law leads ultimately to a study of two sets of community bonds wherein human reality develops. There is (i) our community with God or naturing nature; and then there is (ii) our community with the other modes of natured nature. Human laws based on the latter community (ii) are sound in the degree that they fulfill a double condition. Their proper functions are: to enable men to act appropriately as distinctive members of the modal world, and to do so in such fashion that they strengthen mankind's union with God or community (i). Only when we harmoniously integrate our law-regulated responses to both sorts of community can we begin to perceive the actuality of that community of nature-as-a-whole which embraces the two. Consequently, laws are liberative and enhance our reality when they knit human actions and relationships into the full community between God and the modal universe.

Spinoza summons all his epistemological and ontological ideas on nature when he inquires *how* the two aspects of community are manifested to us. In the case of community (i), our communion with God does not come about directly through the lower types of cognition: external signs and words, experience and imagery. But when employed within a corrective methodology, they do orient us toward God. Their function has its symbolic representation in Rembrandt's painting of the sage, whose chamber has a dark and winding staircase leading toward the source of light. The actual attainment of community with God requires, however, the direct imparting of God's essential being to the human understanding. Describing this union in the *Short Treatise*, Spinoza shows a notable preference for nonvisual language. He calls God's manifesting act an intimate touch, and calls our responsive recognition of community with God a taste of such union. Although Lowlands mystics and others also employ such terms, Spinoza's expressions are governed by his philosophical doctrine on nature. The language of touch and taste is an effective, peculiarly human way to convey something about the self-communication of naturing nature, as well as the effective use of our understanding as a peak operation of natured nature in finite form.

The practico-active-affective use of our mind also achieves the realization of community (ii), especially when the other modes of natured nature are specified to be other human beings. When I have a true understanding of God through his own immanent activity, I tend to share with other men my knowledge and love of God, my sense of the living power of naturing nature. If there is reciprocal communication of this understanding and its happiness, Spinoza holds that we are freely "constituting one and the same nature, always coming into accord in all things."[31] This is the supreme form of the harmonious modal community among human agents. Yet it cannot exist in isolation, since it intrinsically involves some community relations with the rest of the modal universe accessible to us, as well as with God the nurturing foundation of every living union.

The naturizing of God and man is an essential part of Spinoza's philosophical formation. But he cannot move at once from there to doctrinal arguments on the metaphysical and ethical, religious and political implications of his conception of nature. To work out his further positions, he must make methodical use of the several modes of cognition. Hence, Spinoza is now under philosophical obligation to develop an explicit methodology, one that is suited for establishing the basic instruments and order in reconstructing the theory of nature.

CHAPTER FOUR

Method Naturized

IN A LATER AGE that confidently transformed Newtonian physics into an imaginative framework for including man and his arts within nature, Alexander Pope based *An Essay on Criticism* (1711) upon the following premise:

> *Unerring Nature*, still divinely bright,
> One *clear, unchang'd,* and *Universal* Light,
> Life, Force, and Beauty, must to all impart,
> At once the *Source,* and *End,* and *Test of Art.*
>
>   .   .   .   .   .   .
>
>   Those RULES of old *discover'd,* not *devis'd,*
> Are *Nature* still, but *Nature Methodiz'd;*
> *Nature,* like *Liberty,* is but restrain'd
> By the same Laws which first *herself* ordained.[1]

Although Spinoza lived a half-century previously, he probably would have found this poetic vision congenial. For it presents nature as a living, unifying force that expresses itself in universal laws, including those which get reformulated in the arts and sciences of mankind.

But when these lines are extended from poetry and physics to the realm of philosophy, they are likely to arouse some misunderstanding. Pope himself intended his banner words *Nature Methodiz'd* to signify that scientific laws and artistic rules are reaffirmations of nature's own order, not aboriginal creations of the human mind. Still, one may hastily construe these isolated words as implying that philosophical methodology is autonomously framed by men and imposed upon nature. This opens a split between man and his methodological work on the one side and nature on the other. Spinoza aims at healing this split by including man and his philosophical reflections entirely within nature itself. Hence, it is fitting to reverse the poet's words and assign to Spinoza the motto *Method Naturized.* His methodological reflections are themselves specific acts of nature and receive their validation only from the order present in nature.

There was no dearth of philosophical treatises on method during the century 1550–1650, but they failed to adapt radically enough to the reality of nature. Such Renaissance thinkers as Leone Ebreo and Bruno rhapsodized poetically about man's relations with nature, whereas Ramus and the textbook writers tried to impose a purely logical set of definitions and schemata upon nature. Bacon did indeed accept the standard of nature. But this commitment got subordinated to his search after forms and restricted by his effective exclusion of God and the human spirit from the scope of nature and philosophical inquiry. Contrariwise, Descartes centered philosophy so strongly upon the relationship between God and the human self that the unity of nature is fractured and the methodological study of nature becomes secondary. All these faulty approaches authorized, after midseventeenth century, a fresh attempt at developing a theory of method squarely centered upon nature and upon man's task of opening up its meanings to knowledge and action.

This ideal animates Spinoza's own *Treatise on the Emendation of the Understanding*. It is his chief contribution to the theme of "method naturized," which requires a thorough proportioning of rules of method to the human enterprise of understanding nature and living in accord with it. To show how deeply Spinoza's methodology corresponds with this intention, I will examine four primary topics to which he addresses himself. The *Emendation* offers a distinctive invitation to philosophy; it locates the crux of methodology in a theory about nature and mind; it makes a critique of skepticism; and it states the definitional conditions for a humanly approachable wisdom concerning nature and our role in it.

1. Invitation to Philosophize

A reading of the initial seventeen paragraphs of the *Emendation* is likely to be a disconcerting experience.[2] This introductory section is apt to puzzle us in several respects, running counter to our expectation. We are unprepared for its tone, its scope, and the very title of the treatise wherein it is found. Not until we reflect upon how these features are related to Spinoza's general investigation of nature can we perceive their functional purpose and rightness for this phase of his project.

A surprisingly personal note is sounded at the very outset and permitted to resonate throughout the *Emendation*. This seems to run counter to Spinoza's use of impersonally stated arguments, especially his growing predilection for demonstrations made in the geometrical manner and order. Yet such mode of proof runs the danger of isolating itself through the very act of showing its universal rigor. Unless a philosopher can arouse the interest and concern of others, he may never get them to weigh his work seriously and then engage in reflections of their own. For touching other people's sense of intellectual participation, Spinoza realizes that nothing is more effective than to reveal his personal stake in finding the most fruitful use of the human mind. That is why, already in the *Short Treatise,* he occasionally permitted personal exclamations to erupt. He testified there about how great a love and strength arise from having a true idea of God as naturing nature, even though one's knowledge of God and the whole of nature is far from being exhaustive.

In the opening pages of the *Emendation,* Spinoza deliberately placed himself in the tradition of ancient and early modern exhortations to philosophize. This tradition felt that any exhorting would ring hollow, unless the philosopher himself showed his own engagement and spoke personally to others. Thus in the early seventeenth century, Bacon wrote as a personal advocate for and user of his new organon for the advancement of our knowledge and control of nature. Similarly, the allure of Descartes' *Discourse on Method* sprang from its autobiographical opening part on his own schooling and his hitherto unsatisfied quest for wisdom and the improvement of human life. It might be argued, of course, that these exhorters were merely employing the "dramatic I" as a rhetorical device to gain interest and sympathy for their philosophical programs. Doubtless, this aspect of I-language was present and artfully used by the long line of exhorters to philosophize. But, just as certainly, it was not the sole reason why such language was employed. Especially in the case of pioneers, they were concerned to communicate their own sense of dedication and excitement at moving back the boundaries of the unknown.

As for Spinoza, he combines the tradition of an I-language approach to the kinds of goods in life with a contagious conveyance of his own intellectual and moral search for the truth about nature and man. For appreciating the personal manner in which the *Emendation* begins, we should bear in mind his tutorial relationship with students of the University of Leiden. His critique of Descartes only clears the ground for communicating to them, and more especially to his own widening circle of friends, the positive motivations prompting him to seek a distinctive philosophy. Spinoza's references to "my philosophy" and its proportionate method have a personal ring to them, not reducible to a mere literary device.[3]

He was also following the counsel of a then well-known textbook account of what a good introduction to philosophic method should do. This academic model was proposed in *Logical Praxis* (third edition, 1657), by Adrian Heereboord, the leading professor of philosophy at Leiden.[4] Spinoza himself may have attended his lectures briefly and was certainly familiar with his writings. Heereboord deliberately taught and wrote as a philosopher who came after the schoolmen and Descartes. He sought to treat philosophical themes in a way that would liberate the mind from prejudgments and that would substitute the ideal of seeking the truth of an issue for the debater's glory in contention and victory.

The *Logical Praxis* presents this aim as being ethical as well as logical or, rather, as a purification of logical method through its adaptation to an ultimately ethical formation of mind. To achieve a logico-ethical reform, a philosopher ought methodically to reshape his basic operations of: (1) meditating, (2) discussing, and (3) writing. For these are the three active resources available for developing and sharing his thought.

Modes of Inquiry and Expression

1. Solitary and private reason *(solitaria ac privata ratio)*, expressed in personal reflections and meditations.
2. Social and public reason *(socia ac publica ratio)*, expressed in oral discussions and disputations.
3. Social and public reason, expressed in written texts and published treatises.
    The inquirer must seek, and the author must furnish:
    (a) information on the latter's
        (i) life-situation *(vita)*,
        (ii) specific occasion for this writing *(occasio scribendi)*,
        (iii) cause *(causa impulsiva)* spurring him to treat this theme;
    (b) an initial statement or introduction *(inscriptio aut exordium)* setting forth the items of (a), and specifying the foundation, object, and scope of the author's written treatise.

This Heereboord model is presented here as an example of the procedures ordinarily expected of conscientious philosophers by the groups with which Spinoza became associated. His call for an intellectual reformation is not just a conventional gesture but proceeds from a mind that is itself engaged in personal, self-critical reflection. And his detailed methodological arguments are forged through his participation in tutoring, question-and-answer sessions, and wide correspondence. Spinoza circulates his manuscript drafts for comment, tries to meet the criticisms proposed by visitors and correspondents, and constantly revises his manuscripts so that in printed form they will represent his best thinking on the issues at hand.

In particular, the introductory paragraphs of the *Emendation* serve as an *inscriptio aut exordium*. They convey information about the author's life-situation, his occasion for writing, and his impelling cause for correction of our mind. All this is done through a use of I-language that befits Spinoza both as personal thinker and as persuasive author. Following the tradition of Aristotle, Stoic moralists, and religious sources, he registers the attraction of sensual desires, riches, and social repute. But he also holds out the hope of obtaining release from these pursuits, through his mind's reflective experience and persistent search for something giving supreme and unfailing joy. That hope rests on the unquenchable presence of several modes of cognition in Spinoza himself and in every man. Plural kinds of perception offer a moral as well as a speculative yield. They open up prospects for a new arrangement of practical living, based on a methodically cultivated power to rethink and reorient.

This moral phenomenology gains dramatic quality from the reflective agent's eventual recognition that he cannot forever maintain a straddling posture on long-term goals. Either he must let his mind get forever absorbed in the fruitless scramble after sensuous pleasure, riches, and honors, or else he must reduce them to the instrumental status of goods-in-passage within the setting of a *novum institutum,* a new beginning and basic refounding of his life. But Spinoza warns that such a refounding requires energetic thought and patient reeducation of one's responses and relationships. Everything depends upon the twofold process of detaching one's fundamental love from perishable things and ordering it instead toward an eternal, infinite, and inexhaustible source upon which it can forever feed.

By weaving all these considerations together, Spinoza specifies the *occasion* for writing the *Emendation*. His artistry consists not only in conveying the graduality of any moral redirection, based on the healing of our understanding, but also in keeping at a minimum his initial account of our basic act of love, our search for enduring felicity, and the eternal reality toward which that love is directed and from which the happiness is drawn. For in this way he incites us to ask more about the philosophical principles underlying the entire program.

This is a question about the *scope* of Spinoza's treatise and the kind of introduction it contains. His designedly brief response consists of five points. First, the scope and sole aim of his philosophizing are to show that human perfection derives supremely from ''cognition of the union

which the mind has with nature as a whole."[5] Coming so early in the
Emendation, this is an enigmatic declaration. It is intriguing enough to
draw our special attention, and yet so compact that it elicits a flood of
questions. The text arouses us to ask about the following: the type of
cognition that can be thus efficacious, the precise meaning of *tota natura*
or nature as a whole, the structure and practical consequences of the
relationship between mind and nature, and the paradoxical sense in which
the mind must come to know this union that it already *has.* Spinoza
succeeds in getting us not only to raise these queries at the threshold but
also to keep returning to them throughout the entire exposition of his
philosophy.

Second, Spinoza confesses that he feels a certain impulsion (similar to
Heereboord's impulsive cause) to communicate to others, as far as he can,
his thought about where our chief satisfaction lies. This impulse is the
moral philosopher's personalized version of the old axiom that the good is
diffusive of itself. Even to devote one's energies to an inquiry about the
mind-nature union is to take the moral turn. For it demands moral discipline to concentrate our reflection upon the human sense of that union and
upon how it engenders love toward an eternal, infinite reality. And since
in principle the moral turn involves all human agents, Spinoza as
philosopher experiences an impelling motive to impart his reflections to
others.

A third consideration is that social conditions must be sufficiently
stable and supportive to permit men to meditate upon the question of
where their felicity really lies, as well as to encourage their joint efforts to
attain it. Spinozan discourse on nature and mind is not rarefied, exotic,
and purely private. It addresses people living in society, and does so in
spoken and written forms that have a public as well as a private dimension. Although Spinoza alludes here only in passing to the social conditions conducive to philosophizing, these conditions are implicit in the
Short Treatise's teaching on man's community with God and with the
modes of nature. These relationships will come to the fore in the
Theological-Political Treatise and the *Political Treatise.* But already in
the methodological context Spinoza counts a good society among the
conditions, as well as the content, of a maximally developed theory of
nature.

The fourth factor is similarly mentioned but not elaborated in the
Emendation. There are practical disciplines that aid us in seeking our
well-being and doing so within a relatively favorable social fabric. They
include: technology, a program for improving health, an intelligent plan

for the education of youth, and the particular maxims generated by moral philosophy itself. Their conjoint task is to shape a society where a large number of individuals can more easily and securely live in nature and reach their moral stature within it.

Last, Spinoza qualifies all the considerations given above with some postponing phrases.[6] He says that each matter will be formally treated "later on" or "in its place." This or that topic is to be treated "more accurately" at the appropriate place for its systematic analysis. And actual demonstration of the general issues involved is delayed for the main body of what Spinoza calls "my philosophy," as distinct from this introductory sketch. These qualifying remarks help to define the intent of the *Emendation*'s opening paragraphs. They constitute an introduction to his *entire* philosophy, not just to his treatise on method. Consequently, we may legitimately anticipate that Spinoza's philosophy will: center upon the mind's union with nature as a whole, try to communicate this theme to the human community, concern itself with the best social and political conditions for thus communicating, and encourage disciplines that aid a healthy, well-educated humanity to make good use of natural resources.

Thus the practical precepts with which Spinoza rounds off his introduction supply us with provisions for the arduous route of his philosophizing. Unlike Descartes' provisional rules of morality, however, they are not proportioned to a universal doubt. Rather, they are provendary for actively fashioning a method, a systematic doctrine, and a way of living which together lead man to comprehend his relationships within nature as a whole.

We can now comment on some odd features of Spinoza's title for his methodology: *Treatise on the Emendation of the Understanding*. Along with the broader scope of the opening paragraphs as leading into his whole philosophy, there is also the more restricted function of preparing us for the present "treatise" or orderly set of reflections and arguments constituting a philosophical method. Since its goal is to secure man's well-being and happiness in nature, the method necessarily involves some "emending" of our ordinary ways of thinking. That the emending process consists in both the healing of a wound and the correction of a practice is clear from Spinoza's own description of his project. "But before all else, there must be devised a way of healing the understanding and, as much as is allowed at the outset, of purifying it, so that it may understand things successfully without error and in the best manner available."[7] Since the method is designed for our error-ridden and often mediocre way of thinking, it is accurately designated here as a *modus medendi intellectus, ipsumque . . . expurgandi.* Spinoza is recommending some drastic correctional measures for mending and purging the understanding. The severity of the remedy is not watered down by the qualifying phrase *as much as is allowed at the outset.* No immediate cure is promised, but rather a therapeutic course that will ultimately enable the understanding to recognize its union with total nature and to act accordingly.

The really troublesome word in the title and in the above quotation is *understanding.* That term becomes the more difficult to construe the more one becomes informed about the distinctively Spinozan division of nature. Descartes had encountered no great problem about reforming the understanding. For he distinguished sharply between divine and human understanding, as well as between divine wisdom and even the supreme kind of human wisdom attainable through philosophic method and doctrine. In his dominant theory of nature, however, Spinoza has a twofold connotation for "understanding." It signifies both the immediate, infinite, eternal modal expression of substance, considered under the attribute of thought, and the causally mediate, finitely constrained, and temporally embroiled modality which we constitute and recognize as our own finite mind. It is this latter intellective mode which the *Short Treatise* identifies specifically as "the human understanding," and which Spinoza calls (in the *Ethics* and elsewhere) "the human mind."[8]

The therapeusis promised by his method is not intended to emend the infinite understanding which, regarded in its own act, steadily knows and lives its union with total nature. Yet this referent is formally ruled out neither by the Latin title of Spinoza's treatise on method nor by the ordinary Dutch and English references to an emendation of "the" understanding. Hence, for clarification we must employ the terms of distinction provided by the theory of nature. We have to state explicitly that the purging and healing process concerns only the finite mode of understanding, the idea of the human body which is none other than the human mind.

Starting with his title, however, Spinoza himself does not institute textual determinations everywhere in his methodological essay, so as to remove all ambiguity on what is to be emended. His reluctance to do so rests on three grounds. First, he finds it useful at the outset to tolerate some ambiguity, lest he distract and discourage people who are simply seeking methodic aids against their cognitive deficiencies. They can be brought more expeditiously to the true source and order of healing if they will reflect upon the familiar operational meaning of understanding, unburdened at first with complicated distinctions tied to the Spinozan theory of nature.

Next, it is not Spinoza's intent to drive a wedge between infinite understanding and the human mind. To do so would be to deprive the latter of any hope of correcting and improving itself. Spinoza has to bring the human mind gradually to recognize its finite causal relation with the infinite understanding. Any methodic healing of perceptual and passional defects depends upon the affirmation of an active unity, existing in nature, between finite and infinite understanding. Our mind gains strength from coming to discern the interrelation between the precepts of methodology and the ways of nature. Emendation is proportional to the actional power of our understanding to discover and live by the truth concerning human nature, seen within nature as a whole.

The third basis for Spinoza's initial use of unspecified language in the title of his treatise is that the method therein propounded will not work automatically and isolatedly for our intellectual betterment. Its efficacy requires a reordering of our practical lives, at least sufficiently to provoke reflection upon man's relations with the universe. In order to underline this reciprocity between a definite method and a definite view of reality, the introductory paragraphs of the *Emendation* are thoroughly saturated with nature-terminology. As the latter cascades upon us, we gradually realize that Spinozan methodology gets its distinctive vigor from being correlated with a complex account of nature. Spinoza seems to be saying to us: As a sign that philosophical reflection on the understanding and the happy life must be guided by a perception of nature, I will now employ a language best suited for arousing and refining that perception. His performatory act expresses itself in at least these six characteristic phrases: (1) *in sua natura*, (2) *talis natura* and *talis societas*, (3) *aliqua natura humana*, (4) *ordo quem naturaliter habemus*, (5) *aeternus ordo et certae leges naturae*, and (6) *tota natura*.[9]

As is appropriate for a treatise on mending our human understanding, the greater portion of this language concerns finite modes of nature. (1) "In its nature" signifies that we are considering a modal thing, action, or perfection solely in and by itself. The as yet unamended human mind treats a finite being, a deed, or a perfective note, as though it has a separate hold upon reality. To break down this approach which aims at conferring autonomy is a prime aim of Spinoza's method. It seeks to wean our understanding away from an isolative viewpoint, with its supporting stock of discrete images and abstractions. Natural reality is not to be found in a cut-off condition or a claim to independent status for some modal thing taken *in sua natura*, but rather in its interaction with other modes and in their common rooting in the one substance. Methodologically considered, the truth lies in these concretions and not in a breakaway consideration of anything, apart from the rest of nature.

(2) Once the isolational illusion is removed, however, we can legitimately affirm the core truth about the presence of "such a nature." Modal realities do have such-and-such a determinate nature (*talis natura*), be it an essential structure or a particular way of existing, a perfection, or a distinctive way of acting. Here, the truth comes only when the theory of finite modal nature is specified sufficiently to designate this or that particular nature. Such determinateness includes some references to substance and the modal conditions required to realize the particular nature as being this or that one. When the question concerns a grouping of people, Spinoza rephrases his doctrine in terms of "such a society," *talis societas*. This or that society has its characterizing marks, its own way of living and developing. Yet it realizes this unique social pattern through the particular manner of its relations with other societies coexisting in a common world. By conjoining the themes of "such a society" and "such a nature," Spinoza foreshadows the incorporation of his philosophy of political and ecclesial society within the framework of his theory of nature and its modalizations.

(3) "Some human character" is a special usage, reminding us that problems of moral knowledge and conduct should not be cut loose from the general conception of nature. By *aliqua natura humana* is meant some exemplar of human living that can be proposed for our emulation, while we are still en route toward grasping the implications of the human mind's union with the whole of nature. Thus a sage or a saint serves as such a pattern, both to incite and to encourage us toward a fuller moral life. Since we cannot reach our acme at once and completely, we need some steady model of what human nature's urge toward moral improvement can really accomplish. Our active power and freedom are increased along the way, when we inwardly appropriate some human character or pattern of a more blessed sort of living. That this moral symbol is itself an interim stage does not diminish its practical function for man, the gradual self-realizer of his union with nature. Spinoza's acceptance of the role of practical exemplars gives a new pitch to his words "*such* a nature" and "*such* a society." These words are not confined to signifying differentiation. When used in an ethical context, they also signify a peak of human

perfection which we admire and propose to ourselves as a concrete exemplar for personal resolve and social endeavor.

(4) The phrase "the order which we naturally have" (*ordo quem naturaliter habemus*) raises more issues than it can settle at first use. For the reader being introduced to Spinoza's philosophy through the early paragraphs of the *Emendation*, it is yet to be determined how we "have" an order, especially an order dependent upon our union with the whole of nature. Quite as elusive is the term *naturally*. The naturalness can be conventional or liberational. It may describe the customary responses of an individual who is conditioned externally, or it may indicate our own active patterns of striving. Perhaps the term *order* carries a more definite meaning which can reduce the difficulty of the rest of the phrase. For it suggests the presence of relations that overcome an isolational notion of human nature and that connect us with the rest of the universe. The purpose of Spinoza's methodology is to guide us toward those connective relations which optimally realize our human powers.

(5) This is where "the eternal order and fixed laws of nature" (*aeternus ordo et certae leges naturae*) is a useful rather than a decorative phrase. It directs us to look beyond contingent temporal happenings, so as to connect our lives with a permanently existing set of relations. Epistemologically, this means bringing into play those cognitive acts which convey more than convention and imagination can do. In ontological terms, the rootedness of men and all other finite modes is traced to substance and the pattern among infinite modes. In his wording, Spinoza is careful not to separate "fixed laws" from "eternal order." For the fixedness in question is not static but shares in the causal activity and expressive ordering of eternal substance. Spinoza is already preparing us to refer all talk about laws of nature to their foundation in the immanent order of naturing nature or eternal substance.

(6) With "nature as a whole," the circuit is at last welded between nature in the significations above and the human drive toward unfailing happiness. There is an ethical intent at the center of Spinoza's methodology, just as there is a logic and ontology of nature shaping his ethical teaching. Given this reciprocity, it is not surprising that there is a gamut of related meanings for *tota natura*, as that term is used in the *Emendation* and the other writings. Progress in understanding Spinoza's thought can be measured by one's ability to distinguish these meanings, bring them into unitary consideration, and make them effective in the practical sphere.

Depending on the context of his reasoning in the *Emendation* and the *Ethics,* Spinoza uses *tota natura* in at least seven distinct but related senses. (a) At the minimum, "nature as a whole" stands for all bodies or finite modes of motion-and-rest taken together; or for all minds or correlated finite modes of the understanding taken together; or for both totalities conjoined (but without abolishing their mutual distinction). (b) It cosignifies these finite modal totalities along with the mediate infinite mode or pattern of the entire universe. (c) It represents the integration between the extended modal universe and the immediate infinite mode which is motion-and-rest; or that between the correlated modal universe of thought and the immediate infinite mode which is the infinite understanding; or the inclusive union of all those modal expressions of substance under its attributes of extension and thought. (d) Sometimes, the term is broadened to designate even those modes expressive of substance under attributes other than extension, along with their respective modal expressions of thought (thus reaching farther than those modes of understanding which are correlated with the modalizations of motion-and-rest). (e) Synthesizing all the meanings thus far enumerated, "nature as a whole" is a synonym for natured nature in its totality. (f) The term also provides a way of referring to the whole reality of substance or naturing nature, involving all its attributes and properties. (g) At the maximum, it is the divine all-being or immanent causal union of naturing and natured nature that is intended by "nature as a whole."

The art of Spinozan logic and methodology is to render us aware of these several senses of *tota natura* and guide our interweaving of them into a coherent philosophy. Spinoza does not merely report this pluriformity to us as detached observers, but relates it to our quest after well-being and happiness. Hence his method is practical as well as speculative in its intent. Method becomes thoroughly naturized only when it combines an emending of our thoughts about nature with a proportionate ethical response and reshaping of our active life.

2. The Crux of Methodology: "The Mind Itself and Nature"

Spinoza begins his theory of method proper by looking at man descriptively and then incitively. The *descriptive* phase consists in comparing our factual situation with the goal of our cognitive efforts. To bring out the discrepancy between situation and goal, he transposes the moral description of man (given in the general introduction to the *Emendation*) into cognitive terms. The starting point is recognition of human weakness, or *imbecillitas humana*, which continues the theme of "weak souls" broached in the *Short Treatise*.[10] Our weakness shows itself not only in the storm of our passions and conflicting desires but also in that miasma of ignorance and unsurety, doubt and error, which surrounds our efforts to know nature and ourselves. The wonder is that we still continue the efforts and, indeed, that we seek some unifying wisdom about man and God. To compare man's noetic weakness with his noetic aim induces, at the first try, only ironic skepticism. But to keep on doggedly comparing and looking for a pathway from the one to the other stirs the human mind eventually to look for a method of fulfillment.

The *incitive* phase consists in suggesting grounds of assurance that a methodic bridge is not only desirable but also within our capacity to construct. Hence Spinoza takes another look at his account of the modes of perception.[11] His present interest is not to describe and differentiate them again but to point up two implications of their presence in us.

First, all the modes of perception are ways of cognizing. Whatever else we may say about man, he is a cognizing being. He would not be human without including an active principle that drives persistently toward improving his cognition. What he cannot comprehend through one way, he seeks to reach through another. For a being who is thus constituted, the wisdom-goal is not entirely alien and beyond its weak condition.

Second, human cognition is characterized not only by the pluralism of its perceptual ways but also by their interrelation. We have the ability to synthesize our diverse cognitive modes and values into a complex pattern. We learn from reports by other inquirers, from our own experience and imagery, and from reasoning and direct insight. Singly, any one source supplements and corrects the others. When interrelated as is a braided rope, the diverse sources impart the strength of that unified understanding or wisdom toward which our active cognitive principle impels us.

Reflection upon these two traits casts light upon Spinoza's parenthetical, almost offhand statement "for we have a true idea."[12] This assertion requires some clarification about both the having and the truth of the idea. We "have" it, in the sense that our several kinds of perceptual operations are expressive of one active cognitional principle, namely, of that within us which generates and unifies all our ways of perceiving. In this functional sense, a major emendation is already being made in our self-understanding. The human mind *is*, not just *has*, a true idea which manifests itself in the several kinds of perception.

As for the truth-character of this active cognitive principle, it comes through in the interrelational quality of human perceiving. The human mind does not merely express itself in discrete ways of perception. It corrects and expands any one of them by actively adjusting it to the others, so that it can achieve an emended interrelation of the entire cognitive range. Even in its most untutored, methodically minimal condition, our mind is constantly modifying its many perspectives in order to obtain a harmonious synthesis. It is working toward the truth about itself and the world, and thereby deserves to be called a true idea in the context of methodology.

Another of Spinoza's statements (which I have already quoted and shown to be fraught with difficulties) concerns the order we naturally have. We can now see that the human mind *is*, not just *has*, a cognitively active principle of order. In the *Correspondence*, Spinoza calls it "my order."[13] He is stamping his personal mark, of course, upon the distinctive conception of order being set forth in this treatise. But unless something more general were also intended by these words, the results could be dismissed as a private persuasion. Since Spinoza presents arguments and historical comparisons, he uses the words in a stronger meaning that addresses an evidentiary claim to the human community. Each inquiring individual is being invited to reflect upon the complex interrelations in his own cognitive life. He is then presented with Spinoza's interpretation of whatever dynamic patterns are found to be present in the community of reflective minds. Thus, I can verify that the seeds of method are present in the ordering activities of my own mind or, in a word, in "my order" as I perceive and seek to improve it.

For quite a distance, Spinoza follows in the wake of Bacon and Descartes. The stultifying skeptical objection is that evaluation of any particular method depends upon comparison with another method, whose own soundness is judged by yet other methods—leading to an infinite regress without any definite purging and healing of our minds. Yet while we are weak insofar as we do not come equipped with beak, claws, or scales, we do have the ability to make primitive tools and then to use them for fashioning still more effective instruments. Man the evolving toolmaker is the visible image of man the evolving methodmaker. The human mind does not need an extrinsic and infinitely regressive measure, but develops more effective methods through its intrinsic striving for truth and its progressive relation with new means of reaching it.

Once the three philosophers propose the toolmaking analogy, however, they part company over the specific order and scope of reflective method. Spinoza finds no good reason for the Baconian limitation of philosophical method, such that it cannot establish the truth about God and the intellective soul. Nor does he have confidence in the Cartesian order of proceeding from self-knowledge to that about God and only then to the physical world. Instead, Spinoza fashions a philosophic net for including man and the physical world as interrelated expressions of the divine unity of nature. He then makes the throw by drawing them together and strengthening the cognitive ways experienced by human minds. This is the historically differentiating sense of "my order" in its Spinozan usage.

On the reconstructive side, Spinoza clearly posts the yield expected of his method. It must analyze and reorient human perceptions in such a manner that "I may begin to recognize simultaneously my powers and the nature which I desire to perfect. . . . [The best method aids us] to recognize exactly our nature, which we desire to perfect, and simultaneously as much about the nature of things as is necessary."[14] These two carefully constructed and similarly worded statements tell a good deal about the functions of a nature-directed method in emendating the human mind.

Spinozan method is an intellectual instrument commonly shared by the standpoints of "I" and "we," of "my" and "our," so that what is originally proposed as "my nature" and "my order" can become perceived as "our nature" and "our order" of rectified understanding. The two sentences under comment use the same infinitive form *to recognize* (*noscere* or *nosse*), signifying a process of getting acquainted with and acknowledging something. The methodically strengthened mind becomes acquainted both with its own powers and with other things; it acknowledges the reciprocity between grasping the true nature of these other things and gaining true perception of its own nature. The adverb *simultaneously* binds together the two poles of this enlightenment, lest there be a severance between learning about ourselves and learning about other natural realities.

A sense of starting on a long journey is conveyed by the verb *begin*. We do not leap at once to an intuition of the whole of nature, but must advance step-by-step in an orderly, yet arduous, process of reflection. Spinoza's repetition of the phrase *desire to perfect* signifies both that his method of investigation responds to a deep-seated striving within us and that its goal is to satisfy our need to act morally as well as to know. The function of the restrictive words *as much . . . as is necessary* is to keep our study of the rest of modal nature bound up with our self-realization. Precisely how a better understanding of "the nature of things" helps to perfect ourselves as moral agents, as well as inquirers, will be a major question in the *Ethics*.

But here in the *Emendation*, Spinoza places a fivefold demand upon a method seeking to be philosophically true and humanly helpful. (a) It must furnish an accurate recognition (*exacte nosse*), one that (b) clarifies our powers and desire to perfect our own nature (*natura nostra*), and one that (c) also illuminates the nature of things in the world (*natura rerum*) and (d) has simultaneous discernment (*simul*) of the mutual relations between our own nature and that of things in the world; (e) finally, all these tasks converge in the fundamental purpose of all Spinozan methodology—to lead us to true and effective knowledge of *se et natura*, of "the mind itself and nature," considered in their union and active relations.

The ability to develop the composite theme of the mind itself and nature is Spinoza's norm for judging the truth and worth of any philosophical methodology. Descartes falls short of this measure, since he looks for the criteria of truth in the doubting mind's self-relationship alone. Such marks would be extrinsic to the mind-nature relationship, and hence would require an order of reasoning that leads from our mind to God and only thereafter to the physical world of bodies. But for Spinoza, a true method is intrinsic, insofar as it *is* precisely a reflection upon our mind as being always objectively referent to our body and the rest of nature. Otherwise stated, method consists of an orderly reflection upon the human mind as being a true idea of its own body and, thereby, of things in nature. Hence, a true method proceeds simultaneously, rather than separatively, so that its every phase increases our understanding of the mind and the rest of nature in their union. Each methodically achieved advance opens a conjoint perspective on the power of nature and the power of one's own mind.

Spinoza's position is also clarified by contrast with university textbook versions of method as a means for understanding the causes of things. What he finds unacceptable here is not the study of causes and of relationships based on them, but rather the view that methodic inquiry terminates in the notion of God as the cause who is completely transcendent of nature. On this point, Spinoza's account of the meanings of nature and natural things leads him to an immanently inclusive method of relating God to the totality of natured beings, including the human mind. That philosophic method is the best one that leads us to reason in an intrinsic, simultaneous, and immanently inclusive manner about nature as a whole. For this method makes our mind fully reflective about the truth concerning nature. That is why Spinoza conceives of his method as being itself *the idea of the true idea of nature as a whole*.

At the outset, any individual human mind falls far short of realizing this reflective knowledge and its proportionate activity and happiness. Methodologists and moralists alike warn that a long journey is required to bring our minds to fulfillment. Spinoza's problem is to transform this commonplace into his own uncommon view of gradual and orderly progression. In a rather long passage, he gives some distinctive methodological precepts that are consonant with his theory of nature and mind.[15] For the sake of analysis, I will divide his text into five parts, each of which embodies a principle of his naturized method.

(1) The principle of direct proportionality. "And since it is clear through itself that the mind understands itself just so much better as it understands more things about nature, it is thence established that this part of the method [on the order of inquiry] will be just so much more perfect as the mind understands more things, and then will be most perfect when the mind attends to cognition of the most perfect being, or reflects on it." Here, Spinoza holds that there is a direct proportion between increase in our cognition of natural things and increase in our self-compre hension. We do not advance in self-understanding by withdrawal from other things but by improving our grasp upon them and widening our scope concerning them. Spinozan reflection makes no break with things in the world, seeks no closure of privacy unconnected with them. Instead, it continues to inspect and meditate upon them and upon ourselves together, until it recognizes that our mind and other things belong to the same natural reality. For us to understand more things means to understand more about nature and about ourselves.

Spinoza regards this direct noetic ratio as being clear *per se*, by its own power and through its own presentation to us. It carries intrinsic clarity within the frame of his conception of nature. For in that context, the human mind comes to recognize itself as included among the finite modal expressions of nature. It discerns its kinship with other finite modes, amid whatever differences also come to notice. Far from losing sight of itself in a study of things in nature, the human mind finds its own reality conceived more clearly within the common whole.

A further point emerges from this proportionality, which is not a static equation but a progressive growth in one's power of insight and one's hold upon the truth concerning mind. Because method is a reflection upon a true idea, our development in self-understanding is also a development in philosophical method. The more we come to know the relationship between the human mind and other things in nature, the more we also learn about methodic ways of improving this basic knowledge. And because methodic betterment is proportioned to the mind's grasp of natural

realities, the best method is that based upon our grasp of the most perfect
being, or naturing nature. The principle of direct proportionality provides
Spinoza with a standard for comparative judgments about philosophical
methods, a way of determining the unconditionally most effective one for
gaining truth about the mind's union with the whole of nature, and hence
an unsurpassable pattern for ordering our reasoning and our action.

(2) The principle of intellectual power and natural order. "Hence the more
things the mind gets acquainted with, so much the better does it understand both its own powers and the order of nature. Moreover, the better it
understands its powers, the easier it can direct itself and propose rules to
itself; and the better it understands the order of nature, the easier it can
restrain itself from useless matters." Here, Spinoza specifies the mind/
things correlation as being concerned precisely with simultaneous increase in cognition of the mind's *powers* and nature's *order*. This reciprocity holds valid for all the ways in which the mind exercises its powers
and for all the ways in which nature structures and achieves its order.
Hence the correlation permeates every aspect of Spinoza's systematic
development of philosophy—metaphysical and ethical, religious and
socio-political.

In the *Emendation*, however, he restricts himself quite properly to the
methodological consequences. As our mind deepens its awareness of its
own capacities, it finds itself able to formulate ever more fruitful rules of
research and to adhere to them. That the process of methodic purging,
healing, and investigating is self-generated comes through unmistakably
in the emphatic reflexive phrase "can direct *itself* and propose rules to
itself." These words convey the distinctively methodological form of
experiencing the mind's own power. Such experience will stand us in
good stead when we get buffeted by events and enslaved by passions. If a
sense of powerlessness threatens to discourage our plans for active reform, Spinoza can enlist this confident recognition of the mind's self-
generated power to formulate progressively more effective instruments
both for studying nature and comprehending ourselves.

Constant improvement of knowledge brings with it an increase of
action. Expressed methodologically, the latter is seen in our ability to
refrain from "useless matters" or, in more positive terms, to adhere to the
ideal of economy and self-control. Rule-regulated action enables us to
advance from an inchoate relationship with nature to one that keeps pace
with our always-increasing recognition of the orderliness of nature and
the mind's inclusion within that order. In the *Ethics* and elsewhere, Spinoza spells out the practical consequences of regulating the human mind

by rules founded in a better understanding of nature's order. Our power of acting is heightened by our method-governed move from the outlook of chance and oppressive forces in nature to that of nature's liberating order for reflective human agents.

(3) The principle of non-discreteness. "An idea comports itself objectively in the same manner as its ideatum comports itself really. Therefore, if there were in nature something having no commerce with other things, even if there were its own objective essence which ought to agree entirely with the formal one, still it [the objective essence] would have no commerce with other ideas. That is, we could [Dutch: understand nor] conclude nothing about that very essence." In the midst of his positive statements about mind, nature, and method, Spinoza is careful to insert this negative text as an admonition. Its purpose is to rule out a line of speculation that the best method is to achieve a complete cognitive adequation between the human mind and its body, by isolating them from everything else in nature. Briefly put, Spinoza's reply is that such an isolation would destroy both our self-knowledge and the truth about nature.

To reach this conclusion, he employs three of his basic pairings.[16] First, "idea/ideatum" distinguishes between some definite act of meaning (the idea) and the referent thereby intended and affirmed (the ideatum). In man's case, the idea may be a particular meaning, a systemic group of meanings, or the unifying mind itself (which is sometimes called the soul). The ideatum may be some particular feature of the extended world, a unified body (especially *my* own body as affirmed by *my* mind, which is often called the soul of *this* body), a mind itself or a meaningful idea insofar as they are being reflectively considered, or even some other expression of nature that may conceivably fall within consideration.

Next, "objectively/really" is a correlative functional distinction. It holds between an idea, taken in its signifying reference (or "objectively"), and an ideatum taken in its own constitutive structure and interrelations ("really" or "in nature," in the sense of being that to which a designating intention refers). These paired terms concern ways of taking something under consideration. In this correlative-functional usage, "really" and "in nature" (elsewhere, "naturally") specify that something is being viewed in its distinctive components and connections themselves, without thereby narrowing down the whole of reality and nature to this perspective. It is an operational designation made within the totality of nature, which itself also includes the objectively specifying act. Both poles of the distinction are *entirely immanent* to nature's actuality and significance. Any further determination of this couplet depends upon the context within which Spinoza uses it.

Third, "formal essence/objective essence" aids the method in specifying more closely our discourse about that which necessarily constitutes something as being what it is and as acting the way it does. When that principle is taken just in its own structural constituents and relationships, it is denominated the "formal essence." And when that principle, along with its structure and relations, is considered precisely as being known or being the grounding terminus of a cognitive act, it is denominated the "objective essence." There is no profligate multiplication of essences here, since the same structure and relationship can be signified now in its own being and now in respect to its being known (whether by something else or in a unifying act of reflection).

So that these binary distinctions can serve a useful purpose in his theory of nature, Spinoza introduces a common rule holding good for all their members. Some *commercium* or interworking must be present within the realm of ideata, as well as within that of ideas. He further states that "to have commerce with other things is to be produced by the others, or else to produce the others."[17] There is the same latitude in the ways of being produced and producing as there is in the things so related. As far as concerns man and human experience, the finite things under direct consideration are modes of understanding (minds and ideas) under the divine attribute of thought, and modes of motion-and-rest (bodies and their properties) under the divine attribute of extension. The relationships of being produced and producing obtain among the modes of understanding themselves and in the manner appropriate to these latter modes.

As thus cautiously stated, the commerce itself is intramodal, a productive bond holding among modes under the same attribute and appropriate to these ways of expressing this attribute. Such relations do not constitute a causal derivation of the modes of thought from those of extension, or the converse. Yet within the full scope of Spinoza's theory of nature, there is indeed a proportional ordering between these two series of intramodal connections of being produced and producing. The main condition for perceiving this proportional order is to emend our reflection sufficiently so that it will grasp the kinds and components of commerce within the context of modal nature. Causal community among things produced and producing is a way to conceive nature as natured and naturing.

The manifestations or active expressions of the unique Spinozan substance under different divine attributes constitute the one modal universe, within which these produced and producing modal series are mutually proportioned and ordered. Thus the commerce among ideas both connects the intramodal constituents and is also intermodally correlated with, and informative about, the commerce among ideata expressive of another attribute. This correlation follows from the orderly unity of nature as an active whole, grounding the truth of human perceptions of the extended world. The truth of our knowledge in general rests upon the intramodal commerce (coherence), upon the intermodal proportion (an actively correlative sort of agreement), and upon the distinctive ability of our minds to reflect upon both these aspects of self-unifying nature.

In the first sentence of the text of the third principle given above, Spinoza affirms the general pattern of intramodal commerce and intermodal correlation. It is this reasoning which underlies his well-known declarations made respectively in the *Emendation* and the *Ethics:* "The proportion [*ratio*] which is between two ideas is the same as the proportion which is between the formal essences of those ideas. . . . *The order and connection of ideas is the same as the order and connection of things.*[18] These texts suppose our familiarity with the doublets of idea/ideata and objective essences/formal essences, as well as the sense in which "things" can be taken as bodily modes as distinct from the ideas which refer objectively to these bodily things.

Within each side of the contrast, the intramodal commerce gets expressed as a proportion or ratio, an order, and a connection. These relations are determined by the process of being produced and producing, a process that becomes diversified within each modal series without losing its correlation with the other series. That there is correlational sameness rests ultimately, for Spinoza, upon a view of these bonding series as belonging together in natured nature and as expressing together the actively ordering power of naturing nature. The implications for the logic and method of human cognition are spelled out in the *Emendation*. But the consequences for problems of divine causality, human unity, and the conversion of man as much as possible from relations of being produced to those of producing are reserved for the *Ethics* and other writings.

The second sentence in our third principle is formulated as a counterfactual condition. It states the results that would follow were a certain state of affairs to hold in nature. "Nature" here signifies the world of bodily things, considered by us precisely as formal essences that specify motion-and-rest and hence that belong to natured nature under the attribute of extension. Spinoza says: Let us suppose that some thing would be present in nature, considered as the world of bodily modes, and yet would have no connective relations of interchange with the other things also presumably there. That supposed entity would be isolated from the rest. Its own formal essence would be completely discrete, unengaged in any transactions involving other formal essences in this modal world of extension. In my metaphysics, we can also suppose that this isolated thing or formal essence has its own objective essence or idea commensurate to itself. What would be the consequences for an objective essence of this sort?

Spinoza spells out the conditional consequences, both in a general way and then in quite specifically human terms. The very fidelity of the objective essence to its formal-essence referent means that the former would itself be isolated from other objective essences expressing the modes of understanding. It would be unconnected by any commerce with other ideas. Its discrete character could furnish no grounds for relating this objective essence to the interworking modal world of thought. Such an essence would be just as sterilely cut off from the interplay among ideas as its referent would be cut off from the interplay among bodies. The supposed body and its idea would not belong to the modal world and, thus demundanized, would not belong to the reality of natured nature.

The situation would be intensified, not ameliorated, by asking what the human mind could do with an objective essence or idea totally sealed off from commerce with other objective essences or ideas. We human reasoners could conclude nothing on the basis of this isolate, since we could not draw it into a net of inferential relations. The Dutch addition to the text at this point is even more emphatic: we could neither *understand* nor *conclude* anything about a totally discrete objective essence. For to understand this essence in itself, we would have to grasp it as actively involved in the commerce among ideas, the modifying and interrelating of assertive meanings—which runs counter to the supposition of unconditional discreteness. Such a supposition frustrates both a cognition of the objective essence itself and any act of reasoning and concluding something else from it. The supposition cannot be squared with our method-making, our inferential activities, and our gradual improvement in understanding things. In a word, it would remain impervious to philosophical emendation and truth.

These experiences support the principle of nondiscreteness in the interpretation of nature. Whether "nature" and "thing" are taken restrictively to denote modal expressions of extension or more broadly to include modal expressions of thought and perhaps other attributes of substance, the designated reality is actively related and interconnected. Spinoza dissolves the counterfactual condition in order to help us perceive more strongly that nature is an operative and unitive order, throughout all its modalities.

(4) The principle of fruitful connectivity. "Contrariwise, [formal essences] which have commerce with other things, as do all that exist in nature, will be understood. And their objective essences will also have the same commerce, that is, from them will be deduced other ideas, which in turn will have commerce with others, and thus instruments for proceeding further will increase." By the very wording of this principle, Spinoza identifies that which alone is powerful enough to revoke the fictive supposition that there may be a something in nature (*aliquid in Natura*) which lacks all ties of interchange with the rest. The supposition about isolated ideata and ideas is overcome through attending to the self-affirmation of "all that exist in nature" (*omnia quae existunt in Natura*). All natural beings enjoy the act of existing under the condition of working together and thus sustaining relations within the context of nature. Not discreteness but interconnectivity marks all natural existents.

Here, Spinoza relies upon the supple, yet determinate, meanings in his theory of nature. Principles three and four together are directly concerned with human ways of considering natured nature. The supposition of something isolated occurs to us when we view the vast multiplicity of modes of natured nature, and do so through an as yet unemended way of perceiving them. But since the question of isolation-versus-connectivity is posed by the human mind in regard to its proportionate referents, "all that exist in nature" must be specified still further. It refers to extended natured nature in all its modes, finite and infinite, with special stress upon the human body. Once we recognize the latter's involvement in many sorts of intramodal bodily forces and in the inclusive whole of motion-and-rest, we can also see the fictive or else erroneous status of the assumption about a wholly discrete extended thing. This use of the meanings of nature illustrates the process of purging and healing the understanding, by making the process measure its suppositions against the active self-affirmation of nature in the presently relevant sense.

That same basis of relatedness within modally extended nature strengthens the case for relatedness among ideas in modal nature's expressions of thought. We can listen reflectively to the self-affirmation of natured nature also in this realm. It testifies to the connection among ideas and hence to a valid ground for our inferential use of mind. Only when our ideas or objective essences affirm their own connections can we have emended and true knowledge of thinking nature itself as a modal reality. The intramodal commerce among ideas permits the drawing forth ("deduction") of ever further relational knowledge of nature as natured under the attribute of thought.

Spinoza is now well-positioned to strengthen his hopeful theme of a continual improvement of philosophical methodology and knowledge. Taken by itself, the analogy of man as toolmaker and improver of tools is a striking image that still searches for philosophical certitude. Rational justification for concluding to the human mind's intrinsic vigor comes only within the theory of naturing nature as expressing itself in modes of understanding. The relations betwen ideas or reciprocal relations among ideas lead the mind onward and possess a cumulative dynamism toward developing ever more effective intellectual tools or levels of methodology. Philosophical progress (which Spinoza here calls a process of "proceeding further") is not just a brave Baconian slogan of *plus ultra*, but is a fruitful consequence of the connectivity principle. Used in the study of intramodal relations among ideas and minds, this principle gives a footing in the theory of nature for continual emendment and advance in human concepts.

(5) The principle of exemplarity: "Further, from this last point which we said, namely that an idea ought to agree in every respect with its formal essence, it is again evident that, in order that our mind reproduce in every respect the pattern of nature, it ought to bring forth all its ideas from that one which reproduces the origin and source of the whole of nature, so that this idea itself may be also the source of the other ideas. . . . That method will be most perfect which shows the norm of the given idea of the most perfect being whereby the mind must be directed." This complex principle performs three key functions in Spinozan methodology and theory of nature.

First, it generalizes the relationship between idea and formal essence to achieve maximum unity and order. That relationship reaches beyond the proportion between different sorts of modes. For the entire modal world can itself be considered as natured reality, having a formal essence expressive of the active power of naturing nature. Hence a philosopher must search for that idea or objective essence which encompasses a reference to the originative source of all the correlated modes of natured nature. Spinoza is here on the trail of the ultimate foundation, in his conception of nature as a whole, for the previously stated principles of nondiscreteness and fruitful connectivity. In the last analysis, isolated entities (be they bodies or ideas) are ruled out because of the unifying reference of all modal realities to naturing nature. Their connectivity within their own modal realm is actively fruitful because of this same reference. The goal of methodmaking is thereby seen to lie in developing an idea of the whole of nature which will truly express this origination of natured from naturing nature. Philosophical progress is measured by the degree of approach to a method which will yield such an idea and its reasoned explication.

By stressing degrees of approach among guiding ideas and methods, Spinoza makes allowance for a second consequence. He admits a pluralism among sciences and philosophies, based not only on the several ways of cognition in man but also on the relative adequacy of ideas and methods to grasp the relationships in nature as a whole. This basis of ranking permits Spinoza to use both normative language and the superlative, in regard to the *best* method and its animating idea. Within his conception of nature and of the relation between objective and formal essence, the best philosophical method draws its ideas in orderly fashion from that idea which signifies the active font of modal nature. All our philosophical skills *must* concentrate upon the emergence of modal realities from naturing nature, an emergence which inwardly shapes every demonstrative argument. This standard of philosophical demonstration makes Spinoza simultaneously critical of other paths of reasoning and also appreciative of the actual accomplishments of scientists and philosophers.

The third, more long-range function of the principle of the exemplar is to provide direction for enjoying the mind's union with the whole of nature. When our mind aims methodically at reproducing in every respect the pattern or exemplar of nature (*omnino Naturae exemplar*), it also seeks to realize our driving thirst for happiness. Although the *Emendation* does not unduly emphasize the ethical consequences of its portrait of the best philosophical method, it does in fact furnish an ideal for the entire course of inquiry in the *Ethics*. There, Spinoza transfers the theme of exemplarity from theism's freely creative God to striving human minds. Insofar as the latter succeed in reexpressing the origination of all modal realities from naturing nature, they gain a true conception of God and the whole of nature with which they are united. This is the path toward the peak of man's knowledge and blessedness.

Assisted by the five principles stated in this section, Spinoza can conclude that "my order" of philosophizing leads to the desired knowledge of the union between "the mind itself and nature." This proposition is the crux of his methodology, since it places within our grasp that pattern of nature as a whole which transforms human passions and weakness into actions and strength. There still remain many specific problems in the method and logic of repatterning our mind to think philosophically about nature. But before treating these issues, Spinoza must first face the broad assault of skepticism upon his cognitive claims.

3. The Skeptical Mind and Its Purifiers

At first glance, Spinoza's treatment of skepticism appears to be too hasty, casual, and dogmatic. But in fact the challenge of skepticism is constantly with him; his counterapproach is carefully designed and complex in structure; and his response is sensitive to the strains which are placed by the skeptics upon his view of nature.[19] Although he is just as concerned about skepticism as are Descartes, Locke, and Leibniz, nevertheless he follows his own way of dealing with it.

It is helpful to make a preliminary distinction between mentioning and treating the problem of skepticism. Spinoza *mentions* it frequently, indeed at almost every stage of his investigation. These references serve to unsettle what Hume would subsequently call the careless dogmatism of those who recognize no need for philosophical arguments, especially concerning the foundations of knowledge and method. However, Spinoza does not launch into a full-scale study of skepticism in any random passage in which he happens to mention it. In most instances of reference, he gives it just enough recognition to fuel our active interest in philosophical questions and just enough delay to set us seeking the means for analyzing the attitude and arguments of skepticism. Not until the process of naturizing the conception of God, man, and method is well under way does the propitious moment arrive for a formal *treatment*. Spinoza delays his response until we are beginning to become aware of our power of understanding and the means for perfecting it within the limits of man's place in nature.

One might suppose, however, that the question of skepticism loses its bite and simply vanishes in the wake of our attainment of this basic awareness. But Spinoza is sufficiently attuned to his own century to realize that no such automatic dissolution of the issue can realistically be expected. On the contrary, the crisis of skepticism as a philosophical alternative ripens simultaneously with our still rudimentary desire to know and act more effectively, so as to improve our relationships with other realities in nature. For we also experience a blockage against satisfying this aim. Skepticism draws strength and plausibility from this frustration. Hence, Spinoza's judgment about the proper timing for meeting the skeptical interpretation is determined by this predicament in which the human effort at self-realization finds itself.

That effort usually comes to grief through a failure to integrate our avenues toward cognition, at the critical phase in their growth when they could strengthen each other and overcome each other's shortcomings. The two broadest cognitive pathways already developed by mankind in advance of Spinozan philosophy are *internal meditation* and scientific *investigation of nature*, the inward and the outward vectors for bettering our knowledge and quality of life.[20] Spinoza's ideal is to achieve their interpenetration as a methodological imperative. We must open up our meditations to the discipline of the physical universe's actual conditions, and —conversely—we must put our findings about the physical world at the service of the entire range of human concerns. But the stark fact is that men seldom attend to this complementary imperative. Only rarely are the two paths unified in individual lives, let alone placed upon a general methodological course toward their integration. Spinoza perceives that, until a synthesis is reached, his account of God, man, and the physical world will seem to contain only a tangle of paradoxes exposing it to skeptical doubt.

To meet the interim situation and gain a fair hearing for his philosophy, Spinoza relies quite heavily upon *meditatio*. He broadens its meaning, so that it is no longer the special preserve of religious people and Descartes but is a commonly shared human operation. It signifies the energies of understanding, as it stirs everyone's mind toward some acts of reflection and pursuit of lasting happiness. People of every sort feel called upon to engage in some meditative activity. This encourages Spinoza himself to hope that people will give a fair hearing to his corrective precepts of method and his ordination of our mind to a union with the whole of nature. When meditation is assiduously cultivated and conjoined with the scientific investigation of nature, it undermines skeptical and Cartesian doubt by leading us to reflect upon the truth about nature and our well-being therein.

There are three widespread obstacles against completing this Spinozan turn: prejudice, lack of acute and accurate distinctions, and volatility of social conditions. Unexamined presuppositions engender a dogmatic cast of mind which may refuse even to consider Spinoza's rectification of conventional opinions about nature, God, and man. But even the abeyance of prejudice is no guarantee that it will be followed by positive acceptance of his naturizing emendation. For the latter requires some distinctions and arguments which often cannot be followed by minds unaccustomed to close thinking. For lack of intellectual discipline and reflective skills, even the best-disposed persons may be unable to follow the course of Spinoza's reconstructions. And finally, the influence of family, state, and church upon one's mind is ambiguous. It may seem to fall entirely on the side of prejudiced entrenchment of customary opinions, but this is not the entire story. In times of intellectual crisis and power shifts (as in the seventeenth century), these establishments are likely to crumble from within, producing a state of confusion and doubt in the minds of those who had looked to them for guidance. Taking these three obstacles together, they may well lead to a skeptical lack of commitment to Spinoza's naturizing program. They block him from moving directly from the impetus of meditation to his methodic presentation of truths about nature.

Hence, Spinoza follows an indirect route, organized around the theme of the purifiers of our understanding.[21] In the actual history of mankind, the opposite drives toward meditation and toward the investigation of nature have impelled men to develop three ways to push aside the obstacles listed just now, and thereby to enable them to build a road toward Spinoza's philosophy. Following his employment of a medical figure, these ways are purifiers, and they are (a) mathematics, (b) mechanical philosophy, and (c) the Bible. Each one makes a unique contribution toward keeping the human mind alive, in touch with the rest of natural reality, and able to shake free in some degree from both dogmatism and skepticism. Jointly, they encourage a thoughtful consideration of human intellectual abilities, the order of nature, and our native urge toward finding some beatitude in life. This meditative reorientation does not bring everyone into formal philosophical agreement with Spinoza, but at least it starts them on a path where they can give some liberating attention to his method and doctrine.

(a) Mathematics contributes in several ways to humanity's intellectual liberation—a matter upon which Spinoza and Descartes agree. Euclid offers a type of knowing that is distinct from sense perception, since it reaches to necessary and general properties of figures. This suggests to the reflective mind that our cognitive activity is not confined to reporting only about our passing sensations, images, and feelings. Development of mathematical reasoning brings with it the henceforth inextinguishable idea of cognitional pluralism, the recognition of man's ability to know in different ways. Moreover, there is nothing in this pluralizing process which inherently confines human knowledge to the perceptual and mathematical kinds. There is continuity between them, but nothing that authorizes a closure restricting our mind to these two expressions. As we move from a rote use of geometrical theorems to a grasp of the arguments supporting and connecting them, we begin to experience the power of reason and to envisage other uses of it. Mathematics opens one path for exercising our understanding in a philosophical manner.

More specifically, Spinoza appeals to mathematical knowing as an instrument for overcoming two hindrances to the philosophical study of nature. First, mathematical discipline controverts the view that we are insuperably ignorant of all but our own impressions, just because we cannot discern moral purposes and a divine design for all natural phenomena. This limit would have frustrated our desire to know nature, "if mathematics, which is not employed about ends, but only about the essences and properties of figures, had not manifested another norm of truth to men."[22] We can indeed make some progress in the study of nature by using mathematical means and by measuring our work in accord with this other norm.

Reflection upon mathematical developments helps us also to weaken the second hindrance, namely, the methodic cultivation of doubt. The latter is insufficient to bring our truth-seeking to a halt or to concentrate it solely upon the Cartesian thinking self. For the shift from teleological to mensurational and equational inquiries suggests that we have intellectual resources not yet fully employed in the investigation of nature. Although mathematical demonstrations are directly concerned with number and figure, they testify indirectly about our mind's power to reach a new conception of truth that is fruitful in interpreting nature and hence that renders skepticism superfluous.

(b) Mechanical philosophy continues the process of purifying our intelligence and providing it with new grounds for assurance. Spinoza is very careful to broaden the scope of this purifier enough to include ancient as well as modern representatives.[23] He credits Democritus, Epicurus, and Lucretius with exerting a corrective influence against skepticism across the centuries. By their steady concern with "the nature of things" they countered the skeptical limitations of inquiry to the perceiver's own images and sentiments. The ancient atomists located man and his entire perceptual life within the compass of nature, with its intrinsic structures and movements. Only when human sensibility and desire are viewed within the prevailing order of nature can they be truly understood and used for our welfare. Thus the Greek and Latin proponents of a mechanical philosophy set the pattern of bringing man within the context of active nature, where his cognitive and conative acts could be better judged.

Spinoza was well aware that Bacon and Gassendi had revived the fundamentals of the classical atomistic philosophy of nature, man, and ethics. But he also wanted to include the modern meaning of mechanical philosophy within his account of the second purifier of the human understanding. During the first two-thirds of his own century, that meaning was associated chiefly with the scientific work of Galileo and Descartes, Harvey and Boyle.

Without overstepping our present topic of the mind's purifiers, we can see four advantages in Spinoza's updating of the denotation of mechanical philosophy. First, its modern vigor shows that this opening to nature has contemporary import, not just historical significance. The seventeenth-century mechanical philosophy displays the human understanding's ceaseless power to increase its toolmaking, conceptualization, and explanation. A speculative appeal to skepticism cannot halt the investigation of nature in a variety of fields, ranging from astronomy to rudimentary microbiology. While Spinoza is not satisfied with the resultant conception of nature, neither is he so dissatisfied with its positive features as to abandon them for skeptical suspension of all claims to know traits of nature.

Second, Spinoza's already-quoted remark about mathematical provision of "another norm of truth to men" becomes more sharply specified by modern mechanical philosophy. The latter seeks to exhibit just how mathematico-mechanical concepts and models increase our understanding of the sensible and infrasensible features of physical nature. Mechanical laws forcefully support the notion of a general order of nature, to which man must conform but which can be made accessible and useful to him. For mechanical disciplines generate not only pure knowledge but also the technological means for enhancing human welfare within nature so viewed. This aspect of our happiness would be unattainable were we to abandon the mechanical approach to nature and withdraw into private feeling.

In the third place, the intellectual effort required to formulate and improve the laws of motion and the mechanical theory of sensible qualities leads us to acknowledge the human mind's capability and to expect still further knowledge about the physical world. The passage from the everyday to the mechanical view of nature opens up a further prospect. Mechanical generalizations can dispose a reflective mind to accept Spinoza's philosophical interpretation of extended-and-moving nature. His theory of the bodily modes in natured nature and the general pattern of all physical changes can at least be reasonably entertained by a human mind purified through the notions found in ancient and modern mechanical philosophies.

In a letter to Henry Oldenburg, Spinoza distinguishes between two sorts of notions used in accounting for nature. (i) Notions fashioned from unreflective common experience "explain nature, not as it is in itself, but insofar as it is referred to human sense."[24] These unpurified notions tell us only about the condition of our own sensibility, without being corrected by any scientific method of investigating the rest of bodily nature. Because they simply project our unsifted sense perceptions upon the physical world, such notions supply fertile materials for the skeptical criticism of the human mind.

(ii) Chaste notions are those which undergo the discipline of mathematics and mechanics, so that in some measure they do "explain nature as it is in itself, not indeed as related to human sense." These purified notions belong in the rational mode of cognition and include the main concepts of mechanical philosophy. They are "chaste" in several respects. They cleanse our sense experience so that it is not exclusively propriocentric; they embrace the mathematico-mechanical view of the qualities of bodily nature; they weaken skepticism itself by methodically depriving it of easy examples of the anthropomorphic outlook; and they help the human mind to pursue undistractedly the search for knowledge of itself and the rest of nature, including a contextual reflection upon the role of human sense perception. The mechanical philosophy employing these chaste notions gives only a limited interpretation of extended nature, but that is enough to clear away many misconceptions resulting from common prejudice, ignorance about the various referents of our notions, and suspensive doubt.

The fourth distinctive contribution of modern mechanical philosophy to Spinoza's critique of skepticism comes from the scientific use of hypotheses and hypothesis-guided experimentation. As the *Emendation* remarks, our human mind constantly devises fictions and frames hypotheses. Taken by themselves, fictive activities can lead to harmless reverie and sometimes to great works of imaginative art. Epistemological difficulties creep in only when we fail to recognize these entities of imagination for what they are and thus fail to curb their unconditional reality-assertions about nature. When we people these fictitious worlds with imaginative entities and mistake them for real ones, we become entangled in fantasy and error. The skeptical tactic is to describe this tendency and, on its basis, declare our cognitive powers to be untrustworthy.

Spinoza counters that this is a case of epistemological overkill. All that the situation warrants is a set of monitory precepts of method. Recognize the fiction-making operation of our mind; restrain our tendency to endow with ontological implications its imaginative constructs; and channel it within definite bounds, beyond which the mind can legitimately go only with the aid of reformed and purified concepts. Spinoza sums up these admonitions in a statement about the inverse proportion between knowing nature and feigning about it in uncritical fashion. "The less men know nature, the easier they can feign many things. . . . The less the mind understands, and yet perceives many things, the greater power of feigning it has. And the more things it understands, the more that power [of feigning] is diminished."[25] The only way to cut back on an irresponsible framing of fictions and hypotheses is to purify our perceptual imagery and put it at the service of chaste rational notions and a philosophical understanding of nature.

There are three specific instances where knowing and feigning are in direct conflict with each other. First, feigning is altogether incompatible with that complete knowledge of nature ascribed either to the God of theism or to the Spinozan infinite mode of understanding. Next, there can be no valid feigning or Cartesian doubt about our own existence, once we recognize our own mind to be the affirming idea of its body. Lastly, it is inappropriate to feign about those truths which are eternal in the sense of involving eternal necessary existence, when this involvement is known to us. In these cases, the act of feigning would respectively try to combine a play of alternatives with complete knowledge of necessary actuality, a dreamy lack of self-understanding with existential self-awareness, and a suspensive method with the understood presence of grounds for necessary assent. These efforts cannot intrinsically weaken Spinoza's conception of naturing and natured nature.

On the positive side, he does admit several legitimate uses of hypothesizing and other forms of cautious, reflective feigning. They are a helpful, and indeed a necessary, means of aiding the human mind in its mixed condition (where it perceives many things experientially and problematically, seeks to increase its reasoned knowledge, and does attain to some proper understanding of nature). In order to cope with this complex situation, we often frame hypotheses for unifying and interrelating our perceptions of "diverse things and actions existing in nature" (a phrase from the *Emendation* which conforms with the doctrine and language of the *Short Treatise*).[26] Even when we do not as yet relate these things and actions to their essential structures and to the eternal order of nature, we can nevertheless devise some descriptive schemata and probable explanatory hypotheses useful for organizing our perceptions. Spinoza cites the framing of careful hypotheses in astronomy, where we consider celestial phenomena within a framework of types of motions. His only caveat is against regarding some prevailing hypothesis as essential knowledge that the nature of heavenly bodies *must* be of this sort. The kind of supposition used in astronomy provides for amendment and perhaps replacement of every accepted pattern.

By admitting a valid role in human life for fictions and hypotheses, Spinoza avoids the skeptical dilemma of cognizing everything or nothing about nature. Some truths about naturing and natured nature do come within our strict knowledge, and about these we cannot genuinely feign. This upper limit restricts Cartesian universal doubt and the appeal to a very powerful deceiver. And the function of hypotheses in mechanical philosophy supplies a lower limit against skeptical despair over the clashing theories about experienced phenomena. It is unrealistic and intemperate to regard the human mind either as a demigod that knows everything about nature and does not need to hypothesize at all, or else as so bereft of any reasoned knowledge and understanding that it generates only fictions about nature.

Spinoza never revoked the above four contributions of ancient and modern forms of mechanical philosophy. He consistently maintained these functions, even when he criticized Boyle and the work of the Royal Society. He rejected their methodological claims to reach essential knowledge of bodily nature, while at the same time he acknowledged the usefulness of their actual procedures and general concepts in purifying the human mind and fortifying it against unconditional skepticism.

(c) The Bible also figures prominently in Spinoza's canon of purifiers.[27] He includes both Old and New Testaments, augmented by the long tradition of Hebrew commentaries. Biblical religion elevates the vision and hope of large masses of people who remain formally untouched by mathematics and mechanical philosophy. It gives practical direction and encouragement amid the travail of human history and the disheartening chorus of the skeptics.

Specifically, this religious and moral current in culture helps to counteract the third barrier against receiving Spinoza's philosophy: the mutability of human customs and societies. The crumbling of accepted social forms arouses a practical skeptical attitude that tends to erode all human ideals and codes of conduct. Sometimes, institutional religions try to counter a practical skepticism by imposing upon society some fixed set of religious and moral precepts. Spinoza disallows the competence of any religious establishment—be it a chosen nation or a church—to determine practical truths formally as such. Yet even in the *Theological-Political*

Treatise, where such truth-claims are most extensively opposed, he concedes that the religious image of a people of God-as-lawgiver purifies and spurs on our search for just laws and stable social conditions. In this manner, biblical religion counteracts the skeptical undermining of confidence in our ability to reach some staying truths about virtuous social living, despite cultural changes and disasters.

Another purificatory influence of the biblical outlook flows from its theme of the living God and of our sharing in his eternal life. The religious orientation of people toward eternal life operates as a counterweighing force against skeptical restriction of our minds to temporal flux. For the truth about living eternal reality and our relations with it, however, Spinoza looks to his own philosophical reflections on nature. Like mathematics and mechanical philosophy, biblical religion actually helps to dissolve skeptical arguments and attitudes. But before their philosophical significance can be appreciated, all the purifiers must themselves be reinterpreted in the light of Spinoza's conception of nature.

Hence, the *Emendation* invites us to view the skeptical mind itself from the philosophical vantage point of naturing and natured nature. As the skeptics of every age insist, skepticism is not merely a set of arguments, but rather a whole way of life. Spinoza is not psychologizing away the problem, therefore, when he considers more concretely the predicament of skeptics. Despite their suspension of judgment and adhesion at most to probable opinion, their daily lives require them constantly to think and act in ways requiring discernment. They have to maintain or oppose or concede many points, including those that bear upon their own being and its relationships. Comparing their praxis with their official position, Spinoza draws a twofold conclusion about skeptics. "[1] They are not perceptive about their own selves. . . . [2] They even doubt about their own states of wakefulness: which happens because they have never distinguished between dream and wakefulness."[28] People who accept this life pattern become like mindless automata, even when they must discern and decide matters of practical living.

These two judgments state exactly how Spinoza views the skeptics from the standpoint of his method and doctrine on nature.

(1) He uses strong wording—*neque seipsos sentiunt*—to convey the depth of their self-alienation. To follow the skeptical ban on attempts to form absolutely certain judgments on reality is to suffer ultimately the loss of self-understanding, of true and feelingful perception of themselves. Spinoza realizes that this evaluation is made in the face of exquisite

skeptical recording of their own opinions and sentiments. His point is, however, that the scar of Montaigne cannot conceal the skeptics' failure to grasp the significance of viewing men within the process of nature. Skeptics are ready enough to liken our opinions to the growth and decay of cabbages and to the organic changes in our body. But they are loathe to draw out the general reality-implications of affirming the presence of one's own body in its changing physical milieu. Thereby, they deprive themselves of a true perceptive apprehension of human reality within nature. They lose the opportunity of knowing natured nature and of emending their transient opinions through this knowledge.

(2) Descartes and his skeptical critics had become helplessly entangled in debate over dreaming and waking. Their impasse would consign people to a condition of dreamy wondering or, at best, to energetic sleepwalking which could take care of practical needs but could not distinguish between dreaming and being awake. At this juncture, Spinoza intervened with the question: What would count as our waking up to something?

His reply is closely bound up with his first criticism of the skeptics. They are imperceptive about themselves in the degree that they fail to analyze thoroughly the acts which affirm their own bodies and the many things that satisfy their exigencies. An individual remains unaware of self and a little dreamy, until he recognizes that his body is both resonant of further activities in the bodily world and proportionately responsive to his own striving ideas and aims. Someone "comes to," when he reflectively apprehends his involvement in these actions and relationships or, in Spinoza's technical vocabulary, when he recognizes himself as individually existing and acting within natured nature and its naturing source. Such recognition enlightens this man about his distinctive reality and activity, thus constituting the Spinozan criterion of the wakeful condition as distinct from dreaming.

4. Wisdom in Defining

Spinoza speaks very sparingly about wisdom. He wants to avoid the pretensions of both the dogmatic and the skeptical treatises "On Wisdom" and, at the same time, to underline his own careful remarks on the topic. In grading the kinds of methods, however, he does characterize the general purpose of his philosophy to be attainment of supreme joy and the peak of wisdom, insofar as our mind can reach them.[29] He always seeks a joyous wisdom and a wise joyfulness, in a reciprocity that Nietzsche could appreciate. Philosophical reflection upon nature is meant to satisfy our striving for the highest knowledge and happiness in a unified act, rather than in separation or opposition to each other.

On several grounds, nevertheless, Spinoza remains cautious about assigning a prominent role to the theme of wisdom. The very abundance of a sapiential literature in the Bible and in Jewish and Christian religious tradition raised many questions of interpretation from the standpoint of his philosophy. He sees some value in the view that wisdom is a gift of the spirit. But he opposes any inference that revelation bears fruit in a strictly *super*natural sort of cognition, in a religious wisdom that even Descartes held to be above the capacity of philosophy to confer. Just how to relate the spiritual gift of wisdom to Spinoza's own goal of the peak of wisdom must await his general treatment of revelational religion, as set forth in the *Theological-Political Treatise*. Yet already it is clear that he will ultimately interpret even the gift of religious wisdom as being *intra*natural in its source and significance.

From another quarter, Charron and contemporary skeptics were urging that the only wisdom accessible to man has a solely practical worth. But whether this practical wisdom be fideistic or freethinking in coloration, in Spinoza's judgment it remains essentially flawed. For it presupposes a split between the practical and the speculative orders, along with a denial of speculative knowledge of reality to man. Spinoza's counterposition that we can and do attain some speculative knowledge of nature, and that such knowledge has practical consequences for action, leads to a nonskeptical conception of wisdom. The wisdom sought by his philosophy is speculative and practical alike or, as the *Ethics* will state it more precisely, is that sort of adequate idea of ourselves and the rest of nature which transforms our striving into morally powerful action. This development of knowledge into practical moral power is Spinoza's alternative to the skeptical sort of practical wisdom that remains unconnected with any speculative certainties about nature.

Still further complications arose from the current philosophical textbooks which did admit a speculative component in wisdom, in accord with the Aristotelian and Cartesian traditions concerning metaphysics. As reformulated by Spinoza, three primary questions were discussed about the nature of metaphysical reasoning.[30] (a) Is metaphysics mainly a study of first causes and principles of reality? (b) Or is it chiefly concerned with the most general truths about being as such and its transcendental attributes? (c) And in any case, how does metaphysical inference depend upon definitions that substitute for the model of (are a *locum tenens* for) defining through genus and specific difference? These queries confronted Spinoza with a mined harbor through which he had to steer his own carefully charted course. He could not identify his method and doctrine on nature simply with a metaphysical wisdom, any more than with a religious or a purely practical wisdom. He had to clarify whatever was distinctive in his pursuit of a wise understanding of nature and the mind's union with it.

(a) The Spinozan study of nature is not unqualifiedly a search after first causes. On the face of it, this is a puzzling demurrer. It is not intended in a skeptical sense, since Spinoza not only admits our capacity for gaining causal knowledge but also makes causal analyses and inferences central to his philosophizing. Yet he does exclude from his aim any cause whose firstness consists in a claim to subsist apart from nature and to originate nature as a realm of being that is entirely other than itself. His method is not shaped for seeking out *such* a first cause of causes.

Instead, its proper task is to ascertain, distinguish, and relate the various causes which internally constitute nature as a whole and operate within its all-inclusive reality. Every ordering among causes is guided by this view of the causal investigation. However elaborate the distinction among causes becomes in the *Metaphysical Thoughts* and the *Ethics,* it never leads to recognition of some first cause whose primacy would lie in its transcendence of nature as a whole. There is a highly practical consequence here for Spinoza. His conditions placed upon causal inquiry guarantee that metaphysical inquiries always remain a phase within an ethically actionable wisdom about man's relations within total nature.

(b) On the second question, Spinoza loses no opportunity to dissociate his metaphysics of substance and active modal things from a theory of being as such and its transcendental notes. As he interprets it, the latter theory is filled with abstractions and universals which, however stretched and differentiated, are impositions placed upon nature and distortions placed upon our cognition of it. Spinoza is careful not to attribute the impositional and distortive functions to the mere presence of abstractions and universals. The latter do have a legitimate employment in logic and elsewhere. But metaphysical fantasies and errors come from trying to apprehend the real beings in nature by means of abstract universal notions and figures of imagination. Out of this confusion is generated the conviction that metaphysics consists of these notions of being and its transcendental notes, somehow used analogously.

Here, Spinoza's emendation of our understanding consists in replacing the analogy of being and the transcendentals (as thus generated by imagi-

nation and promulgated by logic-book definitions) with the analogy
among things internal to nature. Correspondingly, he replaces a
metaphysics of imaginary transcendence of nature with his theory of
nature as the all-embracing whole of real agencies. No loss occurs when a
study of substance, things, and actions is purified of those imaginary and
abstract elements which populate treatises that are metaphysical, in the
sense of claiming to reach beyond nature.

Spinoza must then face the retort that his kind of purification deprives
the human understanding of its means for generalization and, hence, for
attaining philosophical wisdom at all. His response to this objection in the
Emendation sets a pattern for his other replies to it.

The problem is not that of having or not having general concepts but,
rather, that of distinguishing between two sorts of generality about nature
which I will call diremptive and interpretive. Diremptive generality results from tearing some features away from the actuality and order of
nature so that these traits can be universalized. But this is done at the cost
of constructing meanings which are empty of nature's actualities and
isolated from nature's causative interconnections. On the contrary, interpretive generality comes from reflecting upon nature in a way that
expresses the active order and connectivity of nature, by remaining interior to it. Spinoza's logic and methodology are proportioned to this latter
sort of generality. Only interpretive generality yields metaphysical truths
about nature by conveying to us the *formalitas naturae*, the intrinsically
meaningful pattern of nature as a whole (including our self-understanding
of belonging to, and acting within, this pattern of nature).[31]

Two of Spinoza's precepts of method are specifically directed toward
mending the ravages of diremptive generality and obtaining the interpretive kind. The first rule concerns how to obtain the *prima elementa*, the
first elements of a philosophical system. They are not found either in the
mathematical indivisibles or the physical indivisibles of ancient and modern atomism, either in the simple natures of Descartes or the nominal
definitions of Hobbes. These meanings are already constituted within
natured nature, so that their relative primacy and elementary character are
restricted to some particular area. Instead, Spinoza identifies the unqualifiedly prime elements of philosophical wisdom with the font and origin
of natured nature. To begin philosophizing with the prime elements
means, therefore, to begin with the idea of the originative source of
nature—that is, with the idea of naturing nature. The foundation of this
idea is unique primal actuality rather than an abstract universal, just as it is
the immanent powerful source of nature's interconnected order and unity

rather than an entity set apart from them. In the *Ethics,* Spinoza will further develop this theme of generality and the prime elements of philosophy by means of his theory of naturing nature as the unique, immanently causative, infinitely powerful substance.

The second specific rule concerns how to prevent the valid use of fiction and doubt from degenerating into self-deception and error about things. Spinoza recommends that investigating minds make a double move. We should consider a thing's existence in a more particular manner—that is, in its close concrete proportion with that thing's essential structure. And simultaneously we should attend to how a particular natured thing is bound up essentially and existentially with the relational order of nature as an active whole. When we do understand something both more concretely and more interconnectively than universals and transcendental notions permit, then we increase our hold upon interpretive generality and reduce the margin of deception and error. Our journey toward philosophical truth is advanced in the degree that we develop the intellectual power to execute this double move.

(c) The third general question raised by metaphysical discussions of wisdom concerns the appropriate type of definitions to use. For Spinoza, proper definitions are those which (in accord with the crux of methodology treated above in Section 2) guide our philosophical reasoning toward reliable knowledge, as much as is humanly achievable, of the mind itself and nature as a whole. Hence, the rules of definition are obtained by reflecting upon the most manifest traits of nature and of mind functioning in it.

For Spinoza, this means that an adequate theory of nature begins, not from some abstract and universal propositions, but "from some particular affirmative essence, or from a true and legitimate definition."[32] The definitional starting point bears three marks: *essential,* or stating that which is necessary to the being of the natural reality; *particular,* or expressing the distinctive singular actuality of the thing being defined; and *affirmative,* or suitably conveying the causal presence and power of naturing nature in itself and throughout the modal world. Insofar as these conditions are met, the primary definitions will enable us to clarify, distinguish, and fruitfully interrelate our ideas in inferences that hold valid for natural reality. The interlinking and order among such ideas will refer objectively and truly to the interlinking and order in nature as a whole and in its humanly accessible portions.

From this operational approach to definitions in his doctrine on nature, Spinoza reaps four benefits. (1) It strengthens his position on the interpretive generality that such a doctrine gives. This generality does not arise from extrinsic denominations, relations, and circumstances. Rather, it comes

> from fixed and eternal things and, simultaneously, from the laws inscribed in these things as in their true codices, in accord with which all singular things both come to be and are ordered. Indeed, these mutable singulars depend so intimately and essentially (so to speak) upon these fixed things that, without the latter, the former can neither be nor be conceived. Hence although these fixed and eternal things are singulars, nevertheless, because of their presence everywhere and their very broad power, they will be for us as universals, or genera of the definitions of mutable singular things, and as proximate causes of all things.[33]

From this nature-pervasive *praesentia* and *potentia* flow the interpretive generality of Spinoza's basic definitions and their primary elements. In his basic definitions, the presence and power of eternal things take the place of abstract universal genera, just as the same immanent presence and power also enable the work of proximate causal differentiation to go on. Hence, inferences made in accord with Spinozan definitions will both concern singular realities and hold true for the entire order and connections in nature.

(2) The phrase quoted above, *they will be for us as,* cautions us concerning the noetic limitations under which our finite human minds labor in philosophizing about natural things. Spinoza does not casually use these words or add the cognate statement, "And then our mind, as we have said, will refer as much as possible to nature."[34] These qualifiers emphasize the inherently limited ability of our human mind to comprehend the significance of its true and legitimate definitions for a theory of nature as a whole. Although this theory establishes some truths about the order and laws of nature, nevertheless "to conceive all things simultaneously is far above [*longe supra*] the powers of the human understanding." In terms of the kinds of knowledge, this means that we must use the inferential path of philosophical reasoning, even though it aims at evoking some intuitive knowledge of nature and some action consonant with such intuition.

Spinoza is even more cautious than Descartes about achieving a simultaneous grasp of all things in nature. Yet the vitality of Spinoza's philosophizing about nature lies in its twofold acceptance of both the goal of a wisdom of nature as a whole and the unblinking awareness of the limits under which the human efforts to realize this wisdom must operate. One point stands out clearly in reflecting on this situation. To admit that perfect attainment of a single intuitive vision of natural realities is *longe supra* our intellectual powers is to allow for some transcendence within the cognition of nature. Yet it does not legitimate, for Spinoza, any appeal to a supernatural source of enlightenment. Man's proper attitude is to endure and enjoy the tension between intent and reach, in his efforts at knowing nature and practically responding to it. We have to continue to explore and utilize the hopeful relationship between the human mind and the infinite mode of understanding.

(3) Whatever his admonitions against an uncritical intuitionism, Spinoza affirms that some genuine philosophical advances can be made in the investigation of nature. His conviction rests upon a complementarity between the naturizing of God and man and the naturizing of the methodic theory of definition.

An initial sortal distinction is made between defining uncreated things and defining created things.[35] This corresponds to the distinction made respectively between naturing and natured nature, now regarded as that which is to be defined. Taking full advantage of the latitude in his usage of "thing," Spinoza assigns the name "uncreated thing" to that which is the primal causal power or activity, namely, naturing nature. And he designates as "created thing" that which is the caused outcome or modal expression, namely, natured nature. The *Emendation*'s task is not to delve more particularly into the kinds of causality, the relationships they sustain, and the import of this entire analysis upon human praxis—topics which constitute the province of the *Ethics* and the treatises on politics and religion. It is sufficient at the present stage to characterize broadly the sorts of definitions appropriate for uncreated and created things, so that some developmental routes for philosophical inquiry can be indicated.

The conception of naturing nature guides Spinoza's precepts both for definition in general and for definition of an uncreated thing. His most general requirement that a true and legitimate definition be essential, particular, and affirmative finds its archetypal realization in the idea of naturing nature. For the latter signifies that which is primordially necessary and eternal, unique in its actuality, and unlimitedly powerful both in its own existence and in its expressive manifestations constituting the modal universe.

By reflecting on these traits of naturing nature, Spinoza formulates four specific and distinctive rules for defining an uncreated thing. First, a true definition expresses this thing's own act-of-being (*esse*) in such a way as to exclude reference to anything else as a cause. The naturing act is signified as sufficient for the defining account because, in the real order, that which is uncreated grounds itself in its own act-of-being.

Seond, when an uncreated thing's definition is thus set forth, it leaves no room for raising the separate existential question: "But is it? Does it exist?" The existential act is already included in the act-of-being, on the part of naturing nature. Once our mind apprehends this self-grounding reality under definition, it also recognizes that there is no real basis for making distinct queries here concerning the essential *what* and the existential *whether*.

Next, the wisely defining mind is also constrained from using any substantives which could be converted into adjectival form, since the adjectival terms would be abstract and would require a founding principle in some other subject. This rule respects the concrete unicity and substantiality of naturing nature. The latter's attributes are not to be construed as universal traits shareable among several substances.

Lastly, it is requisite that all the properties of an uncreated thing be inferred from its definition. Spinoza has to qualify this rule considerably, since he must now take into account a distinction between the definition itself (which concerns naturing nature) and the defining human mind (which belongs to natured nature). What holds for the former, considered in itself, is not absolutely realizable from the standpoint of the latter and its limitations. For us to know naturing nature in accord with the first three rules does not mean that we know it exhaustively in all its real properties. We cannot derive them all from the true definition of naturing nature. Thus the problem of the human mind and its cognitional limits remains at the heart of Spinoza's logic for defining uncreated nature.

His rules for defining a created thing are also permeated by his general theory of nature. The two main requirements for a definition here are that it include a reference to its proximate cause, and that it state all of the thing's properties, even when it is being considered alone and not in conjunction with other created things. One can detect here the influence of the Spinozan view of natured nature as a whole. The "naturedness" of any particular created thing consists of its being constituted by a proximate cause and, indeed, constituted through and through in the ensemble of its own properties. These two conditions must be reflected in any definition intended to meet Spinoza's standard of the truth about anything in natured nature as a whole. Further considerations for understanding some particular thing will depend upon its relations with the rest of nature.

A good example of improving the means of cognition comes when Spinoza asks reflexively how to increase the yield of ideas formed by our defining mind itself. By considering the human mind in itself and in reference to the infinite understanding as a causal mode of nature, we can determine which properties of our ideas will improve our knowledge of nature as a whole.

Spinoza develops an epistemic model for emendating our ideas. He incorporates eight traits into this model.[36] (a) The ideas must be certain —that is, they must be informative about both formal structures and objective meanings. (b) These ideas must have an intrinsic significance and integrity of their own and not be merely a mosaic of references to other things. (c) Reformed ideas are expressive of infinite reality and are not confined solely to finite things and meanings. (d) Such ideas are basically positive in their significance, even when they may be expressed in negative language. (e) They are clear and distinct, in the Spinozan sense that they inform us about beings and distinctions really present in nature. (f) Such ideas manifest something about the necessity and power of our own human nature considered as a determinate outcome of the necessity and power of nature as a whole. (g) Emendated ideas emphasize the perfections present in an object, but without overlooking its limitations and defects. (h) In the case of ideas formed from consideration of other things affecting us, such ideas make us aware of many different ways of imagining the things that thus modify us.

The corrective knowlege of nature sought by Spinoza cannot develop from any one of these factors taken separately, but only from a reasoned and artful synthesis of them all. Any one note by itself leads to imbalance, but in modifying interaction with the others it enables us to realize the power of our own mind acting in unison with the totality of nature. Our emendation is guided by submitting our ideas to this eightfold, nature-regulated test and making inferences in accord with this standard. It regulates every phase in Spinoza's argument in the *Ethics* and elsewhere.

(4) There remains a final characteristic of the Spinozan way of defining, namely, its *interrelatedness*. Unlike most contemporary treatises on logic and method, the *Emendation* is not loaded down with theses about the distinctions among relations. Spinoza is deliberately frugal here on this topic. He avoids planting an artificial jungle, that might confuse and entangle the mind in a maze of artificial schemata on relations. On the contrary, his intention is to allow the doctrine on relations to develop gradually out of his inquiry into nature. Already, that inquiry uses relational language and concepts. The transition from use to explicit theory is hastened by Spinoza's encounter with acute relational problems, such as the different cognitive ways of regarding a modal thing (especially the human mind) in itself and in connection with others.

Spinoza's theory articulates his recognition of the relatedness between

naturing and natured nature, as well as between the various modes comprising our experienced world. His emended theory of relations is involved in questions about the tension between singularity and generality,
the reference of objective to formal being, the interplay between a created
thing's properties and its proximate cause, and the ordering of our understanding toward nature as an interconnective whole. It is from reflections
provoked by these definite issues, rather than from general logical definitions, that the fundamental meanings of "relation" spring. He proposes a
similar, nature-oriented reformation of our talk and thought about "perfection," taken both in a general way and in special reference to human
actions.

These discussions lead Spinoza steadily toward a convergence of the
naturizing of method with the naturizing of God and man. Their actual
conjunction is the comprehensive task of the *Ethics* and its associated
treatises on politics and religion. In these writings Spinoza states, as well
as he can, his conception of the humanly accessible wisdom on nature.

CHAPTER FIVE

A Nature-Reading of *Ethics I–II*

IN HIS FINAL NOVEL, Flaubert arranges for his two avid but indiscriminate copying clerks, Bouvard and Pécuchet, to pounce upon Spinoza's *Ethics* just as they would upon a standard reference work on geology, Roman history, or gastronomy. Their brief tour of Spinoza's work is predictably disastrous. "All this was like being in a balloon at night, in glacial coldness, carried on an endless voyage towards a bottomless abyss, and with nothing near but the unseizable, the motionless, the eternal. It was too much. They gave it up."[1] Their disorientation is not so unique and imaginary as to be confined to the fictional world. A similar feeling of vertigo is likely to creep over anyone who plunges directly into the *Ethics* without some preparatory study of Spinoza's other works and without having some theme to focus upon.

Genetically considered, the several drafts of the *Ethics* overlap most of Spinoza's early writings which we have been examining. The latter serve as trial runs which state the issues, test the types of argument and presentation, distinguish his own position from that of other philosophers and, in general, prepare the soil and tools for his most sustained reasoning. For quite a while, the draft *Ethics* consisted of three parts, roughly corresponding to the threefold subject of the *Short Treatise on God, Man, and His Well-Being*. Due account also had to be taken of the logical and methodological contributions made by the *Emendation*. In the *Ethics* as we now have it, Spinoza devotes Parts I and II respectively to his doctrine on God and man. But the topic of human well-being and happiness is so complex that it forces him to expand his original third section into the present Parts III–V of the *Ethics*. My own division between this chapter and the next one respects the history of Spinoza's planning and development.

There are several master themes weaving their way throughout the *Ethics* to give it continuous structure and intellectual thrust. Because the theory of nature is only one of these themes, it cannot exhaustively capture the meaning of that book. Nevertheless, it does permeate the argumentation sufficiently to serve as a study guide and a unifier of what would otherwise seem to be detachable outriders of Spinoza's speculation.

This is the functional sense in which to conduct a "nature-reading" of the *Ethics*. It inspects some texts that treat of nature explicitly and implicitly and traces out some main ramifications of that topic in the *Ethics*. But the relationship is reciprocal between that work as a whole and its thematic treatment of nature. For while an emphasis upon nature helps to bind together many principles, propositions, and excurses into an orienting interpretation of the *Ethics*, that book in turn specifies and develops the Spinozan meaning of nature in some important ways. The book is not merely a passive receptacle for previous findings but is itself an active and original development of the language, method, and leading concepts in Spinoza's theory of nature.

1. Definitions for Reasoning about Nature

The *Ethics* opens with disconcerting abruptness by proposing a crucial set of definitions. They seem to come from nowhere and to assign arbitrary meanings for the basic terms to be used throughout the treatise. That initial impression can be corrected only by considering the internal source of these definitions, the way in which they are being proposed to us, and at least one of the prime aims they are intended to accomplish.

Although the *Ethics* begins with a set of definitions, they themselves have an internal source in Spinoza's previous and concurrent writings (not to mention the analogues to be found in other philosophers). With respect to this working context, the specific task of the *Ethics* is to rethink and unify his emendation of method and his theory of God and man. The definitions with which that book starts constitute the first step in weaving together his methodological and doctrinal correctives. Right from the outset, their intent is to prevent any sundering of procedure and content. The defining process begins with "cause-of-itself," for example, both to ratify the precept of making our thought reflect the order of beings and to reaffirm what for Spinoza is most significant about the first being.

As for the abrupt manner of proposal of the definitions, it is an economic act for disposing us prospectively toward the kind of philosophizing to be expected and tested in the main body of the *Ethics*. As a precondition, Spinoza does two things with his previous account of the different kinds of cognition. He trims it to a threefold distinction between experience (sensory and imaginative, as expressed in language), reason, and understanding or intuitive knowledge. Simultaneously, he implicates this distinction fundamentally in *all* his philosophizing, so that it will never be lost from sight in our interpretation of what he is doing in the definitions and everywhere else.

Definitions themselves are accomplishments of the human mind, not dictates of divinity. Their soundness is to be determined by their use in argumentation, where our reason must also rely upon its peculiar ways of experiencing and understanding. The "Explanations" that Spinoza introduces into even his primary group of definitions symbolize the process of reflecting, distinguishing, and using all his other cognitive resources to establish precisely these defined meanings. As used in the inferences in the *Ethics,* the definitions get clarified and modified by experience of the human condition and its imagery, by the drive toward singular existents, and by the search after a systematic understanding of nature. In turn, our judgment about the definitions has to await their actual uses in this philosophy.

For seventeenth-century readers, the geometrical order of reasoning was a compelling model. Spinoza adopted it cautiously and only after experimenting with various other uses of mind and modes of expression. His commitment to this order did not entail regarding it either as an automatic generator of demonstrated truths or as a mere facade, reflecting no more than a time-bound cultural taste. Spinoza had not hesitated to alter Descartes' geometrical approach to God's existence. He made the alteration on the twofold ground that it would bring more coherence into the Cartesian philosophy and would sharpen Spinoza's own criticism of the same. Similarly, the geometrical order of reasoning in the *Ethics* did not render that work immune to criticism by others and incapable of improvement by its own author (who made several drafts of it).

Nonetheless, Spinoza judged that the geometrical order of reasoning was the best intellectual instrument at hand for meeting the demands of rationality in a philosophy of God and man within nature. Stating one's primary definitions, axioms, and postulates in explicit form is both a good requirement for the author and a ready means of inspection and evaluation by others. Moreover,the statement and proof of a proposition, along with its corollaries and lemmas, build up links with preceding arguments and implications issuing in subsequent ones. The continuity of inferences and the cross-strands bring a high degree of systemic unity into the philosophy thus developed. Yet it is a system that does not overwhelm our intelligence but invites the latter to weigh every stage of the argument.

An effective way of testing a systemic philosophy is to look at its primary aims. We can regard the *Ethics* as Spinoza's way of executing his purpose (announced in the early sections of the *Emendation*) of awakening us to the union of the mind with the whole of nature. To redeem that promise, he must now regulate his philosophizing by the ultimate requirements of the idea of the active source of all natural realities, such that from this supremely generative idea will be seen to follow the ideas of the other things in nature. Hence, the *Ethics* must begin with a treatment of God as naturing nature. This is not just an optional difference from starting with Bacon's sensible world or Descartes' Cogito, and not just an aping of some theological treatise on the revealing God. Rather, it is a necessary philosophical response to the purpose and method Spinoza has set for himself. Part I of the *Ethics* must treat of God in a foundational manner that will enable us to understand, as much as is humanly possible, the relationship of God and man within total nature and the moral struggle of man to become satisfyingly related with God, in the whole reality of nature.

Once we are furnished with these preliminary leads, we have a setting within which to receive and interpret the initial definitions of the *Ethics*. They function within that sort of theory of God which expresses the idea of naturing nature and, hence, which works as the active source of ideas about the rest of nature, seen in human perspective. Consequently, we are to expect from these definitions that sort of meaning which best contributes toward understanding our own relationships with God in this whole of nature. There is no section of the *Ethics* that is unaffected by the definitions set forth in Part I. Hence, there is laid upon us, as interpreters of Spinoza, a corresponding imperative: Bring the "that-sort-of" qualification to bear upon all particular argumentations. For, explicitly or implicitly, every text is pervaded with these definitions and their systemically mounting consequences.

    I. By cause-of-itself I understand that whose essence involves existence, or that whose nature cannot be conceived except as existing.

   II. That thing is called finite in its own kind which can be limited by another of the same nature. For example, a body is called finite because we always conceive another greater. So an act-of-thinking [*cogitatio*] is limited by another act-of-thinking. But a body is not limited by an act-of-thinking, nor an act-of-thinking by a body.

  III. By substance I understand that which is in itself and is conceived through itself, that is, that whose concept does not need the concept of another thing from which it must be formed.

IV. By attribute I understand that which the understanding perceives of substance as constituting its essence.

V. By mode I understand the affections [*affectiones*] of substance, or that which is in another through which it is also conceived.

VI. By God I understand absolutely infinite being, that is, substance consisting of infinite attributes, each one of which expresses eternal and infinite essence. *Explanation:* I say absolutely infinite, not however [infinite] in its kind. For of whatever is infinite only in its kind, we can deny infinite attributes [Dutch: that is, one can comprehend infinite properties which do not belong to its nature]. However, to the essence of that which is absolutely infinite pertains whatever expresses essence and involves no negation.

VII. That thing is called free which exists from the sole necessity of its nature, and is determined to acting by itself alone. But [that thing is called] necessary or, rather, compelled which is determined by another to existing and operating in a fixed and determinate manner.

VIII. By eternity I understand existence itself, insofar as it is conceived to follow necessarily from the definition alone of an eternal thing. *Explanation:* For such existence, like the essence of a thing, is conceived as an eternal truth. And hence it cannot be explained through duration or time, even if duration be conceived to lack beginning and end.[2]

This primary group of definitions already inclines the *Ethics* toward renewing and enlarging the question of nature. Such an orientation is manifest in three aspects: the method of defining, the grouping of definitions, and the presence of cues to be used in developing the Spinozan theory of nature.

(a) ***Definitional method and content.*** The rules of definition set forth toward the end of the *Emendation* are prolonged and rendered operational in the actual definitions that introduce the *Ethics*. It is as though the unfinished business of the former treatise is resumed and instantiated in the opening pages of the latter. The *Ethics'* eight definitions are rule-governed formulations which adhere strictly to the methodological canons for healing our understanding, or making it aware of the mind's union with nature as a whole. This adherence of the *Ethics'* opening definitions assures not only a general agreement with rules of method but also a quite specific ordination of our mind toward the truth about itself and nature.

In the *Emendation,* the main division is into rules for defining an uncreated thing and those for defining a created thing. This corresponds to the *Ethics'* definitions respectively of cause of itself (I) and (conjointly) a thing finite in its own kind (II) and things infinite only in their own kind (VI, Explanation). All other distinctions between uncreated and created things are here subordinated to the one ineradicable contrast between that which has no cause and explanation outside itself and that which does indeed require some distinct cause for its reality and significance.

This reduction readily satisfies the first rule for defining an uncreated thing, namely, exclusion of the idea of a cause as an explanation outside the thing defined. By starting with the definition of cause-of-itself, the *Ethics* strengthens its hold upon this rule. For whereas the *Emendation* simply states that, in the case of an uncreated thing, the exclusion of every cause means requiring nothing else "except its own active-being [*esse*],"³ the *Ethics* positively characterizes this *esse* as a self-causing or self-affirming essence. To qualify as cause-of-itself, an essence must "involve" existence in the sense of actively maintaining it through that essence's intrinsic power alone, independent of any other agency. Spinoza could find no more effective way of conveying to us the existential power and self-maintenance of naturing nature than by reserving his very first definition for cause-of-itself. Moreover, the proposed meaning of cause-of-itself is noetic as well as ontological. One cannot truly conceive of cause-of-itself as being nonexistent or as requiring some causal explanation apart from its own essence. This composition of the ontological and the noetic aspects of cause-of-itself is paradigmatic for the other definitions associated with naturing nature.

Clearly, this compound reference to what-is-and-is-conceived enables Spinoza to satisfy his second rule for defining an uncreated thing, namely, that the definition leaves no room for doubt about such a thing's existence. When we reflect upon the definition of cause-of-itself, we come to see that doubt is not a fundamental method and act of response. It depends upon some conditions that affect only created things, which are themselves accounted for by reference to cause-of-itself.

The impropriety of doubting the existence of an uncreated thing follows also from the definitions of substance, attribute and God (III, IV, and VI). Substance "is in itself," in the insistential way that the essence of cause-of-itself necessarily and autonomously involves its own existence. When our mind truly apprehends substance as self-affirming and self-standing being, we see that any existential doubt is because of a misplaced abstractness of questioning. This exclusion of doubt is in no way weakened by turning to attribute, since the latter manifests something about "substance as constituting its essence." No matter which attribute is grasped, it communicates to us something about the active, necessary, and self-grounded affirming of substance's own existence. Our understanding cannot acknowledge this existential truth and still engage in radical existential doubt about the attributes of substance.

Furthermore, Spinoza's explicit definition of God serves to synthesize the meaning of substance and that of unconditionally infinite attributes. This reinforces the incompatibility between the understanding's grasp of existential truth in this area and a method of universal doubt. The statement that each divine attribute "expresses eternal and infinite essence" points toward eternity (as signifying existence which follows necessarily from truly defined essence) and toward infinity (as unqualified real affirmation of existence). Since naturing nature is likewise to be signified by these same defined terms, no real footing will remain for asking in a primarily doubtful way: Does it exist? (*An sit?*)

The third rule of definition of an uncreated thing is that it not be explained by anything abstract. This is of immense importance for capturing Spinoza's intent in the definitions in *Ethics I*. He does not treat "cause-of-itself," "substance," and "God" as category terms that have many instances and many sources of individuation. Their meanings do not express the mind's abstraction from the concrete, but rather the mind's perception of that reality which is most concrete and powerful. In the already-quoted phrase of the *Emendation,* these meanings furnish the basis for drawing philosophical conclusions "from some particular affirmative essence, or from a true and legitimate definition." In this respect, the *Ethics* involves its definitions in a sustained argumentation which uses them as signifying particular affirmative essences, establishes thereby some truths about nature as a whole, and in the process makes them recognized as legitimate.

Fourth and last, the definition of an uncreated thing must be such that, from it, all the thing's properties can be concluded. Spinoza adds that failure to reach actual knowledge of all the properties does not invalidate the definition or interrelated set of definitions. This is not a casual concession but a reminder of the need to correlate the *Ethics'* definitions with the degrees of cognition open to the human mind for which, after all, these definitions are proposed and put to inferential use. Such properties as free thing (VII) and eternal thing (VIII) are indeed specified as following from the true definition of a thing that is cause-of-itself and substance. Other properties are left for propositional inferences to determine, but nowhere does Spinoza forget the limits of human understanding by foolishly claiming that Part I gives the complete sum of properties belonging to God or naturing nature. There is a distinction between knowing that God is substance consisting of unqualifiedly infinite attributes, knowing under human conditions only the two attributes of thought and extension, and the methodological ideal of knowing all the attributes and properties of uncreated naturing nature. Spinoza is unwilling to surrender either this ideal or the restricted approach to it which his conception of nature attains.

In the case of a created thing or a being that does have a proximate cause, there are only two rules of definition. The definition must include reference to the proximate cause; and when the concept or definition of the created thing is considered alone, not in conjunction with others, all its properties can be concluded from it. The first rule is carefully observed in the *Ethics'* definitions of finite thing in its kind (II) and mode (V). Finitude in its kind involves reference to something greater or more powerful within the same order, be it of body or of mind. And the designation of mode as "affections of" reads into its meaning both an ontic and an epistemic reference to substance. The precise sense in which God as naturing nature is cause of modes or natured nature is left for the theorizing in *Ethics I–II* to determine. Similarly, the knotty problem of ascertaining modal traits from a study of created things will have to be unraveled in *Ethics II,* where man's ways of becoming related to other bodies and minds are formally treated.

(b) *Grouping of definitions.* The terms chosen by Spinoza for definition at the outset of the *Ethics* have two tasks to perform. More immediately, they must signify the meanings needed to develop a theory of God as naturing nature. And in the longer run, their meanings must be put to use in constructing the theory about nature as a whole. We can grasp this double intent by attending to the several ways in which the definitions are grouped in respect to our primary concern with nature.

The course to be followed in the systematic reasoning is set at once by presenting together the definitions of cause of itself (I) and finite thing or thing finite in its kind (II). Thereby, Spinoza disposes our mind in two ways. First, we are to expect that the doctrine regarding God considers the divine being and attributes in their causal power and outcome in finite reality, rather than in an isolated and perhaps transcendent fashion. God is approached here precisely as nature in its actively naturing significance. Second, the sequential defining of cause-of-itself and finite thing directs our reflection toward joint consideration of nature as unbounded and bounded power, as that which consists of naturing and natured components together. This complex apprehension detracts neither from the powerfulness of what is naturing nor from the integrity of what is being natured.

The next grouping takes an interior journey into the two terminals of nature. Thus the definition of substance (III) sharpens our understanding of cause-of-itself. The latter is now affirmed to be self-sufficient in its own being, as well as to be the very principle from which our knowledge of nature as a whole must flow. With his definition of attribute (IV), Spinoza renders more specific this correlation between being and being known in the most reliable way. Attribute signifies the opening of substance (and hence of cause-of-itself) to the adequate cognitive act of the understanding. The latter can truly affirm something about substance by perceiving its essence through the attributes of thought and extension. Just as the understanding can gain a truly attributive knowledge of what constitutes the essence of substance, so can it truly know mode (V), when conceived as the affections or causal outcomes of substance. The sense in which modes are present in substance must be consonant with the self-sufficiency and power of substance as cause-of-itself. Mode signifies the reality of natured nature, which is a causal expression of naturing nature and which is rightly conceived only through reference to the causal activity of naturing nature.

Thus these two groupings of definitions (I–II, III–V) prepare an inquirer for articulating the distinction between naturing and natured nature. That distinction helps to relate and put to systematic use the terms thus far under definition. Cause-of-itself, substance, and attribute elucidate Spinoza's concept of naturing nature, to which they are exclusively bound. Likewise, finite thing and mode provide a meaning and a language to guide his further analyses of natured nature. And the effort to bring together all members of the two groupings gives the impetus for developing the concept of total nature.

But the third grouping of definitions (VI–VIII) shows that Spinoza does not underestimate the difficulties lying in the path of his theory of nature. What is most striking about this third group is the *contrastive* structure of each definition.

The defined meaning of God (VI) does serve, indeed, as an integrating center for the other constituents of naturing nature; cause-of-itself, substance, and unconditionally infinite attributes. But this involves some explanation of the difference between "absolutely infinite" and "infinite in its kind." The former is reserved for naturing nature, that is, for the Spinozan God with its attributes. Yet since some modal realities are infinite in their kind, natured nature is a mixed region including modes infinite in their kind as well as finite modes or things that are finite. How to relate these modes among themselves, especially in the case of infinite understanding and the finite human mind, looms already as a major problem concerning the human aspect of natured nature.

The definition of free thing (VII) begins the process of examining the properties of God or that which exists and acts from the determination of its own nature alone. This holds unqualifiedly for naturing nature. Still, "free thing" is one member of a pairing whose contrasting member is "compelled thing." The realm of natured nature (which is determined to exist and act in fixed fashion by the power of cause-of-itself) is surely the homeland for compelled things. But is there any appropriate sense in which some of its inhabitants can lay purchase upon the meaning of free things, and do so without ceasing to belong to natured nature? Spinoza the moral philosopher cannot suppress this question, which arises from both the human experience and the philosophical topic of our passage from servitude to some sort of freedom.

Eternity (VIII) too is so defined that more complications for the theory of nature can be foreseen. As with the other definitions, the reality being defined and the way of conceiving it are kept inseparable. In fact, Spinoza approaches eternity by contrasting two conceptions of existence. The opposition here is stated between viewing "existence as following solely from the definition of a nondurational, nontemporal thing" and viewing "existence as explained by time and duration." Eternity (i.e., the view of existence given first) is a property of naturing nature. In experiencing and trying to explain things in natured nature, however, we have recourse to the temporal and durational character of their existence. Is our reliance upon the latter explanatory mode owing solely to the use of imagination? The danger is that natured nature may then be regarded as a construct of imagination alone, or else that the cognition of eternal truths and the search for eternal life may be regarded as acts of abandoning natured nature rather than of transforming our conception of its irreducible reality. This would lead to the internal collapse of Spinoza's doctrine on nature as a whole.

(c) *Cue words and phrases.* Upon revisiting the initial definitions after having read through the *Ethics,* one notices how skillfully their wording contributes to one's linguistic education. Spinoza loses no time in furnishing the words and phrases that are essential for his immediate argument on various topics. It helps to notice, however, three less-obvious tactical movements that prepare our minds for following the development of his conception of nature.

(1) Noticeable by its absence is any reference to nature in its comprehensive sense. The crucial thematic term *tota natura* is not included. There has to be a gradual buildup both in Spinoza's inferential use of other defined terms and in our ability to follow his arguments before the need for an inclusive complex meaning of nature can gain forcible recognition.

However, a beginning is made with a restricted use of "whose nature," in the sense of either substance or of this and that kind of mode. Eventually, the attentive reader of *Ethics I* will be linguistically disposed to include God and modal things within the broadest meaning of the whole of nature.

(2) The formula most frequently used in the definitions is "By X, I understand that which." From the very threshold, Spinoza is affirming the inseparability between knowing and being known, indeed between my emended human ways of knowing and the realities that get defined or demonstrated in the *Ethics*. In contrast to the Cartesian *Cogito*, the Spinozan *Intelligo* affirms the oneness between the order of being and the proper order of understanding the reality of nature. That this connection also affects the human ways of acting and our practical relationships with the whole of nature becomes progressively clearer as the investigation moves along.

The "I understand" can best be grasped as situated between upper and lower noetic activities, in both of which it participates. The upper reach of noetic perfection is signified, in definition IV, by the term *intellectus*. This points toward the distinction between finite modes of understanding, or the human mind, and the infinite immediate mode of understanding (which has the right to be unqualifiedly called "the understanding" or "understanding"). It is altogether essential to Spinoza's account of nature that this distinction not be exploited to create a division. For it is the understanding which truly conceives of God or substance through the latter's attributes, and our human mind must be able to share in this activity in order to have knowledge of divine substance and some of its attributes. The language of "I understand" and "the understanding" disposes the reader to accept this sharing relationship and thus to gain access to naturing nature.

The definitions are replete with expressions of the operations of the mind within its own humanly characteristic way of cognizing. The acts of human understanding are here stated to include: conceive, comprehend, explain, and deny. Of special interest is the wording of the contrast between free thing and thing that is called "necessary or, rather, compelled" (definition VII). This phrase signals the need for correcting our thought and language, and for doing so in a methodic way which spurs us toward constant emendation of cognitive materials and expressions. These materials come from our sense experience, imagination, and daily conversation, marking the lower noetic limit of the intellectual life.

The Spinozan Intelligo assimilates all these acts and corrective measures. It stands for a reflective integration of all that tests out as sound in the three types of human cognition: sense experience and imagination, reason and methodic reform, and intuitive knowing. Hence, from the pedagogical standpoint, the "I understand" is not merely a stipulative but a recapitulative expression. Readers of the *Ethics* cannot be expected at first, however, to apprehend the recapitulative function of that phrase, especially insofar as it brings home the reflective reasoning about natured nature on the part of its most complex finite mode, the human inquirer. Hence, readers must examine the reasoning whereby Spinoza justifies for his definitions his own axiomatic requirement that "a true idea must agree with its ideatum," that is, with that which the idea intends and affirms.[4]

Here is where the last part of the recurring phrase "By X, I understand that which" shows its importance. In his reasoning about something, Spinoza does not force the pace but refers to it in terms of *that which* (*id quod*). In *Ethics I,* the "that-which" procedure is quite apparent in gradually determining certain traits about substance and then concluding that these traits apply to God or naturing nature. Similarly, the train of argument establishes that divine causality has many implications for that which is caused, namely, for natured nature. Thus Spinoza employs the "that-which" procedure in his inferences about both naturing and natured nature. His repeated dictum that something "is and is conceived to be" as it is defined or demonstrated, combines the *id quod* and the *intelligo* already associated proleptically in the definitions.

(3) Finally, there is a relationship between an entire family of verbs and a lone adverb. The verbs used in the definitions are: *involve, express,* and *follow.* They signify that powerful consequences flow from cause-of-itself, which is to say from substance and its attributes. Their expressive and manifestive activity is a prominent part of the meaning of naturing nature. From the latter, there follow those determinate outcomes in existing and acting which constitute natured nature. The involvements embrace both being and knowing. The acts of cause-of-itself give rise to all modal things in the ontic order, just as they give a specific foundation to our philosophizing in the noetic order. Hence, the entailments represented by these verbs can be restated in Spinoza's other favorite term *affirm,* just so long as that term is acknowledged to hold alike for being and knowing. Indeed, there is no split in natured nature, since cognitive acts are themselves a distinctive sort of modal being.

Spinoza wants to prepare us, however, for the complexities which these relationships introduce into his philosophical analyses and inferences. The anticipatory sign of these complexities is the adverb *quatenus,* "insofar as." He introduces this term in his definition of eternity, which is existence itself insofar as it is conceived to follow necessarily from the definition alone of an eternal thing.

This account is remarkable for several reasons. It explicitly links "insofar as" with "follow" and its cognate verbs, thus suggesting that the adverbial qualifier is required because of the causal and cognitive involvements of the naturing principle. Its expressive power constitutes, permeates, and becomes reexpressed in natured nature. Since this many-sided relation binds naturing and natured nature together, the term *insofar as* is a linguistic integrator leading us toward the unifying theme of nature as a whole.

Moreover, the definition of eternity implies that the human mind may take other views of existence. We may try to identify eternity with prolonged time and endless duration. It is no accident, then, that Spinoza should locate his understanding of eternity after his definitions of infinite thing and free thing. This sequence suggests two points. First, the human mind is a finite mode of the understanding, which is infinite in its kind but not in every respect. We attain knowledge of eternity only insofar as we correct our durational imagery by the infinite understanding's conception of the nondurational derived existence of the understanding itself. Second, our true conception of eternity depends on our ability to distinguish between an existential and actional necessity determined by the thing itself and an existential and actional compulsion imposed by something else. Only insofar as our mind clarifies itself sufficiently to distinguish the essential necessity from the external compulsion can it understand the meaning and share the reality of free thing and eternal thing.

The qualifier *insofar as* aids us to gain a true conception of both the distinction between naturing and natured nature and their operational unity as a whole reality. Since this distinction and unity are reflectively apprehended precisely through man's struggle to emend his cognitions, *quatenus* will get maximum use in *Ethics II* and thereafter. This adverb is the Spinozan icon of our need to discern the effective workings of God or naturing nature within the modal universe. It also stands for our consequent power to live and act in accord with the prospects thereby opened up for natured nature.

This signified relationship between God, man, and the rest of the universe is bound to be complex and multivalent in its philosophical interpretation. We can sympathize with William James's caustic remark that "Spinoza's philosophy has been rightly said to be worked by the word *quatenus*."[5] James suspected this word of cloaking a failure to relate God

and man intimately and to maintain the integrity of the temporal, historical, plural world of ours. But Spinoza himself incorporates the term into
his opening definitions not as an escape mechanism but as a cue to the
difficulties to be encountered and the careful distinctions to be used in
developing the stages of his inquiry into nature and its modalizations.

2. Placing the Queries about God in Sequence

The propositions and demonstrations that make up the main body of
the *Ethics* can be regarded as reasoned responses made to queries about
the topics being investigated. This procedure with its implied questions
and answers (sometimes formalized in an erotetic logic) makes us attentive to the presence of Spinoza's own inquiring mind. His awareness of
problems is also expressed in the numerous corollaries, lemmas, and
scholia, since they constitute aspects and implications of the primary
queries and responses which they elucidate. Especially in the prefatory
remarks, the appendices, and even some of the scholia, Spinoza uses
first-person address, which emphasizes his role as questioner. He displays
a keen personal sense of obligation to raise the main difficulties on an
issue, as well as to keep his responses relevant to his queries.

Two major problems concern adequacy and order. First, what will
count as an *adequate* response to a query?[6] Spinoza sometimes asks this
about the adequacy of an idea. It becomes clear enough and distinct
enough only when it affirms something contained in, or consonant with,
or ampliative of, the meaning of nature which is gradually evolving in his
philosophy. Some aspect of querying about nature is eventually stated in
propositional form. The demonstration and other forms of argument
count as adequate resonses when they bring to bear upon the issue at hand
those aspects of the logic of nature, so far established, which are shown to
have consequences here. If the response does draw out the implications, it
will also develop that logic itself and expand the context for raising
further queries and working out further responses that can be incorporated.

This accounting of adequacy involves the second problem: what *ordering* of queries and responses best meets the aims of Spinoza's philosophy?
He has already treated this matter in the *Emendation*, where he maintained that the best order of philosophizing is to start with the idea of that
being from which the rest of reality is necessarily derived. This is only an
initial general precept, however, which results in beginning the *Ethics*
with Part I on God or naturing nature. The problem of order must now be

restrictedly rephrased as one concerning the relationship between queries internal to the broad topic of God.

Within the query-and-response frame, we are asking about the sequencing of queries and resonses about God as expressed in the propositions of *Ethics I* (without denying that Spinoza's doctrine on God continues to grow in the subsequent parts of the *Ethics* and elsewhere). The sequencing does not solely concern a numbered series of propositions moving along a flat horizon. This is primarily a question about what experts on computers call the pyramiding or peaking process. Within any part of the *Ethics,* Spinoza works noticeably toward some definite peaks of doctrinal emphasis. An entire group of propositions mounts toward some culminating position, which is then shown to have definite implications for the arguments that follow.

Depending upon the theme under study, several such climaxes are reached in *Ethics I.* Scholars interested chiefly in the problem of God's existence, for instance, have noticed that propositions 1 through 11 converge upon the demonstration that God necessarily exists. Instead of plunging straightway into this issue (as he had done in the *Short Treatise*), Spinoza now takes the preparatory steps of showing that substance is the unique unproduced cause of itself, whose essence necessarily involves existence and affirms its own existence in the absolutely unhindered way appropriate to infinite substance and attributes. Proposition 11 follows the methodological rule concerning the existence of an uncreated or unproduced thing, by showing that existence follows necessarily from the definition of God as *"substance consisting of infinite attributes, each of which* [necessarily] *expresses eternal and infinite essence."*[7] Spinoza reworks several proofs of God's existence in a manner that makes these proofs conform with both his methodology and his peaking process of reasoning.

My attention is drawn to another culmination that occurs later on in *Ethics I.*[8] In the scholium to proposition 29, Spinoza distinguishes nature into that which is naturing and that which is natured. This distinction is immediately put to work in the very formulation and demonstration of proposition 31, and its force is felt throughout the remainder of the *Ethics.* Why does Spinoza use the general theory of nature, and why does he delay introducing it until he is over halfway through *Ethics I*?

The latter part of this double question concerns the strategy of *postponement.* Spinoza postpones the explicit statement of his comprehensive view of nature as long as he can, that is, until the difficulties entailed in doing without it mount to an intolerable level. This is a matter of judgment, but the judgment concerns both Spinoza as source philosopher and ourselves as interpreters. In effect, the scholium declares that he cannot carry on *his* reasoning beyond this point without the aid of his general conception of nature, except by piling up ambiguities and cumbersome indirections that become self-defeating. At the same time, the scholium suggests that *we* cannot follow Spinoza's philosophizing any longer without making explicit advertence to the naturing-natured distinction and its multiple precisions of his thought. To make us perceive both the internal systematic need and the interpretive one for employing the distinction is the strategic purpose behind the delayed presentation.

This brings to the fore the first part of the question just formulated, namely, why Spinoza feels obligated in philosophical conscience to employ the general theory of nature at all in *Ethics I*. One reason has already been intimated in the previous analysis of the definitions. The doublets cause-of-itself and finite thing, again, substance-attributes and mode, signify that *Ethics I* is to treat of God's essence, existence, and actions through some use of these coupled meanings and their allied definitions. What does not get stated at the definitional stage, however, is the basis for the unified theory of God that should emerge from this approach.

As the actual demonstrations proceed, the problem of supplying this unifying basis becomes increasingly urgent. Three developments help to articulate the problem and make a search for its resolution unavoidable.

(a) The first contribution comes from the concept of *cause-of-itself,* which Spinoza makes more and more prominent in his treatment of substance. In order to demonstrate that "*it pertains to the nature of substance to exist,*"[9] he argues that the unique and unproducible substance is cause-of-itself, namely, affirms its own existence necessarily and without hindrance. This unhemmed causal power of substance or God also necessarily produces the entire reality of other things. "In that sense in which God is called the cause-of-himself, he must also be called the cause of all things. . . . *God is the efficient cause not only of the existence of things but also of the essence*" of these things. The latter are produced modes rather than unproduced substance or cause-of-itself. Granted that the designation "cause-of-itself" is reserved for divine substance, the query must then be pressed concerning the causal unity-without-identity between substance and modal things, naturing and natured nature.

(b) Clearly, the doctrine on *modes* is the second factor prompting the search for a unifying theory of nature. In *Ethics I*, Spinoza asks about their reality, their inclusion of the understanding, and the manner in which they follow causatively from substance. Each step of the inquiry leads to complications that cannot be treated satisfactorily without the context provided by considering nature as a whole.

Prior to proposition 29, there are at least four major texts affirming the reality of modes.

[1] Apart from the understanding, there is nothing except substances and their affections. . . . [2] For in the nature of things [*in rerum natura*], there is nothing except substances and their affections. . . . [3] However, modes (*Definition* 5) can neither be nor be conceived without substance; wherefore they can be in the divine nature alone, and can be conceived through it alone. But apart from substances and modes, there is nothing. . . . [4] For apart from substance and modes, there is nothing (*Axiom* 1 *and Definitions* 3 *and* 5); and modes (*Proposition* 25, *Corollary*) are nothing but affections of God's attributes.[10]

Although these texts are used in demonstrating different propositions, they are similarly worded and raise similar difficulties about the scope and union of real beings.

In the first three quotations, use is made of "substances" in the plural. This usage must be interpreted within the continuous sweep of inferences in *Ethics I*. Thus texts [1] and [2] come before the unicity of substance has been established. And although text [3] does appear right after demonstration of substance's unicity, it still falls within Spinoza's continuing effort to induce people to regard thought and extension as attributes of the sole substance. In this respect, text [4] is the most accurately stated. For it compresses into a few words Spinoza's position that there is but one substance, that all other real things are modes, and that modes are related to substance by "affecting" the latter's attributes through being their various expressions.

Nevertheless, problems crop up when each quoted text is restored to its inferential setting. The reference to the understanding in text [1] is a way of asking about those formal essences which are intended by the understanding and its objective essences or ideas. What the understanding's ideas affirm as real entities, having their own essential and existential act, are substance and its affections or modes. But we are still left wondering about how substantial and modal realities can be brought together and related by the understanding, without one of these meanings becoming absorbed into the other. A comprehensive view of nature is needed to embrace these different yet related ways of being.

At first glance, such a general basis would seem to be supplied by the explicit mention of nature in text [2]. But although the expression *in rerum natura*, "in the nature of things," is used several times in propositions 5 and 6, it fails to meet the expectation of a unifying principle. At this early stage of the *Ethics,* the expression stands midway between its colloquial or idiomatic use to signify the real order of things, or the total universe, and the Spinozan treatment of nature and things in their full systematic range. We are still left asking about what does indeed hold good, as being real in the nature of things.

Up to this point in the argumentation, "in the nature of things" performs a largely negative function. It is a brief way of saying that, given the reality of substance and modes, we ought not to regard attributes as a third sort of entity. This bars us from holding either that there could be several substances sharing in the same attribute, as a real ground for their distinction, or that one substance could be produced by another substance by means of the same attribute serving as a mutually real basis for causation. Thus at this phase of the sequencing, *in rerum natura* buttresses the unicity of substance and the fact that it cannot be produced, but does not yet specify the causation and internal differentiation of modes.

A further step is taken in text [3]. It specifies that the trait of modes, that they exist in another, means their presence precisely in the sole substance and their knowability by reference to this sole substantial reality. Spinoza further states that this manner of modal being means *in sola divina natura esse,* "to be in the divine nature alone." God's essence and existence are one and the same reality; cause-of-itself affirms its own existence through the same eternal, necessary, and infinite power wherewith it affirms its own essence. This can be said of God alone—that is, of substance alone. That is why there is only one substance, as well as why modes have essence and existence in and through the essential-existential affirming act of substance. The latter is appropriately called divine, condensing an entire skein of reasoning into the term *divina natura.* Nevertheless, Spinoza's reference is still restrictively intended for the sole substance, "the divine nature," in which modes have their being and through which alone they are adequately conceived. The famous Spinozan phrase *Deus sive Natura* is functionally referred to a context of the restricted or nonmodal signification of divine naturing nature given in the present text. What still remains to be achieved is a conception of total nature as being divine, so that "divine nature" includes both substance and modes.

In respect to the peaking process of sequenced inferences, text [4] comes to the very limit of what Spinoza can do, without explicitly using his theory of naturing and natured nature. For here, modes are regarded from the perspective of being affections or active expressions of the attributes of God. The denial that attributes comprise a third order of being does not render them metaphysically and epistemologically otiose. On the contrary, reflection upon them is the best means for clarifying how the modes follow from substance, have their being in substance, and are known in reference to substance. Without a theory of attributes, Spinoza could not conceive of substance and modes together, and therefore could not reach philosophical knowledge of nature as a whole.

But it is also true that the topic of attributes introduces a heavy burden of distinctions concerning both substance and modes. No human philosophy can be satisfied with an isolated treatment of substance, taken without any reference to our modal world. Spinoza's thematizing of attribute is his recognition that we search after a view of substance precisely as giving rise to our experienced modal world of minds and bodies. Attributes signify the essence of substance truly so viewed by the understanding. Hence in text [4], modes are regarded as affections of their respective attributes, that is, as causally revelatory access routes to the essence of substance.

The assignment of modes under their proper attributes renders more precise, but does not resolve, the problem of unifying substance and its modes. The difficulty of their integration becomes increasingly pronounced in propositions 21 through 29 of *Ethics I*.[11] Here, Spinoza is grappling with the fact that the singular things (*res singulares*) perceived in our experience are finite and have a terminal limit for their existence. How can they follow causally from the unconditionally infinite, eternal, necessary being and causal activity of substance?

This query compels Spinoza to begin the work of internal differentiation among kinds of modes. Those things that originate directly from some attributes of substance are themselves the immediate, infinite, and eternal modes. But the infinite modal pattern that arises from attributes, considered as being already modified by the immediate modes, is unavoidably mediate and further differentiated from eternal substance. Thence springs a world of finite modes or singular things, each of which determines and is determined by other finite modes in the same series, coming from the appropriate attribute and infinite modes. Yet with every stage in this modal differentiation, a greater distance seems to grow between substance and the cascade of modal entities.

In order to mend this fracture, Spinoza makes his own use of the distinction between remote and proximate causes. He interprets this distinction as one holding between different standpoints of our consideration. God is called a remote cause only from the inadequate perspective of the modes themselves, and only as a means for differentiating among modal things in their various relationships with each other and with their respective attributes. But from the basis in divine active power, God is the immanent, proximate cause that is most intimately operative and pervasive in all modal things. How to heal those breaks and assure the primacy of God's immanent causal presence and determination of all modal essence, existence, and activity—this is the task leading inevitably to Spinoza's doctrine on nature as naturing and natured.

(c) To reach this peak of his sequencing, Spinoza must involve his *theory of the infinite understanding* in every moment of his reasoning. He cannot define "attribute" in a way that retains its grounding in reality and yet does not become a third form of being without appealing to a unique relation between substance and the infinite understanding. The latter knows substance, and what the understanding knows as constituting the true essence of substance is nothing other than attribute. Only through this affinity between understanding and the attributes can an internally complex account of modes be given, without gradually estranging them from substance.

The linguistic signs of the infinite understanding's indispensable contribution to *Ethics I* are: "fall under" and "conceive of," "consider" and "distinguish." Thus Spinoza launches his detailed treatment of divine causality of modes by correlating the infinite number of modal things, produced in unlimited ways by the necessity of the divine nature, and "all things which can fall under the infinite understanding."[12] He then relies upon his account of the understanding to discern which sorts of causality apply to God's activity and which do not. The correlative office of this reference to the understanding is to consider different kinds of modes by their relation to the divine attributes and to each other.

There are several good reasons why Spinoza cannot proceed further without explicitly situating the infinite understanding within his framework of nature as naturing and natured. First, he has now completed the initial task of distinguishing reality into substance, infinite modes, and finite singular modes. The question arises whether the understanding itself belongs within this division, or whether it comprises yet another sort of real being. For Spinoza, there can be no tampering with his repeated statements that nothing real is given except substance and its modes. Just as his theory of attributes does not add to this division, so also his theory of the understanding does not proliferate it. The understanding does *not* belong within the sphere of substance, and it *does* come within the sphere of infinite modal reality. To reinforce this point, Spinoza assigns the understanding not to naturing nature but to natured nature alone.

Second, he wants to reap an immediate advantage from this assignment. For it means that understanding, desire, and will (in any intelligible sense) cannot be attributed properly to God, and hence cannot be the source of divine causality. The modal world proceeds primordially from the necessity of the divine naturing nature, unqualified by any act of understanding and will. Naturing nature acts freely only insofar as it remains uncoerced by natured nature, including the understanding. But this very freedom from coercion means that divine causation or creation expresses the necessity of the divine nature and provides no ultimate ground for contingent existing and acting, on the part of modal things.

In the third place, the inclusion of the understanding within natured nature imposes the latter's internal differentiation upon the former. Thus, although there is an infinite and eternal understanding, it is not identified with God's attribute of thought but is an immediate modal expression of God's power within the natured world. The mediate causal and finite expressions of naturing nature, considered under the attribute of thought, are finite modes of understanding or minds. Just how the infinite and finite modes of understanding are mutually related cannot be established solely from a causal consideration of thought. To illuminate this difficult issue in some degree, Spinoza will have to specify that the world that we experience involves the natured modal expressions of extension and hence ultimately a proportionment between the finite human body and the finite human mind. This points toward the inquiries to be undertaken in *Ethics II*, on the human mind.

Yet even in *Ethics I*, Spinoza has a fourth set of reasons for including infinite as well as finite understanding within natured nature.

[1] *The understanding, finite in act or infinite in act, must comprehend the attributes of God and the affections of God, and nothing else. . . .* [2] *The understanding in act, whether it be finite or infinite, and likewise will, desire, love, etc., must be referred to natured nature, not indeed to naturing* [nature]. . . . [3] The reason why I may speak here of the understanding in act [*actu*], is not because I grant that there is any understanding in potency [*potentia*], but, because I desire to avoid all confusion, I do not wish to speak except about a thing perceived by us as clearly as possible, that is, about the very operation-of-understanding [*intellectione*], than which nothing is more clearly perceived by us. For we can understand nothing that does not conduce to the more perfect cognition of the operation-of-understanding.[13]

In part, the first two texts reaffirm Spinoza's position that substance and modes comprise reality and set the scope of even an infinite understanding, and that the understanding in all its realizations belongs entirely within natured nature or the domain of modes. But taken in conjunction with the third text, these propositions make a notable advance in his theory of the understanding in its relation to nature as a whole.

The quoted passages speak conjunctively about finite and infinite understanding. This is a paradigm for Spinoza's discourse on any modal line within natured nature. Whatever the difficulties about how the finite modes originate from the infinite ones, there is a cohesive unity among the infinite and finite modal expressions of the same attribute of substance. Together, these modes constitute an internally related causal order within natured nature.

Furthermore, Spinoza uses the technical term *intellectus actu*, "the understanding in act," in referring to both the infinite and the finite understanding. Text [3] is the scholium where he states his distinctive meaning for this widely used term. It is not part of a theory setting off an active intellect from one in potency. This rules out any interpretation of "understanding in act" as being identical either with a separate agent intellect or with the actuation of an intellect initially in potency, as the realistic tradition on human abstractive knowledge maintains. Spinoza usually uses the term *potentia* to signify active power rather than capacity for actualization. In the present text, the intended contrast is an epistemological one between the clear, true knowing (whether finite or infinite in its mode) and an obscure inadequate perception. In effect, understanding-in-act inserts the doctrine on the three modes of perception into the heart of Spinoza's treatment of natured nature.

The nuance added by text [3] is that the understanding-in-act constitutes reflexive cognition of the very operation-of-understanding or *intellectio*. No excessive claim is made for the latter, insofar as it is a human activity. Intellection is characterized relatively (as much clear perception as is possible for us), proportionally (we improve this cognition with every act of perceiving other things), and negatively (we perceive nothing more clearly). Spinoza's caution on this point is doubly motivated. It enables him to convey the point that, in cognizing something else, we simultaneously strengthen our understanding's operational grasp upon itself as an active finite mode of cognition. And by way of anticipation, it binds our self-understanding with what will be said, in *Ethics II*, about our basic perception of the bodily world and the human body.

Taken together, these three texts furnish a gloss upon Spinoza's stated aim of making us aware of the mind's union with the whole of nature.

With every cognition, the human mind grasps itself as finite understanding-in-act. It also perceives its operational union with infinite understanding, a union that is one principal component of natured nature.
The human mind's acquaintance with the bodily world and its own body
deepens, rather than depletes, its own reality as *intellectio*. Hence text [2]
can be reformulated more positively as an affirmation of our increasing
knowledge of natured nature. "Natured" does not have a purely passive
significance, but conveys the causal activities of understanding and of
bodies as expressing the power of substance. The positive affirmation of
text [1] is, therefore, that our finite understanding-in-act does attain to
some clear, true knowledge of the attributes of God or substance or
naturing nature, as well as of God's modal affections or natured nature.
Weaving these strands together, there is a sound foundation for basing
human happiness upon the mind's union with the whole of nature.

I will conclude this section by giving the scholium which regulates the
entire sequencing order examined above.

> Before I proceed further, I want to explain here, or rather to call to mind,
> what we should understand by naturing nature, and what by natured nature.
> For already from what has preceded, I deem it to be established, surely, that
> by naturing nature we should understand that which is in itself and is
> conceived through itself, or such attributes of substance that express eternal
> and infinite essence, that is (*Proposition* 14, *Corollary* 1, and *Proposition*
> 17, *Corollary* 2), God, insofar as he is considered as free cause. However,
> by natured [nature] I understand everything that follows from the necessity
> of God's nature [from the necessity] of each of God's attributes, that is, all
> the modes of God's attributes, insofar as they are considered as things which
> are in God, and which can neither be nor be conceived without God.[14]

Here, Spinoza does some stock taking. He looks retrospectively at what
he has already shown (in *Ethics I* and perhaps in the other writings
familiar to his study group) about naturing and natured nature, as well as
prospectively at the clouded vision of those who ignore this doctrine and
at the further reasoning needed to rectify their thought.

As he plunges into the study of man, Spinoza will use the two divisions
of nature as beacons and norms of truth. Naturing nature consolidates his
position on substance and attributes, eternally existing and infinitely
powerful essence. This will govern his *quatenus* propositions about God,
his consideration of God precisely as free cause of our world of bodily
things, including man. And natured nature will bring to bear upon the
coming analysis of man the implications of regarding all modal things as
proceeding from the necessity of God's nature or essence, which is identical with the divine power of being and acting.

3. Man's Passage from Madness to Sanity about Nature

From the vantage point of nature-theory, the appendix to *Ethics I* is
something more than an afterthought or a polemical interruption of the
main flow of reasoning. It makes an essential contribution that is enhanced
by Spinoza's personal form of address. In structural terms, it welds together the later propositions of the first part and the opening propositions
of the second part. This it does by reminding us that the previous treatment of God established much already about the modal world, as well as
by preparing us to expect that propositions on the human mind will
further evolve the doctrine on God. Thus the appendix serves as a useful
bridge for maintaining continuity in the *Ethics*.

The most prominent transition is that from the passions and our bondage to them (Parts III and IV) to active freedom and happiness (Part V).
But this grand transition in the moral order depends upon the reform of
human thinking urged in the appendix to Part I and demonstrated in *Ethics
II*. This appendix renders explicit the intellectual changes entailed by
Spinoza's reasoning in the propositions which it links together. Most
far-reaching among these emendations are those concerning the way in
which men view God, the physical world, and their own responses.

In the *Ethics* and elsewhere, Spinoza states bluntly that the basic
passage is from an insane to a sane conception of nature. He ascribes the
madness to our imaginative belief in final causes, supposed to be operative throughout reality. To support this belief as literal truth, we concoct
numerous maxims. That is why an attack upon the use of maxims in our
thinking about nature is a prominent part of Spinoza's critique. Teleologists are specially fond of the maxim that ''nature does nothing in
vain.''[15] As a meaning for what would count as a vain or frustrated course
of action, proponents of final cause specify that which would be detrimen-
tal to human welfare over the long course of events. Hence the root of
madness consists in an anthropocentric finalism, a conviction that everything must work eventually for man's benefit.

This self-serving finalism is set on a collision course with any realistic
appraisal of the human condition, which is burdened with frustrations and
sorrows. Out of the conflict between the wishful and the all-too-prevalent
comes a severe contraction of the significance of nature. Instead of unifying reality within nature as a whole, there is a threefold division of reality
into physical nature, man, and God (or the gods). This runs counter not
only to Spinoza's theme of total nature, but also to his usage of *res
naturales* or natural things. The latter is a sliding term employed by

Spinoza to designate sometimes the world of modes of extension, sometimes the world of modes of thought, and sometimes both modal regions as constituting a unified order and connection (*omnia naturalia*). But to account for the misfortunes of humanity, the teleologists tend to contract *res naturales* to the physical world, against whose defects man is pitted and with whose purposive tendencies man is cooperative.

Once this step is taken, the consequences are not only disruptive of the unity of nature but also generative of all sorts of superstitious beliefs. In his attack upon finalistic thinking, Spinoza shares the passion and often the language of Lucretius, even though the two philosophers part company in their systematic views of nature and God. Superstitious people let reality seep into their minds just sufficiently to convince themselves that they are not the original makers of natural things (in the Spinozan language, this modal world of bodies). Hence, they must look elsewhere than to themselves for the power to direct nature finalistically toward serving human needs and desires.

Spinoza identifies four stages in the genesis of belief in final causes.[16] (1) Instead of probing instructively into the immanent order and connection among all beings in nature, people seek foolishly outside of nature for "some ruler or some rulers of nature." They picture the *rector naturae* as transcending the order of nature and as freely directing nature toward ends beneficial to mankind.

(2) In order to characterize more closely this purposive reshaping of natural things, some men cannot avoid setting themselves up "as interpreters of nature and of the gods." The *interpretes naturae* criticized by Spinoza are those who deem all natural happenings to be contingent events, signs of a divine transcendent purpose, and the means of a divine intervention in the order of nature. Final causes are thus associated with the contingency of nature's order and the free use of nature to realize the plans of an outside divinity on man's behalf.

(3) Spinoza is now able to turn the tables on those who criticized him as degrading God through his doctrine on extension as a divine attribute. Rather, it is his critics, the exponents of final causality in nature, "who feign God [to be] like man, consisting of body and mind and subject to passions." It no longer suffices Spinoza to argue that body, mind, and passions belong exclusively to natured nature. Now, he maintains that a representation of *Deus instar hominis* (God as like man) is essential to the teleological view of nature. For God is pictured as using nature as an instrument for attaining his own useful good. To employ the natural course of things as a means of realizing his providential plans for man-

kind, God must seek a good that is useful for himself. Like man, he aims at an end that satisfies his need or indigence in this respect. Every interpretation of the divine purpose, even that made in terms of a communicative good or an assimilative end, still remains in the same man-shaped pattern of God as gaining some satisfaction from his rule and governance over nature. The anthropomorphic model for envisaging God's relation to natural things dominates every theory of final causes in nature.

(4) What sort of status does finalism have among human perceptions? Spinoza calls final causes "human figments," because they do not concern any order in nature except that which affects our imagination. Telic notions are modes of imagination or ways in which imagination gets affected. These notions do not inform us about the nature of anything in the physical world, therefore, but only about the constitution of the human imagination.

Unfortunately, believers in final causes refuse to submit their images to clarification and correction by methodic reason, but confuse them with things existing apart from imagination. This confusion prompts Spinoza to refine his terminology by calling finalistic notions "beings, not of reason, but of imagination." In this sense, *entia rationis* undergo and survive the purifying scrutiny of reason, which uses them in the experiential and rational study of nature. Taken by themselves, *entia imaginationis* are open to similar critical use, even though it be a more limited one. But partisans of finality do not make the distinction or accept the limits of imagination, so that they espouse an uncriticized and hence inherently confused outlook. Their purposive view of the actions of physical things, men, and gods is totally vulnerable to the skeptical judgment of insanity. But this does not warrant the further conclusion of skepticism, that every philosophical conception of nature suffers from the same delusion, if it claims to deliver truths about things in nature.

The bridge-building quality of the appendix to *Ethics I* is evident in the new currency it gives to two themes already broached in the *Emendation:* becoming aware of oneself, and developing a new logic of man in nature. The former theme is retrospective, whereas the latter one sends forth connectives into the subsequent path of reasoning in *Ethics II* and thereafter.

Those who accept final causes are sleepwalkers. They may even wander among the demonstrations of *Ethics I* without ever really comprehending the argument or appreciating what its denial would entail for themselves and natural reality as a whole. Spinoza has used many approaches to show that natured nature comes forth, with unqualified necessity, from God. There is no ground for distinguishing between God's absolute power and his ordinate power, because there is no presence of understanding and will within the divine nature that might justify this distinction. God produces the modal world in continuity with the act wherewith he exists, an act that enjoys the unconditioned necessity of his power and essence. Because his power and essence are absolutely the same, God acts causally to produce natured nature from the necessity of his own nature alone, or (if one uses legal language) from the sole necessity of the laws of the divine essence or naturing nature.

Spinoza even turns against itself the objection that such causation would detract from the perfection of God. *Perfection* is not a primary term or concept from which anything can be independently concluded. Its reasoned philosophical meaning is entirely governed by the theory of power and essence, existence and causal act. Hence there is "no cause which, extrinsically or intrinsically, incites God into acting, except the perfection of his own nature [Dutch: but that through the power of his perfection alone, he is an efficient cause (*causa efficiens*)]."[17] The Dutch version drives home the point with clarity and precision.

Divine perfection signifies precisely the power and essence of God. The necessity of God's essential act of being prolongs itself in his causal action, which directly expresses the power of efficient causality alone. There is neither need nor room for the intervention of purposive motives, designs, and decisions. Hence to ascribe final causality to God is to detract from his own perfection. That is why Spinoza heatedly criticizes those confused people who imagine that God must make a purposively free choice among possibles, in creating *this* rather than *that* contingent order of natured nature. If the latter could be causally constituted to exist and operate in some other manner, then God's own essence and power could be otherwise than they actually are. In that case, naturing nature would be mutable and perhaps plural (many gods for many kinds of cosmic order). Spinoza regards this consequence as the highest pitch of madness affecting those minds which allow their finalistic imagery to run unchecked. Any logic of possible worlds (Cartesian or otherwise) must either declare itself to be only a nonontological play of imagination or else be declared aberrant in regard to nature.

Already the contours of *Ethics II* are being shaped. Spinoza will not permit his theory of man to be influenced by any teleological view of nature, however modified. Instead, it is necessary "to destroy that entire fabric, and to think out a new one," which will completely supplant the telic prejudices about nature.[18] The fresh fabric or context for understanding man is woven by the new Spinozan ontology. It regards the structure and activity of natured nature as being the necessary causal expression of God's own power, essence, and perfection. Mathematics and mechanics (which we previously saw to be purifiers of the understanding) have begun our reeducation by dispensing with final causes in their explanations. But only the philosophic conception of nature can furnish the foundation in reality for a sane and thorough rethinking of human life.

4. Man in the Perspective of Singular Things

Better than in any other writing of Spinoza, we can observe in the *Ethics* just how strenuously he must work to achieve systematic continuity between the theory of God and that of man. It is not enough that they both belong within the theory of nature, since in its most general statement this theory relates the infinite causal power of God to a vast range of produced kinds of things. The problem is to observe the methodological rule of beginning with God and yet to lead the argumentation into a definite focus upon man. Hegel's criticism was that "in the system of Spinoza all things are merely cast down into this abyss of annihilation [absolute substance]. But from this abyss nothing comes out."[19] But the real difficulty is that myriad footsteps lead out from Spinozan naturing nature in such profusion that the pathway to human reality seems to be only arbitrarily distinguished, in any degree of specificity, from the rest.

Spinoza addresses himself to this question in *Ethics II*. Whatever the particular issues treated in that part, its overriding responsibility is to interpret our experience of human life in the light of the previously established positions and their implications. Spinoza gradually proportions his view of naturing nature to the reality of man, considered as an integral yet distinctive component of natured nature. It is from this standpoint that I will examine some peculiar features of *Ethics II*.

(a) *Title and prologue.* This part is entitled "On the Nature and Origin of the Mind." We are thereby forewarned that Spinoza is shifting his perspective, doubtless in consequence of the appendix to *Ethics I*, to a study of that sort of caused entity which entertains images of free choice and finality and which even projects such images into a notion of how God acts as a cause. "Mind" has already been operative in forming and attributing these images, as well as in developing Spinozan philosophical principles and propositions which furnish grounds for rejecting the application of free choice and purpose to God. But now we are probing directly into the nature of this humanly minded being.

"Nature" is being taken here in a restricted sense. It connotes some essential traits which constitute the human mind, which distinguish this sort of thing from others, and the absence of which would also spell the removal of mind. The kind of nature under investigation is at least broadly specified by the term *origin*. Thereby, Spinoza signals his transition from unoriginated being to mind as a kind of being that does have an origin. This mark of causal origination from God affects the entire study of the essential traits, activities, and relations of mind. An explicit passage is being made from naturing nature to one form of finite natured nature.

Instead of plunging directly into definitions and axioms, however, Spinoza opens *Ethics II* with a prefatory remark or prologue: "I pass now to explaining those things that must follow necessarily from the essence of God, or the eternal and infinite being. Not indeed all things, for we have demonstrated (*Part* 1, *Proposition* 16) that infinite [kinds of] things must follow from this selfsame essence in infinite ways; but only those things which can lead us, as it were by the hand, to a cognition of the human mind and its supreme beatitude."[20] This prologue is in the form of a carefully worded performatory statement. Spinoza tells us that he is proceeding with a forward thrust into new topics. His progress is made possible only on the strength of what has already been established about God or naturing nature and its necessary consequences. Yet he is not attempting to explain all these consequences; they are infinite in kind and number, far exceeding the capacity of human philosophizing to grasp in a distinct manner.

Thus the remainder of the *Ethics* has a severely limited scope. Although retaining whatever has been said in general about natured nature, it will concentrate effectively upon those modal realities that have some ascertainable bearing upon *our* cognition of the human mind and its search for happiness. Operating here are both a principle of limitation and a principle of selectivity. A theory of modal nature is limited, in its further development, by the intellectual reach of ourselves as gathering leads from the bodily universe and our own activities therein. Even under this condition, however, our philosophical inquiries could lead in several directions.

In the *Ethics*, therefore, Spinoza selects those lines of inquiry that can safely guide us (as Virgil led Dante) to a certain sort of understanding, characterized in threefold fashion. First, it is a "cognition," which is inclusive of contributions from all the modes of perceiving. Next, this cognition concerns the "human mind," that is, a finite modification of the attribute of thought. There is no intention here of excluding the infinite mode of understanding, but only of relating it to that finite mode which is the human mind. Similarly, the bodily world is included insofar as it also is essential for comprehending the nature of our mind. And finally, the philosophical explanation is ethically oriented toward cognizing the human mind's "supreme beatitude." Although perhaps not readily noticed in Part II, queries and responses are selected which provide a guideline for treating the subsequent moral topics of passion and virtue, freedom and the blessed or happy life, or the actively aware union of natured with naturing nature.

(b) **Man's mind within nature.** *Ethics II* is a very closeknit unit of reasoning. It does not wander at all from the task of analyzing the human mind, and yet the path it follows is peculiarly shaped by Spinoza's resolve to conduct the analysis within the context of his own view of nature as a whole. The course of inquiry responds both to the specific topic and to the distinctive requirements of the general theory of nature. My aim in the remainder of this chapter is to show how the latter consideration affects the organization, as well as the content, of this approach to the human mind.

(i) *Definitions-axioms-postulates*. The *definitions* in *Ethics II* have an immediate dispositional effect upon an attentive reader, as well as further uses in the ensuing demonstrations. Thus *body* is defined as "a mode that expresses in a fixed and determinate way the essence of God, insofar as he is considered as an extended thing."[21] In this short compass, Spinoza sharpens our intelligence on several points. He locates bodies in the realm of finite modal nature; he reaffirms that extension is an attribute of God or naturing nature; and he restamps his own mintage upon the words *express* (signifying God's active causal presence in natured nature), *consider* (indicating that a theory of body and mind is not ready-made but requires our reflective inferences), and *insofar as* (warning us in good time to be alert to the precisely restricted intention of statements on human nature which would be puzzling or inconsistent if we were to disregard the frequently used qualifier *tantum quatenus,* "only insofar as").

There is a similar freight of useful meaning in the definition of *idea* as "a concept of the mind which the mind forms because it is a thinking thing."[22] Spinoza explains that he uses *concept* rather than *perception,* because the former term signifies an action of the mind (a conception or act of formative conceiving), whereas the latter term seems to indicate that the mind passively undergoes some reception from the object. Both here and in the definition of *adequate idea* as "an idea which, insofar as it is considered in itself without relation to an object, has all the properties or intrinsic denominations of a true idea," the intent is to direct our consideration toward the intrinsically active resources of our ideas and minds. Such reassuring emphasis is needed, if human knowledge of nature (human as well as physical, infinite as well as finite) is ever to turn the corner from patent inadequacy and error to an adequate, certain act of understanding.

Spinoza is not cutting off the real reference of ideas to their ideates in bodily objects. But he does want to ground our consideration of true ideas upon the mind's own vigor and upon the interplay of ideas themselves, rather than upon a passive, extrinsic mirror relationship. The larger question looms concerning whether natured nature is a purely receptive domain or has, through the divine presence, the ability to operate within each of its modal lines (not solely to make correlations among caused series). Spinoza's support of the latter view becomes increasingly articulated in the definitions and reasonings of *Ethics II*.

To appreciate why and how man is considered among the singular things, we must weigh the last definition given in the second part. "By singular things I understand things which are finite and have a determinate existence. And if several individuals [Dutch: or particulars (*Singularia*)] so concur in one action that together they are all the cause of one effect, I consider them all, in the same respect and so far forth, as one singular thing."[23] Spinoza the individual philosopher announces his own presence as the definer through the phrases *I understand* and *I consider*. This is appropriate both as a reminder of the personal activity of the *Intelligo*, required to formulate and acknowledge definitions, and as a reflexive sign that human beings belong among the singular things or particulars under definition. By including the human mind as a component of the human singular thing, Spinoza treats the mind as a modal reality within finite natured nature. Its existence is bound up with that of the human body; its coagency with its body constitutes them as one singular thing (this or that human being); and active concurrence among several human beings is the basis of a society or particular human community within modal nature.

Spinozan *axioms* are, epistemologically viewed, a very mixed lot. They agree in being readily accepted at the place in the system where they are proposed. But the grounds of their aceptance, and hence their cognitive strength, vary widely. Sometimes a statement functions as a working axiom in one place and yet figures elsewhere as a proposition requiring demonstration. A statement may gain axiomatic standing through removal of a prejudice, through its pragmatic convenience, or through its registration of a fact that is undeniable but also unanalyzed. Spinoza uses this variety of meanings to prevent imposition of prejudices and commonplace maxims, disguised now as certitudinal axioms about nature in general or about some sector of natural reality. He is just as prompt as Boyle or (later on) Leibniz to question and deflate the plethora of supposed axioms about nature itself.

A sampling of three axioms advanced in *Ethics II* will show how problematic these statements are, apart from the general conception of nature.[24] First, "the essence of man does not involve necessary existence. That is, in accordance with the order of nature, it can so happen that this and that man may exist as that he may not exist." One might infer from this that, at least in regard to existing, the order of nature admits of contingency and real possibility. To criticize this position, Spinoza must eventually distinguish the common order of nature (beclouded by our ignorance of existential causes and connections) from the eternal order of nature (elucidated by our knowledge of the necessary and all-inclusive power of naturing nature).

Another axiom states laconically: "Man thinks [Dutch: or otherwise stated, we know that we think]." But acceptance of the fact does not guarantee discernment of its complex significance. The axiom concerns man, not the Cartesian ego; it enters at some distance from the systematic starting point, thus reinforcing Spinoza's contention that the best order of philosophizing about nature begins with God and not with the Cogito; and the Dutch text reaffirms the reflective, methodically conducted interpretation that must permeate the factual admission. Human thinking both testifies about the divine attribute of thought and manifests an operation shared by man with the infinite mode of understanding.

Lastly comes this axiom: "We feel, nor perceive, no singular things [Dutch: or nothing of natured nature (*natura naturata*)] except bodies and modes of thinking." This involves several theoretical points about particular existents. They belong within and entail all of the previously established traits of finite natured nature. There is no exclusion of determinate modes of natured nature other than bodies and their respective ideas, but they would remain outside the scope of human feeling and perception. Since the only modes we can actually feel and perceive are bodies and their proportionate modes of thinking, our theory of the nature of the human mind must observe a similar proportionment to the human body and other bodies which variously affect the latter. Yet our philosophizing does not confine itself to feeling and perceiving but also uses the ways of reason and understanding (intuitive knowledge). The corrective operation of these other ways enables us to integrate the theory of mind with the view of nature as a whole, thus permitting the passage from a less-adequate to a more-adequate grasp of human knowledge and action.

As for the postulates of *Ethics II*, Spinoza employs the dramatic technique of postponing their presentation until after he treats of bodies. This dispersal of the geometrical procedures shows how essential a study of the human body and its causal relations with other bodies is to the proper theory about the nature of the human mind and its search for improved self-comprehension and happiness.

(ii) *Propositions 1–7 and 8–13.* A reading of these propositions in terms of nature brings out their double grouping and the smooth passage from the initial group to the next one.

At first glance, Spinoza seems to be retrogressing in propositions 1 through 7 of *Ethics II*, since they deal with God. But it soon becomes evident that their job is to make the general theory of nature more clearly pertinent to the study of man. The first move is to reformulate those attributes of naturing nature which express themselves in the determinate mode of human nature. Instead of just repeating that thought and extension are attributes of divine substance, Spinoza proceeds to call God a "thinking thing" and an "extended thing," within the scope of naturing nature.[25] This point has definite implications for the modal nature and unity of man. For although whatever thinks and is somehow extended holds claim upon existence, it does not thereby also hold valid claim upon *substantiality.* Other considerations must be brought in to determine whether the thing under investigation is substantial or modal.

Spinoza invokes his previous proofs of the infinite essence and uniqueness of substance in order to conclude here that man, as a thinking bodily being, is an existing mode rather than a substance. Furthermore, just as the unicity of substance is not violated by regarding God as both a thinking and an extended thing, so also the unity of human nature is not destroyed by man's being a thinking thing and a bodily extended thing. Indeed, when man is viewed in relation to the active presence of naturing nature there is good ground even for regarding man as "one thing," for both human thinking and human bodily traits are causal expressions of the selfsame divine substance.

Spinoza's next move is to establish the anthropological significance of

his theory of the immediate infinite modes of natured nature. This procedure runs counter to the Cartesian attempt to build a theory of man and the
human mind solely from the relationship between God and the finite
modes of natured nature. But without including the infinite modes, we
misconceive the relation of God and man, as well as the origin and nature
of our mind.

What does it mean to attribute thought to God or to regard him as a
thinking thing? This is an affirmation that ''he can form the idea of his
essence and of all things that follow necessarily from it. But every thing
which is in God's power, necessarily is (*Part* 1, *Proposition* 35); therefore such an idea is necessarily present, and (*Part* 1,*Proposition* 15) is not
present except in God.''[26] It requires several pages for Spinoza to unpack
the significance of this reasoning for his main topic in *Ethics II,* namely,
the human mind.

The ''idea of God'' is one that is both formed by God and directed
toward an understanding of God's own essence and the infinite sweep of
things that follow necessarily and in infinite ways from the divine essence. Negatively stated, this idea is *not* an archetypal plan which must
insert itself between the divine essence and causal power in order that
God may actually produce the universe. This would be a relapse to the
already-criticized position that God creates through deliberative planning
and willing. On the contrary, ''we have shown God's power to be nothing
else than the actuous essence of God.''[27] Spinoza's striking phrase *Dei
actuosa essentia* (which was so attractive to Hegel that he applied the
noun-form *Aktuosität* to infinite spirit) means that the divine essence by
itself is productively effective. It acts just as necessarily as it exists, and its
infinitely various effects flow necessarily from this essence, as actuous
power, without mediation of knowledge and will. For Spinoza, this is the
only way to escape the dilemma that the divine power is either an-
thropomorphically imagined (''which shows God to be conceived by the
crowd as a man or as like a man'') or else even involves impotence
because of its need for deliberative will.

Spinoza points us positively toward the conclusion that the idea of God
is something formed and necessarily produced by the actuous divine
essence. Hence it belongs in natured nature. And, indeed, it is the same as
the immediate, eternal, infinite mode of understanding. When that understanding is regarded in respect to its unified object, it is termed (using the
objective genitive) the idea of, or *about,* God. Infinite understanding has
actual knowledge of God's attributes, along with all the modes that follow
necessarily from them. This is the supreme realization of intuitive knowl-

edge and unity with the whole of nature. It is the telos toward which we are always striving in our acts of knowing, loving, and enjoying.

In order to make his general theory of modal nature more available for the study of man, Spinoza next makes two carefully worded distinctions.[28] First, he sets off the formal actual-being of ideas (*esse formale idearum*) from the formal actual-being of things that are not modes of thinking (*esse formale rerum quae modi non sunt cogitandi*). There are proportionate ideas for *all* these latter modes, not only for modes of extension, since the infinite understanding comprehends the divine essence in all its attributes and their causal expressions in natured nature.

The second distinction is between the *objective* or *cognition-yielding* relation between ideas and their ideata and the *formal* or *causative* relation in modal nature. Ideas are caused by other ideas alone, as expressions of the attribute of thought, and not by things that are not modes of thinking. Similarly, members of any distinct sort of these latter modes are caused by other modes in the same series of expressions of their respective divine attribute, rather than by ideas or by modal operators expressive of other attributes. Objective and causative relations are not to be confused, even though they may concern modes (such as human minds and bodies) that are closely united in natured nature.

These two distinctions permit Spinoza to make controlled use of his *tantum quatenus* and the language concerning God's causal development in natured nature that accompanies this expression. God is cause of infinite and finite modes of thought or ideas only insofar as they express, and are constituted by, his attribute of thought. The causation is intramodal and engages divine power only in respect to this attribute. Something similar holds for any other intramodal causation as involving God only insofar as his constitutive causal power is regarded under reference to the appropriate attribute. Yet while these *causal* lines of involvement remain distinct, they also shape the unity of the *objective cognitive* reference of ideas to their ideata—insofar as our minds become aware of the components as co-present in natured nature.

The scholium to proposition 7 is quite remarkable. The scholium's aim is to defend the sameness of the order and connection among ideas and that among things, a sameness apparently threatened by the distinct lines of causation among ideas and among things (ideata that are not modes of thinking). In a meditative mood, Spinoza begins by recalling to mind a previously demonstrated point: that there is but one substance. One can refer to God as "thinking substance" and "extended substance," but these are only different ways of denoting the selfsame unique substance.[29]

All modal orders and connections arise from this unique substance and express the sameness of their causal source, along with the difference in our attributive consideration and inference. Both the sameness and the difference remain in full force, so that emphasis upon one of them never cancels out the truth of the other.

Spinoza applies this conclusion at once to our way of thinking and speaking about nature.

> And hence whether we conceive of nature under the attribute of extension, or under the attribute of thought, or under any other [attribute], we will find one and the same order, or one and the same connection of causes, that is, the same things to follow in turn. . . . As long as things are considered as modes of thought, we must explain the order of the whole of nature, or the connection of causes, through the attribute of thought alone. And insofar as they are considered as modes of extension, the order also of the whole of nature must be explained through the attribute of extension alone. And I understand the same about other attributes. Wherefore, of things as they are in themselves, God is the veritable cause, insofar as he consists of infinite attributes; nor for the present can I explain this more clearly.[30]

This text introduces some notable refinements in the general conception of nature, as well as in the linguistic resources at Spinoza's command.

First, any thorough consideration of natured nature must eventually view it in reference to God's attributes. One can then speak about the order and connectedness holding for natured nature, viewed as embracing a causal sequence of ideas and of other modes. No bifurcation of nature occurs, since the proposition about the same order and connection among ideas and among things holds for the unification of natured nature under the attribute of thought and under that of extension.

Second, there are several meanings for "the whole of nature." Depending on the context, it can embrace both naturing and natured nature. But in the present scholium, "the whole of natured nature" is the intended sense of the shorter phrase, since it concerns the unity of modal things alone. And the delimitation goes still further. If modes of thought are gathered together under the attribute of thought alone, then this concerns "the whole of natured nature in its modes of thought." If the unification is made under the attribute of extension, then the expanded phrase is "the whole of natured nature in its modes of extension."

These differentiations are well founded in the attributes and modes intended by them. But they do not dissolve the inclusive whole of nature, since they are valid only under the condition that the divine essence itself consists of all the attributes and causes all the modes being differentiated.

For understanding Spinoza's further development of the theory of nature in its bearing upon the human mind, however, it is necessary to persist with the analysis of still other features of this scholium.

In the last clause of the quoted text, why does Spinoza advert to the limits of what he can presently elucidate? One reason is that he has referred twice already to any other divine attribute or attributes there may be, along with thought and extension. This point had raised difficulties among his friends and other readers of the manuscript drafts of the *Ethics*.[31] They wondered whether the unbounded power of the divine essence must express itself in any other attributes, as well as whether (through union with the infinite understanding) our minds can get to know something about such other attributes and their modal worlds. In line with his theory of God, Spinoza can only reply conditionally that, if the divine power or essence is not exhausted by thought and extension, then there must be other attributes and their modes which are known to the infinite understanding.

But the problem also concerns whether the scope of our minds can be similarly enlarged. Spinoza cannot specify this side of the cognitive equation any closer until he formally treats the domain of finite modes. Thus the inner logic of his inquiry requires him now to make his third move: from the theory of divine attributes and infinite modes to that of finite modes. Each of these moves advances his conceptual and terminological adjustment to the origin and nature of the mind, that is, to the general theme of *Ethics II*. In the case of divine attributes, the characteristic adaptation is stated in terms of God considered as "thinking thing" and "extended thing." The adaptation of the infinite mode of understanding gets expressed in the analysis of "infinite idea of God." And now Spinoza treats of finite modes through his discussion of "singular things." He has already defined them as things that are finite and hav a determinate existence—traits that fit the reality of man.

We are at last in a position to specify the Spinozan sense of explaining philosophically the origin and nature of our mind. It does not consist of tracing out a temporal-historical genesis or a psychological description, useful as those methods may be. To obtain a philosophical understanding of our mind's origin and nature is to follow the proper order of philosophizing about human reality. It consists in making this gradual triple move from God considered as extended and thinking thing to the idea of God, or the infinite understanding considered as having the divine essence as its object, and thence to finite modes considered as singular things or existing finite particulars. Within this threefold context of incorporated principles and our own self-experience, Spinoza develops his philosophical argumentation about the mind's expression of these principles (origin) and its act of being (nature).

In addition to the other qualifications placed upon *the whole of nature*, then, the phrase is often intended to mean the order of the entirety of singular things or finite modes. One must determine from the textual context whether the whole of singular things includes both finite minds and bodies or is restricted, for purposes of inquiry, to one of these modalities. The repeated word *considered* is a reminder that the intent of human inquiry must always affect our philosophical talk about ''the whole of nature,'' in its several related acceptations. It should not be surprising that our way of considering a finite modal thing through its rooting in some divine attribute specifies our meaning for the whole of nature. For just as the meaning of the attribute itself includes our view of the divine essence, so also does our conception of the whole of nature include our consideration of the causal order of finite modes under an attribute. Thus there is an effective reciprocity between Spinoza's theory of God's attributes and his theory of the whole of singular things in modal nature. The understanding's considerative activity is the bond between these two theories.

Once Spinoza treats man and the human mind within the perspective of the singular things in finite modal nature, he also commits himself to a study of body and of the human body in particular. The movement of inquiry from the formal actual-being of man and the human mind to the human body is already ordained by three features of the meaning of a singular thing: its existentiality, determinateness, and concurrence.[32] First, the human mind is that sort of existent which itself affirms an *existing* reality. The human mind is the idea of its body, and its primordial intrinsic act is to affirm the existence of its own body.

Second, the human mind is a determinate existent which can perceive its own body as a *determinate* existent. By itself, this note of determinateness in a finite mode is unremarkable, except for involving the determining series of its own causes. But in the case of the human mind, account must also be taken of its habit of regarding a thing's existence as indefinite in duration. Hence, there must be an inquiry into the human mind's modes of perception, especially into that of imagination whereby it forms the image of temporal duration or indefinite continuance of existence. Such inquiry affects the mind's ways of cognizing its own and other bodies.

Third, the concept of singular things enjoys a certain operational flexibility. Whenever things *concur* or cooperate to effect a single action, so far forth they are considered as a singular thing or particular existent. This synergic operation can hold between the human mind and its own body, when their action and ordering are seen to be harmonious. They are then truly to be regarded as one singular thing (which is their unitive and perfective way of being finite modal expressions of the selfsame unique substance). From this standpoint, Spinoza concludes that what basically "constitutes the actual being of the human mind (*esse humanae mentis actuale*) is the idea of some singular thing existing in act (*idea rei alicujus singularis actu existentis*), namely, the human body.[33] There cannot be a closer union and proportionment among finite modes than that which holds, and is consciously affirmed to hold, between the components of the singular human existent.

This path of reflections on how the meanings of nature focus upon man leads into the long series of axioms and lemmas following proposition 13.[34] They do not comprise what Spinoza would regard as a formal "philosophy of nature," in the sense of a philosophical physics or general theory of bodily nature, such as that presented under this title in the university textbooks on natural philosophy. This is a special part of philosophy, one which Spinoza constantly postpones and never gets around to working out. Rather, these axioms and lemmas are instruments chiefly for understanding the human body and the human mind. They also contribute to the subsequent theory of man's passions, actions, and union with naturing nature. Their immediate function, however, is to prepare us for the long-delayed *postulates* of *Ethics II,* which are on the human body.

Spinoza explains the composite individual being of the human body through his paradigm for thinking about the composite individual being of the whole of corporeal nature. The basic individuals in the bodily world are the most simple bodies, which differ from each other only in motion and rest, speed and slowness. Several of these most simple bodies can unite together to form a composite individual of the same nature, provided only that they are in contact and communicate motion to each other in some fixed proportion or homogeneous pattern. In turn, several composite individuals of different natures, or differing ratios of motion and rest, can join together to constitute a composite variated individual involving heterogeneous natures. It retains its form as a complex individual on condition that the differing components continue to retain a reciprocal proportion in their interchanges.

Spinoza then adds: "And if we thus proceed forward towards the infinite, we may easily conceive nature as a whole to be one individual, whose parts—that is, all bodies—vary in infinite ways, without any mutation of the whole individual."[35] Here, *tota natura* is the entirety of bodily modes in natured nature. It can be conceived as that sort of synergic individual which is composite (consisting of many individuals) and variated (consisting of individuals of various kinds), and yet which also manifests a perduring unity and dominant set of relations amid all the changes. This is a way of envisaging the mediate infinite mode or macrocosmic pattern of the whole universe. It constitutes a dynamic individual reality, which both expresses the immediate infinite mode of motion-and-rest and regulates the active, steady order of changes in the bodily world. On a microcosmic scale, the human body itself is a complex, existing individual, which affects other bodies and is affected by them in countless ways. Throughout the whole process of change, however, this human body never loses its form as an individual, any more than the whole of bodily nature loses its overall structure of mechanical laws.

(iii) *Propositions 14–31 and 32–49*. The approach which insists upon the priority of nature encourages me to make these two groupings of the later propositions in *Ethics II*.[36] The two groups are not sealed off from each other but serve, rather, as partners in a dialogue about the relatively inadequate and the relatively adequate aspects of human knowledge. Taken together, they contribute toward our grasp of the nature of the human mind and form a basis for launching into the topics to be treated in the next chapter. The mingling of inadequacy and adequacy in our cognitions prepares the way for a study of the mingling of passional misery and actional grandeur in our search for the blessed life.

What characterizes Spinoza's account of human cognitive shortcomings (propositions 14 through 31) is the constant reference to "God precisely insofar as" he is causally expressed by the world of bodies and modes of thinking. This argumentative procedure is not arbitrary but is strictly regulated by the emendated order of philosophizing. That ordering of inquiry not only begins with God or naturing nature but continually develops new aspects of its involvement in the modal world, especially in human nature and its composite strivings.

By following this route, one can avoid the two errors attendant upon every effort to begin philosophizing about man through an immediate analysis of singular things. One extreme is to remain forever transfixed by these things and to read into them all the traits of divinity. This has the disadvantage not only of confusing naturing and natured nature but also of glossing over the defects and illusions of human belief. The other extreme consists in excluding God so completely from philosophical anthropology that the resources of naturing nature are never utilized to overcome these defects and illusions, or to attain relatively adequate human knowledge. In short, one can make sense out of our cognitional situation only by interpreting this mélange in the light of the conception of nature as naturing and natured. God does not belong to the essence of modal things, but his power constitutes them and strengthens their actions.

Spinoza attacks the myth of the human mind's primary and fully pellucid knowledge of itself, as bracketed off from the rest of reality through some Cartesian method of doubt. This supposed self-lucidity runs contrary both to the correlation of the divine attributes of thought and extension and to the correlative divine causality of the connective order among ideas and among bodily modes. The hold of the myth of the human mind's immediate and perfect self-knowledge can be broken by spelling out some consequences of the position that the human mind is the idea of the human body, which itself belongs within corporeal natured nature or the causal web of other bodies.

The ways of negation and contextuality govern Spinoza's reasoning on the issue. (1) The human mind is ordered toward a cognition of ideas of the affections of its own body, which is perceived only along with many other bodies affecting it. The ideas we have of these external bodies tell us more about the constitution of our own bodily ways of being affected than about the nature of the other bodies affecting us. For although the order and linkage of the affections of our own body involve the nature of other bodily things, that order and linkage cannot independently explain the nature of these other things.

(2) Altogether crucial is the focus taken by the human mind. It can consider the ideas of affections of other bodies in a quite isolated manner, that is, apart from both the broader causal nexus among bodily modes and the specific contribution of these affections to our own affected body. Insofar as these isolating conditions prevail, Spinoza denies that the human mind knows the affections of its body, the human body itself, and even the human mind. This shows how radically dependent our self-knowledge is upon a relational and contextual perception of the ideas of corporeal modifications.

(3) To find even a small remedy for our ignorance, we must reform our way of considering the latter ideas. This reform begins by perceiving some bonds between ideas of corporeal nature as a whole, those of the other bodily affections bearing upon our own body, and the ideas of affections of our own body. When these ideas are reintegrated in some

degree, they manifest something of naturing nature's power in shaping our own body, as well as in shaping our mind (the idea of this body). In the same degree and manner in which we relate the ideas of bodily affections, we achieve a measure of cognition of our body, of the human mind, and of the reflective idea of the mind itself. This reflective idea is the start of methodic discipline in thinking, a discipline which builds upon progressive consideration of God "precisely insofar as" the necessary causal power of naturing nature is seen to determine correlatively all bodily and thinking modes in natured nature.

Spinoza draws a somewhat bleak picture of the quality of our perception, just before we begin to make the methodic turn. "Thence it follows that the human mind, as often as it perceives things in accordance with the common order of nature, has an adequate cognition neither of itself nor of its body nor of external bodies, but has only a confused and mutilated cognition."[37] Such flawed cognition results from permitting our mind to be molded uncritically and almost entirely by imagery about the surrounding world of bodies. We imagine them to have fluctuating, fortuitous relationships that exert an extrinsic power over us. This world-view is confused because it reads the limits of our imagery into the very structure of modal reality. And it is mutilated by remaining cut off from the necessary connections in natured nature as well as from our mind's power of knowing and loving God. *The common order of nature* is not a domain of reality in its own right, but is precisely this undisciplined and short-sighted way of regarding modal nature and man in it.

Yet such an outlook holds sway only conditionally over us. The human mind is constrained only "as often as it is determined externally toward regarding this or that in accordance namely with a fortuitous meeting of things, and not as often as it is determined internally (that is, from the fact that it regards many things together) toward understanding their agreements, differences, and oppositions. For as often as it is disposed internally, thus or in another way, it then regards things clearly and distinctly."[38] Spinoza holds before us the prospect of making a transition from the outlook of uncriticized imagination to that of reason and understanding, or from the common order of nature to the eternal order of nature.

Propositions 32 through 49 search out the noetic grounds for thus transforming our conception of nature. The impetus for the transition has already come from *Ethics I*, with its order of philosophizing from God to singular things. Now in a rapid series of propositions, Spinoza looks for resources in ourselves as finite bearers of God's power and necessity.

The human mind is itself a unified idea adequately expressing the actuous essence of God. In its complexity, our mind actively forms ideas that affirm truths about their objects as modes of natured nature, as well as truths about their naturing source. Repeatedly, Spinoza contradistinguishes these ideas from mute pictures on a slate. Ideas essentially say something, make affirmations about reality. We are able to test, correct, and improve these affirmations by relating them to the order of the understanding and the three kinds of cognition. Those ideas that express traits common to all bodies yield adequate knowledge, or truths in which all men basically share. When we recognize that these truths and the proportionate ones about the mind ultimately say something about God's attributes of extension and thought, we achieve that sort of necessary reference to naturing nature which marks eternal truths and gives us access to *the eternal order of nature.*

The distinction between the common order of nature and the eternal order of nature is not between two kinds of ordered nature, but is between two ways of viewing and relating ourselves to the one selfsame order of nature. It is a noetic (and, as the next chapter will show, a moral) distinction which marks our transition from inadequate to adequate knowledge of the order in the whole of nature. We come to know that God's *vis* or enlivening force produces and permeates the entire modal world, which therefore has a necessary pattern of interconnecting causes. For us to share in this eternal order of nature, we must discern and respond to the same divine *vis.* This we do through understanding that naturing nature is causally constitutive of modal nature and involves itself in all the latter's activities. Such a transformation of our outlook upon naturing and natured nature is an achievement of our mind and its true ideas, not a work of any separate faculty of free will.

Through these reflections on the transition from confused and mutilated cognition to clear and integrative knowledge of nature, Spinoza sets the course for his account of human passions, liberation, and beatitude. We must next consider how his treatment of these latter themes incorporates his conception of nature and also endows that conception with some fresh increment.

CHAPTER SIX

A Nature-Reading of *Ethics III−V*

As ORIGINALLY PLANNED, the first two parts of the *Ethics,* treating of God and man, were to be followed by a concluding third part on man's moral conduct and well-being. Spinoza never abandoned this latter topic, but he did find it too complex to deal with satisfactorily in a single part. The complexity was intrinsic to the subject matter, which embraced the passions and actions of man along with his virtues and happiness. But its origin was also traceable to the distinctive methodology and theory of God and man which were to serve as foundations for the ethical doctrine. Having reworked his method and view of God and man as portions of a general theory of nature, Spinoza now found it necessary to rework the ethical topics within this same framework.

Bringing the topics and the framework together required a more sustained and intricate inquiry than could be conveniently stated in a single part. Spinoza had already altered the relationship of God and man so profoundly that he was obliged to develop its moral consequences into what eventually became the last three parts of the *Ethics.* He had to reinterpret the passions and man's plight of servitude within the context of his several meanings of nature. Then he had to search among these meanings for some grounds of liberation and increase in man's actional power, yet grounds that would remain consistent with his general account of man in nature. And the same rules of consistency were required to govern any culminating view of the happy life that might emerge from this whole course of reasoning.

Although the later parts of the *Ethics* are thus multiplied, they still achieve a definite unity among themselves and with the rest of that book. Among themselves, they specify the problems involved in the common theme of attaining our well-being amid the conditions of everyday existence. And their solutions are reached in harmony with the general conception of substantial and modal nature, within which the human search for moral action and fulfillment gets intentionally pursued.

In turn, my primary focus here is upon the interrelations between the specific issues and the broader methodology and doctrine of nature. Whatever strictures Spinoza passes on final causes, he does achieve an inner coherence and purposive unity among the parts of the *Ethics*. He offers that sort of view of ethical living which is most consonant with his naturizing of both God and man, and hence which his principles aim at realizing.

1. Moral Epistemology

Reversing a famous statement of Rousseau, we may say that Spinoza regards men as being everywhere enchained by their passional affects and yet as being born with the seed of moral freedom. Their task is to cultivate a fuller understanding of these affects and of the ways leading toward a growth in human freedom. Spinoza is sufficiently schooled in the Stoics and Descartes to seek the conditions of moral liberation in his conception of knowledge and nature. The Stoics had directed their logic and physics toward ethics, and Descartes had used his metaphysics and philosophy of nature to make passage from a provisional to a definitive morality. But Spinoza's distinctive positions in the speculative order get translated into a distinctive approach toward ethical issues.

The Socratic injunction of "know thyself" is as deeply imprinted upon Spinoza as upon any other moral philosopher. But everything depends upon the path whereby this moral knowing is sought and upon the significance and relationships of the self thus attained. For this reason, there is an ethical intent motivating Spinoza's extensive criticism of the Cartesian Cogito as the way to self-knowledge. It is with the ethical aspect of this criticism that I am now concerned.

The basic defect of making primary use of the method of doubt to bracket the physical world and to affirm the pure thinking self is that it overlooks the unity of natured nature as a whole. If the latter is set aside, then there is no real foundation for an understanding of the human mind and body and their practical activities. Spinoza has already shown that, when considered solely in itself, the human mind can know neither its own nature (which *is* the idea of the human body) nor the nature of the human body and other bodies in the world. Instead of misstarting with the Cogito, then, we have to build upon our perception of the affections of the human body.

Our ideas of these affections do involve the human body and mind, as well as the other bodies that affect the human body. But our initial reflection upon these affectional ideas yields only a meager cognition. We perceive the affections themselves, the human body as existent and as variously modified by other bodies, and the human mind as having the ideas of these bodily affections. However, such perception is a confused and inadequate, rather than a clear and adequate, knowledge of the natural realities involved together. This weakens our practical relations with the rest of natured nature.

Spinoza takes a direct ethical interest, therefore, in the two reasons for the inadequacy and the remedies that overcome it. One source of the inadequacy is that we relate the ideas of bodily affections to the mind alone and then reflectively consider the mind only in itself (in Cogito fashion). This viewpoint leads one initially to overestimate the mind's control over these ideas and then, when they still remain unruly, to despair about the mind's power to govern itself. To overcome this oscillation between extremes, Spinoza appeals to the complex unity of modal nature in all its manifestations as graphed by the Spinozan Intelligo.

The moral reality is neither the bodily state alone nor the idea alone, but rather their composition, for which the technical term *affect* is reserved. "By affect I understand the body's affections, whereby the power of acting of the body itself is increased or diminished, helped or restrained, together with the ideas of these affections. *If therefore we can be the adequate cause of any of these affections, then I understand by affect an action, otherwise a passion.*"[1] Thus actions and passions are kinds of affects, distinguished by whether we are or are not the adequate cause of the body's affections. Moral self-governance is proportioned to our becoming adequate causes and having actional affects.

Spinoza establishes a close relation between human causality and understanding. We are adequate causes and have actional affects in the degree that, "from our nature, something follows in us or outside us which, through the sole same [nature], can be clearly and distinctly understood."[2] Where such causal understanding does not attain clarity and distinctness, we are only the inadequate causes and are subject to passional affects.

Hence, it is morally crucial to specify the second reason for cognitive inadequacy and the way to remedy it. The problem arises from the very multiplicity of our bodily affections and their ideas. Even after some particular affection and its idea are seen together, they must still be joined with the other affections and their ideas which shape our moral life. We can establish an order and connection among bodily affections by referring them either to imagination and memory or to reason and intuitive understanding.

A purely imaginal-memorative basis of unification is deficient, since it fails to reach the necessity of existing and acting in natured nature. Lacking a knowledge of our own power and that of modal nature, we remain inadequate in self-knowledge and causation and hence are buffeted by the passions and their imagery. But insofar as we achieve some ordering around reason and understanding, we grasp the power and order of nature, attain some self-understanding and adequate causality, and bring out the actional and liberational character of human affects. Through the influence of affects which are actions, Spinoza hopes to heal both the cognitive and the practical ineffectuality of the split between the Cogito and the bodily world.

We are now in a better position to seize upon the moral implications of his theory of error. In the methodological context of the *Emendation*, he had traced the causes of error to four major sources.[3] (a) The imagination is exposed to opinions reflecting the many external forces working upon man. (b) Our minds are partitive and tend to confuse a fragmentary with a whole view of nature. (c) We rely too heavily upon universal concepts and abstract reasonings which are often substituted for the reality of nature, instead of clarifying it. (d) The proper order of investigation is violated when we fail to begin with that which is truly primary and to bring ourselves into a satisfactory relationship with primary positive reality. The recommendation of the *Emendation* is that we use the idea of God to rectify all these roots of error. And Parts I and II of the *Ethics* deliberately treat of God and man in a manner calculated to displace error by truth. Thus, Spinoza reasons his own way to a doctrine on God and man; he keeps the unity of the whole of nature central; his account of the one substance and its modes adheres to their concrete definition and actuality; every subsequent demonstration is squared with the initial reasoning about God and never strays from an ultimate reference of modes to the divine substance.

Now, from the perspective of the last three parts of the *Ethics*, we can see how the reform of moral thinking also counters the tendencies toward error. There is a correspondence between the four bases of error and the four divisions of the present chapter. This is as it should be, because Spinoza regards error as the breeder of human weakness and unhappiness, just as he regards the truth about nature as the radical ground of our moral power and happiness.

(a) This present section argues for the ultimately moral intent of Spinoza's epistemology and ontology. The theory of the affects is a prolongation of his teaching on the degrees of perception and the modal unity of man.[4] If we rely in a primary unreconstructed way upon imagination, we become passive in regard to external things and interpret ourselves as being at the mercy of chance, contingency, and possible happenings. To surrender to this world picture is to shape our bodily affections and their ideas according to the order of imagination. In this situation, our life is in bondage to the passional affects in their most debilitating and demoralizing form.

Yet, although Spinoza states that imagination is a cause of error and passional bondage, he is equally insistent that imagination is not itself inherently erroneous and vicious. After all, it is a cognitive power of man and hence is open to emendation by, and integration with, his other ways of cognizing. This point is morally important, because it means that there are some internal active resources available to any mind that reflects critically upon its imagery and passional affects. It can reinterpret and transform them in accord with the ordering set by reason and understanding. This is not a purely speculative reorientation, but a practical one that increases our activity and union with nature as an active whole. Upon this reconstitution depend our virtue and happiness as moral agents.

I correlate the other three causes of error with the three following sections of this chapter in order to underline the continuity of Spinoza's ethical reasoning with the rest of his view of man within the whole of nature. Thus (b) he will not deny or otherwise abrogate the partitive nature of man but will probe into those aspects of it that aid our moral search (section 2 below). (c) Similarly, Spinoza will reexamine our cognitive strengths to develop an encouraging model of human action within a framework of practical ideals that are not pejoratively abstract and universal (section 3 below). And (d), Spinoza will interpret the rule of starting with what is primary, in a way that can elicit from us a moral union or love toward the eternal God (section 4 below).

2. Moral Man as Part of Nature

Part IV of the *Ethics* confronts us with but a single stark axiom, which is followed by an equally uncompromising proposition. The axiom states: "There is no singular thing given in the nature of things, than which there is not another more powerful and stronger. But, for whatever thing is given, there is another more powerful by which that given thing can be destroyed."[5] This is axiomatic in the sense of being sufficiently well-evidenced, at this stage of the inquiry, to be accepted in itself.

It represents a confluence of the Spinozan conceptions of "singular thing" and "passional affect." The former is a finite mode within natured nature, a particular entity that is limited in being and power. To view this singular thing's bodily constitution just as being determined from without by other extended modes, without our having a clear understanding of the causes involved, is to regard it passionally. The bodily affections and their ideas are considered as being caused by other forces in the rest of nature. Hence, as so regarded, any singular thing is subject to others that can overpower and destroy it.

Lest it be supposed that man is immune to this condition, Spinoza advances an unequivocal proposition. *"It cannot happen that man be not a part of nature, and that he can undergo no changes except ones which can be understood through his nature alone, and of which he is the adequate cause."*[6] This proposition could be directly controverted only if men were not singular things, and if none of their affects were passions. Both experience and reason attest, however, to our limited modal reality as parts of natured nature, as well as to the mixture of actions and passions in our affective life.

Spinoza's demonstration of the proposition draws heavily upon his general theory of nature and its finite modal expressions of power: "The power whereby singular things [conserve their actual-being], and consequently man conserves his actual-being [*esse*], is the very power of God or nature (*Part* I, *Proposition* 24, *Corollary*), not insofar as it is infinite, but insofar as it can be explained through the actual human essence (*Part* III, *Proposition* 7). Hence man's power, insofar as it is explained through his actual essence, is a part of the infinite power, that is (*Part* I, *Proposition* 34) of the essence, of God or nature." Fundamentally, man cannot evade a partitive status in natured nature, because his actual essence is a partitive modal expression of naturing nature's infinite actual essence or power.

If the divine power were totally expressed in the human essence, then from sole consideration of that power as manifested in the idea of some man, one would be able to derive the order of the whole of nature under the attributes of thought and extension. That such total derivation cannot be made is indicative both of man's partitive reality and of the intermixture of passions and actions in his finite affective life. Just as man's essence is not an infinite actuality or power, so the changes involving him are not unalloyed actions arising from an infinite knowledge of causes.

There is an indirect way of trying to minimize the consequences of acknowledging man as a part of nature. Spinoza calls this the notion of an empire-within-an-empire, which was popularized by the Stoics and

Descartes (and which was to be continued, after Spinoza's time, in Leibniz's frequent references to a kingdom-within-the-kingdom-of-nature).[7] In this imagery, man is able to carve out a domain of his own, one that is made by his own will and governed by his moral freedom rather than by the necessary laws of nature.

Spinoza regards this as an illusory escape hatch, which he opposes on at least three grounds. First, man has no separate faculty of will, but only some particular acts to which a universal name is often attached. Our ideas are not inert reflections but are themselves active affirmations requiring no reduplicative faculty of will. Next, modal nature under the attribute of thought embraces all expressions of the human mind, including those called volitions. Ideational-volitional acts are developments within this seamless modal nature, rather than rents in its enveloping reality. And finally, moral freedom comes from our reflective acceptance of the necessity of nature as a whole, not from an attempt to escape from it or set one region of it apart from the rest. Man is that kind of a part of nature who actualizes himself through recognition of his union with nature, as the infinitely powerful and necessary totality.

Nevertheless, Spinoza finds something symptomatic in the enclave attitude toward ethics. It represents a doubt whether men have the capacity for so exalted a knowledge, whether as parts they can come to understand the whole of nature and draw happiness from it. Spinoza is very careful in treating this practical sort of doubt, since it calls into question the ethical significance of his entire theory of nature. His response is threefold: to offer some guiding imagery, to reformulate his method in explicitly ethical terms, and to underscore the immanent actional basis for every increase in human power and well-being.

(a) *The worm's-eye view.* In correspondence with Spinoza, Oldenburg (writing as spokesman for Robert Boyle) wants to learn more about the interconnections in nature,but without getting into any metaphysical discussions. He echoes the demand of scientists and moralists to be shown, solely on practical grounds, that men can know about their union with nature as a whole. The exclusion of metaphysics prevents Spinoza from using his theory of the uniqueness of substance as the unifying source of all modal existents. Yet he does not fall silent but works at the imaginative level of his questioners. Using this medium, he cannot communicate to them precisely what he knows about the union of modal parts within total nature. But he does devise some guiding images that can convey, by analogy, some grounds for his being persuaded about the interconnective relations binding together all things and actions in the unity of nature. He puts to good use the power of framing imaginative hypotheses, which have some suasive power as long as their limits are also noted.

Let us feign the presence of a worm living in the bloodstream—a supposition not difficult to make in the age when so many unsuspected bodies were being found by use of the microscope.[8] Let us further suppose that this worm has the intelligence to observe lymph, chyle, and other particles in the bloodstream, as well as to observe how these various particles modify and are modified by each other's motions. All these relationships are viewed as contributing to the general health of the blood, which in turn requires that the particles adjust and accommodate to each other. This observed mutual coherence may then lead our somewhat cogitative worm to conclude that no other causes are required, that the circulating blood constitutes a sufficient system of its own, and that the lymph, chyle, and worm itself are parts of this living whole.

There is an analogy here between the worm's viewpoint and that of the human scientists and ethical theorists. The latter observe bodies interacting with each other in fixed patterns and proportions of motion, or moral agents working together under social laws. From the mutual accommodations and agreements, the coherence of bodily nature can be conceived as that obtaining between parts and whole. A similar coherence can be affirmed in minded nature, which also tempers, harmonizes, and holds in union its agents as parts within a whole.

Spinoza is bound to warn, however, that the worm analogy breaks down at the point where the self-sufficiency of the blood system is stipulated. Actually, there are other causes distinct from this system and interacting with it in a more encompassing whole. Similarly, the coherence of observed bodies must be incorporated within an entire mechanistic world picture, just as the coherence among minds belongs within a larger pattern of intellectual life. Spinoza cannot further advance this reasoning without appeal to his own philosophical method and his doctrines on substance and attributes, infinite and finite modes of natured nature. But he has brought the analogy along far enough to suggest that partitive man can find the evidence of coherence and can make the rational inference to the whole of nature, considered unconditionally and yet as sustaining a union of parts with infinitely powerful nature.

Elsewhere, Spinoza uses the metaphors of the triangle, the circle, and the stone as being endowed with reflective consciousness. But in these examples, his aim is primarily critical. We can suppose that the conscious entity will become aware of mutual adjustments and cooperations, thus reaching the concept of a coherent whole of things like itself. Yet this supposed center of reasoning may then go on to conclude either that such a totality comprises the entire universe or at least that its essential characteristics belong to the whole universe. In Spinozan language, this inference would mean reducing all nature to triangularity, circularity, or lapidarity, or else reading these traits into the whole of nature. The part-to-whole relationship would lead to the reduction of naturing to natured nature or to the attribution of modal traits to the unique substance itself. Such is the case, for instance, when human passions are ascribed to God, thus replacing naturing nature with an idol made in the image and likeness of man.

Thus the worm's point of view and its variants are useful metaphors that nevertheless have their limits. They remove the charge of arbitrariness from Spinoza's talk about the interconnections and unity of nature, since they supply an analogy for how a part can have knowledge of a particular whole and can attain a closer union (*arctior unio*) with its whole. From the analogy of physical and moral nature, the human mind is thereby encouraged to know and unify itself more closely with naturing nature and the whole of nature. In doing so, however, our mind must be careful lest it mistake extended and thinking modal nature for the whole of nature, and especially lest it read its own limits and causal mixture, imagery and universal notions, into God.

(b) *The ethical import of naturized method.* My chapter on Spinoza's *Emendation* was concerned with the naturizing of his methodology. Although this process was examined there mainly in respect to speculative issues, it was also intended to include the practical aspects, so as to achieve a total reform of philosophy. Just as the *Emendation* makes several references to "my philosophy" as a whole, so does the Preface to *Ethics III* speak correlatively about using "the same method." In this way, Spinoza explicitly prolongs his own naturizing of methodology into the moral order itself. It now becomes necessary to weigh the contribution of these later passages in the *Ethics*.

Over the last three parts of that book, Spinoza casts a net of texts explicitly characterizing his method. They are intended to support the comprehensiveness of his methodology as a guide toward the study of nature as a whole, at least as far as the latter can be investigated by a reflective part of nature, namely, by man. Their further general function is to draw the treatment of God and the human mind in *Ethics I–II* more closely together with the moral analysis of man in *Ethics III–V*, thus strengthening the unity of the entire work.

(i) The preface to Part III is a carefully worded charter for the methodology used in the remainder of the *Ethics*. Spinoza acknowledges that he will be derided by misanthropes and practical skeptics for planning to deal with human passions and actions, vices and irrational impulses, by means of his "geometrical manner" and his demonstration through a determinate proof or "fixed reason."[9] He appeals to his view of nature, nonetheless, in support of the continuity of method throughout philosophy.

> But this is my argument. Nothing happens in nature which can be attributed to a defect of nature itself. For nature is always the same, and everywhere its strength and power of acting are one and the same. That is, the laws and rules of nature, in accordance with which all things happen and are changed from one set of forms to another, are everywhere and always the same. And so also there must be one and the same account [*ratio*] for understanding the nature of whatsoever sorts of things, namely, through the universal laws and rules of nature. Hence considered in themselves, the affects of hatred, anger, envy, etc., follow from the same strength and necessity of nature as the other singular things; and consequently they admit of fixed causes through which they are understood, and have fixed properties equally worthy of our cognition as [are] the properties of whatever other thing in the contemplation alone of which we take delight. Hence I shall treat of the nature and forces of the affects and the power of the mind over them by the same method whereby, in the preceding [Parts], I treated of God and the mind, and I shall consider human actions and appetites just as if it were a question about lines, planes, or about bodies.

It is made abundantly clear here that Spinoza cannot carry on his ethical investigations without his naturized method and its warrant in nature itself.

The last sentence quoted above is a famous declaration, but three nuances have to be noticed. First, it starts with the word *hence,* indicating that this is not an arbitrary stipulation but the consequence of a line of reasoning. Spinoza is led to treat human actions and passions in a definite way because of procedural consequences of his view of nature. Because of nature's own self-consistency and pervasively steady power of acting, the laws and rules according to which it operates have an import that is general and the same (everywhere and always, to use the language of human experience). Hence the philosophical method reflectively developed to treat natural things, in all their modes, need not and indeed cannot properly make an exception in the case of those things called human actions and passions. The strength of nature manifests itself in this region as the power of reason, working to form and reform man's affects. Thus, a philosophical study of human emotion, activity, and morality makes headway only by using the one same nature-oriented method for getting to know natural operations at work in our affective life.

Second, the reference to Spinoza's previous treatment of ''God and the mind'' reminds us about the proximate context within which the theory of human servitude, liberation, and blessedness functions. This reference affirms the continuity of principles and the consistent inferences to be carried over from the theory of naturing nature and of natured nature under the attribute of thought. Moreover, the preceding parts furnish a working model of that sort of reasoning in the geometrical manner which functions also in questions about our passions and moral activity. The sameness of method has to respect the diversity of moral expressions of naturing nature, so that procedural adaptations are required for obtaining philosophical truths about man the moral being in nature.

Third, Spinoza makes an unaccentuated distinction when he likens the study of moral man to a question about lines, planes, ''or about bodies.'' Of course, this last phrase in the sentence under comment can refer to a purely geometrical account of solids or to the use of geometry in the dynamics of bodies. But it also reaches over into Spinoza's analysis of bodily modes (which analysis uses a geometrical diagram on the motion of the simplest bodies). His theory about bodies is required for understanding not only speculative problems on the mind and the human composite but also practical problems on the affects, which concern bodily modifications as well as our ideas about them. Indeed, there is a twofold similarity between the theory of the mind and that of the emotions. In both cases, an affirmation of one's bodily reality is basic for human existence and operations; and in both cases, Spinoza pursues the investigation of the bodily component only up to a point that clarifies our basic moral endeavor, postponing further examination of corporeal particles and combinatory affects for some other systematic occasion.

In a subsequent analysis of particular passions, he makes the following cross-reference to the above text:

> But the laws of nature have regard for the common order of nature, of which man is a part; which I wished to remark about here in passing, lest someone should think that I am telling here about men's absurd deeds and vices, rather than that I wished to demonstrate the nature and properties of things. For, as I said in the Preface of Part Three, I consider human affects and their properties in the same way as other natural things. And indeed, if human affects do not show human power, at least they show the power and workmanship of nature no less than do many other things which we admire, and in whose contemplation we take delight.[10]

There is an important equivalence between the term *other natural things* *(reliqua naturalia)* used here in Part IV, and *other singular things (reliqua singularia)* used in the preface to Part III.

Perhaps the simplest way to explain Spinoza's claim to be using one and the same method throughout the *Ethics* is to say, therefore, that he regards human passions and actions as singular natural things, which are to be treated like all other singular natural things. The passions and actions, which constitute our moral life, belong to man who is himself a part of nature. Human affects are "things" (in the sense of being modal realities compositely expressing the attributes of thought and extension together); they are "singular" or finite expressions; and they are "natural" as belonging within natured nature and as being regulated by the latter's general order and laws. As traits of partitive man, the affects themselves come within the causal patterns of finite modal nature. Through them courses the power of naturing nature, and by reason of them it holds that *moral* man is both a receptive and an active part of nature and natural causation. Moral reasoning is itself regulated by principles and considerations that obtain among singular natural things. This naturized method in ethics is not radically different from reflective inquiries about the rest of nature, and the results yield a similar delight to behold.

(ii) There are four internal phases in Spinoza's actual use of his method of treating moral man as a part of nature. Each phase is marked by a characteristic procedural term.[11] Although Spinoza does not always adhere to these namings, he uses them with sufficient strategic prominence to signal his move from one to another of his stages of analysis and argument.

Methodus. His first step is to consider human affects or emotions in a comprehensive yet somewhat indeterminate manner, without yet dwelling at length upon their distinction into passions and actions. Here it is that he prefers to use the term *methodus,* "method," to convey that his entire methodology of naturing and natured nature applies synoptically to man's several practical relations with the rest of nature. He also speaks about this inclusive approach as a *ratio,* in the broadest sense of an "account" based on his integral theory of nature. Appropriately enough, the most general uses of "method" and "account" are found in the (already quoted) preface to *Ethics III.*

Via. The second phase of the inquiry studies human weakness, vacillation, and relative impotence in moderating and governing the affects. There is a predominance of the passions, that is, of those affects which are due to our inadequate understanding of our bodily affections, or the causal power of other bodies, and of our mind's ability to moderate affective forces. After plunging directly into an examination of the passions in *Ethics IV,* Spinoza pauses long enough in two scholia to permit our methodological orientation.[12] He calls his procedure in this phase a *via,* a "way" into a philosophical understanding of the passions. This way into the passions yields only a limited view of the affects, since a prolongation of this "same way" considers the passions mainly in the context of natured nature and with emphasis upon the latter's power over the human mind. Yet the intermezzo furnished by these scholia also assures us that this way is not the sole path available to us in interpreting and using the affects. Prospectively and encouragingly, Spinoza mentions a *prolixior ordo,* a "more developed order," which he will subsequently unfold. The purpose of *prolixus noster geometricus ordo,* "our developed geometrical order," will be to demonstrate how the balance in our affective lives can be tipped from the dominance of passions to that of actions. But simply to hold out this perspective of an action-weighted order does not yet bring philosophical reflection beyond the way of analysis of the passions.

Ratio. Spinoza's third step is to make us meditate on the fact that, even when we are in the grip of the passions, we can nevertheless formulate some rules of reason to reshape our lives. He employs the term *ratio* now, not as broadly signifying a nature-based account or method in ethics, but in a much more determinate sense. *Ratio* acquires a very distinctive methodological meaning in the closing demonstrations and the long appendix of Part IV. There, the venerable Stoic and Christian ethical phrase *recta vivendi ratio,* "right reason or pattern of living," becomes a helpful theme for Spinoza.[13] It signifies that, even when man is being disoriented by the sea of passions coming from his unclear comprehension of natured nature, he can still forge a model of reasonable living. In Spinoza's naturized method, this means that partitive man is not bereft of the power of reason to meditate upon those other aspects of nature which help him to formulate right rules for a reformed humane life. Thus his practical reason gets righted or trued in regard to his moral activity.

Modus, sive via, ad libertatem: Prolixior ordo. The fourth and climactic phase in this ethical interpretation of method is the keynote of *Ethics V.*[14] In the very first sentence of the preface, Spinoza makes another linguistic refinement by using the classical term *modus,* signifying a "manner" of using our practical reason in respect to human affects. One cannot avoid associating the ethical methodological meaning of this term with the metaphysical definition of "mode" with which the *Ethics* begins. This linkage is not merely verbal, since modes in general are affections of substance and since the procedural manner under discussion concerns a transformation of the moral quality of human affects, or a modal composite of bodily modifications and ideas.

Precisely what that transformation achieves is suggested by specifying the manner as being a certain type or *via* of "way." Whereas previously Spinoza had directed attention toward the way-into-passions, he now centers analysis upon the way-into-actions and our access to freedom. The culminating phase of ethical methodology is to use our power of understanding in a manner that will convert a large portion of our affective life from a passional to an actional relationship within nature. Such a transition goes from human servitude to human liberty, and reflection upon this transition enables Spinoza to redeem a previously made promise to furnish a *prolixior ordo*. The axioms and propositions of Part V embody his "more developed order" of inquiry; they express the route and the findings of "our developed geometrical order." In its actual elaboration and unfolding, the Spinozistic order of philosophizing finds its goal in the doctrine of our active union with God and the whole of nature.

(c) *The actional turn: naturating nature.* How can man make the turn from a mainly passional to a mainly actional way of living? In trying to meet this question, it helps to distinguish between beginning this turn and carrying it through as far as can be done. Postponing a study of the latter process until sections 3 and 4 below, I will concentrate here upon Spinoza's account of *the start* of this moral reorientation.

In discussing passional and actional affects, as well as the move from the one to the other, I have used several qualifiers that reflect Spinoza's usage. Man is never in a *purely* passional condition but in a mixed condition that may be *predominantly* passional. Similarly, any moral transformation modifies a large portion of his moral life, so that as far as is humanly attainable it becomes actional. Not purity but blending in different proportions characterizes the human situation, whether at start or at finish of a lifetime of practical endeavor. What this mélange means is that weakness and strength, passion and action, are variously ordered and interrelated in our lives. The passional affects can never attain such complete dominion that they quench the actional affects, thereby also extinguishing our drive toward conscious union with the whole of nature.

That drive always energizes us, because the power of naturing nature operates as a steadily activating presence in men and the entire modal universe. In order to mark the active modal response elicited by this presence, I will introduce the term *natura naturatans* or "naturating nature." This term does not signify any real entity in addition to substance and modes, naturing nature and natured nature. But it does sharpen our philosophical perception of natured nature itself. The latter is never merely a passive receptacle or inert mass. Whether it is an infinite or a finite mode, every reality in natured nature partakes in some way in the modal expression of God's activating power. The word "naturating" expresses both aspects of every modal being: that it is a necessarily caused reality, and that it is caused in such fashion as to be itself an active cause of some sort within the universe.

There is no exception to this fact that all modal beings present themselves under two aspects, although each of them is a naturating actuality in its appropriate manner. Thus, the naturating quality of human life manifests itself in our moral actionaı turn. Our responsiveness consists in trying, with awareness, to achieve the primacy of actional over passional affects in our relationships with the rest of nature. For this is the distinctive actuation of naturating nature on the part of composite singular things having a conscious appetite or desire.

What enables men as singular things to respond to God's operative power and thus to start (from the very outset of their existence) the actional turn? For Spinoza, the answer does not lie in a separate faculty of will, an appeal to which can yield only a figment or fictional basis of action. Instead, it lies in the practical significance of his metaphysical reflections on essence, existence, and actuality.

The *primum* or true foundation of responsive action of any singular thing, or determinate modal expression of naturing nature's active power, is that thing's own actual essence or *conatus*. "The power or conatus of each thing whereby it, either alone or with others, does or endeavors to do something, that is (*Part* III, *Proposition* 6), the power or conatus whereby it endeavors to persevere in its actual-being [*esse*], is nothing else than the given or actual essence of the thing itself."[15] The actual essence is constantly striving, making the effort to maintain its act of being and increase its naturating activity. In a specifically Spinozan sense, the conatus or prime intrinsic ground of endeavor is identified with the actual essence. A modal thing's essence is nothing other than its persevering try to share in the eternal order of nature, or the unceasing necessary causation coming from naturing nature, rather than to have some limited temporal duration within the common or imaginative order of nature.

Once more, we understand man as a distinctive instantation of naturating nature and its conatus, rather than as an unaccountable fantastic exception to them. His actional turn is a naturating response arising from his own conatus, his actual essence endeavoring to persevere in its own actual-being. From this effort comes his emendation of the understanding, the improved clarity and distinctness of his ideas, and thereby the increase of his active affects. Within the human composite, the mind's naturating conatus operates in an appropriate way. It actively endeavors to affirm: its own actual-being and that of the whole range of its adequate and inadequate ideas; itself as the idea of the human body; and especially the actual existence and activity of its own body and bodily affections as they are related to itself within the eternal order of nature.

Throughout this argument, Spinoza follows his methodological precept of starting with that which is first in the order of being. God or naturing nature is that which is unconditionally first in every account of nature. On the side of man as moral agent in natured nature, the probe does not reach a rock foundation until it comes to the human actual essence considered as conatus. Deep calls to deep in the ethical relationship between naturing nature and the human conatus. It is from the core of the actual human essence or conatus that the naturating response is consciously made. The naturating view of man is the obverse side of Spinoza's *quatenus* approach to God. For it is insofar as his power communicates moral strength to naturating man that God actually expresses himself in human life.

As it were in passing, Spinoza adds a remark that reaffirms his theme of the human community. A person's naturating response is strengthened, not diluted or corrupted, through a social union with like-minded people. The ethical conatus thrives more upon fellowship among human agents than upon their isolation or conflict, a topic to be developed in Chapter Eight.

3. The Free Man as a Moral Exemplar

Readers of the last three parts of the *Ethics* are sometimes disconcerted by what seem to be Spinoza's capitulation on some key moral terms and his compromise on the moral ideal. The two issues are indeed bound together, since he cannot discuss moral patterns without making some use of ordinary moral vocabulary. But the point to be emphasized here is that he reforms the meaning of the main terms and takes a comparative approach to several ideals of moral living. Since both moves are regulated by his developing theory of nature, they deserve a brief analysis here from that governing standpoint.

Once he sets forth his concept of the affects and the conatus of naturating nature in man, Spinoza is able to work out a transformational lexicon and grammar. Terms and syntax that would otherwise lead to fictions and errors can now be given rectified meanings and rules of use.[16] The italicized words in the next two paragraphs mark the content and scope of his linguistic reform, insofar as it involves his thought on moral man in nature.

The underlying considerations are that the human mind can become conscious of its conatic desire to affirm the human body's existence and the bodily affections' activity, and that this desire changes considerably in accord with man's ways of being involved in the causal operations of natured nature. His consciousness of the human conatus enables him to consider it in three ways. It can be viewed in respect to the human mind alone, in which case the conatus can be called *will (voluntas)* (but with no claim for a special faculty or for special kind of acts distinct from those of understanding and endeavoring to make ideas more adequate). Again, the conatus can be considered as an endeavor of the natural singular thing composed of human mind and body together, that is, as *conscious appetite (appetitus cum ejusdem conscientia)*. That the appetitive conatus in man is precisely a conscious one gets specially affirmed by using the term *desire (cupiditas)*.

Man is a desirous being. This is not only a descriptive statement but an argued essential truth about the nature of the human singular thing, whose very conatus is thus identified. "Desire is the essence itself of a man, insofar as it is conceived as determined by whatever given affection of his to do something."[17] With respect to being a determinant of human action, desire is a primary affect along with *joy (laetitia)*, (a man's transition from a lesser to a greater perfection) and *sorrow (tristitia)*, (a man's transition from a greater to a lesser perfection). The conatus or basic desire differs from one to another human constitution, and within the same human being there are conflicting impetuses leading to an increase of either joy or sorrow. Spinoza feels confident enough now to speak about *perfection (perfectio)*, as the existing and acting reality of the actual essence, as well as about *good* and *evil (bonum* and *malum)* as denominating respectively something useful that is conducive to our joy, and something not truly useful to us and hence that frustrates our joy. *Virtue* is the same as power. "As it is referred to man, virtue *(virtus)* is the very essence or nature of a man insofar as he has the power (*potestatem*) of affecting something which can be understood through the laws alone of his own nature."[18] Thus a man becomes virtuous in the degree that his actions arise from more adequate ideas concerning his role in the whole of nature, and in the same degree he attains freedom and power within this active whole of nature.

What accounts for this outpouring of rehabilitated moral concepts and language? Spinoza holds that he is both permitted and required to make this transformational recovery. It is now permitted, because there is no longer a danger that such thinking and discourse must direct us toward something beyond the totality of nature. All the meanings are related to the conatus, especially the human modality of it. And this conatus is itself the nuclear responsiveness of naturating nature. The recovered lexicon expresses the human modalities that increase or decrease the power of natured nature to understand and act in accord with naturing nature. For a reflective mind, then, these terms signify our ways of becoming related with the whole of nature, rather than any fictive project of transcending the latter.

Moreover, the renovation of moral vocabulary is imposed upon Spinoza by his need to develop an encouraging moral model for pilgrim man. He must now make the transition from an account of how we begin the actional turn to one of how we sustain and increase its domain, that is, sustain and increase our power or virtue as moral agents en route. Spinoza elucidates the process of moral growth through his theory of the moral exemplar, which is a major theme in *Ethics IV*. Although this theme is sometimes criticized as a surrender to shortfall morality and as a deviation from his own stated search for beatitude, it is presented under safeguards intended to blunt just such criticism. He uses three kinds of safeguards drawn respectively from methodology, from the general theory of nature, and from the deliberate peculiarity of his exposition of the theme itself.

(a) Already in the opening pages of the *Emendation*—pages intended to introduce and give a preview of his philosophy as a whole—Spinoza observes that moral liberation from disordering passions and pursuits comes only with a clear understanding of the terms *good* and *evil*, *perfect* and *imperfect*. They do not denominate an object taken by itself in isolation, but are referential terms designating a thing's relationships within the eternal order and fixed laws of total nature. Furthermore, he points out that we cannot arrive at one bound at an adequate understanding of nature's eternal order and thereby instantaneously achieve our fullest human perfection and good. In other words, we must make a gradual and method-guided approach toward cognition of the mind's union with nature as a whole.

During the journey, however, there is a definite move that one can make to gain assurance and proper orientation. ''In the meanwhile a man may conceive some human character [*naturam*] much firmer than his own and, at the same time, may see nothing so to stand in the way that he may not acquire such a character."[19] What Spinoza calls here *aliqua humana natura* is a moral model which serves an intermediate function. It is a type of human nature or character which comes closer than does one's present condition toward realizing the perfection available to human agents. Its purpose is the interim one of proposing a practicable degree of power or virtue, a concrete pattern of actual affects within one's own reach. This moral exemplar can then be regarded as a staging area leading one toward yet a fuller recognition and possession of the mind's good. Far from substituting itself for the highest ideal, it serves as a directional lead and incitement toward the plenary goal of the human conatus.

As a moral philosopher, Spinoza is sensitive to the human tendency of conceiving practical models by which to measure, and towards which to aim, one's striving after the blessed life and happiness. His *methodological* safeguard is an insistence that all such images of the moral man are instrumental in status, are means leading beyond themselves. Hence he speaks somewhat indefinitely of ''some'' human character or pitch of human nature, lest any particular exemplar be illegitimately absolutized as the completional term of our moral endeavor.

(b) Part IV of the *Ethics* does not move at once to the sketch of a moral exemplar. Instead, it probes into two interpretations of practical model-formation which lead to conflicting views of nature itself. First, there is an anthropological analogy which reads into nature our own process of forming ideal constructs. We stress similarities among singular things, form universal standards, and then declare the natural particulars and the outcomes of our own workmanship to be perfect or imperfect in the degree that they agree with *our* standards. It is an easy step to project this entire process upon nature as a whole. We suppose that nature sets up universal exemplars; that nature envisions these exemplars as goals which *it* strives to realize; and that whenever the ideals fail to be perfectly achieved, nature itself is defective and somehow sins against its own ends.

To avoid the inference about nature's deficiency, Spinoza is always wary about universals, transcendentals, and finalities. They are traceable to human cognitive conditions and to human desires in the domain of efficient causality, but they cannot be imposed upon nature as a whole. If they are uncritically imposed thereon, they only lead us to bemoan the faultiness of nature, attributing to it our own moral failures. This attitude saps our moral conatus and enslaves us to the passions.

By sharp contrast, the second analogy for interpreting practical model-formation is based explicitly and unequivocally upon the intrinsic human drive to increase our actional power. Spinoza readily admits that *"we desire to form an idea of man as an exemplar of human nature which we may envision."* [20] This is a legitimate and indeed necessary function of our finite conatus. The ordinary moral terminology of perfect and imperfect, good and evil, refers to our approach toward or retreat from this exemplar. But we do not forget that the moral model arises from our own desire and serves its effort. Hence we refrain in principle from extending to naturing nature and the eternal order of nature as a whole that terminology which is appropriate to human desire.

Spinoza reinforces this limitation rather vehemently when he declares to Oldenburg: "I do not deem it right for me to laugh at nature, much less bewail it." [21] It is without either tears or laughter that Spinoza philosophizes about total nature, regardless of how intense his reflections get. Nor does he ridicule or deplore human nature itself, even when men fall far short of their exemplary view of moral conduct. To treat of human passions and actions in a manner similar to the study of planes and angles means here to refrain from substituting mockery for understanding of human conduct, as well as to persist in trying to learn more about how human nature is partitively related to the eternal order of nature. The analysis of a moral exemplar cannot allow itself to be deflected by disparagement and despair concerning man as a part of total nature.

(c) The last seven propositions and appendix of *Ethics IV* provide a constructive approach to a moral model and its supporting arguments. [22] The propositions themselves delineate the traits of a free man. And the appendix restates the course of reasoning in a unified set of chapters to aid our effort to actualize the exemplar of a morally free agent, even under conditions where the passions largely hold sway. The peculiarity of Spinoza's exposition is found in this unusual blending of propositional demonstrations and informal thoughts or short descriptive chapters.

"Have you observed," asks one character in Balzac's *Human Comedy*, "how readily, in childhood or at the beginning of our social life, we set up a model for ourselves, spontaneously and often unawares?" [23] Spinoza would answer warily in the affirmative: man is not born totally free and autonomous, and hence is prone to form and follow some practical model. But it is unwise to rely uncritically upon spontaneity and unself-consciousness, since they may express only our passional affects and opinions, thus subjugating us to the model of a servile way of life. Instead, one must reflectively set forth the frame of mind and pattern of living of the free man, a task which Spinoza performs in the seven concluding propositions of *Ethics IV*.

(i) A free man lives solely by the dictates of reason, directly desiring the good as previously defined. That is, he seeks to act, live, and conserve his actual-being or what is basically useful to him. Here, Spinoza writes his famous sentence that *"the free man thinks of no thing less than of death, and his wisdom is a meditation not on death but on life."* [24] Behind this apothegm lies the whole of Spinoza's reasoning on nature. As a mode of natured and naturating nature, man has a conatus seeking primarily to unite him with naturing nature. Since this is a life-giving union, his primary rational motivation is to persevere as *part of the living whole* of nature, rather than to become preoccupied with death or the extinguishing of his participation in this living totality.

(ii) Freedom has to be achieved through endeavor, rather than imagined as a birthright. If men were born free, they would never have inadequate ideas and hence would never form conceptions of good and evil. Such a condition would obtain only for God considered as the cause of human nature taken by itself. But in fact and in accord with the Spinozan doctrine on natured nature as a whole, human nature never exists and never gets truly understood except as a part of natured nature. The necessary struggle toward moral realiztion of partitive man shows itself here. Our cognition cannot but be a mixture of inadequate and adequate ideas; we cannot but form concepts of both evil and good, as applied to our responsiveness to nature as a whole; and consequently the essence of man is conative and desirous of liberation.

In the biblical story of the fall of man and the deliverance of the people of Israel, Spinoza sees a religious symbol of the free man's liberational striving. For freedom comes to people "as led by the spirit of Christ, that is, the idea of God, from which alone it depends that man be free, and that he desire for other men the good which he desires for himself."[25] In the religious imagery, one can discern the need for rejoining the human mind with the infinite modal understanding, for recognizing one's own good to lie in this union and its ordination toward naturing nature or God, and for trying to share this freedom with the rest of the human community.

(iii) In the remaining five propositions, Spinoza makes more concrete his theory of *fortitudo* or firmness of mind. Of the three primal affects (desire, sorrow, and joy), sorrow remains a passion always since it consists essentially in a transition toward diminution of one's power and perfection. Since desire and joy signify the latter's increase, they can undergo transformation from passional to actional affects. Spinoza uses the term *fortitudo* to designate "all actions which follow from the affects that are referred to the mind, insofar as it understands."[26] Because the free man perseveres at increasing the scope of his understanding and actions, he must be portrayed as eminently having firmness of mind. From this it follows that he also gains individual courage and social generosity, which are the two aspects of fortitude. Courage (*animositas*) is the strong desire whereby each one strives to conserve his own actual being, as prompted solely by the dictate of reason concerning what is useful to the agent. Generosity (*generositas*) is the desire whereby each one strives (solely from reason's dictate about what is useful to another) to assist other men and join them to himself in friendship.

The character of the free man binds these definitions to the morally developing individual and relates them not only to each other but also to his situation in nature. He needs firmness of mind, since he lives in a dangerous, overpowering world where it is fatal to be either overfearful or rash. His modal finitude is brought home to him by his need for human aid in the necessities of life, aid that he must often seek from intellectually and morally ignorant men from whom he must nevertheless thankfully accept benefits. But he is most bound in gratitude, friendship, and generosity with those other men who are also free, strongminded, and generous in their turn.

From the standpoint of nature theory, it is crucial to accord such prominence to the functions of *fortitudo* or firmness in building the free man's character. Insofar as it signifies strength and presence of mind, courage is the great persevering power which keeps the individual's conatus steady in the midst of danger, enables the conatus to become largely an active affect striving toward what is truly useful and liberating, and thus permits his human mind to give a naturating response to naturing nature. Insofar as one's moral firmness has the aspect of generosity, it enlivens the social dimension of the move from passions to actions. Natured nature has a unity, which shows itself in our generous social relations.

If the courageous person had strength of mind alone, he might foolishly try to make the journey alone in his active search for the good and happy life or, at the most, might try to reach it only in the company of similarly strong minds. But Spinoza insists upon the aid that the free man has to obtain even from men moved by opinion and passional affects. Human beings of every individual and social condition have something to contribute to the moral efforts of other people in the shared situations of life. This broadens the base of generous solidarity among all finite human modes, even though the closest generosity and gratitude are reserved for the union of free men (in the plural) among themselves. The pervasive social influence of naturing nature upon men is expressed in their need for common laws, the state, and the various forms of human community and friendship. Thus, in its two aspects, firmness not only traces out a character study of the free man but also brings us one step closer to the union of naturating with naturing nature.

(iv) The appendix to Part IV of the *Ethics* is remarkable for restating in thirty-two concise chapters of straightforward prose the unifying thread of doctrine which had been just previously argued in geometrical fashion. Spinoza senses the need for expressing his thought in the portable form of a moral handbook not less accessible than the vade mecum of a Seneca or an Epictetus. The very last chapter of the appendix synthesizes the Spinozan reflections on a moral exemplar.

> But human power is quite limited, and is infinitely surpassed by the power of external causes; and hence we do not have the absolute power of adapting to our use the things that are outside us. But yet we shall bear with equanimity those things that befall us contrary to that which a consideration of our advantage requires, if we are conscious that we have performed our duty, and that the power which we do have could not extend itself so far that we could avoid those things, and that we are a part of the whole of nature whose order we follow. If we understand this clearly and distinctly, that part of ourselves which is marked out by intelligence, that is, the better part of ourselves, will entirely acquiesce in it and will endeavor to persevere in that satisfaction. For, insofar as we do understand, we can desire nothing except that which is necesssary, and can acquiesce absolutely in nothing except in true things. Hence in the measure that we correctly understand this, in that measure the endeavor of the better part of ourselves agrees with the order of the whole of nature.[27]

Armed with these thoughts, a person of experience and reason can adhere to a practical model for moral living.

In this text, Spinoza recapitulates his analysis of our struggle to develop a moral character even in a situation where we seem powerless. His first point is that we are not unconditionally lacking in power but, rather, that our power is greatly limited in the way that a singular thing has only restricted capabilities within natured nature as a whole. Yet even in this particulate relationship, we can interpret what is happening to us and develop a stable attitude toward our predicament.

Hence Spinoza's second consideration is that, even when external forces and hence the passions loom so very large, we have the inner resources for attaining what the Stoics call a certain equipoise, a balance of mind or equanimity. But this virtue comes only if we fulfill a certain condition: Become self-aware. This veiled imperative is always present in the *Emendation* and the *Ethics*, yet everywhere Spinoza also argues that its fulfillment comes about through understanding ourselves within nature, not through methodic doubt or some intense resolve of will. We must become conscious not only that we are performing our office in life and are unable to avoid some disadvantageous circumstances but also, and indeed primarily, that we are part of total nature and adhere to its order. Conscious adherence to this causal ordering leads us toward an increasingly active participation in the living whole, as distinct from a passive or reluctant servitude thereto. Our naturating nature draws its moral self-awareness and power from its naturing principle, acknowledgment of which enables us to keep our situation in perspective and to discern a pattern useful to our own reality.

The third theme specifies more closely how we reach this perspective and what further moral qualities it fosters in us. Spinoza correlates our active response to nature's eternal order with his moral meaning for intelligence (*intelligentia*), which is capacious enough to include a rectified imagination working along with practical reason. Working together in some measure, they not only envision a detailed moral model but also achieve its embodiment as shaping a considerable portion of our affective life. In this complex and morally active sense, intelligence designates "the better part of ourselves" (*pars melior nostri*), a value-laden phrase that becomes increasingly important as the *Ethics* moves toward its climax. With this language, Spinoza signifies more than the partitive relation of man as a singular thing to nature as the totality. Both epistemologically and conatively, clear and distinct ideas constitute man's better part. For they arouse our mind's true understanding and acceptance of the order of total nature—an understanding and acceptance which actionally transform much of our mind's affective life, even though not its entirety.

Intelligence, or that better part of ourselves which perceives and welcomes nature's ordering, attains the moral quality of repose or satisfaction (*acquiescentia*). This is a peaceful satisfaction having an active connotation, in contrast with mere resignation. The acquiescent mind joyfully accepts and interiorizes the eternal order of nature. The latter's necessary causation is no longer regarded as an intruding and threatening force. Instead, we come to recognize that this necessity and its implications constitute our permanent basis of action and guide for endeavor. In this steadying influence upon the mind's conatus, satisfaction and constancy and equanimity reveal themselves as virtues working mutually with firmness. What unifies these traits of our better part is their intelligent apprehension of, and joint action in accord with, the whole of nature as Spinoza conceives it.

(v) *Ethics V* deals with the understanding's power or human freedom, but it does not break continuity with the previous sections. Spinoza cannot allow a rupture to occur because the earlier parts lay the groundwork in a doctrine on God and man, nature and a moral exemplar, without which our mind would lose support and bearings in its quest for freedom. Hence toward the beginning of Part V, there is a long scholium on what measures to take when we lack perfect cognition of our affects and hence cannot perfectly arrange and connect the body's affections in accord with an order directed toward the understanding itself.

What this scholium advises us to do is, in effect, to retain and strengthen the previously elaborated moral exemplar. Our safest procedure is "to conceive a rectified pattern of living or fixed precepts of life, and commit them to memory, and continually apply them to the particular things frequently encountered in life, so that thus our imagination may be broadly affected by them and that they may always be at hand for us."[28] The model developed by moral intelligence is not kept apart in a sanctuary of its own. On the part of people involved in the world, it has to be engraved upon memory, enriched through practice, and enlivened imaginatively for individuals and societies.

Here, perhaps more than anywhere else previously, we find Spinoza appreciating the positive value of experience and imagination, memory and varied application of general precepts. He becomes attentive to what "experience no less clearly than reason teaches." The epistemology of moral exemplars rehabilitates the first mode of cognition, joins it with practical reason, and thus helps the human agent to meet confidently the changing circumstances and encounters of everyday practical living. Only with these aids can one attain sufficient stability and tranquillity to reflect upon the ultimate questions of freedom, beatitude, and union with

God—all of them considered within the context of Spinoza's view of nature.

4. *Our Ethical Telos in Nature*

Spinoza begins *Ethics V* unceremoniously with the declaration that it is the other part of ethics.[29] This refers to the distinction, noted above, between starting the moral journey and continuing it as far as is humanly possible. To conceive the moral exemplar of the free man is already to engage in the continuation process: to form one's moral character upon this pattern is like building a fort that can withstand the changing fortunes and assaults of the world. But our conatus urges us toward the more positive goal of developing our powers to their utmost and enjoying the deepest satisfaction life can bring. Spinoza devotes his concluding inquiries to this topic, and his treatment is highly teleological in two senses: systematic and ontic. Systematically, there is a recovery and convergence of many concepts strewn throughout his other writings and the earlier sections of the *Ethics* itself—concepts now shown to have practical implications and an inner tendency toward unification. What makes their synthesis effective is the ontic drive of men toward their maximal moral realization in relation to the rest of nature. My present analysis must concentrate selectively upon man's ethical telos within nature.

As further specification of his perspective, Spinoza states that he leaves to logic a purely theoretical study of perfecting the intellect, and to medicine a study of curing the body. He does this so as to concentrate here upon the mind alone, that is, upon our power to elucidate and reshape the affects and thus reach human freedom and blessedness. Such concentration does not exclude the body, both because the human mind is the idea of the human body and because the right ordering of the affects concerns bodily affections as well as our ideas of these affections. But it does emphasize the mind's own resources for achieving emotional moderation, together with the mind's cultivation of acts that do not arise from a confused perception of bodily existence and duration.

The broadest and most readily grasped division of Part V is into a study of reason's power over the affects, and the mind's freedom and beatitude.[30] Hence the present section considers respectively the two themes of remedial reason and beatitudinal mind. Taken together, they give backing to Spinoza's affirmation of the superior strength of wisdom over ignorance and hence the telic import of the morally wise man.

(1) *Remedial reason*. The previous account of the free man has already begun to manifest our ability to develop a character of stable moral nature, which centers the affective life on an order proposed by the understanding rather than imposed by external forces and the flow of circumstances. But Spinoza is not satisfied with this exemplar, since it is limited by an imperfect cognition and affective response in respect to nature. What more can we do, then, to improve our moral situation?

The reply is terse and to the point: We can understand ourselves and our affects more clearly and distinctly, thus leading to a love toward God. A free man's stability rests upon his clear and distinct knowledge of the common properties of bodies, a knowledge that reaches to all the affections of his own body and that he shares jointly with all other men who use their reason. But he often fails to contemplate sufficiently, to the point of referring his bodily affections and his own affective ideas to the idea of God. This spells his failure to recognize that bodies and their ideas belong in natured nature, whose necessity and causal order come from naturing nature. But the mind that does regard itself and its affections clearly and distinctly within the context of total nature rejoices in this knowledge, includes a specific reference to the idea of God as naturing cause, and thus rejoices in and loves God himself.

What pragmatic differences does it make to include an explicit love toward God (*amor erga Deum*) in the expanding moral pattern? As far as strengthening the power of reason over the affects goes, Spinoza draws several consequences. Our love toward God unifies the bodily affections so that they can be more comprehensively ordered by the mind. Furthermore, this love springs from the adequate idea of God. The love itself and the contemplation upon which it thrives are actional and are conatively all the more actional in proportion to our greater understanding and love. Because of its foundation in true knowledge of ourselves in nature, this love is neither dependent upon the passional affects nor superable by them. It has no contrary passional force by which it can be expelled but, rather, it is what Spinoza calls "the most constant of all affects."[31] In his love toward God, therefore, man finds an unshakable constancy, which is the real foundation of all other forms of constancy and virtue in our mutable world. It engages the greatest part of our mind, renders the passional affects into the least part of our affective life, and is the highest good dictated by reason and common to all men, regardless of any invidious distinctions.

Yet Spinoza also sounds a cautionary note, lest we confuse this love toward God (as characterized within the framework of remedial reason) with the full account of the mind's blessedness. For one thing, the love in question issues from knowledge of God that is founded upon either the second or the third kind of cognition, that, is upon reason or upon intuitive knowing. Spinoza's analysis concentrates on a reason-generated love toward God, postponing for a while a study of the distinctive quality that intuitive knowing brings to our love relationship with God.

Moreover, the constancy of reason-based love toward God is established by relation to conditions prevailing in this present life. The phrases *haec praesens vita* and *ut praesens* are precise technical expressions.[32] As Spinoza uses them here, they do not signify primarily a contrast between our life now and an afterlife. Rather, their first aim is to designate one specific way of viewing our life now: as involving bodily passions to be controlled, and a temporal-durational way of existing which comes to a definite end with death. Faced with an image of the unstable common order of nature, we orient our lives firmly toward God. Such a human mode of presence intermingles rational contemplation and imagination in a manner that permits the love toward God to emerge, but not to gain as complete a clarification and actuation as lies in our power to achieve.

Since our love toward God remains under these human conditions of presence, it does not seek reciprocal response of the same sort from God. To do so would be to import into God an affective love involving a mixture of adequate and inadequate ideas, as well as a passage from passion to action and a continual increase of conatic power. This would mean the anthropomorphizing of God, combined with a premature cutoff of our own striving to improve upon the human love for God. Reformulated in terms of nature-theory, this kind of reciprocity would obliterate the distinction between the operations of naturing nature and those of natured nature. It would transform the divine naturing act into a naturing response. Simultaneously, it would restrict the human naturing act of love to what the second sort of knowledge permits under temporal conditions. For Spinoza, this double consequence would subvert the actuality and truth of nature as a whole. The proposed remedy would lead to incoherence about nature and hence would not be a constructive act of human reason.

(2) *Beatitudinal mind.* Just as previously it was asked what further contribution reason can make to the moral exemplar of the free man, so now it is asked whether anything more lies in man's power to improve upon his rational love toward God. In response, Spinoza's last group of propositions in *Ethics V* shifts the emphasis from the mind's influence

over the affects to its direct active pursuit of eternal blessedness. Indeed, this is the ultimate focus of all previous investigations, insofar as they are resonsive to the mind's search for closer union with total nature. Such an analysis sharpens the Spinozan doctrine on nature in regard to three topics: our eternal being, the intellectual love of God, and the wise man's strength.

(a) A major component in our ethical telos is to reach a lively conviction that our mind is, in some respects, *eternal*. To energize and give moral significance to this conviction, Spinoza summons the resources of both reason and experience, insofar as they can be made instrumental to intuitive knowing and loving. Reason is asked to rethink some of its earlier demonstrations about God and man, while experience is asked to bring home their actual application to ourselves as striving moral agents.

The way of reason supplies some pertinent assurances, both negative and positive. Negatively, it argues that we cannot follow the trail of reminiscence back into an eternal preexistence. For that trail reaches no farther than does the temporal duration of our body, a span that is fixed and limited in its coming to be and passing away. That part of our mind which is considered coevally with our body's duration shares in the latter's temporally limited and perishing hold upon existence. Memory and imagination are thus blocked from being avenues to cognition of our share in eternal being.

On the constructive side, however, reason has frequently used the distinction between the common order of nature and the eternal order of nature. Now in the last part of the *Ethics*, Spinoza makes prominent use of these two ways of regarding natured nature. The common order of nature is a view of existence through duration (*per durationem*), whereas the eternal order of nature views existence under the aspect of eternity (*sub specie aeternitatis*) or, more concretely, in relation to our mind insofar as it is eternal (*quatenus aeterna*).[33] Because the human mind is the affirming idea of the human body, it can eventually develop an adequate idea of the essence of the body as apprehended without the confusion and mutilation caused by temporal duration. Hence, our mind comes to know both the body and its own essence in their actuality and truth, that is, under the aspect, form, or look of eternity. Human reasoning establishes (as in Parts I and II of the *Ethics*): that the human mind and body are modal realities which are in the divine substance and conceived through it; that they depend in their essence and existence upon the active power of God; and that the actual and true existence of their essence is necessarily caused by the actuous eternal essence of God. These findings satisfy the Spinozan definition of eternity and of regarding our mind, body, and the modal world under the form of eternity.

But this inferential approach does not entirely satisfy our thirst for the eternal. We must grasp, as concretely as we can, our actual passage from the durational to the eternal consideration of things. This transition has to be engaged in and experienced by us in a familiar way, not just reasoned about through general demonstrations: Only when experiential acquaintance with this transit is conjoined with demonstrative reasoning does Spinoza declare:

> But nevertheless we feel and experience ourselves to be eternal. For the mind does not feel the less those things which it conceives by understanding [them] than those which it holds in memory. For the mind's eyes, whereby it sees and observes things, are the demonstrations themselves. Hence although we do not recollect ourselves to have existed before the body, yet we feel that our mind, insofar as it involves the essence of the body under the aspect of eternity, is eternal and that this its existence cannot be defined by time or explained through duration.[34]

Only the involvement of our mind with our body's essence and with God's necessary, eternal causal order is able to define, explain, and bring home forcefully our eternal being or actual presence in the eternal order of nature.

Three comments need to be made on this quoted text. First, Spinoza uses the cue-word *insofar as (quatenus)* to qualify what we grasp about the mind as being eternal. That part of the mind which is proportioned to the body's essence, and which knows that essence and itself in respect to the divine necessary causality, manifests itself to be eternal. Hence, Spinoza designates this eternal part of our mind as "this something" or "something of it" (*hoc aliquid* or *ejus aliquid*), "its greater part" or "the eternal part of the mind" (*major ejus pars* or *pars aeterna mentis*).[35] This partitive usage corresponds to what he said previously about our better part, except that now it specifies that the better moral quality expresses the power of eternity in us. What religious discourse calls immortality is here seen to be an eternality that we can feel and experience now, in our clarified act of existing. The question of whether our experienced eternality retains any individual character is best treated in the context of our intellectual love of God.

Second, to know that some part of our mind is eternal constitutes an important component in our *self*-knowledge. Since this self-knowledge involves our relationship with God, Spinoza proceeds immediately to the proposition that "*the more we understand singular things, the more we*

understand God [Dutch: *or we have understood more of God*]."[36] The
direct proportional more/more type of statement is frequently used. In
previous places its main intent was to reassure us that a study of singular
things does not diminish, but rather increases, our knowledge of God.
Now, Spinoza specifies that the direct proportion concerns a study precisely of that in ourselves and other things that evinces the immanent
causal power of the eternal God. We cannot complete the move from
viewing our own finite modal nature under the aspect or form of duration,
to viewing it under the aspect or form of eternity until we recognize its
essential and existential dependence upon the necessary causation of
naturing nature.

Last, this increase in our understanding of ourselves and other singular
things by reference to the eternal God fulfills the conditions for the third
kind of cognition. There is a peculiarly Spinozan meaning here for "'intuitive knowledge" *(scientia intuitiva)*. When the mind is imbued with the
eternity of total nature, it understands the essence of natured things from
the standpoint of their active ground in naturing nature. Thus the aspect or
form of eternity signifies a cognition that expands its vision from an
adequate idea of God's engendering attributes of thought and extension to
an adequate understanding of the actual, true essence of engendered
things comprising our modal world. To develop this third sort of cognition
of things is the mind's supreme virtue and conatus—that is, its highest
power and endeavoring nature. What Spinoza calls here the mind's highest "'nature" is that character, aroused by our very awareness of being in
the eternal order of nature and acting in accord with its power and pattern.
Within this character are integrated all the intermediate models which
help the human mind to reach and retain its naturating apex.

(b) Spinoza is now in possession of all the elements required to determine his meaning for the intellectual love of God *(amor Dei intellectualis)*. He trades heavily upon the ambivalence inherent in this phrase,
which taken as an objective genitive signifies our love for God, and taken
as a subjective genitive signifies God's own love for himself. (We have
previously examined a similar ambivalence about "the idea of God.")
Each sense of the phrase has its own difficulties, toward the resolution of
which it helps to bear in mind the pertinent concepts about nature.

Our love of God springs from the third kind of cognition of ourselves
and God and hence surpasses, at both poles of the agapic relation, the
previously considered love toward God generated by the second sort of
cognition through reason. The adequate formal cause of the mind's intellectual love of God is the mind itself, insofar as it is eternal and is

distinctly aware of its eternality. Through the dynamism of his own conatus, each one increases his understanding's intuitive knowledge of himself and God, strengthens his love of God as the eternal naturing cause, and thus is more perfect and more blessed.

The problem is that this increase is difficult to communicate in time-laden language, while also maintaining that the mind is eternal in its act of cognition and love under the form of eternity. To make the issue easier to understand and explain, Spinoza makes a remarkable twofold method-ological move. Without thinning his certitude that we are eternal, he nevertheless frames two contrary-to-fact suppositions or counterfactuals.

The first supposition concerns a way of viewing the relation between our mind and the third sort of cognition. ''We shall consider [the mind], as we hitherto did, as if it were now beginning to be [*tanquam jam inciperet esse*], and were now beginning to understand things under the aspect of eternity.''[37] Spinoza has recourse to this fictive device in order to bridge the gap between the temporal and the eternal ways of interpreting the mind's actuality. Within the framework of the finite modes of natured nature, the mind *is* eternal, even though its eternality is obscured and miscontrued by the imagery of temporal duration. No matter how ignor-ant or confused a finite mind may be, it is never entirely lacking in a dim awareness of its eternal actuality and a telic endeavor to clarify this nuclear awareness. When reason and intuitive knowledge do uncover the grounds in nature for acknowledging this shared eternity, Spinoza treats the mind as though it were only just beginning to be and to understand under the form of eternity. He uses the temporal language of a beginning and a becoming to express the self-affirmation of our eternal *esse* or actual-being.

The second supposition follows since our active affective life is also transformed by the mind's self-understanding. To convey the radical impact of viewing our affects in the light of eternity, Spinoza revives the affective language used in the *Short Treatise*. Not only do we feel and experience joy in our strengthened endeavor. When this joy is joined with the idea of the necessary, eternal cause of our modal actuality, we respond with an intellectual love of God rooted in our intuitive knowledge of the causal connection between naturing and natured realities.

Even though this act of love is just as eternal as our act of being and knowing, Spinoza again finds use for a counterfactual supposition.

Although this love toward God did not have a beginning [*principium*] (in accord with the preceding *Proposition*), yet it has all the perfections of love just as if [*perinde ac si*] it has commenced, as we feigned in the Corollary of the preceding Proposition. Nor is there any difference here except that the mind had as eternal these same perfections which we feigned to accrue now to it, and that too along with the concomitant idea of God as eternal cause. If joy consists in the transition to a greater perfection, blessedness ought properly to consist in the fact that the mind is endowed with the perfection itself.[38]

In affective terms, then, the life of the virtuous mind is compounded out of joy and blessedness, regarded respectively as a transitional increase of power and an eternal possession of perfect love. That love toward God which reason based on the transitional *increase* is now emendated as the way whereby our naturating mind gets to acknowledge its *possession* of an eternal knowledge and love for naturing nature or God. At least this emendation comes to fill the better part of our natured mind, whose endeavor continues ever more inclusively to recognize its fulfillment in that knowledge and love.

Once these two suppositions serve their clarifying purpose in his conception of nature, Spinoza's path is cleared for treating the other major meaning of the intellectual love of God, namely, God's love for himself. This is a delicate task, since the objections previously adduced against applying to God our reason-generated notion of love are never retracted. They could not be withdrawn without injecting into God the conditions holding for modal nature. But the situation is somewhat ameliorated, now that we see the benignly fictive status of talk about only just now commencing our intuitive knowledge and intellectual love for God. I say "somewhat," however, since Spinoza himself interjects the remark "if it still be allowed to use this term." in connection with his treatment of our joy as participants in God's infinite love.[39]

What Spinoza strives to find is, in fact, some analogue for joy and love which can be applied to God without confusing him with the conatus of our natured nature. This project requires six steps.

(i) An important meaning for God's absolute infinity is that the nature of God *enjoys* its own infinite perfection. It affirms its unbounded actuality, the self-possession of which supplies a meaning for joy which does not rest upon any increase of perfection.

(ii) God necessarily exists, in the sense that his essence involves existence and hence that his nature cannot be conceived except as existing. This fulfills the meaning of God as unconditioned or self-grounding *cause-of-himself.* Hence the nature of God is explicitly involved in the meanings of divine joy and cause. Naturing nature is also the unself-depleting cause of the actual being of things comprising natured nature. In no meaning of cause properly applicable to God does there enter any dependence of his actual nature upon the causation of anything else.

(iii) Joining together these emendated meanings of joy and cause creates a naturing analogue for what Spinoza has called intellectual love. It involves no struggle with passional affects and no endeavor to increase any actional affects. Hence, it is a supremely intellectual love of God for himself.

(iv) Spinoza can now safely apply to human love for God the same *quatenus*-method previously used in treating modal nature and human cognition. Our loving action of the mind, contemplating itself in conjunction with an idea of God as cause, is a part or facet of God's self-contemplating and loving action—insofar as the divine action can be expressed by the human mind. Since in loving himself, God loves men precisely insofar as they are modal expressions of his causal action, it follows that "God's love toward men and the mind's intellectual love toward God is one and the same."[40] This conclusion does not confuse God and man, since the originative action of naturing nature and the responsory action of natured nature are here being considered in the causal union signified by nature as a whole. In this philosophically specified context of nature as a whole, no modal traits of our naturating love are projected into God's love toward men.

(v) Immediately after the inferences stated above, Spinoza permits himself to make a sun-flare exclamation: "From these we clearly understand in what our salvation, or blessedness, or freedom consists, namely, in a constant and eternal love toward God, or in God's love toward men."[41] There is a deliberately religious tenor to this declaration. What the religious believer calls rebirth and salvation finds its truth manifested in the freedom and blessedness won by the philosopher.

Both the believer and the philosopher seek their realization in the unitive love between God and men. But the Spinozan way of explaining this love moves arduously beyond any anthropomorphic notion that would ascribe our affective conditions to God. The meaning of the loving union is reconceived to conform with Spinoza's theory of nature. He founds our liberation and blessedness upon precisely that sort of relationship holding between God the naturing principle and our naturating selves. The only genuine mutuality is that of our *quatenus* inclusion in God's infinite love.

Spinoza also points out the religious and philosophical connotations of the words *a constant and eternal love* in the text just quoted. In the sacred Scriptures and their commentaries, this love is called "glory," whether it refers to God or to our mind. But in Spinoza's philosophy, this glory is not truly distinguished from *acquiescentia* or joyous acceptance and satisfaction of mind. The doctrine regarding intellectual love determines more exactly, however, that the basic, originative joy and satisfaction lie in naturing nature's own self-possession and necessary causality. Our satisfying acceptance of that causality enables us to share unitively in the divine love and eternal life, which we discover experientially to provide the foundation of all our power and virtue, courage and constancy.

(vi) The last step in this explication brings to the fore a portion of Spinoza's view of nature that was left somewhat recessive until now. If all the propositions about beatitudinal mind are synthesized and held in steady view, "it is manifest that our mind, insofar as it understands, is an eternal mode of thinking, which is determined by another eternal mode of thinking, and this again by another, and thus to the infinite; such that all taken together constitute God's eternal and infinite understanding."[42] Thus, when we consider the mind apart from the body's existence, we do not abandon all thought about our body but positively view our mind within its own line of causality.

We reaffirm that our mind is modal and not a substance, that it is a finite mode within natured nature, that it expresses the divine substance or naturing nature under the attribute of thought, and that our finite mind belongs within the infinite and eternal mode of understanding. To regard our mind as a causally determined expression of the infinite mode of understanding helps us to make the crucial turn required for the third kind of cognition and hence for grasping our liberational and beatitudinal way of acting. At long last, Spinoza establishes the ethical significance and power of the understanding as an immediate, infinite mode of natured nature, a doctrine which seemed previously to have only an ontological import. Like a massive, arching movement in a Bruckner symphony, the theory of the infinite mode of understanding gradually performs its ethical function of enabling our mind to grasp and enjoy its eternal active origination in naturing nature. Only then does man become liberated, blessed, and truly cognizant of bodily nature's practical role in moral life.

Within this complexly qualified context of modal nature, Spinoza now safely uses the superlative form, in saying that "the greatest part of the mind" is affected and occupied by our intellectual love of God. Anyone thus actively responsive "has a mind whose greatest part is eternal."[43] That portion of the mind which perishes along with our body is the imagination, whereas the eternal part of the mind is the understanding whereby we act.

Spinoza pointedly refrains from speaking about "personal survival." The term *survival* is correlative with preexistence and signifies the prolongation of imagination and image-based memory. Also, here he steers clear of the term *personal,* so as to avoid the usual connection between person and individual substance. Instead, he refers to "each one" (*unusquisque*) and "each singular thing" (*res unaquaeque singularis*), in order to treat our mind in the framework of his general theory about finite modes or singular things existing in natured nature.[44] In the case of our mind as an eternal singular thing, it comes to regard death as being of the least moment or importance when viewed in the light of the eternal. The eternality of *our* mind and *its* action is compatible with the inclusion of all finite modes of thought within the unique, infinite, eternal understanding. Individuality remains a function of the unity of action, thus accommodating not only each one's mind as an agent but also the total expressive agency of the understanding, taken as an immediate infinite mode of natured nature under the divine attribute of thought. Spinoza has a *sui generis* conception of our mind as eternal or immortal.

(c) In the scholium to the very last proposition of the *Ethics,* Spinoza treats of the wise man's strength (*sapiens potior*). Readers who come this far are often just as disappointed as are readers who come to the concluding section on absolute knowing in Hegel's *Phenomenology* and his *Encyclopaedia*. And their disappointment rests on similar grounds: just as students of Hegel expect him to elaborate something more than and different from what went before, so do students of Spinoza expect something more and different to come out. But such is not Spinoza's intention in writing his closure.

The Spinozan wise man is a figure of the "nature" or exemplary cast of mind that the author hopes to imbue us with, if we follow reflectively the sinuous course of the five parts of his *Ethics*. It is not by chance that the term *via* appears here one last time, since the book seeks to induce in us a sense of "the way."[45] A pilgrim route must be followed and incorporated in its entirety if we are to learn that blessedness or intellectual love for God is not a separate reward for virtue but is that virtue itself or that power of mind arising out of this whole argumentative and reflective enterprise.

Spinozan wisdom combines the endeavors at demonstrating with those at meditating upon the mind's union with the whole of nature. All three kinds of cognition--experiential, rational, and intuitive--make their distinctive contributions and thus earn their permanent place as components in this wisdom of nature. No one of them can be discarded, any more than can nature as naturing or as natured. For the wise man is he who holds together every aspect and meaning of nature. He recognizes that total nature embraces all the modal acts (including our cognitive and affective modalities), along with divine substance in its immanent causal activity. Spinoza expresses this catholic scope of man's ethical telos in nature in his often-repeated requirement that the wise man must be "conscious of himself, and God, and things through a certain eternal necessity."

Two traits of this comprehensive wisdom stand forth with special clarity in the concluding pages of the *Ethics*: its internal differentiations and its systemic openness. The former is linguistically expressed through relations of direct and inverse proportionals (more/more, less/less, more/less, most/least), which register the gradual ascendancy of action over passion in the character of the courageous wise man. Yet this ascendancy never leads to total obliteration of the existing mind's body, passions, and vulnerability to the causality of the rest of bodily nature.

Spinoza keeps enthusiasm well within bounds through his parenthetical remark that "we live in continual variation."[46] Hence his last references to the union of the more apt mind and the more apt body of the wise individual are linguistically marked also by an abundance of adverbial qualifiers. The sage "scarcely" fears death and regards everything referring to imagination and memory as being "scarcely" of moment by comparison with the goods of the understanding; he tries "exceedingly or above all" to improve his body in proportion to his mind's maturation; he avoids the condition of the libidinous individual who is unconscious "as it were" and who "hardly" knows himself, God, and things in nature; for the drive of wisdom is precisely to make one "greatly" and "unusually" aware of oneself, God, and things as being all bound into the unity of nature as a whole.

This noticeable piling up of cautionary adverbs—*vix, apprime, quasi, fere, multum*—serves not only to keep alive all of Spinoza's distinctions and comparisons regarding nature but also to keep his systematic analysis of nature open for further investigations. The *Ethics* is not, and is not intended to be, his last word about nature. To prevent any premature termination of his master theme, he devotes his penultimate proposition to a vindication of piety and religion, as well as of everything that fosters steadfast courage and generosity (marks of that firmness of mind whose traits must be conserved and enhanced in the life of wisdom). Hence, the philosopher must attend, specifically and at length, to human religious and social institutions. Without a study of them, Spinoza's doctrine on nature would be incomplete and adjudged to apply only to a restricted area of human activity. My next two chapters are intended to remedy any such misconception.

The antithesis of the Spinozan wise man is the crowd embarked in Brant's *Ship of Fools*. One passenger proclaims: ''None of us sees wisdom's light.''[47] The fool-literature of Brant, Erasmus, and their tradition takes its sampling from every sector in society. Spinoza is equally inclusive in finding weakness and obstacles in all our social forms. But he does not turn away satirically and fideistically from the social tendencies toward foolishness. His philosophical method is not only diagnostic but, in some measure, curative of the aberrancies of institutional life. He does make us pay heed to the social aspects of wisdom and the resources for social therapy afforded therein.

Ethics V offers several considerations that have a social implication and support a hope for social reform. (i) At last, it becomes clear that temporal duration is not dismissed outright, any more than is imagination. What Spinoza rejects is an *absolutist and exclusionary adherence* to temporal duration, one that interprets all reality confusedly and exclusively under temporal-durational imagery. This viewpoint would admit no emendation by the knowledge of nature reached through the second and third sorts of cognition. But when these cognitive ways do arouse the endeavor or desire for an understanding of nature's eternal order, they affect the social interpretations of our temporal-durational existence.

(ii) Insofar as it is itself an eternal mode, the mind is the formal cause of knowledge under the form of eternity. To deny such causal power entirely is equivalent to demodalizing the human mind itself, to depriving it of its true reality and action within nature as natured and naturating. But no one's modal reality is ever *totally* suppressed in the affirmation of one's bodily existence and social relations. Spinoza's insistent use of qualifying terms here (that each one's mind is only quasi-unaware of itself, God, and other things in eternal nature, or that one is indeed somehow conscious of being eternal despite confusion and obscurity) holds true for all manners of people joined in all manners of social enterprise. Social encrustations never entirely thwart philosophical analysis and its ensuing practical reorientation.

(iii) Spinoza manages to maintain a fine balance between the differentiation of conative activity in human individuals and the mutual strengthening of endeavor in social groups. There is something distinctive about the endeavor of philosophers, but it is not insulated from the aims of other people. Within the causation of nature as a whole, mutual needs exist and social ties are helpful to us all. No thoughtful mind can avoid reflecting upon the needs, ties, and problems raised by human union in various sorts of communities.

Consequently, Spinoza interrupted his revision of the *Ethics* long enough to compose treatises on religious and political issues. Such issues do not lose their urgency for anyone who becomes aware of his own ethical power and blessedness. One always remains a wayfarer requiring peaceable company. The wise individual's salvation does not consist in being removed from religious and political realities, but rather in critically and coherently including them within his emendated vision and way of acting. I must now turn to the contribution that Spinoza's account of these matters makes to his still-developing conception of nature.

CHAPTER SEVEN

Religion within the Totality of Nature

DURING THE INTELLECTUALLY CROWDED YEARS 1665–70, Spinoza took time from his revision and expansion of the *Ethics* to write a separate study of religion. His *Theological-Political Treatise* (1670) was published anonymously, but its authorship became known in a few weeks. He distributed copies of it to Oldenburg and Boyle in England, clarified its meaning to numerous correspondents, and was only mildly discomfited by having it banned at home along with Hobbes's *Leviathan* and his friend Meyer's *Philosophy the Interpreter of Holy Scripture*. The book hit its mark squarely by disturbing the ecclesiastical authorities and those civil authorities who felt obliged to defend some form of church orthodoxy.

Although the compound term *theological-political* has an odd ring to it today, it was the most succinct adjective to convey one of Spinoza's major concerns in writing his treatise. Among the reasons he gave for composing it was the condition of the times, further specified as the impudence or undue influence of preachers and theological considerations upon the use of political power. In this sense, the *Theological-Political Treatise* was a tract for the times, showing a historical sensitivity toward particular situations which was never suppressed by Spinoza's criticism of temporal imagery and his dedication to nature's eternal order. In the longer time span, there was a full century of European wars and civil strife arising in some measure from theologically formulated religious differences and aimed partly at reaching ecclesial uniformity in a national state. That this passion for theological-political order disturbed other philosophers can be gathered from the protest of Spinoza's contemporary, John Locke, against the "religious rage" of Englishmen. "Why then does this burning zeal for God, for the Church, and for the salvation of souls—actually burning alive at the stake—pass by, without any chastisement or censure?"[1]

Spinoza was in no position to answer Locke's question on chastisement, and was inclined toward censure only insofar as he could offer reasons against theological prejudice and for civil toleration of diverse thinking and talking on religious issues. What brought the matter uncomfortably close to home, however, was the sharp division of opinion and policy among Dutch political rulers on how to deal with religious differences. Leaders in the United Provinces were disunited on this practical question, some hewing to Calvinist orthodoxy, others being more hospitable to dissenting groups. Spinoza sided with the more tolerant policy of Jan de Witt, even though the story of the philosopher's acquaintance with and influence upon the statesman lacks a factual basis.[2] It was enough that the philosopher had his say, that it was supportive of de Witt's refusal to silence the various remonstrant or dissenting sects, and that the reasoning was appropriately philosophical in tenor. Spinoza addressed himself explicitly to philosophically minded readers who could follow the argumentation on its own plane. During his lifetime he prevented the publication of vernacular translations, which might disturb the practicing believers whom he admired and did not want to discourage from piety and good works.

The Bible was also intimately involved in the discussion, because all parties in the theological-political controversies of that age appealed to it for support. Hence, Spinoza had to propose a way of treating the Bible that would be consonant with his own philosophy, with the role of religion in society, and with civil peace and freedom. Along with Isaac La Peyrère and Richard Simon, he pioneered some principles of Biblical interpretation that later became commonplace. The Old and New Testaments were to be treated exactly like other historical sources. Their constituent books had an internal textual meaning adapted by their respective authors to the particular mentality, cultural condition, and linguistic pattern of the intended audience. Spinoza argued that these limiting conditions prevented the imposition of belief in some one theological interpretation upon all the citizenry, let alone upon all philosophers.

Thus the *Theological-Political Treatise* is a many-faceted work. It can be read as a theory of religion, as a guide to biblical criticism, and as part of a larger political theory. But what unifies these aspects and also sets limits on their independent development is their common bearing on the freedom of philosophizing. This convergence of purpose is made clear in the book's subtitle: "Containing several discussions whereby it is shown that freedom of philosophizing not only can be granted without harm to piety and public peace; but that it cannot be abolished without also abolishing public peace and piety itself."[3] In conducting these discussions, therefore, Spinoza does not feel that he is wandering away from his main activity of philosophizing. Rather, his arguments seek to prevent any blockage of that activity made in the name of religion and the state. He is intent upon showing that his general view of nature has implications sufficiently determinate to safeguard the freedom of himself and others to reflect upon socially sensitive questions and publicly report their findings.

My approach to the book can now be specified. I will consider how Spinoza's own sort of free philosophizing on theological-political issues stems from, and is regulated by, his act of meditating and arguing about nature. His theory of religion and biblical interpretation, of theology and reason, is examined here only insofar as it involves his broader consideration of nature. The involvement itself is a two-way affair. It concerns both an application of our previously determined conception of nature and some new developments of that conception made in the course of meeting the problems of religion raised in the *Theological-Political Treatise*. Any strictly political aspects are postponed until the next chapter.

Sometimes the *Theological-Political Treatise* is regarded as having an esoteric method and meaning owing to Spinoza's study of Maimonides and the Kabbalah.[4] Without underestimating his concern with these sources, I nonetheless suggest that two characteristics of Spinoza's own philosophical practice contribute to the difficulty of following his train of argument in this book. A consideration of them helps us to make a straightforward philosophical reading within his own textual boundaries.

The first practice can be called the carry-over effect. Since Spinoza was making use of the *Emendation* and further elaborating the *Ethics* simultaneously with his composition of the *Theological-Political Treatise*, he incorporated many elements from the two former works into the latter. His sense of methodological continuity found expression, for instance, in his remark that obscure sayings of the prophets can be investigated and elucidated "from our method."[5] And the impact of the *Ethics* is felt in his appeal to the workings of the idea of God and to different sorts of cognition and union with God.

The second practice can be denominated the gradual presentation process. Like Descartes and other system-minded philosophers, Spinoza had a strong sense of what could be established about an issue at one particular stage of the inquiry and what had to be postponed. Initial statements of a position pointed toward their refinement and qualification at some subsequent phase in the order of investigation. Although the numerous cross-references in the *Ethics* seem cumbersome, they do furnish the means for avoiding some interpretive problems raised by the lack of such references in the smoother-flowing *Theological-Political Treatise*. Nevertheless, this *Treatise* is a prime instance where the process of gradual presentation is observable.

These two practices furnish the basis of division within the present chapter. Its first section examines a major instance of the carry-over effect, namely, the use which the *Theological-Political Treatise* makes of the positions on religion and piety advanced in the *Ethics*. The chapter's other sections consider some main phases in the process of gradual presentation as it operates in the *Theological-Political Treatise* itself, in order to develop still further the theory of religion within Spinozan nature.

1. Religion and Piety as an Ethical Theme

A nature-reading of the *Ethics* cannot avoid noticing the prominence of the topic of religion and piety. It threads its way through the whole book and becomes an increasingly important avenue for understanding how man orients himself and increases his ethical power. There are three main stages in Spinoza's unfolding of the theme of religion and piety: its legitimation, definitions, and incorporation within the blessed life.

(a) *Legitimation*. Spinoza realizes that his doctrines on God's necessary causality, man's necessitated workings in modal nature, and the denial of free will expose his philosophy to serious practical objections. Hence, at the very end of *Ethics II* he not only criticizes the hypostasizing of human will, apart from particular expressive ideas, but also argues that his own theory best serves the needs of human life. For it helps us to bear with life's difficulties, by assuring us that the entire course of natured nature issues necessarily from God. It also encourages us to aid other people and join with them in social endeavors which are a rational response to the kinship among human individuals within modal nature.

In full harmony with these practical advantages of Spinoza's doctrine on God and the human mind, moreover, is the firm support it lends to a religious reading of human existence.

> [1] It teaches that we act from God's bidding alone, and that we are sharers of the divine nature, and the more so in the degree that we perform more perfect actions and understand God more and more. [2] Therefore this doctrine, besides the fact that it gives the mind repose in every respect, also has this consequence, that it teaches us in what our supreme felicity or beatitude consists, namely in the cognition alone of God, whence we are led to do only those things which love and piety advise. [3] Hence we clearly understand how much those people stray from the true estimation of virtue who expect to be recompensed by God with the highest rewards for virtue

and the best actions, as though for the utmost servitude—as if virtue itself and servitude to God were not felicity itself and supreme freedom.[6]

Thus Spinoza forestalls any easy dismissal of his thought on God and man, understanding and will, on the ground of its being incompatible with a religious attitude and the practical aim of our life (*ad usum vitae*, the Cartesian code word for cultural, moral, and religious practicality). What an emending philosophy must do is to interpret religion in the light of an adequate, true conception of nature.

The three sentences in the text quoted above are as finely chiseled as the articles in a creed. [1] God is the empowering source of human activity. Everything is done at his bidding, but this bidding is not an arbitrary act of will. Naturing nature expresses itself with necessary active power throughout natured nature, including the human agent who therefore owes all to God. Religion is the vehicle of our basic awareness that we are participants of the divine nature. The phrase *participes divinae naturae* makes philosophical sense insofar as men are finite modalities of the infinite eternal modes of understanding and motion-and-rest, which are themselves the direct causal manifestations of the divine attributes of thought and extension. Thus, our entire being shares in the divine nature, insofar as we are finite modal expressions of the active causal being of the unique substance. Spinoza also regards men as constituent realities within nature as a whole, and hence as "sharers in divine nature," taken in the sense of the dynamic totality of substance and all its modes together.

It is also a religious discernment that partakers must take part in a continual struggle and journey toward God. This translates the Spinozan teaching on the human conatus, its striving toward an actional rather than a passional relation with external forces in modal nature, and its persever-ance at the task of increasing at least the predominance of actional power in one's life. Such increase gives a definite measure for "more perfect" actions, which depend upon improving our perception of man's active role in nature. That this improvement consists fundamentally in gaining an increasingly participative understanding of God and our relationship with him is another way of stating Spinoza's account of how our knowl-edge of naturing nature intensifies our own self-activity or naturating nature.

[2] Whether the consummation is described as Stoic tranquillity or biblical peace of soul, it is a concrete way of designating the mind's peak activity. To evoke this liberating and saving response is the ultimate aim of the *Ethics*. All its reasoning leads toward a culminating knowledge of God, which is recognized to be the very core of lasting human happiness.

When we shape our actions in accord with this God-centered cognition, we have the sufficient principle of love and piety for effectively regulating our conduct. The promptings of religion are anchored in, and illuminated by, what the philosopher recognizes as the true knowledge of God.

[3] Spinoza's final statement sounds a polemical note, in keeping with his correctional and healing method. Given his view of virtue as actional power, he does not look elsewhere for our felicity and freedom. Men attain them precisely in virtuous activity, which is not an instrumental means leading to something else as a reward. Indeed, we would demean virtuous activity by treating it in terms of trial and subjection, from which burden we are to be relieved in an afterlife and given a reward for our travail. Spinoza repeats the words *virtue* and *servitude*, in order to aid our emended religious meditation to see that virtuous living *is* our real happiness, and that service to God *is* our true liberation from a life dominated by the passional affects. So keenly does he feel on this point that, in the penultimate proposition of the *Ethics,* he returns to a satirical contrast between the common opinion of the crowd and the precepts of reason as to whether piety and religion are burdensome or intrinsically felicitous for the virtuous individual.[7] Spinoza's philosophy acknowledges the intrinsic worth of religion and piety, against the grain of common prejudice which pictures beatitude as a removal of the severe regimen of virtuous and pious practices.

(b) *Definitions.* His formal treatment of religion and piety is crucially situated in, and paced by, the discussion of human affects. *Ethics III* establishes that the primary affects are desire, joy, and sorrow; that all other emotions are combinations or consequences of these basic ones; and that our firmness of mind increases with joy and decreases with sorrow. The task of *Ethics IV* is to inventory more closely our resources for passing from passion to action, from a lesser to a greater strength of mind. This passage depends on our acceptance of the dictates of reason, especially the principle that the primary and unique foundation of virtue consists in the endeavor of conserving oneself, and hence of understanding what does conserve and profit the mind. The greatest obstacle against acceptance of the principle is the widespread opinion that such an intensification of human power is impious rather than virtuous and pious. Hence, the emendation of our meaning for religion and piety is an integral part of developing a true idea of man that can serve as the incitive ''nature'' or model of moral living.

Spinoza proceeds gradually to show that his moral model is other-regarding and not selfishly exclusionary and contentious. That which is supremely useful, good, and virtuous for the mind is to understand God. By its very structure, this act of cognizing God accords with reason, fulfills the human essence, and thus increases man's active power. It is therefore a good that we seek to hold in common, one that brings our individual natures into agreement through a sharing of the highest actuality available to us as men guided by reason. This sharing is not a contingent effect but a necessary consequence of satisfying the prime endeavor of the human essence. The greater an individual's participation in the knowledge of God, the more strenuous is his effort to communicate this good to others and to rejoice in their joint realization of the human mind's natural drive.

It is within this context that Spinoza offers the following specification and definitions:

> He who endeavors to guide others by reason acts, not by impulse, but humanely and kindly, and is supremely in accord with himself. Hence whatever we desire and do, of which we are the cause insofar as we have the idea of God, or insofar as we cognize God, I assign to religion. Moreover, the desire of doing well, which is generated by the fact that we live in accord with reason's guidance, I call piety. Hence the desire whereby the man who lives in accord with reason's guidance is held fast, so that he joins the rest to himself by friendship, I call honorableness [*honestatem*].[8]

These meanings of humaneness and religion, piety and honorableness, are carried over as touchstones in the *Theological-Political Treatise*.

Several aspects of the treatment in *Ethics IV* should be noted. Spinoza does not approach religion and piety as subclasses of justice but as being more directly rooted in the basic affects. They are ways of bringing desire under the activating influence of reason, so that we can gain an increase in action and the virtuous life. Hence, they have an affinity with joy rather than with sorrow, with active power rather than with passivity and impotence. In this respect, the true virtues under consideration are contrasted with the passions of humility, repentance, and pity. Traditionally, these latter states of mind are associated with religion. Anticipating Hume and Nietzsche, Spinoza regards these passions as dispiriting modalities of sorrow, as lesseners of our active power, and hence as paths to human impotence and passional ineffectuality. *So regarded,* they work contrary to truly understood religion and piety.

Yet in the concrete situation, one can also perceive in the above Spinozan definitions a proper estimation of human modal limits (the salvageable element in humility), a resolve to emend one's manner of judging and living (distortedly present in repentance), and a humane concern to do

well for others (the active core masked by pity). Even the tracing of
religion to fear and hope—a suggestion of Lucretius, Machiavelli, and
Hobbes—is not decisive. For fear serves a monitory function in the modal
world of physical incursions and civil tyrannies. And hope can be rechan-
neled as the emotive accompaniment of our perseverance under adver-
sities and our search for fuller knowledge. Thus, the Spinozan approach
through the affects is intended both to criticize the current portrayal of the
devout life and to rescue anything therein that can turn sorrow into joy
through the enhancement of reason-ruled endeavor.

Within the interpretive setting provided by the general theory of nature,
the quoted text achieves even greater precision. It is concerned with
perfecting that complex union of finite modes of natured nature which
constitutes our *humanity.* Hence, there is emphasis upon acting in a
humane and well-intending fashion, without confusing human reality
either with modes that lack reason or with God. Rational self-consistency
is the mark of a well-conducted human life, provided that such practical
consistency actuates our own affects and our kind of naturating endeavor
to share in the divine nature.

The two traits assigned here to *religion* are carefully delineated by
Spinoza with an eye for their nature-significance. First, religion belongs
in the compound area of human desiring-and-doing. It arises from the
basic affect of desire, which constitutes our human essence and differentiates each individual's being. But it cannot consist solely in desire but
must lead to overt deeds, since otherwise it would thwart the active power
of naturing nature which inclines a modal being toward active doing.

Second, a religious sort of desiring and doing is a causal response
called forth by the idea of God in us. Since the human mind is a finite
realization of the infinite mode of understanding, it shares in the latter's
idea concerning God or naturing nature. Reflection upon this idea enables
the human mind to develop from a mainly passional condition to a largely
causal, actional state. In the broader sense, this transition toward virtuous
action is a religious rebirth and growth, grounded in our knowledge of
God and aiming at our love toward God in various ways and degrees.

Spinoza never separates religion from *piety.* Their joint consideration
is part of his strategy to assure that religion has a practical significance
and that its praxis consists, not in a vague prescription of activism, but in
moral well-doing. The systematic linkage of religion and piety is his main
precaution against superstition, which either transforms religion from a
practical into a speculative doctrine or else directs religion toward practices divorced from a straightforward moral meaning for doing well. Not

unrestrained imagination and pity, but practical reason and the active
desire arising from joy in moral fulfillment provide the proper guidance
for a philosophically acceptable piety.

Piety and honorableness are explicitly governed by one's conception of
nature.

> He who rightly knows that all things follow from the necessity of the divine
> nature and come to be in accordance with nature's eternal laws and rules,
> will surely discover nothing that merits hate, laughter, or contempt, nor will
> he pity anyone. But as much as human virtue brings about, he will try to do
> well, as they say, and to be joyful. . . . For he who is moved neither by
> reason nor by pity to be of aid to others, is rightly called inhuman. For (*Part
> 3, Proposition* 27) he seems to be unlike a man [Dutch: or to have all
> humanity drained out].[9]

ın effect, Spinoza tells us that piety must prove itself in probity. Only the
man of moral integrity or honorableness has a rightful claim upon piety.
His knowledge of necessity in nature leads him neither toward quietism
nor toward an incapacitating sort of pity. Rather, in harmony with the
idea of God and the commonality of mind, he is led as far as human power
or virtue permits to help other men increase their own share in the
natured-and-naturating mode of understanding. Religion and piety do not
dehumanize us as long as they give rise to active concern for the well-
being of other people, thus fostering friendship within the human community.

In the passage just quoted, there are two unobtrusive yet significant
phrases enabling Spinoza to meet the objection that his notion of religion
and its associated virtues is too rarefied and elitist. His passing remark *as
they say* indicates his recognition that ordinary people have some sound
understanding that religious piety must meet the test of good works and
friendship, lest it turn into hypocrisy. And his words *neither by reason
nor by pity* remind us that there is something redeemable in pity after all,
that the ineffectuality included in its definition does not always prevent
one from actively aiding others.

These qualifications are imposed upon Spinoza because he approaches
religion in the light of his view of nature. All men enjoy some share in the
power of naturing nature; they are all constituted as finite modes of the
understanding, with a nuclear idea of God and a sense of kinship with
their fellow men; and hence in principle they all can develop at least a
religious attitude analogous to that portrayed by Spinoza as being under
reason's guidance. The split is never completely made between the
philosopher's view of religious existence and that of everyday believers

and doers of the word of God. Otherwise, the very structure of natured nature in its human modes would get fractured and dispersed.

(c) *Incorporation.* What has been said about religion and piety thus far is still open to the opinion that it holds good only for Spinoza's model of the free man. If this were so, religion and piety might be confined to the rules of reason. Spinoza must now establish their relationship with his account of intuitive kowledge of God and hence with the life of human beatitude. This he does concisely and firmly in the closing pages of the *Ethics*.

Ethics V has a tripartite structure. Its main topics are: the mind's power over the affects; the mind's liberative awareness of the eternity of the best part of itself, and its reposeful love of God and of itself as an eternal mode of thought; and the beatitude which consists in a love toward God springing from the third or intuitive kind of cognition. The main proposition in this last section states that our beatitude is *not* the reward of virtue but is virtue or morally active power itself; and that we do *not* delight in such blessedness because we restrain our lusts, but, on the contrary, we restrain them because of our delight in beatitude or love toward God and the eternal order of the whole of nature.[10] Here, the double negative and the reference to restraint serve as reminders that Spinoza is discussing human freedom as a struggle to secure the primacy of the best that is in us. He cannot afford to leave out *any* sort of knowledge or virtue that will strengthen our conscious effort to increase the right ordering of desire and the dominance of our love toward God and beatitude.

Hence he buttresses his affirmation about beatitude with this proposition: *"Even though we did not know that our mind is eternal, we would regard as primary, nevertheless, piety and religion and unrestrictedly all that we have shown in the Fourth Part to be concerned with courage and generosity."*[11] Spinoza never underplays the difficulty of the way to beatitude. To adhere to that strenuous path requires all the firmness of mind we can muster. As we have seen, moral firmness consists in courage (the endeavor to seek what is useful for oneself) and generosity (the helping of others and the joining of them to oneself in friendship). Religion and piety reinforce these virtues by relating the idea of God to one's search for the useful and by giving friendly help to fellow humans. Hence, the man of moral firmness finds his courage and generosity strengthened by religion and piety together. This alliance is consolidated in *Ethics III* and *IV* even before the eternity of something about the human mind is established, and even though a particular individual may not be able to follow the formal argument for such eternity.

Thus Spinoza incorporates into his final affirmation of beatitude every-thing supportive of it in his own previous reasoning and in the develop-ment of human virtues. Anyone striving for beatitude through cultivation of religion and piety makes a contribution, even though his thinking may still have to be purified and philosophically reinterpreted. There is a mighty effort made at the close of *Ethics V* to assimilate the entire vigor of religion and the full range of human modes of cognition, in order to put them at the service of the Spinozan doctrine on freedom and salvation.

2. The Need to Emend Religion

Given the careful treatment of religion in the *Ethics,* there would seem to be no need to devote a separate treatise to it. But the very definitions of religion and piety contain some criterial conditions not always met by people claiming to live in accord with these virtues. Religion and piety concern actions of which we are the cause, insofar as we have the idea of God, follow the lead of reason, and associate with others in an honorable, friendly way. In each respect, one can readily fall short of the measure. That is, one's conduct may be governed by an inadequate idea of God, at odds with the one proposed by Spinoza; and it may lead to social relations of a servile and oppressive quality, manifesting the superstitious rather than the genuinely religious origin of the bond and of its political ramifi-cations. Hence, the analysis of religion can go just so far in the *Ethics,* leaving its more detailed pursuit to the *Theological-Political Treatise* and some of the *Correspondence.*

We must now turn to these latter two sources for the gradual develop-ment of Spinoza's teaching on religion, insofar as his thinking thereon involves his theory of nature. Indeed, his general statements on religion made in relevant letters are replete with references to nature and are philosophically understandable only in the context of a governing concep-tion of nature.

The *Correspondence* prolongs some themes about nature that have already been broached here in earlier chapters. One instance is the topic of purifiers of the understanding, a reminder that Spinoza always incorpo-rates his epistemology and methodology into his doctrine on nature, since the mind's operations and reflective methods belong within nature's own reality. Of the understanding's three purifiers—mathematics, mechanical philosophy, and the Bible—we must now consider in more detail the contribution of the last named. Spinoza did not equate religion with biblical religion, but he gave the latter chief attention because of its personal impact upon himself as well as its deep cultural penetration and involvement in the political life of his times. Along with the Old Testament and traditions of the ancient Hebrews, he included the New Testament (especially Paul's epistles) and the writings of such medieval Jewish thinkers as Maimonides and Crescas.

The Bible is a *purifier* because, when properly understood, it prepares the human mind for acceptance of the view of nature proposed in Spinoza's philosophy.[12] Its imagery and stories dispose us to view our world and every individual entity as components of one encompassing whole, so that we are not entirely at sea when Spinoza discusses natured nature as a totality. Moreover, this reality is not a chaos but an orderly pattern, whose events are governed by divine laws and rules—an anticipation of the idea of nature's order and causal unity. And however distinctive it is, the human soul or spirit is also included within the world order and regulated by God's law. There is life within natured nature, just as there is law governing the desires of man.

Another contribution of the biblical outlook is to regard the universe as God's handiwork. The religiously described universe owes its origin to God and remains open to his creative act. This is a veiled recognition of naturing nature and its productive power, regardless of confusions over the precise relationship of naturing with natured nature. The Bible also fosters the conviction that man is a God-seeker, that man needs help from God's spirit or son, and that in his love for God man finds a new life and salvation, freedom and lasting blessedness. Spinoza's deliberate use of this religious language is something more than cultural accommodation. The images thus verbally stated are dim perceptions of the truth about the human modes of naturating nature, that is, about man's enhancement through union with the whole of nature. The Bible is a chaste and purgative influence, urging men not to be sense-centered and anarchic but to direct their minds to what is real and divine.

At some point in the discourse between philosophers and believers, however, the operative phrase *philosophically speaking* must be applied to biblically grounded religious faith. We can follow Spinoza's application of this phrase in a series of letters which he wrote to the grain broker Blyenbergh in 1665 (when Spinoza was beginning to compose his *Theological-Political Treatise*). The actual exchange between them was somewhat marred by cross-purposes, since at first Spinoza thought that Blyenbergh's questions arose from philosophical reasoning alone. But it soon became clear that the two correspondents differed radically on the meaning and relationships of philosophy, theology, and Scripture. This led Spinoza to clarify his own position on them and on their bearing upon the question of nature and religion.

Spinoza had misidentified Blyenbergh as being "a philosopher pure and unmixed [*een puur philosooph; merum Philosophum*], who (as many, who esteem themselves Christians, admit) has no other touchstone of the truth than the natural understanding, and not theology."[13] Actually, it was Spinoza himself who met this requirement for being purely a philosopher, even in matters concerning religion and Scripture. As he put it, he acquiesced readily to his own understanding and its assurance that everything happens through God's necessary and immutable power. The rooting of the necessity of modal things in the necessary causation of naturing nature served as his sole touchstone of truth. It guided his reasoning not only in metaphysics and ethics but also in the interpretation of scriptural discourse on God and upright human conduct.

In order to rule out any independent scriptural basis for theological criticism of his own philosophy, Spinoza circumscribed the Bible's intent and content.

> *Scripture, since it principally serves for the common people, constantly speaks in a human manner,* since the people are not suited to understand high matters. . . . Sublime speculations, I believe, affect Scripture least. As regards me, I have learned no eternal attributes of God from Sacred Scripture, nor could I learn them.[14]

The Bible is not a metaphysical textbook but a practical guide for living. It serves ordinary people by communicating at the level of human imagery or imaginative perception, and for the sole purpose of fostering pious and mutually helpful conduct among them. Only a pastoral, purely practical theology can result.

One cannot draw from biblical sources any speculative truths about God, the universe, and man, since these sources convey no method for emending the imagery or guiding our philosophical reasoning and intuitive understanding. Nor can there be anything philosophically decisive about an appeal to a particular view of reality as being presupposed or implied by the biblical stories. Such presuppositions would carry no special evidence coercing assent in matters of philosophical controversy, but would be suggestions that must still submit to methodological reform by our own understanding and its intrinsic grasp of the real. Hence, Spinoza finds no grounds in biblically oriented thought for making a correction of his philosophical theory of nature as naturing and natured.

He spelled out for Blyenbergh the main consequences of the principle that Scripture *"constantly speaks in a human manner."* It means that the biblical writers think and write in the language of commandment and parable, perdition and salvation. "They have adapted all their words closely to this parable [of lawgiving-reward-punishment] rather than closely to truth, and have represented God everywhere as a man. . . . Theology has everywhere, and that not without reason, represented God as a perfect man."[15] Spinoza was careful not to add that, from the internal viewpoint of the Bible and its proper theology, this anthropomorphism is merely childish or an arbitrary departure from the pastoral intent. The biblical way of representing God is "not without reason," insofar as it fulfills the practical aim of making most people responsive to precepts about their neighbors, and of helping them to become affectively related to God. The thought and language of Scripture do serve to counter lawless and godless behavior by representing moral life and God in imagery that builds up men of probity and piety.

Dangerous nonsense creeps in only when such law-and-parable talk is translated into a speculative doctrine, a theology making ontological truth-claims to which philosophy must submit. Spinoza recommends that philosophy disengage itself as much as possible from the integral parable situation. He takes three steps toward achieving this disengagement, without discounting the factual influence of his own close study of Scripture and of a long tradition of Scripture-formed thinkers.

First, he describes the procedure whereby God and human nature become confused. The parable mentality uses a method of substitution. It thinks about causes in the images and language of law, and it thinks about effects in the images and language of saving and losing one's soul. Within this schema of law-salvation-perdition, the divine becomes confused with human nature, and God is imagined as a perfect man or a just law-giver. Spinoza's philosophical reform is to make a systematic reversal of this procedure. He rethinks lawgiving within the theory of causes and rethinks the saving or losing of one's soul within the theory of effects. Thus the primary analogate is the relationship between causes and effects, which reduces the tendency to confuse God with the world of human ideals.

Second, Spinoza is very guarded in the use of his century's favorite phrase: "the laws and rules of nature." It appears more frequently in his theological-political writings than elsewhere. Although he cannot avoid this phrase entirely, he interprets it as a way of describing what happens in the modal world as a consequence of naturing nature's productive power and necessary causation. The accent falls upon the active power and causality of naturing nature, rather than upon the descriptive laws and rules of natured nature.

To sharpen our awareness of this reversed emphasis, Spinoza draws a capital distinction between the causal *per* and the descriptive *secundum*, between "through" and "in accordance with."[16] Modal things and events come about strictly *through* the active power and causality of God or naturing nature. The course of natured nature is described as coming about *in accordance with* the mechanical laws of science and the moral laws of biblical theology. Within the total order of nature, mechanical and moral laws are patterns necessarily determined by and expressive of God's causal immanence. If this clarification is kept in mind, it prevents the confused representation of God either as a perfect man or as an absentee owner.

Spinoza's third countermove is to refrain from the religious naming of God as king and judge. Philosophical criticism of the theory of will as a divine attribute is expressed in the religious field as a denial of a separate legislative will of God and his commandments as the basis of moral law and obligation. Similarly, criticism of the separation of virtue and beatitude stands in the way of any religious image of God as judge, doling out rewards and punishments for our deeds. In order to remove the anthropomorphic elements from this picture, Spinoza has recourse to two points in his theory of nature: conatus and virtue. The human conatus, which expresses the immanent activity of naturing nature in us, provides the direct foundation of our moral actions. And virtue is itself the realization of what is humanly desirable and felicific, without waiting for the approbation or disapprobation of someone else as a rewarder.

As a lagniappe in his correspondence with Blyenbergh, Spinoza gives us a concise statement of the religious response made possible by his critical removal of obstacles. "Our understanding offers mind and body to God without any superstition."[17] This is a good rephrasing of the *Ethics'* theme of love toward God, but now enriched by the act of purifying biblical religion. The proper aim of religion is not to teach the truth of a speculative theology but to arouse people to present their whole being to God, and to do so as conscious and obedient agents rather than as unthinking tools. We must now consider how this practical response can be made "without any superstition," that is, without positing anything other than the totality of nature.

3. Scriptural Religion: A Function in Nature

We encounter some strong language in the preface to the *Theological-Political Treatise*. "I believe that most people are ignorant about themselves. . . . And as if all nature were insane along with themselves, they

interpret it in astonishing ways,'' fashioning sacrifices and vows to pla-
cate the gods in regard to happenings whose cause they do not know.[18]
Yet Spinoza did not content himself with describing opposition between
philosophers and people who know neither their own reality nor the rest
of nature. He looked to the power of nature itself to reduce this opposition, not by somehow making all people into philosophers but by providing people with the means to live virtuously and to avoid making foolish
cognitive claims. Nature achieves this modest result through divinely
revealed religion, which in Spinoza's cultural situation means biblical
religion.

He was not aware of the paradox that many beliefs and practices which
he regarded as unfounded and superstitious were themselves developed in
the name of biblical religion. Hence, he undertook the project of reinterpreting and rectifying this religion in the light of his own conception of
nature, clarifying that conception itself in the process. Spinoza aimes at
reenvisioning three fundamental constituents of biblical religion:
prophecy, law, and scriptural teaching. But in order to reformulate these
elements, he had to remove the accompanying belief in miracle which, if
left standing, would bar the entire reconstitution of religion.

(a) *Miracle.* Spinoza's critique of miracle is not made in the spirit of
deism (whose remote deity is at odds with the immanent workings of
naturing nature) or of atheism (taken as a denial of any divine power in the
whole of nature). Rather, his critique depends upon showing that most
notions of miracle are inimical to the truth about integral nature and some
human values attached to that truth. To bring out this incompatibility, he
distinguishes three meanings of miracle which do involve some position
toward nature.[19] I will call them the positions of factual ignorance,
opposition, and transcendence in principle.

The least strenuous analysis is required to treat that meaning of miracle
equated with our factual ignorance of the causes of unusual events in
natured nature. Some degree of unknowing marks our common human
condition. The only real question concerns the response of different
minds to this condition and the wonderment it evokes in us. We can freeze
our response at the level of diffused imaginative wonder, so to speak, but
this only canonizes a factual condition of ignorance and lazy reason. The
other route is to develop the methods for understanding connections
within natured nature and the technologies for putting the growth of
knowledge at mankind's service. Religious motivation is often the source
of the civilizing and educating activity, so that there is no necessary

alliance between religion and this or that condition of unenlightenment and superstition.

More difficult to treat is the oppositional meaning of miracle—that is, the view that miracle signifies a happening against nature. The miraculous event is imagined as occurring because God interrupts or contravenes the order of nature. Many people believe in God only when they consider the course of nature to be opposed and its power to be subdued by a contrary decree, issuing from the divine power and will. Miracle manifests this antagonistic relationship, revealing to us a superior divine reality operating independently and against the order of nature.

Spinoza regards this view of miracle as an unhealthy sign of our ignorance about God and nature, and of ourselves in relation to them. The presuppositions are that God does not act when nature acts in its usual way; that the power of nature and natural causes are themselves otiose or resistant as long as God acts; and hence that the power of God and the power of natural things are two numerically distinct and counter-related powers, the latter of which is created and overruled by the former. Although this schema can be sharply outlined, it rests upon vague imagery that evades reasonable discussion and fails to deliver the desired knowledge about God.

Without strictly rearguing his own positions, Spinoza applies them in the *Theological-Political Treatise* as guideposts to criticism and to the recovery of nature's unity and necessity. On the basis of his doctrine that everything in natured nature follows from the necessity of naturing nature itself, he interprets religious talk about *ordinari* (what is "to be ordered or ordained" by God) as a way of shadowing the truth established in the philosophical language of *fieri* (what is "to come to be" through nature).[20] Thus what religion calls God's eternal decrees are the necessary and true laws of natured nature, in accordance with which all things come to pass and are determined through the power of naturing nature. And what religion calls God's guidance or direction of things is nothing other than this fixed and immutable order of natured nature, this concatenation of all modal agencies and events held together by the power of divine naturing nature.

From this perspective the madness involved in the oppositional account of miracle becomes apparent.

> Hence if anything were to happen in nature that would oppose its universal laws, that would also necessarily oppose the divine decree, and understanding, and nature. Or if someone were to maintain that God does something

against the laws of nature, he would simultaneously also be compelled to maintain that God acts against his nature, than which nothing is more absurd. . . . Therefore, nothing happens in nature that may oppose its universal laws; but not even something that does not agree with them, or that does not follow from them.[21]

Spinoza also presses the epistemological case against such suppositions. Were they to prevail, they would lead us to doubt and skepticism concerning the bases for reasoning to God. God's existence and active power are made known by the steady universal order of nature, not by an imagined event that would oppose this order.

Finally, a miracle essentially involving transcendence would be one that surpasses, but does not oppose, nature. Spinoza finds this meaning somewhat intractable to handle in its own terms, and hence he reduces it to a variant of the second meaning. If that which is to be surpassed refers to natured nature, then the question concerns the latter's relation to naturing nature. This is equivalent to the previous discussion of God's decrees and governance through the universal necessary laws of natured nature.

What needs now to be stressed, however, is the infinite power of the naturing principle and the unbounded fertility of law-regulated modal nature. There is no need to suppose a tinkering supplementary activity on God's part, or a shrinking of natured nature's power to the point where something else can be added that does not follow from its universal laws. Either supposition would be a denial of naturing nature's infinite power and causal immanence. And if that which is to be surpassed refers to nature as a whole, then a miracle would be above or outside of the divine actual-being of naturing nature itself. It would signify only an imaginary act that fails either to manifest God or to elicit from us a religious response.

The examination of miracle makes a special contribution to the theory of nature, since it clarifies the Spinozan meaning for *history of nature* and *narrativity*.[22] This is done by resetting miracle within scriptural narratives. It then becomes a question of how to interpret sacred Scripture. Spinoza states repeatedly that there is scarcely a difference between the method of interpreting Scripture and the method of interpreting nature. The methodological similarity is not only general (that Scripture is to be understood from within its own text and context, and nature from within itself) but also specific, namely, that each is to be approached through its own type of history. Scriptural history is a form of narrativity about what happens contingently in time and under God's decree. It is a concrete instance of how things look in the perspective of the common order of nature, where the image of divine arbitrariness, human temporality, and physical contingency prevails. Miracle stories depend on this imagery.

As a corrective, the philosopher interprets reality as known through the true, eternal order of nature. It is only by reference to this latter order that a philosophical history of nature is made and an emended form of narrativity obtained. Spinoza describes the method for achieving a history of extended natured nature. "In scrutinizing natural things, before everything we try to investigate the things most universal and common to the whole of nature, namely, motion-and-rest and their laws and rules, which nature always observes and through which it continually acts. And from these we gradually proceed to other less universal things."[23] Among these less universal things are those events which Scripture treats as miraculous. But the scriptural story of them must be translated by philosophers into the history of nature, which is regulated by necessary laws always determined by the active power of God or naturing nature.

(b) *Prophecy.* Instead of miracle, Spinoza looks to prophecy for the primary religious analogue to a philosophical healing of ignorance about oneself and God. "Prophecy or revelation is a fixed cognition of some thing revealed by God to men. Moreover, a prophet is that one who interprets the revealed things of God to those who are unable to have a fixed cognition of the things revealed by God, and hence who can only grasp revealed things by sheer faith."[24] Spinoza has no difficulty with the concept of revelation, taken as the imparting of some cognition by God. Under the attribute of thought, God gives rise to the infinite and finite modes of understanding. At the active center of every human mind, there is a germ of the idea of God and the simplest traits of nature. Since all men share in these common fundaments of cognition, Spinoza does not hesitate to affix the name of revelation or prophecy to our natural cognition as coming from God. But he concedes that this goes against the grain of ordinary usage, since most people do not prize and reflect upon their commonly shared cognitive bases (a task left to the philosopher). Instead, they look for something rare and unusual to be imparted in religious prophecy or revelation.

The prophetic character of biblical religion is essential. But it does not provide an independent basis of judging the truth or falsity of philosophical teachings on God, man, and the world. To prevent any veridically autonomous and normative use of biblical prophetic cognition, Spinoza stresses the conditioning role of prophets in conveying its meaning to the faithful.

The prophetic word of religion is determined by a twofold adaptation:

to the temperament and outlook of the individual prophet, and to the cultural situation and capacity of his particular audience.[25] He is not chosen because of an unusually perfect mind and wisdom in speculative matters, because here he may share the ignorance and prejudices of those he serves. What distinguishes the prophet is his extraordinarily vivid power of imagining, coupled with the constancy of his mind's dedication to a good and just way of living. Imagination and piety mark his own openness to divine revelation, and also mark the kind of cognition that he interprets and that others accept through faith alone.

Moreover, the mutual accommodation between prophet and people facilitates, but also limits, the cognition that springs from their encounter. It concerns their good and upright living, but not any speculative truths about God and nature or any ethical demonstrations based on such truths. Thus the faith enkindled by biblical religion leaves philosophers free, in principle if not always in fact, to conduct their own inquiries and determine the truth about the whole of nature.

Once the freedom of philosophizing is guaranteed, Spinoza readily strengthens the structure of revealed cognition within its stated limits. The two major points concern variance and certitude.

(i) Prophets may differ strongly among themselves on cultural and theoretical issues. But they achieve a basic unity on the moral description of a just and merciful God, as well as on our practical ordering of conduct along an upright and other-concerned path. Biblical religion conveys this unified moral conviction, as long as it is not converted into competing speculative orthodoxies.

(ii) It would be inappropriate to seek mathematical certitude in prophecy, since the latter rests on the prophet's vivid imagination which, taken simply by itself, does not yield certitude. But when imaginative strength is joined with something reasonable (*aliquid ratiocinium*), this complex state of mind can attain to moral certitude. ''Hence the entire prophetic certitude was based on these three points: 1. that they [the prophets] imagined revealed things most vividly, just as we in our waking state are accustomed to be affected by objects; 2. on a sign; 3. finally and principally, that they had inclined their mind to the right and good alone.''[26] In accordance with his criticism of miracles as unreasonable, Spinoza does not agree with the prophets that their cognition is really strengthened by appeal to some miraculous sign (point 2). He grants full weight, however, to the synthesis of very active imagination with a whole-hearted devotion to the just, the good, the charitable ideal (points 1 and 3). Herein consists the moral certitude of prophetic cognition and of the faith-act of believing people.

Spinoza even goes so far as to call this cognition a teaching leading people toward the true life (*vera vita*), which is the intent and substance of religious revelation. He feels safe in making this attribution, since it concerns what is useful, right, and good in our practical living, without regulating philosophical judgment on the metaphysics and ethics of nature. In several places, Spinoza also observes that the Hebrew word for *life*, taken by itself, means "true life" and signifies the fruit of understanding or true reason. Yet there is here no encroachment upon philosophy.[27] The biblical version of true life or understanding results solely from disciplining the prophet's imaginative vision by his good practical inclination, unaccompanied by any philosophical method and cognition that might similarly discipline his everyday opinions about natural reality. Biblical wisdom operates within too narrow a compass to exert valid corrective power over the philosopher's understanding and enjoyment of eternal life. A case in point is the limited frame for the biblical conception of divine law.

(c) *Law*. Spinoza acknowledges law to be another necessary component of biblical religion and any other revelational religion, such as the Islamic. It is the means whereby the prophetic word makes itself effective among the whole people formed by the religion. But in his actual treatment of law in the *Theological-Political Treatise*, Spinoza begins with the philosophical foundations and then fits in the religious conception, as a practical way of meeting some circumstances of mass thinking about man and God.[28] The philosophical truth regulates and interprets the religious accommodation, as the ordering of the discussion is intended to show.

Spinoza follows a winding path in order to reach a philosophical meaning for the divine law, in which religion is also interested. Absolutely speaking, the universal laws of nature (*leges universales naturae*) determine everything to exist and operate in a fixed and determinate pattern. But it makes good sense to say that some laws are set by human agreement and mandate. This does not weaken natural necessity, since man is a part of nature and shares in nature's necessitating power. Yet people are ignorant of the coordination and cooperation of many things bearing on their welfare, and hence must agree upon some ordinances and commands (*jussa*) for their security and comfort. In this sense, "law is nothing other than a pattern of living which men prescribe to themselves or others for some end [*finem*]."[29] When this end or aim is the protection of life and the commonwealth, there is human law. And when the aim concerns the highest good alone, or the true cognition and love of God, there is divine law.

There are three good reasons for designating the latter as the natural

divine law (*lex divina naturalis*). First, it is a modalization of the universal laws of nature insofar as they get articulated in our basic human
precept to know and love God. Second, the aim and pattern of living
involved are precisely those that direct us toward possession of divine
life, that is, toward the knowledge and love of God as our supreme good
and beatitude. Third, our knowledge of this law rises from philosophical
reflection upon the human mind and its ultimate endeavor, a reflection
employing the natural vigor of our own mind. The more we learn to
understand our mind's unity with the rest of the modal world and with
God's naturing active power, the stronger ground we have for regarding
this law of love toward God as the fundamental ethical command for us.

The law factor in biblical religion is not intended, therefore, to make up
for any intrinsic deficiency in our philosophical knowledge. Instead,
Biblical law is entirely proportioned to the limits of prophetic cognition.
It is a law that gives practical guidance to believers in scriptural prophecies and historical narratives. Biblical commandments are useful for social living, but they are not a practical expression of our comprehension of
naturing and natured nature. Hence, they do not yield, by themselves
alone, that knowledge and love of God in which our beatitude consists.
The latter comes with recognition of the natural divine law by our liberated and constant mind.

(d) *Scripture*. A sacred scripture of some sort is an essential ingredient
of revelational religion, since it supplies the lasting medium for communicating prophetic knowledge and religious laws. Spinoza is
methodologically interested in this distinctive mode of communication.
For a sacred scripture is neither a learned treatise in some science nor a
wholly undisciplined conflation of words and images. Its use of language
is governed by moral and religious imagination, with the practical aim of
disposing its readers toward worshipful obedience and service to others.
This way of disciplining and structuring human language achieves its own
integrity, which is not dissipated under philosophical inspection and
criticism.

Spinoza defends scriptural integrity within its significational structure,
just as he defends the integrity of his own written conception of nature. To
keep this analogy alive and strong is a major purpose of his hermeneutical
theory.

> Wherefore, the cognition of all these [historical narrations and prophetic
> revelations], that is, of nearly all the things that are contained in Scripture
> must be sought from Scripture itself alone, just as the cognition of nature
> [must be sought] from nature itself. What pertains to the moral lessons that

are also contained in the Bible, although they themselves can be demonstrated from common notions, however, it cannot be demonstrated from these same [common notions] that Scripture teaches them. But this can be ascertained from Scripture itself alone.[30]

The intent of Scripture has to be determined from an internal study of its aims, circumstances, and adaptations, rather than from a metaphorical reading of the text in accord with some imported theories. Even in the case of a scripture's moral teachings, they must be interpreted in the light of the particular textual context, rather than read into the scripture from mankind's general moral insights.

There must be a similar respect for the intent of a philosophical and scientific study of nature, without ascriptions that would confuse and thwart the intent. The cognition of nature must be drawn from nature's own reality and proportionate method. In accepting a difference of intent between a sacred scripture and a philosophical analysis of nature, Spinoza is not propounding a doctrine of two truths. The two intents and cognitions do not lead to a doubling of truth centers. As far as the *intents* are concerned, it remains that "faith does not require true dogmas as much as pious ones, that is, such that move the mind to obedience."[31] The doctrines or pious *dogmata* of faith can exert no correctory force, in the interest of truth, over the philosophical doctrines on nature. From the standpoint of the *cognitions* involved, the same conclusion emerges. The cognition coming from a scriptural source is intrinsically beclouded. What it says about God conveys nothing on his own essential nature, but only on the probity and charity of our human actions. The scriptural pattern of stable living is limited to this human orthopraxis. For an accurate intellectual cognition of God (*intellectualis sive accurata cognitio Dei*), an understanding of his naturing nature in itself and as the foundation for upright and concerned human conduct, we must rely upon the philosophical inquiry into nature as a whole. This alone is where the known truth of the scriptural pattern of true living manifests itself to the human mind.

4. No Handmaid Relationships.

Spinoza was ready, at last, to restate his account of biblical religion in terms most pertinent to his personal encounters and to the cognitive conventions of his age. His correspondents, Albert Burgh and Nicholas Steno, had ardently urged him to embrace a Christian philosophy.[32] But all of Spinoza's study and experience convinced him of the need to keep

faith and philosophy apart. Their separation was not to be based upon
ignorance but upon a close inspection of the internal foundation, intent,
and scope of each. Any attempt to synthesize faith and philosophy could
only result in deforming the cognitive structure of each, as well as in
hopelessly confusing any mind trying to learn the truth about God and
modal nature. Only in the weak meaning of "philosophy," as a meditative thinking about religious teachings, could there be a scriptural philosophy (whether Hebrew or Christian or Islamic) not ascribing a series of
disasters to nature. But this would be different in principle from a philosophical interpretation of nature based on nature itself, with its own
method, aim, and evidential reasoning.

In the *Theological-Political Treatise*, Spinoza addressed himself
primarily to the convention of visualizing the relationship between philosophical reason and theology as that between a handmaid (*ancilla*) and
her queen.[33] There was an elaborate spread of diverse interpretations of
this metaphor. Most of them held that philosophy performs an honorable
and valuable service of methodology, conceptual analysis, and argumentation favoring theology and that, in return, philosophical reason somehow receives strength from the orientation and themes and assurance of
theology.

The Spinozan strategy is not to pursue every particular explanation of a
handmaid relationship but to reject them all. The first move is to distinguish between two views of theology itself: as a knowledge that is both
speculative and practical, and as a purely practical cognition.

Spinoza's entire treatment of biblical religion opposes any
speculative-practical theology, taken in the strong sense of "speculative"
as meaning either the incorporation of a metaphysics or the development
of an inherent metaphysics, which would be used to intervene in philosophical discussions. An incorporated metaphysics would be detached
from an autonomous, nature-grounded cognition as its structuring
principle—the chief objection to any merging of the methods of interpreting the Bible and nature. As for an internally generated metaphysics,
Spinoza admits only two valid meanings for an element of speculation
within revealed religion: opinions that may concern any reality but that
cannot rise above the limits of prophetic cognition and its moral certitude,
and meditations on the basic religious pattern of true living. The former
remains irremediably confined to opinion making, whereas the latter is
indistinguishable from a practical theology unburdened by pretensions to
speculative knowledge.

Spinoza has no quarrel with a *practical* theology, in the sense of a reflective grasp of the fundamental religious model of upright, caring, and devout conduct. But he opposes any expansion and speculative transformation of it with the help of an ancillated philosophy. This is the gravamen of his critique against all theories viewing philosophic reason as a handmaid to theology.

The paradigm for treating this question is Spinoza's concept of *the catholic or universal faith*. The biblical message announces

> that there is a God, or a being that made all things and directs and sustains them with the highest wisdom; and that he takes supreme care of men, that is, of those who live piously and honestly. But he punishes the rest with many afflictions and separates them from the good. . . . There is a supreme being that loves justice and charity. In order to be saved, all men are bound to obey him, and to adore him through a worship [consisting] of justice and charity toward their neighbor.[34]

This declaration can be formulated into articles of a catholic faith addressed to all men. Yet it remains a simple faith, inculcating a worship of God and obedience to him that is found in our acts of justice and love toward our neighbor, where alone we can perceive and turn toward God.

Spinoza then places severe epistemological restrictions upon this scriptural credo and its practical theological explanations. They are subject to a threefold distinction between: *quod* ("that" something is); *quid* ("what" the essential definition or nature of it is); and *qua ratione* ("by what reason" the reality is thus).

(i) Theological reflection on Scripture can affirm the *quod*, that is, the reality of God's existence and infinite active power and our ties of obedience and fellow service. This existential affirmation is a direct confession, not the conclusion of an independent inference in either the everyday or the philosophical way of reasoning. Quite properly, it stands already upon the terrain of scriptural faith and serves to articulate the latter's moral certitude concerning divine and human existents.

(ii) Scriptural faith and its practical theological reflection cannot supply the *quid*, that is, an essential understanding of God and his attributes and our own manner of being. By this denial, Spinoza means something different from the view that we can know that God is but not what he is, or that we can know what God is *not* and that this serves as a substitute for a knowledge of his essence. The function of the Spinozan attribute is precisely to give us a positive philosophical knowledge of what truly constitutes God's essence. The active power of God's essence affirms itself in our mind by giving us insight into the divine essence itself. Spinoza's refusal to grant the status of nonopinionative speculative knowledge transcending mere opinion to revealed faith and its theological elaboration is a way of stating that such religious cognition does not include any essential knowledge of divine substance, attributes, and modes. Hence scriptural faith and theological pronouncements cannot, in principle, exercise any judicative authority over philosophical inquiry into this *quid* region concerned with naturing and natured nature.

(iii) Finally, we cannot look to revealed faith and its practical theology for the *qua ratione*, that is, for the grounding demonstrations about God and man. There is all-too-abundant argumentation in theology, but it does not embody Spinoza's distinctive meanings for "reason." Epistemologically, faith and theology remain proportionate to a practically disciplined imagination, never reaching the resources of cognition through nature-oriented reason and intuitive understanding. Ontologically, there is no footing taken in naturing and natured nature, and hence no comprehension of the necessary causal order and connection of beings. And ethically, this bars a grasp upon the basis for determining a human pattern of life in relation to God and the universe. Taken together, these shortfalls mean that the foundation is lacking for demonstrative reasons concerning the interconnections which comprise the heart of a revelational kerygma.

Yet Spinoza's intent is not to annihilate Scripture and practical theology, which do retain their partial purifying value against undisciplined living, atheism, and skepticism. Rather, the separation of philosophy from faith and theology is just a negative step toward achieving the main aim of the *Theological-Political Treatise,* namely, the freedom of philosophizing. For in marking the cognitive limits of the commitment to faith, we also recognize the positive domain of free philosophical inquiry. This includes a different approach to the above-mentioned *quod* question about God's existence and man's ethical liberation. For Spinoza agrees with theologians that there is no reason why something should not be revealed and also philosophically established, granted the difference and mutual nonsubordination among the respective uses of intelligence.

Philosophical freedom is most striking in regard to the field of *quid* and *qua ratione*.

> What [*quid*] God or that model of the true life is, that is, whether he is fire, spirit, light, thought, and so on, that [matters] nothing to faith; just as also [it matters] not by what reason [*qua ratione*] he is the model of the true life, that is, whether because he has a just and merciful mind, or because all things are and act through him, and consequently we also understand through him and see through him that which [*id quod*] is true, equitable, and good. Whatever each individual has decided on these topics is similarly [nothing to faith].[35]

It is left for philosophy to reason about God's nature, the sense in which things proceed from him by decree or by the necessity of his nature, and the way in which we find our knowledge and freedom and life in him. What we think on these questions is neither indifferent nor beyond the scope of philosophy to determine, since it supplies the method and bases in nature for reaching the truth about them.

I have spoken about handmaid relationships in the plural. Spinoza does not want scriptural faith and its theology to be ancillated to philosophy any more than he wants philosophy to serve as handmaid to revealed faith and its practical theology. The merging of these different bases, cognitions, and methods of interpretation would only destroy the integrity of all the proposed components. Hence a mutual abandonment of the handmaid metaphor and its rationale is a condition for sound faith and philosophical knowledge alike.

To prevent any integration and intrinsic connection of the two, Spinoza states flatly that "between faith or theology and philosophy there is no intercourse and no affinity."[36] People of faith and practical theology should not adopt philosophical concepts and arguments as means of explanation and defense. And although philosophers should carefully study scriptural history, language, and credal convictions, they must keep their own assent disengaged as far as truth claims are concerned. The judgment about the moral certitude of prophetic faith is neither identical with, nor derived from, that certitude of speculative truth which belongs only to philosophy. It is best for all parties concerned to disown the confusing dreams and figments generated by ancillation from either side.

Yet Spinoza does not, and indeed cannot, permit his last word on revelational religion to be negative. His critical objective is to show that the elements of biblical religion—its miracle narrative, prophecies, laws, and scriptural expression—do not breach the unity of nature or the philosophically established account of naturing and natured nature. Once this is accomplished, he must reckon with the fact that his own freedom of philosophizing does not ignore religion but finds a function for it (as distinct from scriptural faith and its theology) within his conception of man in nature. As the earlier sections of the present chapter show, the method of interpreting nature from within nature alone includes a developed theory of religion, piety, and firmness of mind. They help to strengthen and guide our conatus in its drive after steadfastness and mutual help, the union of love toward God and beatitude. This philosophical affirmation of a religious attitude does not water down the principle of "no intercourse and no affinity" between philosophy and scriptural faith or theology, but it does rule out an essential hostility between sage and saint.

Spinoza therefore avoids the dilemma of either handmaid service or hostility as characterizing the relation between revealed faith's practical theology and philosophical reason. Instead, he encourages "each to maintain its domain with supreme harmony [*concordia*]."[37] What keeps this from being just a trite irenic declaration is the threefold way in which Spinoza specifies their concord which is yet no accommodation.

First, the revelational-theological domain has a cognitive structure of its own that does not dissolve under rational inspection. Prophetic faith has a hardiness and rightness about the goals of human living that Spinoza cannot deny. Hence, he often speaks conjunctively about philosophers-and-others, to indicate that the prophets and Christ have a conception of God and man irreducible to, yet in harmony with, the reasoned truth and intellectual intuition of philosophers.[38]

A case in point is the assurance of revealed religion that men can be saved and made blessed solely through obedience to God's word, that is, through acts of faith and piety not dependent upon an understanding of natural things. Since philosophical reason does depend upon the latter understanding and proportions all our knowledge of God and our beatitude to it, Spinoza observes that philosophy cannot strictly show the truth of this religious conviction. Prophets have a singular power above the ordinary, insofar as they proclaim something not perceived by them from the definition of human nature. Spinoza does not hesitate to comment: "But if there were someone who had another means of perceiving and other foundations of cognition, he might indeed transcend the limits of human nature."[39] Such a cognition would not be an absolute transcendence of nature as a whole, however, or even of the infinite modes constitutive of human nature. It would be precisely an unusually strong influx from the infinite mode of understanding, yet an influx that would remain clouded and distinct from the philosopher's knowledge of God and modal nature.

The second consideration is that the revealed word has the power to illuminate minds which remain impervious to philosophical reasoning. Most people cannot develop the habit of virtue, the pattern of true living, through the guidance of reason alone. But they can listen to the message of faith, grasp and obey it, and thus attain human salvation. This leads Spinoza to affirm explicitly the necessity and usefulness of Sacred Scripture, which brings "a very great consolation to mortals."[40] Scripture cannot make philosophers out of the mass of mankind. But it does remove the doubt of philosophers about whether people lacking a philosophical method of inquiry can nevertheless attain salvation and blessedness. Spinoza's own sympathetic respect for the religious practices of ordinary people is grounded in such considerations rather than in a convenient hypocrisy.

Last, he pinpoints one revelational topic that readily provokes a different sort of reflection, adumbrating his own philosophical view of nature's power and the blessed life. In a remarkable Note added to the *Theological-Political Treatise*, Spinoza draws out the following consequence of his analysis of biblical commandments.

> We have shown that divine commandments appear to us as commandments or statutes only as long as we are ignorant of their cause. But when this is known, they cease thereupon to be commandments, and we embrace them as eternal truths, not as commandments. That is, obedience is thereupon transformed [*transit;* French: *se convertit*] into love, which springs from true cognition just as necessarily as light from the sun.[41]

This text is a masterly compression of Spinoza's thoughts on revelational religion and philosophy.

Within the revelational context, God's will is the central reality. He is viewed as a king issuing laws as commandments for us to obey. But those who share Spinoza's philosophical doctrine on naturing nature, or the divine substance and attributes, do not ascribe will to God. They know philosophically that God acts from the necessity of his nature and that the patterns of being and action in natured nature are eternal truths, expressive of the necessary divine power. Such knowledge of the true causal relation between naturing and natured nature gives rise necessarily to our love toward God.

In the ethical order, this involves a transformational process. What were regarded by veiled revelational faith as commandments for our obedience are now clearly known as eternal truths for our love. The transvaluation does not come from revealed religion but from philosophical understanding of total nature. Hence there is no real ancillation or exchange, but there is a harmony between the two cognitions. And the entire relationship constitutes a specific instance of Spinoza's philosophical meaning for rebirth as a human loving response to the truth about the mind's union with nature in its fullness.

CHAPTER EIGHT

Nature as Community of Communities

AT THE TIME OF HIS DEATH IN 1677, Spinoza was still working on his *Political Treatise*. He had done about two-thirds of the planned work, but had written out only a few paragraphs of the final and culminating part on democracy. Political philosophers have tried to compensate for the fragmentary character of this last part by piecing together his remarks made elsewhere on the democratic form of government, and by drawing out some implications. But the lack of Spinoza's own systematic completion has been felt beyond the confines of political philosophy, since his general principles were involved and the other portions of his thought were getting modified in the course of his political reasoning.

The present chapter does not seek to round out that reasoning but rather to consider the broader context within which he conducts his actual investigations of social life and political problems. These treatments have their own specificity but they are also guided by Spinoza's general theory of nature. In his theological-political and political studies, he makes good use of a strand of his nature theory that is woven into his other writings as well. They all contribute something to the theme of nature as community. What the *Political Treatise* does is to make this theme very explicit and concrete, compelling us to recognize its operative presence throughout his philosophy.

My primary focus here is upon some meanings of community involved in Spinoza's naturizing of method, God, and man. These meanings need no longer be kept in the background but can now be brought to the forefront and considered together. When emphasized and synthesized, they are seen to constitute a major element in the Spinozan conception of nature. Indeed, the community approach to nature helps to unify many aspects and lines of reasoning which I had to examine separately in previous chapters.

230

1. The Guiding Model

Already in the *Short Treatise,* Spinoza faced the question of how God communicates with man, a question that he continued to address in his last writings on theological-political issues.[1] The negative portions of his reply were firmly established from the outset. The broadest negation is that God does not make himself known to us through anything outside of nature. Since nature is inclusive of all reality, rather than a differentiated realm within the real, man's awareness of God does not spring from some extranatural or unreal source. But a more restricted negation is also required, owing to the appeal of revelational religion to scripture and miracle. Neither a holy writ nor external signs can properly be regarded as God's special ways of revealing himself to man. They cannot be considered as means which God uses, since they would then reduce God to an employer of instruments for achieving his purposes, a striver after ends that would satisfy his desire. This summons all the objections Spinoza has raised against thinking about God in terms of final cause.

The nonfinalistic affirmation is that nature imparts itself only through itself to the human understanding, taken as a finite mode within nature's totality. When the distinction between naturing and natured nature is considered, then it is recognized that the naturing God imparts himself *solely through himself* to the human mind. This he does only when the human mind comes to realize its proper nature, striving, and actualization. Its act of cognizing God is the very act in which God's manifestation to man accomplishes itself. Hence, God's revealing of himself to man is to be interpreted in the same way as is God's loving of man. Just as it is insofar as man conceives a love toward God that God loves man, so it is insofar as man comes to know God through understanding that God manifests himself to man.

In the *Short Treatise,* Spinoza correlates such understanding with the process of our becoming aware of distinct orders of law governing our life. If we use our mind correctly in reflection upon the order of nature, then we come to realize that our life is governed by the eternal, ineluctably necessary power and order of naturing nature. We also know that we are subject to laws of human society or the human social form of natured nature, although the necessity here allows for some variance and hence is not absolute by itself. By meditating upon these orders of law, we gain awareness of their rooting in the two basic communities in which we participate. The kinds of law to which our actions and works must respond are themselves expressive of the communities that structure our human reality and orient its endeavor.

Spinoza states the communitarian relationship thus: "Man becomes aware of two kinds of law also in himself, I mean the man who uses his understanding well and comes to the knowledge of God. And these [two kinds of law] are caused by the community that he has with God and by the community that he has with the modes of nature, of which the one is necessary and the other not . . . so necessary."[2] In order to impress upon us the paradigmatic character of this distinction, Spinoza repeats the technical phrases "the community with God, . . . a community between God and men" (*de gemeenschap met God, . . . een gemeenschap tusschen God en de mensche*) and "the community with the modes" (*de gemeenschap met de wyzen*).

Four clarifications of the main text can be made. First, this is another clear instance where the theory of nature must include human cognition within its meaning. Such inclusion is not just a self-reference to the theorizer about nature but is a necessary element in the meaning itself under inquiry. Second, human cognition always enters as a complex process, with the consequence that the Spinozan conception of nature is always seen to be in growth and working out its several relationships. Specifically here, man is ceasing to be totally overwhelmed by the forces in physical and social nature; he is coming to realize that these forces are not the sole ones with which he is interconnected and to whose laws he must conform. Third, the condition for enlarging our community consciousness is the right use of understanding. Methodic employment of the modes of human perception leads us not only to the existence, attributes, and properties of God but also to an awareness of our own union with him. Last, we do not merely register a morally indifferent fact of belonging to two communities. We also establish an order between them, such that our community with God is *foundational* for our community with the modes of nature. This means that the laws caused in us by the former community express the unqualifiedly necessary conditions for our moral liberation and beatitude.

But the necessities emanating from our intermodal community are not so unequivocally beneficial to us. For we may regard ourselves as being externally determined by the rest of the modal community and, in particular, by the circumstances and conflicting aims of human social laws or commands. The danger is that, taken by itself, the doctrine of the two communities can generate a dualistic split within human consciousness and practical living. We may feel that our integrity is endangered by our community involvements now with God and now with the modes, and hence we may be tempted to keep them unrelated or even to suppress some one element.

To forestall these consequences, Spinoza speaks somewhat cumbersomely about one's growing awareness of "the community that he has with the modes of nature." Such language disposes an inquirer to rethink the community theme within the context of the main divisions of nature. This move is represented by the following figure.

2. our community with God, i.e.,
   with naturing nature

1. the community of communities,
   i.e., nature as a whole

3. our community with the modes,
   i.e., with natured nature:
   (a) between human and nonhuman
       modes
   (b) interhuman modes

Our knowledge of every component here benefits from this comparison. It advances the theory of nature, while it also knits more closely together the several senses of community.

(1) The community approach to "nature as a whole" helps to mitigate two difficulties in Spinoza's usage. One thing he wants to avoid is an abstract kind of totalization, which would mistake our imagery and language for reality. We can rectify this by considering nature's whole as an active unification of the several communities, all of whose members are distinctive agents working in concert. Their concrete being is neither spun out of, nor dissolved by, some generic and specific notions of community. Just as the cooperation of many agencies constitutes one dynamic individual community, so does the cooperation of many such communities constitute one dynamic individual community, or the community of communities. This concretion is an emended way of signifying nature as a whole. Hence, Spinoza often speaks of our conjoint union with God and with the modes as a unity of all, held together by God's immanent workings in all. This surcommunity is that sort of actuality which requires its composing communities to remain real and operative, each in its own fashion and all converging together. Here is the very broadest meaning of "thing" (thing 5), which does not erase or demote the beingness proper to each agency in the full community of substance and its modes.

The second advantage of the association is to unify the several ways in which Spinoza refers to "nature as a whole." Sometimes, he means the synergic unity of the infinite and finite modes of extension; sometimes, that of the infinite and finite modes of thought correlated with those of extension; sometimes, the whole company of modes caused by God's infinite power; and often, the oneness of modes (whether taken all together or with special reference to the human mind and the infinite mode of understanding) with divine substance. The community of communities draws together these respective meanings, which are not discrete but converge in the unrestricted sense of total nature.

Hence I employ "community of communities" to designate Spinoza's way of conceiving the one and the many. Each community involves the harmonizing operations of many actually existing beings; and all communities join actively together in the unity of the comprehensive whole of nature. Keeping this communal tension alive and effective in our lives is the way to become wise and wisely happy in union with nature.

(2) In discussing our community with God, it is useful to emphasize the word *our*. This is a concise way to capture an important implication of Spinoza's phrase *a community between God and men*. One's self-awareness of the law of God is also an awareness that a human individual's relation with God is not isolated but is shared with other people, in principle as well as in fact, for the mutual enhancement of their lives. The biblical imagery of God's covenant with his people signifies that a socially constituted group, not just myself alone, enters into unity with God. Hence, it is accurate for Spinoza to speak in the plural about God's community with men. God is the sole substance, but no one man can perfectly realize the infinite mode of understanding and its agreement with the pattern of motion-and-rest. There is an essentially communitarian quality about nature viewed as involving the human bond with God.

When we specify that our relationship is with naturing nature, we add a further precision. It helps us to make a balanced interpretation of two statements recurring in Spinoza's letters and treatises: that he cannot separate God and men as do other philosophers, and that he specially avoids conceiving of God as a magnified or perfect man.[3] The community term *between* guards against these extremes. Naturing nature's necessary causal activity establishes an eternal order of union with natured beings, specifically here with men. Our mind can reflectively affirm this eternal, unifying causation and thematize it as a nonseparative community with God. Simultaneously, our reflective consideration sees that this social tie would be destroyed, were its naturing principle transformed somehow into an eminent part of natured nature itself. However exalted, God would then be lacking in the sufficiency and power required for immanent causal expression throughout the modal universe. Thus the key word *between* helps us to do justice to everything involved in the naturing-natured relationship.

(3) Spinoza also asks each of us to meditate upon ''the community that he has with the modes of nature.'' This seems to be the most obvious meaning for both nature and community. We become aware of ourselves only as we become aware of our body and the influences of other bodily things affecting it. Their deep penetration into us invites us to make a deep penetration into them. This journey into modal realities leads us to distinguish three meanings of the intramodal community that gradually become more restricted in denotation.

Broadest in signification is *the community of natured nature*. This comprises the entire universe of modal realities that express God's infinite essence and power, considered under all the divine attributes together. At least in principle, it includes more than the infinite and finite modes of understanding and motion-and-rest, since the divine essence is not restricted in actuality and causation to the attributes of thought and extension. When Spinoza is challenged about whether we could know other divine attributes, correlated with the infinite mode of understanding, his primary concern is to defend the interconnectedness of whatever modal things exist in nature. At stake is the community bond joining all modes caused by the unique divine substance.

Next, there is (3a) *the human-and-nonhuman community* constituted by our experienced world of various sorts of composites, made up of bodies and their proportionate ideas. It is here that our lives are affected by physical forces and that we strive to move from passional bondage to a measure of active power and virtue. Spinoza conceives the attendant problems as a passage from viewing our worldly community in a temporal pattern to viewing it under an eternal one. The latter framework is the eternal order of nature, within which we struggle to organize a morally perfective way of acting that insures our well-being.

The most closely focused point is (3b) *the interhuman community*. Ideally, our social and political relations would be governed by the moral virtues constituting a wise and happy life. But people do not always respond affirmatively to the reasonable vision of moral action and social concord. From their disagreements arise divergent notions of political power and the state, leading to policies that tear apart human societies both internally and between each other. Many of Spinoza's ethical, theological, and political investigations are directed toward elucidating the factors that disrupt or strengthen natured nature, considered as an interhuman community.

The process of distinguishing all these meanings of community could easily lead to a counterproductive fragmentation of the very reality being studied. Confronted with this danger, we can better appreciate the synthesizing function of the general theme of the community of communities. Founded as it is upon the actuality of nature as a whole, it marks the recovery of unity amid the pluralism of communites. Our mind is strengthened by working out the various forms of community, but our reflective comprehension of them depends upon synthesizing these forms into an awareness of total nature's communitarian life. The truth about communities lies ultimately in an active affirmation of their own interconnectedness within total nature.

Spinoza's treatment of community also supplies him with a fresh approach to his recurrent theme of the analogy of nature. There is both internal differentiation and likeness among the several communities in nature. As our awareness grows concerning our own community involvements, we learn both to distinguish the various interconnections and to keep them related with each other. A community interpretation of the analogy of nature (to which we belong and about which we become sufficiently reflective to guide our judgments and discourse) enables Spinoza to criticize anew the defects in two other types of analogy.

One is the way of eminence, where the main stress is placed upon finding a more exalted meaning for terms used about ourselves. When we make an eminent use of such terms in constructing a theory about God, the unavoidable outcome is a theory on God as a projected ideal form of humanity. But the community approach always retains the intrinsic difference between substance and modes in their naturing-natured connection, and always abstains from applying to God the terms proper to an analysis of intermodal communities. For example, Spinoza refuses to imagine God as a judge or king, since these designations belong to the study of human political community.

The other criticized method of analogy is Bacon's interpretation of the universe after the likeness of his own nature. We have already seen that this involves a question of order: whether philosophical inquiry should begin with the Baconian man, the Cartesian self, or the Spinozan conception of God. But there is also an underlying question of community. Within philosophy, Bacon correlates man with the physical universe. Effectively, he examines only the components in the community that we have with the modes of natured nature, leaving to theology a study of our community with God. Descartes does want to extend philosophical reasoning to our community with naturing nature. But his method of doubt isolates the self from the human/nonhuman community affirmed by our bodily existence. Spinoza's way is to reflect upon our twofold community awareness: that of union with naturing nature and that of union with the modes of natured nature, both human and nonhuman. There is no alienation between these forms of awareness, since they articulate the truth of the community of communities, or of nature as a whole. Only as thus regulated by the full guiding model of community can analogical inquiry into nature remove anthropomorphism and skepticism alike.

2. Shaping Our Community Intent

The roots of Spinoza's ethical and political approach to community are sunk deeply into the soil of the *Emendation,* which furnishes logical rules for clarifying and guiding the major intents of our mind. That one of these aims is to strengthen human society is not immediately apparent, however, from the opening lines of that treatise. There, the individual searcher after happiness pits himself against the crowd and its ordinary sources of satisfaction. His responsibility for finding a new basis and ordering of life is stated emphatically in first-person terms. *I* must criticize the pursuit of perishable goals; *I* have to reflect on the perils attached to abandoning them; it is *my* own responsibility to reduce them to the status of controlled means and to seek *my* unmingled joy in the love toward something infinite and eternal. Thus cognitive and moral renovation seems dependent solely upon what Rousseau will later call the solitary walker's reveries, his individual reflection and resolve to attain the true good.

But as Spinoza proceeds from the play of aspiration to the sobering inventory of resources and the labor of execution, he makes a marked shift in perspective and language. His analysis widens from the individual to the human mind more generally considered. The crucial modifier now is *human,* used in both a cautionary and an encouraging sense. Just as even the most acute inquirer is subject to our common human weakness, so also does he gain confidence from recognizing that his happiness centers upon the supreme human perfection open in principle to others. The *we*-form of discourse asserts itself as the appropriate way for Spinoza to discuss the jointly sought target of human striving. "In a word, all our operations, together with our thoughts, must be directed toward this end" of becoming nourished by eternal actuality.[4] The usage of *our* is neither regal nor editorial, but signals an opening up to the community quality of a search after human well-being.

That quality comes to the forefront, once Spinoza identifies the goal of true philosophizing to be the cognition of the union which the mind has with nature as a whole. It is not enough to acknowledge this aim in an abstract and speculative way. One must also work to develop a disposition or character for ordaining everything else in one's life toward permanent possession and enjoyment of such cognition. Spinoza now specifies that there is an essentially social aspect of the manner in which one seeks to attain this frame of mind.

> Moreover, the highest good is to arrive at it in such a way that he might enjoy such a character along with other individuals, if it can be done. . . . This then is the end toward which I tend, namely, to acquire such a character and to endeavor that many may acquire it with me. That is, it belongs also to my happiness to give aid in order that many others may understand the same as I do, so that their understanding and desire may agree entirely with my understanding and desire. In order that this be done, it is necessary [Dutch: first of all] to understand as much of nature as suffices for acquiring such a character [*talem naturam*]; then to form such a society [*talem societatem*] as is to be desired so that the greatest number may arrive at it [that end] as easily and securely as possible.[5]

Since these lines belong in the section probably intended by Spinoza to serve as an introduction to his entire philosophy, they have general import for all parts of his treatment of nature.

Several of his prime concerns are expressed in the quoted passage. (a) Granted that something is called good because of my desire for it and not conversely, yet the mere act of desiring does not entitle me to call it the highest good and unqualified end. Even when what I seek is to establish the stable pattern or character of cognizing the mind's union with total nature, I must take into account the manner in which I go about this task. The phrase *in such a way that* indicates that not just any approach will do, that some ethical qualifications are placed upon how I go about stabilizing my cognitive grasp of the mind-and-nature union. And the phrases *this then is the end* and *it belongs also* reinforce the position that the qualifying notes are essential to the very conception of my highest good, not external circumstances added as an afterthought.

(b) The requirement is that I keep my peak frame of mind open in principle to others. This shareability is not just a theoretical point but a practical task. The verbs *tend, endeavor,* and *give aid* not only underline the strenuous praxis of trying to share but also associate it with my own conatus or basic striving. Unless I do honor the coacquisition rule in practice, I cannot develop that human character which will secure my own power, well-being, and enjoyment of nature. Hence "my happiness" depends essentially upon actually aiding others in a communal effort.

(c) The others in question are "other individuals," human agents engaged in developing "their understanding and desire." Desire is a basic passion denominating the conscious appetite, the conatus of the whole man considered compoundly in his mind and body. The other individuals are human beings, endeavoring to heal and improve their finite understanding and to satisfy their desire for happiness. Hence, the community directly under consideration is the interhuman community. This controls the significance of the correlative terms *I* and *other individuals, my* and *their*. It is toward the building up of the interhuman community designated by these terms that a man of moral power lends the strength and influence of his character. Out of the sought-after agreement of understanding and desire among the members comes a proportional realization of the happy life among men on earth.

(d) But Spinoza is careful not to allow this community intent to dissipate itself in utopian dreaming. For this reason, he employs a series of cautionary phrases to modify the intent of sharing with others. That intent is subject to the practical proviso "if it can be done." The individual's other-regarding efforts are directed toward *many, many others,* and *the greatest number*. Such qualifiers are necessary in view of the conditions to which all relationships among human individuals are subject. Because of their complex nature, these individuals have three basic modes of cognizing that get blended and ordered in various ways. There is also a proportionate ordering among their passions and in their passage toward actional power. The distinctive being of each one's conatus realizes itself through its own blending and developing of these factors. In pursuing my community intent, therefore, I cannot blind myself to these individual differences which specify the varying ability of other humans to acknowledge my helpfulness and to work together for the mutual enhancement of our lives.

(e) Even the agent who intends the best can become discouraged and disoriented by the cross-purposes of a crowd. Hence, toward the end of our text Spinoza states what does lie within our power for improving human communities. His program is condensed in the pairing of *talis natura* and *talis societas*. We have to move along the two fronts of improving our understanding of nature so as to generate a firm character fixed upon the kinds of communities within the community of nature, and of forming that sort of society within which these communal ties will be known, safeguarded, and always broadened in participation. The refinement introduced by the Dutch text signifies that "first of all" I must strive after the requisite knowledge of nature, so that I am not a cistern for which claims have been made exceeding its capacity, promising more knowledge of things than I can deliver. The societal requirement recognizes that agreement in understanding and desire requires stable conditions for communication and interaction. We can regard the *Emendation*, the *Ethics*, and the two political treatises as Spinoza's own good-faith efforts at laying the philosophical foundations for that shared agreement in understanding and desire toward which his conatus and reflection impel him.

(f) Last, we should not overlook the function of the adverbial phrase *as easily and securely as possible*, which modifies the precept "to form such a society." The modifier points up realistically the tension between our reflective *surety* about that true knowledge of nature leading to a stable character and our constant *struggle* to improve the practical conditions favoring this pattern of life and its broad participation by members of a society. We have to strive unremittingly to improve any given social structure, so that it will increase the yield of a safe and encouraging public order.

The criteria of harmony and security in social existence then prompt Spinoza to make inventory of those auxiliary sciences that enable us to meet the requirements and hence that must be incorporated into his fully developed philosophy. As Spinoza the lens-grinder insists, mechanics or technology belong here, because it lessens the hardships and contributes much toward our comfort and effective use of materials. Similarly, medicine (the life sciences) enables us to preserve or recover the health required to pursue the great end of knowing and living in accord with nature. Just as knowledge of oneself and nature rests upon our understanding of the causal influence of the bodily world upon the modifications of our own body, so does the interhuman community develop within the broader human-nonhuman community of the modes comprising our universe. Technology and the life sciences facilitate our living and working in a physical milieu that is often harsh and threatening to our social existence. Spinoza also includes the human disciplines of moral philosophy (practical rules and patterns for fostering mutually helpful actions) and pedagogy or a doctrine on the education of young people. They serve to strengthen, from within, the communal ties among human beings. A good political order is one where these four sciences can freely flourish for a safer, more harmonious way of living together within our world.

Time and cooperative growth manifest their values more forcefully in the Spinozan study of community resources than might be expected from the general contrast between durational and eternal views of nature as a whole. The four disciplines cited depend on a long historical tradition of intellectual work, involving the contributions of many minds over many ages.[6] All this would be lost labor, moreover, were it not for the educational transmission of the human heritage and of methods for reforming and advancing it. Spinoza himself shares, although not always happily, in the enduring effort of education. His tutoring activity at Leiden and his constant engagement in small study circles are experiential sources of his recognition of the need for methodical, critically oriented interactivity of teacher and students. Even his refusal of a university post at Heidelberg rises from his high valuation of the freedom of teaching, which has to be explicitly safeguarded against all theologico-political encroachments upon the educational mode of bettering the human community. From this latter perspective, Spinoza's treatises and correspondence are themselves educative acts contributing to the commonwealth of learning, and doing so despite the hostile reception of his ideas on nature and God, religion and the state.

An intent to foster communities pervades Spinoza's thoughts on emending the understanding. That significance shines through several of his distinctive positions, even when it is not given special emphasis.

At the most comprehensive level, his entire anatomy of error and rules for its cure would be pointless without a community presupposition applying to us all. We are, all of us, in the condition of limited expressions of the infinite understanding, and hence of having the cognitive complexity of imaginative, rational, and intuitive knowledge. Our finitude and cognitive complexity underlie human error, but they also provide grounds for recognizing the causes of error and adopting corrective rules leading to truth. Because we share the grounds in common, we can in principle share likewise in a perception of the corrective rules and a discipline of adhering to them in our judgment and reasoning. The method for understanding and enjoying nature is essentially communicable and cooperatively employed. Spinoza does not underestimate the difficulty of following the path of intellectual reform and the rarity of pursuing it to its terminus in philosophical truth. But neither does he deny the promptings for reform in every human mind and hence his own correlative duty of offering a therapy unrestricted in its invitation, even though individuals and

societies may be blocked by prejudice and passion from following its full
regimen.

The theme of the three purifiers of our understanding also has a community import. The Bible, mathematics, and mechanics encourage intellectual reform only because they are joint achievements of many people
and because their communicative aim is to break through our provincial
separations. The factual operation of these purifiers reaches only a relatively small portion of the human race. But they themselves are essentially structured to help everyone become aware of widespread prejudices
and thus, at least in principle, to be prepared for some sound cognition of
things.

When Spinoza moves from remote preparation to actual acceptance of
his philosophic method, he again uses the community intent to specify the
best order of philosophizing. It must be such as will enable us to know
exactly the proportion between the nature of things and our nature. The
binary relation of *natura rerum* and *natura nostra* defines the purpose of
philosophical inquiry and hence the rule by which to discern the best kind
of cognition and the best method for attaining it. From the standpoint of
that which is to be known, the inquirer correlates a knowledge of the rest
of nature with an interhuman knowledge of "our nature," "our power of
understanding," and "our mind."[7] Thus, in seeking to know oneself and
one's powers, one avoids the Cartesian and the skeptical predicaments by
always further specifying the epistemic goal through the reality and language of community--both on the part of other things in nature and on the
part of ourselves as reflecting upon them. Together, these referents belong to the society of modal nature, which philosophers understand in the
light of the idea of naturing nature as this society's eternally active source
and ground of unity. Insofar as human individuals allow their minds to be
directed by the formality of total nature, they share in the philosophical
knowledge of its many communitarian meanings.

The linchpin holding together these meanings is *the infinite understanding*. It is the immediate living expression of God considered under
the attribute of thought, and its life is to conceive the idea of God known
in his unrestricted actuality and activity. To know God in his actuous
essence is also to know the communal principle of the eternal order of
nature. For we grasp him as the immanent cause of all things and actions
in the entirety of modal nature, including our world of bodies and their
ideas. We can reflect upon the inclusion of our own reality as a complex
unity of the individual human body and its proportionate idea, the human
mind or finite understanding. Our understanding gets emendated in the

degree that it becomes reflectively aware of our inclusion within modal nature, our power of sharing finitely in the knowledge and love toward God, and hence our belongingness within the whole of nature. A sense of such social belongingness is the soul of every epistemic community meaning, just as the naturing-and-natured totality is the basis for every sort of metaphysical and ethical community within which humans are incorporated. Spinoza holds tenaciously to the doctrine of the infinite understanding, because it is so essential to forming and maintaining the community intent in all our inquiries and actions.

Finally, this societal intent is clarified by Spinoza's two uses of the term *common*.[8] The first usage is *common notions,* an account of which Spinoza furnishes in the *Emendation* and the *Ethics.* Since the human mind has or, rather, is a true idea, it actively forms (efforms) sound primary ideas of the basic reality of the common traits of all bodies. These ideas are common notions: (a) as expressing the primary traits of bodily nature; (b) as being jointly shared by all who have a complex human nature including mind and body; and (c) as enabling the human understanding to reflect upon itself, upon modal nature as a whole, and upon the divine naturing nature whose causal power expresses itself in all modal things. Hence, the common notions truly affirm the primary elements of reality that establish the community of total nature. Because these notions signify the actual causal principles of nature, they bear an essentially interconnective communitarian meaning. Their generality arises from naturing nature's self-affirmation and its all-pervasive causal efficacy in our modal world and throughout natured nature. The common notions get stated in true definitions, which regulate all philosophical inquiry into nature as a whole and to which all axioms and postulates are subordinate in properly conducted reasoning. Upon the distinctive commonality and generalizing scope of these notions rests the Spinozan reasoning about our community ties in nature.

The second usage is *common order of nature.* It refers to that view of a durational temporal unity or contingently related order of things in which our imaginative way of perception predominates. Imagination itself is not erroneous, and the human mind never completely dispenses with it. But the common order of nature is at best a story of the imagination's own structure, development, and desires. It should not be confused with the conception of the necessary order and connection in nature as a whole which reason and intuitive knowing furnish us. Nothing is more radically affected by Spinoza's distinction between the common order and the eternal order of nature than is his theory of community. All temporal and

contingent imagery of community interrelatedness must constantly submit to corrective reinterpretation through reflecting on the eternal order of
nature. Always there is a philosophical effort to transform our community
intent, so that it will better integrate with the actual causal relations and
agreements in nature. Only thus can Spinoza reach the philosophical truth
about total nature as the unifying community of communities. We humans may be able to catch only a worm's constricted look at this living
concatenation of nature, but at least the view is faithful to the way things
are and act together.

3. The Societal Motif in Ethics

The demonstrations and summary chapters comprising the latter half
of *Ethics IV* deal with two pieces of unfinished but related business. Why
does it belong to my own happiness to aid other people in their cognition
and desire? And what sort of life is proportionate to the human condition
of engaging in a constant struggle with servitude? By probing these
questions, Spinoza shows how his ethical analysis of man generates the
philosophical perspective for understanding the political community.

(1) Every Spinozan discussion of beatitude or the unalloyed happy life
contains the condition that the human mind be centered ''as much as it
can'' upon knowing and loving God. But one task of the theory of
community is to examine the other side of that condition, namely, that our
mind cannot totally transfigure itself into a knowledge and love toward
God. As long as the mind in question is human, it must also live within
the limits set by our complex human way of existing. That way of existing
involves both some durational and passional aspects and some eternal and
actional ones. The proportions differ among individuals and groups, but
always in terms of a *preponderance* rather than an exclusive presence of
just one manner of perceiving and shaping our life. For us, to exist as a
part of nature is to accept vulnerability as a constant companion of our
effort at liberation, which can change the ratio but not the mixture of
components in human character. In a word, we belong to the whole of
nature taken as the common order of nature, and we also strive toward it
considered as the eternal order of nature. The dynamic relations between
the status of servitude and the striving toward freedom supply the tensions
of moral existence.

The latter half of *Ethics IV* offers some reasons (short of beatitudinal
love directed to God) for joining company with others in order to make
our situation more liberationally humane. Spinoza appeals to everyday

experience, or the first kind of cognition, for perceiving the grounds for at least a minimal social union. Men rarely live by reason's guidance; for the most part they are envious and troublesome toward each other; yet they seldom embrace the solitary life but acknowledge their need for various interchanges with other people. Whatever the inconveniences attendant upon social relationships, "men will nevertheless discover through experience that by mutual help [*mutuo auxilio*] they can much more easily obtain for themselves those things which they need, and that only by [their] conjoined powers [*junctis viribus*] can they avoid the dangers which everywhere threaten them."[9] Thus, the very conditions of human living furnish the underlying learning experience about the need for some social ties. Without this pervasive first-level cognition, Spinoza's societal theme would not be based on considerations of human nature and could not appeal to all men in a social interdependence (one that concerns all members of the interhuman community in modal nature).

Yet there is an ever present danger that an indeterminate appeal to "conjoined powers" will result in tyrannical oppression of the individual's endeavor, rather than in the self-realization and happiness promised by "mutual help." This leads Spinoza to distinguish qualitatively among the kinds of social union. This he does by holding out an ideal for reason to use for guidance, and by characterizing very closely the kind of human association that intensifies our power, virtue, and participation in total nature.

The *reasonable social ideal* is set forth in his short chapters on right reason's pattern of living. The essential consideration is condensed into one stark sentence: "Nor can it come to be that a man not be a part of nature, and not follow its common order; but if he be engaged with such individuals who agree with the nature of the man himself, by that very fact the man's power of acting will be assisted and fostered."[10] Two points in this sentence call for a gloss.

First, Spinoza never separates his thinking about society from his theory about man in nature. Man is not only a part of natured nature but is also subject to the common order of nature. Were he not a composite finite mode of nature, he would not be exposed to other causal powers in nature. And did he not consider this exposure in the receptive and contingent fashion marking the viewpoint of nature's common order, he would not relate his social difficulties to this viewpoint. Critical reflection on the shortcomings of its imagery enables him to conceive of another way (the eternal order of nature) to regard social life and partially ameliorate its burdens on him.

Second, the reform of society and the enhancement of one's power of acting require collaboration with like-minded individuals. In a series of related arguments, Spinoza gives a technical sense to a trait ascribed to such individuals: *"they always necessarily agree in nature"* (*natura semper necessario conveniunt*) with anyone who endeavors to improve his own active power.[11] An agreement or coming together that enhances one's active role in nature is founded upon reason, as rectified and specified by a knowledge of nature's causality and order. To have one's endeavor reshaped and guided by knowledge of naturing and natured actuality fulfills the Spinozan meaning of living under the leadership of reason. The latter prompts one to desire that the highest good, or a knowledge of God, be shared by all other men as much as possible. In the degree, therefore, that the eternal and necessary order of nature animates several individuals, it brings them actively together "always [and] necessarily." There need be no fear that such social relations will extinguish the endeavoring activity which nurtures them or, at the other extreme, that they will shrivel under pressure.

It may be objected that Spinoza has opened a rift between the everyday grounds of social agreement and those based on a rarified view of nature. He has supplied the makings, however, for a methodological and anthropological response to this difficulty. The two views of social agreement are not antithetic but complementary aspects, both of which are required by man's complex being. It is the same human reality that perceives things both experientially and rationally. The latter sort of cognition corrects but does not try to expel the former. Hence, a twofold practical cognition is brought to bear upon the social meaning of conjoined powers and mutual aid. Although the two interpretations of social assistance do not always mesh smoothly, both of them help us to apprise ourselves about human sociality and to improve our ways of embodying its natural benefits.

Indeed, Spinoza goes out of his way to recognize the neediness of reason-guided people for the reinforcement supplied by the everyday social process. He portrays the morally free man as one who declines, as much as possible, to receive benefits from the ignorant (those who follow opinion alone and passional affects) with whom he lives. "I say *as much as possible.* For however ignorant men are, they are nevertheless *men* who, in [our] needs, are able to bring human help, than which nothing is preferable."[12] This is a remarkable affirmation of our common humanity, our shared needs, and the unique value of mutual human help (*humanum auxilium*).

The vigor of the infinite mode of understanding is present in us all; it is more powerful and important than all divisions raised between us; it endows the fruits of our efforts with community significance and hence prompts us to offer them to our fellow humans. As a complex, finite mode of natured nature, no human individual can entirely dispense with the society of the rest of mankind. That is why we all live together and why we all have social needs satisfiable only by others, even if these others have not been liberated by reason and actional affects. Hence, Spinoza softens his severity about declining favors by advising the free man to thank people for their help lest he seem to despise others or avariciously fear to make them a return. A humane society embraces all sorts of people and, in its multifarious interchanges, shows itself to be no elitist utopia. The social strands of our existence are important for everyone, including those who seek what is rationally most useful and virtuous.

(2) Indeed, it is precisely from the standpoint of reasonable ethical living that Spinoza is most insistent upon the need to form social ties of friendship with others. Our moral language and judgments have an essentially social import. *"Things which conduce to the common society of men, or which bring it about that men live harmoniously, are useful; and on the contrary, those which lead to discord in the state are evil."* [13] Thus moral evaluations are made in reference to what strengthens or what weakens social concord, in its contribution to our perseverance and activity. Affects that contribute toward a harmonious society are useful and hence "good," whereas those that weaken or disrupt social harmony run counter to human usefulness and hence are "evil." It is within the context of the community among interhuman modes in nature that Spinoza conducts his analysis of the ethical significance of our emotions and the endeavor to overcome servitude.

A question arises concerning how closely we should construe the above phrase *the common society of men*. Should it be taken broadly to include our communal relations with all the accessible modes of nature, or else be taken more restrictively to designate only the community of the interhuman modes of nature? Spinoza argues for the latter interpretation, in accord with his repeated dictum that human beings are morally most useful and good for each other.

He sharpens the issue by considering the relation between men and animals. (a) In the strictest sense, the conative principle of seeking what is useful to us (*nostrum utile*) bids us "to join in close relationship [*necessitudinem*] with men, but not with brutes, nor with things whose nature is different from human nature." [14] Thus, the concordant friendly society in question obtains properly only among humans. (b) However, it does not follow that the animals are unfeeling. Spinoza holds both that they do feel and that nevertheless we can use them to our own advantage, even though this does not incorporate them into the mutuality of human society. When we consult our own standard of usefulness (*nostra utilitas*) and the contribution of animals and other nonhuman modal things thereto, we are allowed "to use them at our pleasure, and to treat them just as is more agreeable to us, inasmuch as they do not agree with us in nature, and their affects are different in nature from human affects."

These two responses are governed by the Spinozan theory of the many types of community we enjoy with the modes of nature. Human society grows neither in a vacuum without other modes nor in a world where only the union among human beings constitutes a genuine community. Hence, its welfare does not require us to take either an anthropomorphic or a purely mechanistic view of other things in our world.

The Cartesian notion of beast-machine is untenable, since brutes consist of finite modes of extension or bodies, together with the ideas or souls proportionate to these bodies. Yet to acknowledge that the animals feel is not to equate their kind of conscious life with ours. Spinoza refuses to follow the skeptical strategy of reading human affective states into the animals, dilating upon the superior quality of the latter's feelings, and concluding that either there is no difference in kind between humans and animals or that any observable differences favor the quality of social life among the animals. Fabular analogies are human constructs which reflect the storyteller's ideal of social morality, but which do not erode the ontological difference made by man's reflective power and desire for union with total nature.

The specific point at issue concerns whether we can include brutes within the human society based on friendship or the close relationship among like-minded individuals. Spinoza's negative answer accords with his placement of the query. It belongs within the field of social relations in natured nature. Here, a difference prevails between human-nonhuman community relations and those that are solely interhuman. In the strict sense of sharing in the aims of rectified reason, friendship is a societal bond that is solely interhuman in scope. Even the mixed community grounded in experience and reason together consists of cognitions, desires, and actions on the part of members who, in principle, can become aware of the infinite mode of understanding and can share a knowledge of God. In its intrinsic makeup, then, the common society of men does not include our ties with the animals. Those ties do exist, but they instantiate the distinct realm of the human-and-nonhuman community. Just *how* we act reasonably in using animals and the rest of nonhuman natured nature is a special ethical issue, bound up with the proper development of human virtues. Spinoza steers a course between undisciplined empathy and equally unprincipled exploitation of that portion of modal nature which is animate and useful to us, but which is not a component in human fellowship.

In *Ethics IV,* there is a common structure present in the several passages where he leads up to the topic of the state or political society. Spinoza makes this approach through concrete descriptions of what characterizes the reasonable and free man, considered apart from any intuitive understanding of God. Anyone who conducts his life under allegiance to reason needs certain virtues to execute his desire and to be most useful to others and share life's goods with them. Chief among these social virtues are piety and religion, courage and integrity of friendship, and adherence to civil life. In my previous chapter, this confluence was examined from the standpoint of naturizing the virtue of religion. But now the confluence can be seen as leading toward political society.

In his treatment in *Ethics IV* of this latter move, Spinoza does not simply follow Machiavelli and Hobbes but seeks coherence and continuity with his own communitarian view of nature and human relations. Hence, he usually speaks carefully about man "in the natural condition" (*in statu naturali*), rather than "in the state of nature," since the adjectival form indicates that this is not a general account of nature but concerns one situation in interhuman social relations among modes of nature.[15] Moreover, "in the natural condition" signifies a complex texture woven out of the impact of the human-nonhuman community upon the interhuman. Just by itself, a resolve to follow reason's moral judgments is insufficient to secure a harmonious society. For the discordant passions of hatred, fear, and envy are strengthened by external forces in the human-nonhuman relations in modal nature. Hence, such passions have to be overmastered by the power of civil society. What we gain "in the civil condition" (*in statu civili*) is an affective force powerful enough to moderate and order, not just bare conative human individuals, but these individuals as subject to passions uncritically related to external lines of causality in the human-nonhuman complexus of communities in natured nature.

The emendation of our understanding translates itself here as the emendation of our social desires and claims. We perceive that the security and good faith required for harmonious and virtuous living come only within civil society or the state. Only here can we somehow legally determine "from common consent" or "from the consent of all" that which is just and unjust, good and evil. Men are more free when they adhere to the laws of the state than when they remain in solitude and in the contentious natural condition. Spinoza deliberately uses the comparative degree in saying that we are *more* free in civil society. The latter cannot achieve our full liberation and happiness, which depend upon the intuitive knowledge and intellectual love toward God. Hence, in the *Ethics* Spinoza sketches the transition to political society and then calls a halt to that investigation, leaving its further development to political reasoning. Whereas *Ethics V* plunges ahead into the freedom and beatitude coming from our union with God and total nature, the more detailed inquiry into civil society is left for the *Theological-Political Treatise* and the *Political Treatise*, to which we must now turn for what they add concerning community in nature.

4. The Politics of Nature

The last portion (chapters 16 through 20) of the *Theological-Political Treatise* takes up formally the foundation of the state, the extent of its sovereignty in civil and religious matters, and the inalienable freedom of thought and expression that still remains to individuals, especially in regard to religion. These chapters show how intimately Spinoza's reasoning in political philosophy is affected by his larger views on nature. On major political issues he does not hesitate to work out the consequences of positions about nature set forth in the earlier chapters and in his other writings. We are thus afforded a glimpse of the functional use of his conception of nature, as related to a particular group of vexing issues which were dangerous even to discuss at that time.

In *Ethics IV*, prominence is given to the relationship between the interhuman community and the human-nonhuman community in modal nature. Without slighting this relationship, the *Theological-Political Treatise* and *Political Treatise* nevertheless bring to the fore the practical aspects of viewing the interhuman community also in relation to the community we have with divine substance and thereby with nature as a whole. Indeed, political society reveals itself to be the locus of greatest strain between man's mixed and partitive nature and the power of total nature. This tension becomes visible when Spinoza treats of (1) natural right and the right of nature and (2) the state and the order of total nature. The treatment itself is a descriptive analysis, befitting minds accustomed to ordinary juridical and religious concepts but not impervious to philosophical reinterpretation.

(1) *Natural right and the right of nature (jus naturale* and *jus naturae).*[16] Natural right signifies the power and scope of existing and acting on the part of a natural thing. Although Spinoza begins by using his capacious term *natural thing* in order to ensure some philosophical control of the issue, he realizes that people usually think in terms of human natural right. Thus, a man's natural right is specified by, and reaches just as far as, his power and conative desire. This seems to give him limitless authorization to act, but in fact his natural right is restricted by whatever conditions are placed upon his power and its use. He does act in accord with his own power and desire, but not solely in accord with them.

Although an individual may not wish to examine or be intellectually able to examine the source of his power, Spinoza is philosophically bound to search that avenue. Man is a part of total nature, and his power of acting is itself a part of nature's total power of acting. Because he cannot rub out this partitive relationship, he cannot exercise a self-sufficient infinite power or natural right. Promethean claims do not dislodge the ordering power of naturing nature, the active order and right of nature as a whole, and the radical subordination of human natural right to them.

Hence, in the *Political Treatise,* Spinoza makes a reform more in keeping with his philosophical principles. He proposes that there are two referents for natural right: that of each individual thing *(jus naturale uniuscujusque individui)* and that of the whole of nature *(jus naturale totius naturae).*[17] The principle of existing and of perseverance in existing and acting does not come exclusively from the essence of individual natural things, but is the very power of God communicated to them. Theirs is a participated and ordinated natural right that belongs within the wider community of the natural right of nature as a whole.

Spinoza now has provided the materials for understanding his key political concept of the right of nature, or *jus naturae.*

> Therefore from the fact that the power of natural things, whereby they exist and operate, is the very power itself of God, we easily understand what the right of nature is. For because God has right to all things, and God's right is nothing other than God's power itself insofar as this is considered absolutely free, hence it follows that each natural thing has just as much right from nature as it has power for existing and operating; since the power of each natural thing, whereby it exists and operates, is nothing other than God's power itself which is absolutely free. By the right of nature, then, I understand nature's laws or rules themselves in accordance with which all things come to be, that is, the power itself of nature.[18]

With this text, Spinoza grounds the discussion of natural right upon his philosophical conception of the right of nature.

The latter involves a threefold consideration. First, the human individual having a natural right to live and exert some influence in shaping his life must be viewed, along with other natural things, as a part of natured nature. Hence, human natural right is not self-enclosed but, like every other aspect of natured nature, involves an inherently determined reference to God or naturing nature. Second, God's right of nature is proper to his naturing actuality, that is, it is the same as God's power considered as unconditionally free from any other determining causality. This establishes the identity between power and the right of nature in God, as well as their proportion in human individuals and other beings in natured nature.

The third consideration is that God's absolutely free power acts through the necessary causality of his own actuous essence (*actuosa essentia*). Thus, there is no conflict in God between the unlimited power and right of nature and the necessary causal laws governing production of all things. Since the whole of natured nature is structured by these same necessary laws and rules, it imparts them to all individual existents and their operations. For Spinoza, the empowering of human individuals is also their reason for working in accordance with nature's laws and rules. One's right of nature consists precisely in affirming one's power to share actively in the necessary order of nature.

(2) *The state and the order of total nature.* The transition from the right of nature to the state is carefully plotted in *Ethics IV* and the *Political Treatise*. In both places, Spinoza is dealing with human individuals in their everyday condition, not specially with philosophers sharing his theory of nature. People usually perceive that, in their own regard, the right of nature extends as far as their power and is not confined to the precepts of reason. But they often identify their power entirely with impulsive desires and policies shaped by forces outside themselves and in no way critically *appraised by* reason and its humane ideals. Hence, people congregate in the state as an overriding power that is stronger than their own right of nature and their conflicting affective paths. Civil laws determine a common good that enjoys the sanction of this superior social force.

Without revoking the experienced relationship between individual drives and state power, Spinoza nonetheless offers some reflections to prevent the isolating and making absolute of this relationship. He observes that the individual's desire and other affects often generate strong passions that fail to be transformed into human actions, genuinely fulfilling the capacities of our nature. The danger is that the state's constitution, laws, and policies will becloud the distinction between servitudinal passions and those other desires that lead toward human freedom or the greater actuation of our nature. It is the office of wise minds to keep this distinction uncomfortably alive and to work out its concrete bearing upon our governmental forms and social deliberations.

Spinoza pursues this issue right up to the philosophical limits of his *Political Treatise's* standpoint. The doctrine of the right of nature opens up a further avenue of inquiry. If the ultimate basis of the right of nature lies in the divine power, or in God considered as absolutely free, then in what respect does the universal power of nature work toward realizing an analogous modal freedom in our social and political life?

In response to this query, Spinoza clearly does not want to resurrect a view of man already rejected as incompatible with our inclusion in natured nature. The individual human agent does not exercise a distinct faculty of free will or establish a zone of practical choice that is unaffected by other causalities in the world. This would lead to a conception of the state and its laws as carving out an autonomous "empire-within-the-empire" of natured nature.[20] Such a model for the state remains blind to the pervasive causal operations and community ties that determine our social life and that interweave it in the general order of the modal world. It also rests on a defective notion of the divine freedom itself, as though it were an arbitrary power of decision that creates human individuals without regard for the order of total nature.

Even in political philosophy, one must recognize that this order of nature permeates both the power of God and the reason of man. Hence it breaks through the artificial cordon thrown around the state and civil laws (as well as around religion and ecclesial laws). Both divine and human freedom are correctively understood as an adherence to the necessity of one's nature, whether naturing or natured.

> For there is no doubt but that God operates with the same freedom with which he exists. Therefore, just as he exists from the necessity of his own nature, so also does he act from the necessity of his own nature, that is, he acts absolutely freely. . . . And hence I call a man entirely free insofar as he is led by reason, because to that degree he is determined toward acting by causes that can be adequately understood through his nature alone, although he is necessarily determined by them toward acting. For freedom (*as we have shown in Section 7 of this Chapter*) does not remove the necessity of acting but supposes it.[21]

The operative phrase here is *adequately understood*. With these words, Spinoza assures us that his logic and metaphysics of nature are present in full strength within his political thinking. Although men are not led solely by reason to join together in a state, their political life is not impervious to rational evaluation. That state is to be deemed more humanly satisfying which fosters the social conditions for reflecting upon our own nature, for understanding its intrinsic relations with the eternal order of nature, and for contributing thereby to a recognition of the proportion between necessity of action and human freedom within the interhuman community.

The state itself cannot properly legislate any speculative truths about mankind's role within total nature, but it can make society secure and free enough to reflect upon and discuss this role. Hence, Spinoza uses passionately libertarian language in treating the teleology of the state. "It is not, I say, the purpose of the state to change men from rational beings into beasts or machines (*bestias vel automata*). But on the contrary, [its purpose is] that their mind and body may perform their functions in safety, and that men may use their reason unhindered, and neither quarrel through hatred, anger, or deceit, nor bear mutual malice. Therefore the purpose of the state truly is freedom."[22] By this criterion of providing a climate for freedom of judgment and expression, democratic government comes closest among political forms toward satisfying our social needs and telic ideals.

Well-conducted reflection upon our nature and its endeavor will lead us to seek, within the political matrix, a freedom that surpasses the political sort. The search goes on for that highest freedom which *Ethics V* locates in our intuitive understanding and intellectual love of God, and which the *Emendation* further explicates as the mind's union with the whole of nature. Thus, instead of petering out, the community theme recoups itself in the very course of its own development. We come to recognize that community among the modes includes both interhuman society and man's sociality with the nonhuman modal world. Our reflective and endeavoring mind also learns to view all modal types of community within the eternal order of nature, and hence articulates our community with God as naturing nature. In order to bring out the immanent cohesion among all these referents, we must then interpret the mind's union with the whole of nature as a meditative participation in the community of communities.

CHAPTER NINE

A Perspective on Spinozan Nature

In one of his private notations, Kant ruminates on the attitude a philosopher should take toward the rest of the philosophical community, whether these others be his own contemporaries or great minds of the past. "Others are not apprentices, also not judges, but [are] colleagues in the grand council of human reason and have a *votum consultativum*."[1] The sanest policy is to engage in the give-and-take of a discussion group, communicating to others and receiving from others in accord with the exchanges required in a reasonable inquiry.

By anyone's count, Spinoza belongs in the grand council of human reason that represents the history of philosophy in relation to our contemporary philosophizing. What sort of consultative word does he give us to ponder? For a full answer, we would have to listen to all of his complex reasoning. Even in regard to his formal thoughts on nature, I have had to make a selection from among his problems and paths of reasoning and to accentuate them in a particular way. It remains to reformulate this emerging perspective in a manner that will show Spinoza to be offering us his counsel on some issues that continue to elicit our best reflective efforts. My procedure is of a thematic sort. Spinoza's contributions are organized here around six primary themes: cognitive model, query-response, system, telos, praxis, and community.

1. Cognitive Model

The present chapter title includes the words "Spinozan nature." At first hearing, this term has an odd and even arrogant ring to it, as though it implies that the universe itself bears the benchmark of Spinoza or that there is some equating of the universe's reality with what he says about it. However, the meaning is similar to that conveyed by the words *Cartesian nature, Newtonian nature,* and *Leibnizian nature.* There is a general

theory about nature propounded and argued by Spinoza, just as is the case
with Descartes, Newton, and Leibniz. Each one uses and transforms the
intellectual resources available to him and thus gives his own distinctive
form to philosophical thinking about nature in the seventeenth century.

It is accurate enough to include Spinoza in the tradition of philosophers
of nature, then, but only if the proper qualifiers are added. He is not a
throwback to the Milesians who gather all their reflections under the
rubric *On Nature,* but whose thoughts come to us in fragmentary form
and are not yet disciplined by Greek mathematics, mechanics, and
atomism. Yet neither is he comfortable in the company of the early
modern commentators on Aristotle's *Physics.* They hew so closely to
analysis of the definition of nature given in that great source work that
their notion of philosophy of nature remains too regional and depart-
mental. Such a discipline deals only with a portion of the real and does so
in a manner that consigns metaphysical and ethical issues to other
methods and parts of philosophy. Spinoza includes these issues intrinsically in his study of nature, but not in any reductive way that involves the
physicizing of metaphysics and ethics. His theory of nature does not
function as a basis for reduction but as the comprehensive framework
within which any more limited types of inquiry get specified and developed. The Spinozan theory of nature is itself constituted by appropriately inclusive logical, metaphysical, and ethical principles.

It is also difficult to categorize Spinoza's work as belonging to "natural
philosophy." This term symbolizes his century's painful and transitional
efforts to distinguish between the sciences of nature and the philosophy of
nature, and yet to maintain them in some sort of union. He kept abreast of
the best Dutch and British work being done in mathematics and physical
experimentation, practical statistics, and microscopy. But Spinoza held
that the reigning mechanical philosophy had its own broader presuppositions, and hence that the corresponding hypotheses and probable knowledge did not set definitive limits upon our range of investigation.[2] There
was room for other ways of looking at man and the rest of nature. His own
reflections on nature were intended not to contradict particulate and
mechanical principles but to challenge the assumption that they defined
the only legitimate knowledge of reality open to human intelligence. In
this respect, the Spinozan theory of nature is a critique of the epistemological closure sometimes claimed for natural philosophy in his age.

From Spinoza's own standpoint, explicit provision must be made for
human theorizing as a basic contribution. His doctrine about the finite
mind as a modal expression does not encourage the view that our mind

serves no more than as a passive recorder and echo of the processive activities of nature, as a merely Baconian secretary of nature's dictates. Naturing nature and the infinite understanding affirm themselves in man, but they do so through the endeavor and agency proper to man. Our moral concern to attain the power to act depends on our cognitive effort to improve the adequacy and actional range of our ideas. Spinoza has to forge his method inventively, correcting and improving his mind through gradually becoming better acquainted with himself and the rest of nature together. Because of this active correlating process, he has good grounds for regarding his concept formations and arguments as indicators of the human-theory status of his view of nature. It is an achievement of the human mind, even when it includes that mind self-referentially within the intended structures and functions of total nature.

As a linguistic means of consolidating and underlining these considerations, Spinoza uses the term *formality of nature*. It occurs in the course of his discussion of our attempt to make passage from the common order of nature to the eternal order of nature. This transition is not from one realm of things to another, but from one way of regarding the same reality of nature to another. It marks a methodical advance of the human mind toward a truer understanding of itself in relation to the active necessary causation and interordering of the beings comprising nature. To come to know things precisely in this causal interworking is to grasp them under the aspect of eternity, or in their truly known natural being. What is the formal cause of this knowledge of things in respect to their eternal relationship? Spinoza replies that the formal cause is our mind insofar as it is and reflectively grasps itself to be a necessarily generated finite mode in nature. And such knowledge apprehends the formality of nature itself, whose causal unity is founded upon the active, eternal bond between naturing and natured reality. The philosophical study of reality, thus conceived, yields the Spinozan theory of nature.

This point can be reinforced by referring to the theory as Spinoza's idea or active concept of nature. In defining idea as a concept of the mind which the mind forms because it is a thinking thing, Spinoza remarks that a concept (as distinct from a perception) expresses the mind's action. Since his theory of nature is not a passive reflection but the outcome of an intense reflecting and reasoning process, it fits his meaning of idea or concept. To stress this active meaning, I frequently call the theory Spinoza's *conception of nature*. This is a technical expression connoting the work of a philosophical mind as it seeks the truth about nature. The Spinozan theory of nature is not a static structure or closed sort of concept.

It remains essentially open both to the intellectual operation of conceiving or theory formation and to the practical employments that continue to modify and sharpen the significance of nature for Spinoza.

Within this context, it is not misleading to regard his theory of nature as *a cognitive surmodel* that incorporates a reflective act of modeling.[3] It is that sort of cognitive model which results from a method-regulated use of human intelligence and which is essentially at the service of the mind's search to know and enjoy its union with nature as a whole. Spinoza's cognitive model embodies his own logic of inquiry and action. Hence, its significance arises from an active conceiving of epistemological, ontological, and ethical factors in confluence.

Epistemologically, this model of nature functions in accord with the three modes of cognition. First, it has the aspect of an image, a guide for picturing the relations between naturing and natured reality. As rectified and guided by the model, imagination does not breed error but collaborates reliably and steadily with our intellectual activities. Next, the Spinozan model of nature is an expression of our reason, synthesizing some of its basic findings and orienting it throughout further complex argumentations. Just as the *Ethics* uses a cumulative and cross-reference procedure, so does it plot the course by relating a particular problem to the wider plan of reasoning set by the comprehensive model. And the third sort of cognition also makes an imprint upon the model and, in turn, is aided by it. For the model presents our mind with a unifying pattern that spurs us on to gain intuitive knowledge of nature as a whole. Any criticism of Spinoza on the modes of cognition radically affects, therefore, his theory about nature.

The ontological character stands forth clearly in Spinoza's surmodel of nature. Its main intent is to direct our mind toward the articulation of reality as naturing and natured. There are two safeguards against the tendency of cognitive models to impose an artificial framework. First, the division of natured nature into its general and particular phases confronts us with our human particularity in finite nature. We are not permitted to forget the problem of our starting point, since the model rests upon the reflections of the finite human mind proportioned to its own bodily involvements. A surmodel with this basis in reality calls for justification, not for imposition. Second, Spinoza refrains from freighting his surmodel with a cargo of minute specifications. There is plenty of room left for regional ontologies and their submodels. The latter are not deduced but are left for actual exploration of this or that form of natural being.

Finally, the surmodel is crafted to arouse our ethical questioning. What practical difference can be made in our lives by becoming cognizant of this view of the things in nature? Because Spinoza wants us to become thoughtful on this practical bearing, he positions his account of the sur-model just before his treatment of human passions, virtues, and beatitude (in the *Short Treatise* and *Ethics*) and reminds us of it during his social investigations of religion and politics. The pertinent consideration is that man as a singular natural thing is wholly engaged, morally as well as existentially, in the natural process. What he believes or knows about natural causations and relations shapes his passional and actional life, his community ties, and his abiding welfare. Hence, Spinoza's ethics is an integral part of his cognitive model of nature, not something appended to or contrasted with it.

2. Query and Response

It would do an injustice to Spinoza's approach to nature to treat it solely as the presentation of a model. The drawback is that a model gets detached easily from its reflective roots and takes on the appearance of an independent cognitive entity, a content proposed for acceptance apart from any preparatory work or specific arguments. But Spinoza never isolates and renders absolute his surmodel of nature. He develops it within a context of method and discussion that essentially determines both its meaning and its claim upon our assent. The Spinozan surmodel is not the fruit of an acroamatic logic that requires us only to listen to conclusions, but of an erotetic logic that engages us intimately in a process of questioning and answering.[4]

Spinoza uses the erotetic approach out of a conviction that it can improve our understanding of nature and our moral action therein. The *Emendation* rests on the premise that the human mind is reachable and reformable. It can be roused from slumberlike drift by interrogatories about fiction and error and truth, as well as about desire and frustration and satisfaction. But if the questioning is vague and disjointed, the mind thus addressed will stay confused and troubled, never rising above its impotence. Hence, a philosopher's responsibility is to work out a pattern of questions that enable the mind to assess itself truthfully and strengthen its endeavor toward happiness. The differences among philosophers arise from their various ways of patterning the dialogue.

Spinoza engages us in methodic reflection through his governing theme of *oneself and nature*. These components must be jointly investigated at every step. He does not permit the trail into oneself to break its connectives with the rest of natural reality, since this would shut off some relationships helpful to our self-understanding. Neither does he allow the inquirer to lose sight of himself in an eager investigation of the environing world. The emending force of Spinozan methodology leads the inquirer to acknowledge the direct and mutual proportion between coming to know more about the universe and more about oneself. These lines of questioning become coimplicatory as soon as they are located philosophically within natured nature, which includes both the human questioner and the world within a common reality.

But this unifying ground in natured nature is also the reason why queries and responses must be always plural in their act and structure. Spinoza cannot compress the truth about oneself and nature into a single hermetic word, but must elaborate his discourse about them in several treatises. In query-response terms, his philosophy is irreducibly pluralistic. There is no satisfactory way of reducing the issues to a single metaphor, such as that of microcosmic man and macrocosmic universe. Under scrutiny, the microcosm would be found to be exploring the world's complexities, just as the macrocosm would be found to be a matrix for man's complexities. Since Spinoza analyzes such complexities rather than conflates them, he has to employ plural queries and responses. The fact that his querying is organized under the guidance of the idea of natured nature does not dissolve the multiplicity of modes, the differences between kinds of modes, and the correlative differentiation of meanings.

Every initial query-response pattern (QR) incorporated into the Spinozan theory of nature evokes a further query-response effort (re-QR). Taking Spinoza's reflective activity as the center of reference, we can observe this involvement present in both a retrospective and a prospective way. Retrospectively, he regards the Jewish, Stoic, school-manual, and Cartesian views of God, world, and man as past reports that need to be rethought. These sources dealt with questions that are reaskable, and offered replies that incite the mind to seek different responses. The fund of previous QR work invites a re-QR initiative which opens the route for Spinoza's own philosophic work. Both tradition-forming and creativity-reforming approaches to the theme of nature characterize his *Short Treatise, Descartes' Principles, Metaphysical Thoughts,* and *Emendation.*

In the formal argumentation of the *Ethics,* the prospective side of re-QR is clearly visible. Each formulated proposition has two functions: it implies a definite query and it states a definite response. The demonstration immediately following upon the propositional statement gives reasoned support to the indicated response. In the course of reasoning, the response not only gets a backing but also becomes more explicit and determinate. When this happens, Spinoza often sees the need or the opportunity for adding another demonstration. In effect, he now moves from the first demonstrative response to a further query on the issue (re-Q), leading to another form of reasoned response (re-R). Sometimes, this new move is prompted by recognition that the initial demonstration does not fully satisfy the actual questioning on the issue, as often occurs in Spinoza's exchange of letters with a discussion group. There are also intrinsic logical grounds for the re-QR, as when a problem can be related now to more proximate prior reasoning and now to more remote considerations (perhaps in a previous part of the *Ethics*) or to more broadly based premises (i.e., direct use of definitions, axioms, and postulates).

Ultimately, the variation in QR procedure on demonstrations reflects a major point in nature theory. The real order consists of substance and the various modes, along with the actions that respectively bind naturing and natured nature together. In making inferences about this complex reality, Spinoza finds it more effective to stress one constituent or one resulting relationship in some particular demonstration and another constituent or relationship in a further demonstration.

His analysis of a problem is complicated by yet another set of factors. He must reckon with the enormous fertility of the human mind as a distinctive mode. It brings forth an abundance of constructions of imagination, reaching from images and fictions to passional attitudes. To sort these out, weigh their claim to credence, and assess their impact on individual and social behavior, humankind also develops the methods and conceptual tools of reason used in the several sciences and philosophies. In any specific demonstration, Spinoza must select among these materials for elucidating an issue and advancing our understanding of nature. Any particular selection leaves open many other ways of analyzing the issue, and hence other tries at the re-QR effort to demonstrate in accord with his own assessment of human phenomena and resources.

Thus, Spinoza's theory of nature, whether taken in its general divisions or in its account of human cognitions and passions and actions, favors the pluralization of queries and responses. If they are useful queries and truthful responses about some aspect of nature, their pluralization is perhaps a necessary means for advancing philosophical inquiry. I say "perhaps," however, in order to note a difficulty. One might take pluralization merely to mean proliferation of a scatter-shot way of raising queries and furnishing responses. The intellectual eruptions would be

lively but they would not constitute a well-ordered and developing investigation of nature. That is why the QR theme includes the problem of a
methodic clustering and sequencing of queries and responses. Since Spinoza gives so much attention to the starting point and order of human
theorizing on nature, the sequencing is fundamental for any perspective
on his philosophy. It is not just a pendant to other matters but illuminates
his way of thinking and writing.

There are both short-run sequences of questions and answers and long-
run sequences. Spinoza's practice illustrates this distinction. *Ethics II*
studies the nature and origin of the human mind. Hence the long-run
series of queries and responses concerns this topic, viewed from various
angles. But since our mind is essentially an active affirmation of the
human body, Spinoza must include here a short-run series on bodies and
the human body. Elsewhere, the nature of bodies and the human body
may become the main subject of inquiry, requiring a primary set of
queries and responses. But in *Ethics II* they are treated concisely and
instrumentally to elucidate the human mind.

Short-run sequences are regional phasings within a more sustained or
long-run sequence of queries. Both sorts retain their own specificity and
emphasis. At the same time, they have other relationships calling for still
more inclusive contexts of inquiry. Thus, the question of intra- and interrelated sequencing of QRs leads into the theme of system, which will be
separately treated.

3. System

To those who are infatuated with system building for its own sake,
Shaftesbury issues an astringent warning: "The most ingenious way of
becoming foolish is by a system."[5] This admonition applies not only to
system builders but also to interpreters who think that every instance of a
systematic philosophy results from foolish indulgence of a dream.
Against that generalization stands the experience of historical work which
advises us to examine each systematic philosophy in its own design and
effort at validation. Such examination can make good use of formal
criticism of the idea of system, classificaton and comparison of actual
types of systems, and the metaphilosophy of systems analysis.[6] But in
history of philosophy, these aids must be kept strictly subsidiary to the
study of the source philosopher's textual presentation of his own ideal of
system and his attempts to realize and confirm it.

On most issues concerning systems, Spinoza takes a position in con-

formity with his view of nature. This holds for the problems of foundation, orderly continuity, necessity, and inclusion. The relation between
theory of nature and systematicity on these four main issues is not a
one-way deduction but is reciprocal. In fashioning his conception of
nature, Spinoza keeps systematic considerations in the forefront; conversely, his systematic claims are of the sort that have to be shown to hold
for nature. This reciprocity is not surprising in a philosophy that naturizes
both method and theory. The latter are not footed somewhere apart from
nature and looking autonomously at it but are activities developing within
nature and reflecting from within itself.

Discussion about foundationalism is not alien to Spinoza's range of
interrogation. His experience of philosophical dream castles and treatises
presenting ''metaphysical thoughts'' in a rigid order is sufficiently disillu-
sioning to make him search behind every systematic facade. His study of
Descartes disposes him to expect that the search after basic warrants is
often vain. And from the skeptical quarter comes an invitation to abandon
altogether the project of seeking general truths about reality upon which
to build a truth system. Perhaps man's intellectual ability extends only to
careful description of his perceptual states and to a logic of their consequences for practical living. Spinoza's century is not so intoxicated with
systematic enterprises that it fails to offer alternatives to them in the form
of fideistic and nonfideistic skepticism, moralism, and restricted experi-
mental science.

It is in full awareness of this spectrum of viewpoints that Spinoza
persists in philosophizing with the aid of *foundations,* involving some
basic truth claims concerning natural reality. Not to philosophize in this
manner would be equivalent, in his judgment, to turning his back upon
our human intelligence in its emendative power. Basic truths about ourselves and the world do not manifest themselves effortlessly to our indo-
lent gaze. Their accessibility is not postulated upon any easy intuition of
abstract general principles, a supposition that runs in the face of the
ignorance and prejudices and conflicting opinions that abound in human
history. But that same history also includes the growth of mathematics
and mechanics, physical sciences and technology, moral maxims and
religious scriptures. They give joint testimony to the power of the human
mind to remove obstacles against understanding ourselves and the world,
as well as against acting in accord with such knowledge of nature. We
cannot remove the barriers in a flash, but we can attain some ground-
laying cognitions about reality and can forge a reliable method for improving their scope and practical effectiveness. To attain a reflective footing

and work ahead methodically—these are the human acts that are within our power and hence that shape Spinoza's idea of a foundational systematic philosophy.

He does not give an exclusively methodological and preparatory treatment of foundations. To do so would be to isolate our understanding of and assent to them from the actual uses of mind that show their operative presence, as well as from the natural things that determine their meaning. Hence, the cognition of Spinozan foundations is a disclosure process brought about in the course of reflecting upon man's role in nature. Within that context, they manifest their involvement in all our reasoning and hence their capacity to give systematic form and rigor to our philosophizing. Doubt and discussion about foundations occur because of our need to search out the latter and to emend our mixed cognition in their light.

The disclosure approach characterizes Spinoza's emendation of three meanings of foundation. First, it is a search after primary elements. This is satisfied neither by logical particles and principles (which might turn out to be only constructs of imagination or formal rules inapplicable to reality) nor by particles limited to the physical structure of the world. Spinoza suggests that we reach the primary elements of philosophy when we attain a nonabstractive cognition of the actual being of God, considered precisely as the active fount and origin of the whole of nature. Such knowledge comes when we recognize God as naturing nature and recognize ourselves as that sort of minded reality, within natured nature, which efforms or actively brings forth the idea of the naturing God. Gradually, we come to see that our meditation upon God as naturing nature is a grasp upon the philosophical fundament of the theory of nature.

A second meaning of foundation is the use of notions common to humankind. Spinoza delays his clarification until well into *Ethics II,* where he can work out some implications of God's causality of the human mind, the human body, and the corporeal world. There are some traits common to all bodily things, rather than restricted to this or that singular body. In perceiving itself and its bodily affections, its own body and other bodies, the human mind also perceives these shared traits. They function as intrinsic foundations of philosophical reasoning. The agreement within natured nature embraces both the common aspects of bodies and the common structure of our ideas about them. Talk about common notions or ideas is not empty, therefore, but can be interpreted by reference to corporeal traits and naturing nature's interrelative causation of all the finite modes of natured nature. Not the analysis of concepts and usage alone but the nature-analysis of things leads to common notions that yield true, communicable knowledge of natural reality.

In the third place, we seek a foundation for ethical inquiry. Spinoza directs us toward the same source that supplies his other two meanings for foundation: the meanings of nature's actual being or *esse*. *Primary elements* accents the originative causal aspect of naturing nature's actual-being or *esse*. *Common notions* brings out the expressive proportion between the natured structures of the bodily world and the human mind. The latter's whole *esse* is to be the idea of the human body and to express some adequate notions about oneself and bodily nature that are shareable in human reasoning. Finally, *primary and unique foundation of virtue* refers to the basic practical endeavor of every natural thing to conserve its own *esse*.[7] This endeavor is related to both other foundations, since it is the essential response of natured things to the causal life communicated by naturing nature and is that practical actional trait shared by all bodies and minded agents. Spinoza's criterion for right reasoning in ethics is recognition of this convergence among the three meanings of foundation or actual being, as present respectively in God and in our own theoretical and practical actions. The power of this foundational convergence expresses itself, therefore, in both our systematic philosophizing and our desire for the blessed life.

The systematic character of Spinoza's thought also requires an *orderly continuity* in the inferences made and the meanings thereby connected. It is by reference to this note of system that he regulates the criteria of coherence and consistency. As requirements of formal logic, they remain in full force. In criticizing other thinkers, Spinoza never hesitates to point out violations of these criteria and to defend his own doctrine against any charge of violating them. Their negative function is respected and constantly invoked.

Yet taken by themselves, consistency and coherence are not adequate to the positive task of generating the Spinozan kind of philosophical system. An appeal to them still leaves unsettled the ground for an intrinsic agreement and unification of primary meanings. This concerns the constituents of nature as a whole and the relations among them. Hence Spinoza looks for *that sort of* consistency and coherence which best expresses the traits and relationships of naturing and natured nature. Systemic reasoning gets its fundamental guidance from the structure, causal action, and interconnection which constitute the order of total nature. Only when they are reinterpreted through this orderly continuity do consistency and coherence operate within the Spinozan logic of nature. Thus they are included in the naturizing of method as a condition for their specific use in this system and its defense.

Because of the naturizing requirement, Spinoza's system is an instance of neither correspondence theory nor coherence theory. His view of truth cannot be fitted into either member of this anachronistic pair.[8] What makes the choice inapplicable is his inclusion of the human mind as a finite, reflective agency within naturating nature. Because our mind expresses naturing nature under the attribute of thought and within the modal line of understanding, it does not causally receive its ideas from physical things to which its cognition thereby corresponds. Yet neither does its cognition result from a passive reception of ideas from some chain of modes of understanding, with which it is thereby coherent. Instead, the human mind must become aware of its own naturality, its own active power and relationships within nature as a whole. That is why Spinoza equates a true idea with active reflection, as shaped by naturized method.

The human mind works emendationally and systematically toward conceiving the formality of nature in its eternal order. By understanding its own modal reality and action within this order, the mind achieves congruent expression of truth and virtuous living alike. Spinoza aims at a philosophical system whose truth consists in affirming the *esse* and interrelation of the whole of nature. To prevent systematicity from becoming a fantastic and misleading ideal, he balances this noetic goal with a realistic acknowledgment of our intellectual limits and our residual struggle with conditions of servitude.

Spinoza's position on coherence, consistency, and truth determines the sense in which he meets the requirement of orderly continuity in a philosophical system. In the *Ethics,* the visible sign of orderly continuity is furnished by the corollaries, scholia, and explanatory additions to the propositions, as well as by the prefaces and appendices to the parts. A particular proposition might be construed as a discrete atomic statement, were it not for its attendant corollaries, scholia, and explanations. Their function is to serve notice that, although the demonstrated proposition is definite, it is not established in isolation but carries along a further reach of meaning. Its latent implications have to be explicated. Its thrusting quality has to be explored and its forward momentum followed up, so that the inferential process can move ahead into the next proposition. Similarly, but on a macroscale, the prefaces and appendices achieve closer continuity among the parts by making broad reflections upon issues that span the primary divisions of the *Ethics*.

Another essential mark of philosophical system is *necessity.* Not every sort of necessitated thinking leads to a valid doctrine about necessity. Spinoza criticizes those uses of our mind that are governed by the tyranny of individual and social custom, rather than by reflective method. The latter dissolves our enslavement to fate, which is the belief that human thought and conduct are shaped wholly by external causes acting upon us. Our liberation does not come from an equally imaginary and self-estranging belief in contingency, but from a knowledge of that sort of necessary natural causality that empowers us to perceive our own resources and act in accord with them. Our resources consist in our active participation in the power and order of nature, as expressing itself in and through human modal reality. The Spinozan phrase *God insofar as* is a way of systematically conceiving and stating our ability to develop adequate cognition and action through affirming the divine order of nature in our lives.

Hence, the system-generative meaning of necessity sought by Spinoza springs from methodic reflection upon the eternal order of nature, considered as a communication of active power from naturing to natured-and-naturating agents. He measures every theory of freedom by the standard of whether or not it accords with this notion of the necessity of nature. Divine freedom would be destructive of systemic values, were it not understood to be an uncoerced and spontaneous welling forth of the causal power of naturing nature. And human freedom would be similarly disruptive if it consisted in disconnecting ourselves from the natured order and carving out a separate realm. At stake in both instances is the integrity not only of natural causation but also of systematic inference.

There is question of whether Spinoza's emphasis on necessity discourages work in the logic of modality.[9] It need not have this inhibiting effect upon formal research into modality. Spinoza himself distinguishes various logical meanings of possibility, actuality, and necessity in order to mount his own critique and determine which meanings harmonize with his conception of the order of nature. When an ontological claim is made for the results obtained in any particular modal logic, the claim is adjudicated by reference to the distinction between the common and the eternal order of nature. As long as ontological imagery does not ignore or blur this distinction at the point where a reality assertion is made, a modal logic can be elaborated without hindrance from Spinoza's position. His own theory of fictional constructs, counterfactuals, and hypotheses trims back the ontological excesses without restricting the logical study of modality.

Finally, philosophical system concerns itself with *inclusion* or scope. The Spinozan style here is to mingle the intellectually ambitious with the modest. At first glance, the theme of philosophizing about nature as a whole has an inflated appearance. Yet Spinoza qualifies it with several safeguards against foolish claims. He is no universal encyclopaedist but recognizes the need for many disciplines not identical with his theory of nature, although harmonizing with it. Furthermore, he submits the concepts of whole and part to criticism before treating of total nature or nature as a whole. He does not seek a totalizing or all-encompassing generalization based on transcendental and universal notions, since they are never fundamental but are always subordinate in their systematic role. And even when Spinoza bases the scope of his theory upon the causal power of naturing nature, he does not confuse the infinite range of that power with our mind's limited ability to know its effects.

Were the human mind coeval with the infinite understanding, it could comprehend the essence of naturing nature under all its attributes, causal modalities, and relationships in natured nature. One use for the theme of infinite understanding, however, is to remind us of the limits within which the human mind operates. The latter knows reflectively that it has an adequate and true idea of God but not an infinitely comprehensive one. Yet this self-critical sense of finitude is no ground for removing from our philosophical scope some sure knowledge of naturing nature and its causation of natured nature. Such cognition does satisfy the inclusion requirement of the Spinozan meaning of system. But it prevents any vaunting transformation of a study of nature as a whole into omniscience concerning naturing and nature reality, particularly concerning how all the events within our experienced world are interrelated.

Do the cognitive limits placed here upon systematic inclusiveness permit a discussion of possible worlds? Insofar as this is a continuation of the problem of modality, the remarks made above on possibility and necessity apply here as well. Nothing in Spinoza's critique of possibility prevents the logical treatment of imaginative constructs of possible worlds and their accompanying problems.[10] Difficulties arise only when ontological standing in natural reality is claimed from the objects of this logic, beyond being meanings constructed by the human mind. Logical styles are not constricted, but ontological status depends upon having a distinctive nonreductive basis in the natured world.

The new systematic consideration here involves the Spinozan conception of world, or an organized universe of modal entities and actions. The actual modal world known to us is constituted by two infinite, immediate modes of natured nature: infinite understanding and motion-and-rest. Human reality is finitely caused and specified within the pattern of the modal universe so derived. Our mind can know natured nature as actually realized in this modal world, and can know naturing nature through the essential attributes of thought and extension that are pertinent to the causation of this world. Naturing nature is known also to be infinite in its active power, to which we cannot deny the causal power of necessarily producing other modal universes. Their otherness would arise from divine causality expressing itself through thought and some attribute other than extension. The outcome would be another actual world of modes that follows causatively from naturing nature, and yet presents a universe differently constituted from ours.

For Spinoza, therefore, the chief problem concerns whether man can know several actual modal worlds, not just possible ones. It is tempting to argue that, because the human mind shares in the infinite understanding, it has in principle an entrée into knowledge of another modal world organized under the attribute of thought and hence known to the infinite understanding. Although pressed on the issue, Spinoza does not concede that the scope of a philosophical system can be enlarged sufficiently by our mind to give cognitive access to a differently constituted actual modal world. The requisite transfiguration would no longer concern a human mind and the kind of inclusion within reach of a human philosophy.

The use of our logical imagination in modality theory does not people any Leibnizian colony of possible worlds, from which God freely chooses one candidate to actualize. The logic of possible worlds does not spill over into rules of creation for the causal activity of naturing nature and hence does not multiply universes. But it does encourage our reflection upon the many human kinds of theoretical and practical model making within our modal universe. In an accommodated sense, we are constantly engendering actual "worlds" or patterns of a regional sort, such as the human worlds of art and science, religion and politics. They are not insular kingdoms, however, but are modulations within the same natured universe that pervades all the works of human experience and reason.

Within this interpretive context we can also elaborate the regional subtheme of the cross-worlds identity of the human individual. On this comparative topic, Spinoza makes at least one stipulation. There must be some active constant power ensuring a cooperation that persists from one to another meaning of world. For individual identity rests upon at least an analogous pattern of actional union among some elements within each meaning to give to mundanity.

4. Telos

Teleology is highly susceptible to oversystematization. In this area, we tend easily to forget our intellectual limits and hence to mistake our own schemata for reality. Modern philosophers have tried to remove this confusion without also eliminating those features of experience that stimulate teleological thinking in the first instance. This delicate surgery is as necessary in the post-Darwinian era as it was in the seventeenth century.[11] It seeks to heal and strengthen our mind on this theme rather than foreclose its consideration entirely.

There are three general phases in a philosophical rethinking of teleology. First, criticism focuses upon the defects of an already accepted teleology (teleology A). The latter is a given body of doctrine which has lost sight of its genesis in human reflection upon experience. One must remove the illusion that teleological systems are autonomous and their axioms self-evident. Dysteleological features get pointed out, and antiteleological models are proposed. The second phase involves a move from mainly destructive work to a fresh consideration of telic aspects of man and the world. Some new philosophizing examines those telic meanings uncovered in our purged or methodically emended understanding of ourselves and the rest of nature (this or that *telos* in the singular, or these plural *tele*). Phase three consists in a systematically reconstituted teleology that is all the wiser and more modest for the overhauling, but that seeks to make general philosophical use of the telic meanings in a more cautious doctrine (teleology B).

Thus, the modern historical pattern is a move from teleology A to a new inspection of *telos/tele,* and thence onward to teleology B. Spinoza never permitted himself to take the third step in this process. There was still so much support in social customs and institutions for meanings of teleology subjected to his criticism that a systematic reconstruction would have been premature. Perhaps for this reason, his criticism of a teleology A in the appendix to *Ethics I* and elsewhere has been regarded often as his sole contribution. But his position was more complicated, including as it did a readiness to revisit some aspects of our life that do yield telic meanings. He made his own interpretation of some tested senses of *telos/tele,* without allowing them to become firmly systematized as a teleology B.

In rejecting the teleology set forth in Dutch university textbooks, Spinoza gets some support from Maimonides and Descartes. They agree that it is philosophically and scientifically futile to search after the final causes of the visible universe. To assign a general design to the physical world does not advance our understanding and explanation of things. At most, a physical teleology leads to the view that all physical happenings serve man's welfare. This fantasy is not borne out by the harsh conditions of human life. Under scrutiny, anthropocentrism turns out to be a bidirec-

tional symbol. In one perspective, it stands for God's providential governing of the whole universe; in another, it signifies the human activities of
studying and making use of the environing world for our own welfare.
When we seek a final cause for fitting into a providential design, however,
Maimonides and Descartes refer us to God's own purpose. It lies outside
of nature in a region of mystery, to which the human mind is not privy
except through divine revelation and faith.

Here, Spinoza parts company with his sources. Whatever the social
value of belief in religious revelation, it does not supply us with an
independent basis of cognitive truth. For the latter, he looks solely to a
philosophical study of nature that incorporates God rather than treats him
as an extranatural being. The sticking point about teleology is that it
furnishes no meaning of final cause that is appropriate to God as naturing
nature. Finality, taken as that for the sake of which an action is done, is
inapplicable to the Spinozan God. If *for the sake of which* signifies a
fulfilling of some indigency or need on the agent's part, it is incompatible
with the self-sufficiency of naturing nature. But even if that phrase belongs in the order of assimilation, or of securing a likeness of other things
to the agent, it raises other difficulties for Spinoza. The divine purpose
cannot be to wipe out the distinction between naturing and natured nature.
Nor can it be conceived as a striving of intellect and will, for this would
reduce God to a human mode of causal operator.

Since these finalistic analogies fail to safeguard the integrity of the
chief components in nature as a whole, Spinoza abandons finalistic thinking about God. What he specifically rejects is a teleology A having certain
presuppositions. It supposes that telic thought rests upon a general theory
of final causality; that it is primarily a study of the divine providential plan
for the universe; and that our mind can trace out this design in both the
physical universe and human history, using religious faith to fill out gaps
in our understanding of the master plan. Each of these points runs counter
to some feature of Spinoza's theory of nature. The latter does not make
naturing nature conform to a general transcendental principle; it dis-
sociates divine causal activity from any anthropomorphic pattern; and it
does not appeal to religious revelation as a source of knowledge about
man's relationship with God. Spinoza could not but repudiate the set of
suppositions underlying the then-prevailing teleology A.

Nevertheless, Spinoza's thought is not hermetically sealed against
every sort of telic meaning. A telic presence is detectable as soon as he
moves from polemics about God's causality to a direct study of the modal
world, known through experience and reason. The Spinozan theory of

natured nature helps philosophy to make the *telos/tele* turn that goes beyond a rootless, unproductive sort of teleology and its antiteleological counterpart. The more fruitful direction is toward a critical, pluralistic, perspectival study of ends and purposes operating in our world. At least four main themes in Spinoza's conception of natured nature involve some telic considerations.

First, the finite singular thing existing in corporeal nature has an essential structure. In some manner and degree, it is actively engaged in maintaining its own pattern of motion-and-rest. The functional act is more pronounced in the case of more complex bodies, but it is never wholly absent from a bodily existent. There is always some relational interplay between structure and function. It is this intrinsic finality that is affirmed by the coexpressive idea of the bodily reality. The singular modal thing is not reducible to an extrinsic assemblage and not sufficiently knowable through a mechanical model, involving no reference to the proportionate idea or "soul." A philosophical view of the singular existing thing acknowledges its telic pattern of individual structure and function and their coexpressive idea.

A second topic is the distinction between appetite and desire within the Spinozan theory of man.[12] What we share with all finite modalities is the conatus for preserving one's own reality. When that conatus refers to our mind and body together it is called appetite. This is the very essence of man considered as a tendential individual nature, determining him toward actions that conserve his *esse* or actual being. Appetite is not a shove from behind but a persistent inner tendency of our composite modal nature toward continuance and realization. The particular actions expressing this human effort constitute behavior ordered to a goal or purpose. From the analysis of appetite, then, comes the broad telic meaning of goal-directed behavior.

Spinoza then appeals to our experience of being conscious of our appetitive endeavor. Desire is nothing other than appetite taken together with consciousness of it. Actions arising from conscious appetite or desire tend to realize purposes that are intended. The adequacy of our cognition of nature intrinsically affects the quality of our actions, enabling them to comprise an intending type of goal-directed behavior. Human actions become most satisfying when they fulfill our intentional purposes within the order of nature. In his psychological and ethical analyses, Spinoza employs this telic meaning as a guide for determining where our vulnerability and moral strength lie.

This leads into a third theme having telic significance: the moral paradigm. We cannot achieve our moral purposes instantaneously simply by conceiving and desiring them. For the human sort of practical conception has to improve itself through methodic effort, just as the element of desire is a conscious form of our persistent conatus. To sustain the struggle toward liberation, we have to use moral imagination and practical reason in fashioning an ideal or exemplary pattern of virtuous living. Into this practical paradigm are incorporated the tested purposes of moral endeavor, rendered concrete in Spinoza's *natura* or character of the morally wise and free man. Such moral imagery gives unified expression to human ends-in-view, as Dewey calls them. We make moral models in the same degree that we are purposeful agents at work in a world of peril and space to grow.

The fourth telic aspect of Spinoza's philosophy is the intellectual love of God taken as our own act of loving God, informed with our power of understanding. Spinoza surrounds this doctrine with some careful qualifications. Lest it resuscitate anthropocentrism, he does not present it as fulfilling the appetitive tendency of all natural things. For in that case, all of natured nature would revolve around man and serve his desires. Nor does this doctrine render superfluous the painstaking study of human passions and actions directed toward natured nature. They retain their reality, undiminished usefulness, and intrinsic telic significance within the total theory of man in nature. To direct one's love toward God and to achieve intellectual love of God are not supplantive acts undermining the rest of our purposes. Our other *tele* remain fully operative and are not dissolved by the *telos* of loving God. A further reservation is that our love of God involves no breakaway from natured nature, no removal of ourselves from it or transmogrification of ourselves into naturing reality. The closer union sought by this love is never to be confused with an identification with God.

All these cautions find expression in Spinoza's statement that our self-conscious love of God satisfies the better or best part of our mind, its peak ability. Within this purposive context a philosophical use of imagination and reason points toward this love as meeting the human mind's central search after causal efficacy and freedom, moral virtue and the blessed life. This is a thoroughly telic view of how the other cognitive modes encourage an intuitive knowledge, that is, a conviction that our love of God fulfills the naturating power of our mind to reaffirm its own *esse* in the very act of uniting with its naturing source.

Taken together, do these four telic themes supply a grand inductive basis for inferring that God also acts purposively? Several things prevented Spinoza from giving an affirmative reply. He did not ascribe modal traits to naturing nature, although he did hold that whatever we truly attribute to the divine essence accounts causally for our modal world. Another point is that Spinoza's contemporaries did not find the attribution of thought to God so controversial as the attribution of extension. Hence, they did not press Spinoza as hard for his meaning of the divine attribute of thought as they did for that of extension. Consequently, he did not clarify for his correspondents and himself the sense in which naturing nature causes somehow thoughtfully (although not through understanding and will). The metaphor of a geometrical figure giving rise consciously to its own properties was insufficient, precisely because it failed to specify the way in which the causal power of the divine "thinking nature" produces a natured world, itself having various telic aspects. The greatest barrier, however, was Spinoza's apprehension lest any purposive meaning of divine creative causality should restore an anthropomorphic deity and thus undercut his theory of nature as a whole. He did not find any safe way of exploring that meaning without entailing the undesirable consequences.

Hence, Spinoza never made the further move from *telos/tele* to a new teleology B. That project was left for Leibniz, Kant, and Hegel to attempt. Yet although Spinoza developed no teleological system, his systematic thinking and his existential commitment to philosophizing were thoroughly teleological. There is an intrinsic finality in his written works, especially in the *Emendation* and *Ethics* taken together. The former furnishes a methodology and the latter a sustained argument intended to guide people toward that union with nature and that true and fulfilling participation in the blessed life already sketched in the *Short Treatise*. Spinoza's own attitude has two component aims: dedication of all his energies to his life work, and careful regard for other people. He states the vocational purpose from which he permits no deviation: "to live for the true." At the same time, he tries to be faithful to his own teaching in the *Ethics* about one's community relations: "to act humanely and kindly." Hence, I would characterize Spinoza's individual telic pattern as being interwoven with these two aims: *pro vero vivere* and *humaniter et benigne agere*.[13]

5. Praxis

In the case of philosophers who make important contributions to ethics, there is a problem about how their ethics is related to their other work in logical method, epistemology, and ontology. No standard response fits thinkers so diverse as Hume, Nietzsche, and Sartre. The rule of taking each one within his own frame of reference also applies to Spinoza. He distinguishes but does not compartmentalize his positions in the various regions of philosophy, since they all belong within the unity of his conception of nature. It is through this synthesizing referent that he interrelates his arguments on ethical issues with his other investigations. There is a recognizably Spinozan accent upon nature in treating the problem of philosophy and praxis.[14]

Granted the common theme of nature, however, there are at least three ways in which Spinoza might have attempted to join its several components into a unified theory. (a) He might try to begin with a praxis-free method and speculation about the makeup and divisions of nature, seeking thereafter to work out a moral philosophy consistent with this basis; (b) he could attempt to start with a speculation-free ethics and then devise a view of reality as accommodated to his practical requirements; (c) or he could acknowledge the mutuality of speculation and praxis and let his philosophizing be governed always by this premise. Very general discussion of the feasibility of these projects is not as helpful as the historical study of how Spinoza actually proceeded and of how his actual procedure related to his view of nature.

(a) Spinoza does not regard purity from praxis (which embraces theory about practice as well as practical activity) as a desirable ideal or even an open alternative in his philosophy. In whatever sphere, his philosophical efforts are aimed at making the human mind aware of its union with nature as a whole and at acting in accord with this insight. The metaphor of the conscious worm guides our thought on how a particular existent can use its causal connections to reach out toward the wider network of nature. But it does not instruct us on the resource peculiarly available to man, the *automa spirituale*—namely, the making of methods. In the *Emendation,* there is a pragmatic stress on our practical ability to forge and improve philosophical methods. It is a tool for bettering our ideas and reasonings so that they will yield more adequate knowledge and hence more adequate operations. Since Spinozan methodology seeks the reform and improvement of man as knower and as agent, it is shot through with considerations of the modes of human praxis.

The doctrine on God also has a practical as well as a speculative import. What Spinoza loses in his criticism of divine purposive providence he makes up for in his theory of naturing nature. The latter's immanent causality assures the presence of active endeavor as essential to all modal things. There is a practical aspect common to the whole of natured nature, which is actively expressive of the divine power. Hence, human activity has its natural practical context and order. Our ways of practice are distinctively human, but they develop within a theory of reality that formally involves different sorts of practicality related to our own. Thus, the Spinozan ontology of nature is praxis-laden throughout.

(b) But there is a corrupting sort of concern with human values that would simply tailor a speculative doctrine of the universe to the imagery and desires of man. Spinoza marshals all his resources in method and argument against such a pandering ontology. This gives a sharp polemical edge to his revisionary teaching on divine causality and the meanings of perfection and end, good and evil. They are criticized insofar as they make the rest of reality in the likeness of humankind and for its convenience. The heroic aspect of Spinoza's rule "to live for the true" is its persistent effort to overcome the homocentric bias, without stifling our distinctive way of living and acting in relation with the rest of nature.

The truth about natural being is a survival goal for philosophizing. It is that which emerges in the course of mending our thought, action, and discourse. They have to be reshaped, as much as possible, to correct the misperception that our fantasies and desires are laws governing the whole of naturing and natured reality. These fantasies and desires have their place in human life, but they are not the archetypes in accord with which everything in nature is patterned. To tame our projective tendency and its overclaims about the way of things is the intent of Spinoza's conception of the best order in which to philosophize. It is not lost upon him that *we* take the beginning step and do so with *our* idea of God. But his naturized method fosters self-criticism and argumentative rigor in our view of man and morals, lest the rest of nature be reduced to a parable and comfortable support system for ourselves.

(c) Once the interpretive safeguards are introduced, however, Spinoza can make cautious use of the reciprocity model. There is mutual influence between speculation and praxis, as they actually function in his theory of nature. Each permeates the other within the actuality of natural causation. What Spinoza thinks about the ways of human doing and making is intimately adjusted to his broader conception of naturing and natured reality. Conversely, he develops that sort of doctrine on God and the modal world which permits him to make sense out of our practical situation and improve our agency therein.

Praxis is the great educator of mankind. It guides our self-understanding and our efforts to achieve well-being. At no point do we merely exist, without engaging ourselves in the basic action of affirming our own conatus under conditions of limit and struggle. This basal action gives assurance that we are not inert products of some force in nature which permits us no work to do or aims to seek. Rather (in an adaptation of Spinozan language), our conative experience teaches the fundamental lesson that we are *naturating* beings, responsive agents in our own manner. Praxis is not a decoration attached to human life but is our very act of living, which our many doings and makings serve to nurture.

Analysis of praxis helps to make more meaningful Spinoza's distinction between the common and the eternal order of nature. This is not a blunt contrast between error and truth. To view nature under the aspect of duration breeds error only when the durational view is made into an absolute and when indefinite existence is substituted for causal origination and ordering. Behind the durational view is the practical consideration that the human conatus is never instantaneously satisfied by control over circumstances and enjoyment of fulfilled desires. There must be perseverance in a human existence, persistence in struggling to achieve practical knowledge and virtue, and courage of mind and spirit. These three qualities of perseverance, persistence, and courage get perceived by us in the image of moral time. Temporal endurance is an indispensable practical trait of human life, even though it does not settle all cosmological issues. Just as the eternal view of nature incorporates the contributions of imagination concerning concrete individual existents, so it retains the testimony of moral imagination concerning the growth of an enduring virtuous character and the *via* or path it hews through life.[15]

Similarly, there is a distinctively practical significance in Spinoza's talk about "part of nature," "better or best part of oneself," and "part of the whole." Such language does not concern solely a speculative mereology. It also conveys three features of our moral experience.

First, the discussion of servitude in *Ethics III* rests upon the human sense of the vast universe about us and its domination over our lives. Before a Pascal can congratulate us for being reeds that think and stay aware until death, we have a dreadful apprehension of the sway of cosmic, biological, and psychological forces over our conduct. What overwhelms us is not our physical littleness but our relative powerlessness to shape our individual and social lives. Even when scientific research and technology enjoy an exponential increase, their growth does not ensure a proportional development of human freedom. Spinoza's topic of moral servitude thematizes this somewhat baleful practical meaning of man as a part of nature. It signifies that kind of partitiveness displayed when our behavior expresses very little appreciation of human power and intent, but instead represents a submission to estranging motivations.

Nevertheless, the Spinozan passage from servitude to liberation is not accomplished by diminishing or removing our status as part of nature. On the contrary, the liberating process strengthens human partitiveness in nature by means of our knowledge of the distinctively human manner of belonging to nature and acting in accord with it. We educate ourselves into a truer understanding of the order of nature, in which we can share through reasonable human praxis. Thus the moral meaning for being a part of nature consists in the persistent endeavor to transform our life from a narrow passive attitude to one actively interested in and mutually engaged with the rest of the natured world, as well as with the naturing principle.

Second, this process discloses a horizon where the moral agent speaks about the better or best part of oneself. Here, an internal differentiation is needed, even within a reoriented concept of oneself as part of nature. One seeks *as much* praxic fulfillment as falls within the reach of a complex, finite mode. Practical partitiveness involves a reapportioning of actional over passional relationships, but never a total assimilation of the latter to the former. The complex human center of practicality does not become a purely actional entity. The several modes of cognition remain in operation, along with the still striving conatus. Within this always composite human reality, therefore, Spinoza distinguishes that portion which engages directly in the act of knowing and loving God. Yet the better or best part of oneself does not dissever its praxic connectives. It remains part of one's complex selfhood, which in its turn remains part of natured nature.

However, the word *remains* can be misleading, if it implies reluctant submission to fate. For the act of loving God reaffirms and strengthens the human agent in its entire being, just as the humane quality of moral action reaffirms and strengthens human ties with natured nature as a whole. Not disengagement and flight but well-ordered active union of man with total nature is the primary motif in Spinoza's logic of the practical part. The ultimate significance of a praxic part of nature tends to unite, not separate.

This leads to the third phrase, *part of the whole*. When used within the context of human praxis, these words connote a definite sort of part/whole relationship, namely, that which concerns membership in a community. It requires a separate section to consider Spinoza's contribution to this topic.

6. Community

One can scarcely penetrate his approach to this, then, without adverting to his basic teachings on nature. We have a fourfold community involvement corresponding to four main Spinozan meanings of nature.

(a) *Community with nature around us.* There is a strong ecological cast to Spinoza's theory of man. He refuses to ignore or underestimate man's natural matrix, since this would seriously imbalance our grasp of human reality in its relational aspects. Both in his treatises and his correspondence, Spinoza criticizes those who indulge in an emotive denigration of our life in nature. They prefer to ridicule, lament, and despise the human condition taken in isolation from the rest of the natural world, rather than to go about the task of studying the more inclusive processes and patterns affecting our lives. Environmental and social disasters are not an occasion for bewailing nature's weakness. Such challenges incite Spinoza "neither to laughter nor even to crying, but rather to philosophizing and to the better observing of human nature."[16]

The latter is more realistically and holistically observed in its interchanges of reception and initiative with respect to the broader world of nature. Through the physical and biological sciences, technology, and medicine, this constant dynamism gets better known and used to our advantage. But our natural relationships are not solely utilitarian. They get distorted without the leaven of acknowledgment of the environing universe's distinctive (though always interworking) reality.

Spinoza strives to do justice both to the pragmatic side of man-in-nature and to the integrity of each component in this community. The former consideration leads him to restrict the notes of useful good and beauty to the world as affecting us, as interpreted in accord with its impact upon our conatus. But he cannot go too far in this direction without reviving anthropocentrism, under the guise of an exclusively instrumental reading of the natural world.

What enables Spinoza to avoid extremes is his general conception of nature. Man belongs unreservedly within natured reality, is a part of modal nature as a whole, and partakes of its order and power. A distinction must be drawn, it is true, between modal nature as expressive of the naturing principle through infinite understanding and motion-and-rest and as signifying whatever other modal effects may follow from substance. But this distinction reinforces the unity of all modes of natured nature within *our* universe and our experience. Moreover, the human mind's primordial affirmation of the existing reality of the human body tells against any estrangement of man from other experienced natural things, as well as against any diluting of the *esse* and integrity of nonhuman natural things. The Spinozan theory of nature encourages a balanced synthesis of all actualities in the community of man with the other modal realities in our one world.

(b) *The interhuman community.* The city of man is thoroughly permeated by the causal influences and laws governing our universe. Hence, in principle Spinoza admits the legitimacy of studying human society with the aid of mathematical, physical, and socio-biological models. But neither singly nor together do these ways yield comprehensive knowledge of human social reality. That reality has some special traits dependent upon the distinctive manner in which human bodies are affirmed in existence, related in action, and discoursed about in language. Such relational acts are characteristic expressions of the human mind. Beings possessing minds show an ability to gain reflective self-possession, to pursue intentional courses of action, and to use linguistic means of interpretation and practical organization. Insofar as these operations can be shared, they are the basis for the many forms of participation in the interhuman community.

Spinoza's philosophy offers at least four avenues into this meaning for community. I will call them the noetic, conative, paradigmatic, and polar approaches to the theme.

Noetically, the three modes of perception are ways of achieving human cognitive sociality. Throughout its range, imagination functions within a thoroughly social context. This is seen in the important role of signs and testimony in the Spinozan theory of imagination. Even when a critical method rectifies the misleading aspects of signs and testimony, it does so in order to facilitate their more reliable use in shaping human society. Similarly, the imaginative grasp upon concrete bodily existents opens a way for regarding one's own bodily individuality as being mutually related to other individual existents and as drawing meaning from this relationship.

Spinoza's topic of the purifiers of the human understanding has the same communal import for the rational mode of cognition. Why do mathematics and mechanical philosophy of nature supply reason with much needed encouragement? They do so because they are historically developed disciplines relying upon many minds working in concert. These disciplines are communicated through an educational process and are being further advanced within many cultural settings. Social reason is seen here at work. It is an effective sign that human knowledge permits and requires broad participation for its healthy existence and growth. If intuitive knowledge is a culmination, it too must incorporate some factor of shareability rather than retreat to solipsism.

In the *conative* order, Spinoza never weakens his stress upon the individuating character of each one's endeavoring principle. To weaken it would be to suggest that human societal forms are rivals of the individual existent and substitutes for the well-being of individuals. This agonistic relation characterizes tyrannical societies but not those responsive to social discourse. Spinoza conceives the well-ordered state as responding to fundamental needs shared by conative human individuals. The latter can satisfy their full range of strivings only within a secure social order that permits individual ways of self-realization. Because the human conatus expresses one's integral composite nature, it obtains satisfaction within a community relationship and not in the mind's solitude.

To bring home this point, Spinoza elaborates the meaning of nature as *paradigm*. When he first broaches the human need for a certain exemplar or paradigm, he refers it to the individual human striver. But as the theory of servitude and liberation unfolds, it becomes clear that the exemplary nature is a shared ideal. In principle, a moral paradigm symbolizes a way of life that is communicable in meaning and attainable through cooperative effort. The power or virtue required to embody this practical pattern involves the activities of many interrelated people. Their interconnectedness is not homogeneous but a working together on the part of agents needing each other in different respects. Social differentiation weaves a common operational fabric that Spinoza analyzes primarily in its political and religious modalities, but that is not confined to them. The main lesson is that paradigms are best envisioned and pursued by people in a community context, allowing for different types of participation in the jointly held ideal. Moral integrity addresses us all through practical models.

Polarity is a principal hermeneutic tool when Spinoza treats the profusion of meanings of nature proposed throughout human history. His repeated criticism of the enclave view of human society as an autonomous order of its own has a constructive side. Just as political life has to be viewed within the framework set by the underlying study of the ourselves-and-nature relationship, so must every contrastive approach to nature be integrated with this relationship. The contrasting principles are themselves polar elements which we learn to locate internally to the reality of nature as a whole. These elements can be distinguished and even set in contrast for our own purposes, but they do not fracture the community binding our human nature with the totality of natural being.

It is helpful, for instance, to distinguish between what holds by nature and what by human law. This dualism of natural and positive law enables us to appreciate the scope of man's lawmaking activities, but these activities still find their measure in the order of nature. The latter expresses its power distinctively in human reason and desire, which provide a basis for criticizing and improving our particular constitutions and legal systems.

Another dualism studied at length by Spinoza is that between the book of nature and the book of God's revealed word. The Bible (or whatever functions in a culture as a religious scripture representing the divine plan for us) helps to purify our understanding and educate us in the practical order. Its broad appeal testifies to the presence of the human community and the sense of a common calling for all mankind. Spinoza becomes critical of biblically based religion when it fails to rise above the metaphor of the two books, that of nature and that of revelation. This happens when they are regarded as independent sources of truth or when the study of nature (including God or naturing nature) is submitted to the noetic norm of revelation, sometimes backed by political power. Under such conditions, the two-sources view opens up a fissure in the unity of nature; the subordination of philosophical to scriptural views of God and world leaves us without recourse against anthropomorphic imagery; and the politicizing of revelation works against the moral community of mankind. For these reasons, Spinoza locates any Scripture/nature couplet firmly inside the philosophical conception of nature as a whole.

His caution about applying emotive and evaluative terms to the environing universe is due, not to any depreciation of the latter, but to recognition of the human interpretive function. Because of that function, we draw a symbolic contrast between nature as nurturing mother and as vindictive force. Its artistic representations abound in the paintings of Spinoza's own country and century. Rembrandt's *Winter Landscape* and Ruisdael's *Wheatfields* show man as well integrated, through work and play and everyday living, with the rest of natured nature as supportive and nourishing. But natured nature's other face, violent and indifferent by turn, obtrudes in Porcellis's *Stormy Sea* and Ruisdael's *Landscape with Waterfall*.[17] These painters show how variously our passions and interests are affected by the processes of physical nature, and hence give rise to contrasting interpretations of nature around us.

In his own life and philosophy, Spinoza himself showed a sense of the accomplishments of man the artist, taken in both the esthetic and the technological meanings of art. Yet he did not permit this appreciation to become beclouded by any radical split between art and nature. The art/nature polarity highlights the creative initiatives of man in regard to his own structure and that of other natural things. Yet interpenetration rather than dichotomous separation is the rule for human inventiveness, as it operates in constant interchange with natured nature's other modes of activity. All distinctions between culture and nonhuman nature contribute to the total enrichment of the great community of modal nature (to adapt Royce's language).

(c) *Community with God.* This is not a decorative layer superimposed on the other forms of human community. Spinoza's emendative method and order of philosophizing are designed to correct any extrinsic superstructural view of our relationship with God. The path of reflective disclosure uncovers this relationship as a community that we already have with God. It lies at the heart of our own *esse* or actual-being as natural things, as modes sharing in the numinous power and life of naturing nature, and hence as agents attaining to moral freedom.

Biblical religion contributes persuasive imagery to this sense of our communal bond with divine actuality. Religious sources keep human existence open to its eternal roots. Through the image of the people of God, we learn to relate ourselves socially to God as sustainer and goal of human aspirations. The word of God addresses itself to the whole community, which finds salvation and freedom in adhering to this word amid all other relationships in the world. Despite Spinoza's criticism of theocracy and an arbitrarily willful notion of the creator, he acknowledges that most people find in scriptural theism a way to visualize their common participation in divine life.

Should the community relationship with God be fully mutual, so that our love toward him is always proportionately answered by his love toward us? Spinoza's negative reply is consistent with his logic of the passions and the transition from servitude to freedom. For he regards the activity of love as an increase in the lover's perfection and a more vivid recognition of another as cause. If this meaning of love were to prevail, then it would import into God those traits of perfective increase and causedness that run counter to naturing nature.

In asking us to forgo a reciprocal love of God toward us, however, Spinoza does not entirely eliminate love as a quality of the community between ourselves and God. Insofar as we recognize our minds to be finite modulations of the infinite understanding, we share in that understanding's eternal act of loving God. Our concrete feeling of being eternal and of eternally loving God is the supreme intellectual act of our own minded nature. Through this act, individual minds partake most fully of the infinite understanding's vigor. Hence the act of intellectual love characterizes the community among human minds when they are acting at their best. The religious presentiment about God's love for us gets translated into Spinoza's general theory of "God insofar as." God loves us insofar as our intellectual loving act is itself a modal expression of naturing nature at work in the infinite understanding and in human minds. This is as far as Spinoza can go philosophically in securing a loving quality in our community with God.

(d) *Community within nature as a living whole.* Assertions about the death of nature in the seventeenth century are historically incorrect. Not all thinkers rendered absolute the mechanical model and reduced nature to a lifeless machine or a manipulable instrument of human projects. Spinoza regarded the mechanical view of nature as a purifier of our mind but not as its conqueror. Mechanical laws of nature were not ultimate for him. Their prevalence was to be acknowledged but also to be interpreted as one among many expressions of the causal power of naturing nature. From the other quarter, man's distinctive reality did not transform the world into plastic materials, significant only through human shaping and use. Both the visible world and man retained their modal integrity in the Spinozan perspective, which discerned the analogous presence of life in all forms of natured nature.

The communal relations we share with the world around us, with humankind, and with God are incorporative of all the realities involved. Taken as the integral whole, naturing and natured nature is the great community whose joint agency permits it to be regarded as the comprehensive living individual, the all-being sketched in the *Short Treatise* and patiently fleshed out in Spinoza's subsequent writings. This conception of total nature as the community of communities cannot be categorized as a pantheism or a theopanism, a monism, or even a naturalism (unless one specifies his unique theory about nature). It does not violate the distinction between naturing and natured reality, and yet it does not conform with any view of a personal God with which Spinoza was acquainted. His conception of the living whole of nature, within which we reflectively act and attain our well-being, keeps its integrity. We need not try to remove it from criticism or prevent development of other philosophical accounts of God, world, and man. But Spinoza's theory of nature in all its complications and unifications will continue to attract and inspire thoughtful persons approaching it from many avenues.

Wordsworth's reflections on the wedding of man's mind and nature bear some poetic kinship with Spinoza's philosophy. A half-dozen lines in

The Excursion convey the attunement of a meditative person with nature's active reality.

> But he had felt the power
> Of Nature, and already was prepared,
> By his intense conceptions, to receive
> Deeply the lesson deep of love which he,
> Whom Nature, by whatever means, has taught
> To feel intensely, cannot but receive.[18]

Notes
Bibliography
Index

Notes

Abbreviations Used in the Notes

1. THE WORKS OF SPINOZA

AT   *Adnotationes ad Tractatum Theologico-Politicum* (G 3:249–67). Cited by note, and by G volume and page: *AT* 16 (G 3:256–58).

CG   *Compendium Grammatices Linguae Hebraeae* (G 1:283–403). Cited by chapter, and by G volume and page: *CG* 5 (G 1: 303–4).

CM   *Cogitata Metaphysica* (G 1:231-281). Cited by part and chapter, and by G volume and page: *CM* 2:3 (G 1:253–55).

E   *Ethica* (G 2:41–308).

         Abbreviated Constituents:

A	axiom	GDAf	general definition
Ap	appendix		of affects
ApCh	appendix chapter	L	lemma
C	corollary	P	proposition
D	definition	Pr	preface
DAf	definition of affects	Ps	postulate
Dm	demonstration	S	scholium
Ex	explanation		

       Abbreviated References:

       *E*2D3Ex (G 2:84–85)

         [*Ethics,* part 2, definition 3, explanation]

       *E*3P2Dm (G 2:141)

         [*Ethics,* part 3, proposition 2, demonstration]

       *E*4P9S (G 2:216)

         [*Ethics,* part 4, proposition 9, scholium]

Ep   *Epistolae* (G 4:1–342). Cited by letter and by G volume and page: *Ep* 23 (G 4:144–52).

G   *Spinoza Opera,* 4 volumes. Edited by Carl Gebhardt. Cited by volume and page, within parentheses: (G 2:17–25).

KV   *Korte Verhandeling van God, de Mensch en des zelfs Welstand* (G
       1:1–121). Cited by part and chapter, and by G volume and page: *KV*
       2:5 (G 1:62–65).
NS   *De Nagelate Schriften.* Dutch translation of Spinoza's manuscripts done
       probably by J. H. Glazemaker. Cited at the place where quoted in the
       Textgestaltung of G: *NS* (G 2:358).
PP   *Renati Des Cartes Principiorum Philosophiae Pars I. et II.* (G 1:123–
       30). Citation follows the form used for *E*.
TIE   *Tractatus de Intellectus Emendatione* (G 2:1–40). Cited by paragraph
       (numbered divisions of paragraphs introduced into C. H. Bruder's
       edition of *Spinoza Opera*) and by G volume and page: *TIE* 15 (G 2:9).
TP   *Tractatus Politicus* (G 3:269–360). Cited by chapter and section and by
       G volume and page: *TP* 3:7 (G 3:287).
TTP   *Tractatus Theologico-Politicus* (G 3:1–247). Cited by chapter, and by
       G volume and page: *TTP* 7 (G 3:97–117).

2. ENGLISH TRANSLATIONS OF SPINOZA

Correspondence *The Correspondence of Spinoza,* translated by A. Wolf.
                  Cited by page: *Correspondence,* 150.
Elwes   *A Theologico-Political Treatise* and *Author's Notes to the
                  Theologico-Political Treatise,* in Spinoza, *The Chief
                  Works,* transltaed by R. H. M. Elwes, volume 1. Use is
                  made only of those passages not translated in Wernham
                  below. Cited by page only: Elwes, 179.
Ethics   *Ethics,* in Spinoza, *The Chief Works,* translated by
                  R. H. M. Elwes, volume 2. Cited by page only: *Ethics,*
                  110.
Grammar   Spinoza, *Hebrew Grammar,* translated by M. J. Bloom.
                  Cited by page: *Grammar,* 26.
Improvement   *On the Improvement of the Understanding,* in Spinoza, *The
                  Chief Works,* translated by R. H. M. Elwes, volume 2.
                  Cited by page only: *Improvement,* 14.
Principles   *The Principles of the Philosophy of René Descartes,* in
                  Spinoza, *Earlier Philosophical Writings,* translated by
                  Frank A. Hayes. Cited by page: *Principles,* 33.
Short Treatise *Spinoza's Short Treatise on God, Man, and His Well-
                  Being,* translated by A. Wolf. Cited by page: *Short
                  Treatise,* 57.
*Thoughts on
  Metaphysics*   *An Appendix Containing Thoughts on Metaphysics,* in
                  Spinoza, *Earlier Philosophical Writings,* translated by

Frank A. Hayes. Cited by page: *Thoughts on Metaphysics,* 118.

Treastise on Politics A *Treatise on Politics,* in Spinoza, *The Political Works,* translated by A. G. Wernham. Cited by page: *Treatise on Politics,* 273.

Wernham A *Treatise on Religion and Politics* and *Spinoza's Notes on the Tractatus Theologico-Politicus,* in Spinoza, *The Political Works,* translated by A. G. Wernham. Cited by page: Wernham, 121.

3. RESEARCH TOOLS

LS *Lexicon Spinozanum,* 2 volumes with continuous pagination. By E. Giancotti Boscherini. Cited by page: *LS* 47–49.

SE *Spinoza Ethica.* By M. Gueret, A. Robinet, and P. Tombeur. Cited by page: *SE* 198.

Bibliographical information on all publications cited above is provided in the Bibliography.

Chapter One

1. Concise accounts of his life and historical milieu are given by: H. E. Allison, *Benedict de Spinoza,* 15–55; H. G. Hubbeling, *Spinoza,* 24–47; and L. Roth, *Spinoza,* 3–40. For basic biographical research, consult J. Freudenthal, *Spinoza: Sein Leben und seine Lehre,* vol. 1: *Das Leben Spinozas,* and S. von Dunin-Borkowski, *Spinoza,* 4 vols. The special function of Y. H. Yerushalmi's *From Spanish Court to Italian Ghetto. Isaac Cordoso, A Study in Seventeenth Century Marranism and Jewish Apologetics* is to describe the Iberian religious and philosophical background and the diverse intellectual currents in the Amsterdam Jewish community. On the dissenting circles frequented by Spinoza (and later on by Locke), see J. J. Kiwiet, "The Rhynsburg Collegiants" (private circulation, 1976); and G. C. van Niftrik, *Spinoza en de sectariërs van zijn tijd.* J. H. Huizinga's *Dutch Civilization in the Seventeenth Century* gives the general cultural history. Richard H. Popkin recently discovered Spinoza's Hebrew translation of a Quaker pamphlet attacking the Dutch Calvinist view of the Bible.

2. Ep 76 (G 4:320), *Correspondence,* 352. A counterpoint statement comes from David Hume: "We might hope to establish a system or set of opinions, which if not true (for that, perhaps, is too much to be hop'd for) might at least be satisfactory to the human mind, and might stand the test of the most critical examination." *A Treatise of Human Nature,* ed. L. A. Selby-Bigge and P. H. Nidditch, I, iv, 7 (272). Spinoza would accept the last phrase, within his own critical methodology.

3. In *Ep* 15 (G 4:72-73), *Correspondence*, 134–36, Spinoza refers to "my order" of reconstructing Descartes' *Principles of Philosophy* as leading to "another manner" of demonstration and a different doctrine. His avoidance of theological matters marks the newly found holograph "Letter from Spinoza to Lodewijk Meyer, 26 July 1663," edited by A. K. Offenberg, in *Speculum Spinozanum 1677-1977*, ed. S. Hessing, 426–35. This letter is now numbered as *Ep* 12A in the recent Dutch translation of Spinoza's *Briefwisseling*, trans. F. Akkerman, H. G. Hubbeling, and A. G. Westerbrink, 128–29. That Spinoza did express some of his own views in *PP* and *CM*, however, is clear from his subsequent appeals to them. For instance, see *Ep* 19, 21, and 58 (G 4:94, 129–33, 268), *Correspondence*, 150, 173–81, 297.

4. *PP* Pr (G 1:127–33), *Principles*, 3–9.

5. Descartes, *Reply to the Second Set of Objections and Appended Arguments*, in *The Philosophical Works of Descartes*, trans. E. S. Haldane and G. R. T. Ross, 2:48–59. Spinoza, *PP* 1 (G 1:149–80), *Principles*, 21–52. Hence, Spinoza recognizes the genetic factor in definitions and the evidentially mixed quality of axioms bearing on nature.

6. *PP* Pr (G 1:132), *Principles*, 9. The next quotation is from *PP* Pr (G 1:132), *Principles*, 8. See G 1:614 for Pieter Balling's Dutch translation, *Renatus Des Cartes Beginzelen der Wysbegeerte*.

7. Descartes, *Principles of Philosophy*, 2:64 and 3:1, trans. V. R. and R. P. Miller, pp. 76-77, 84.

8. A description of this important but unduly neglected source area is given by P. Reif, "The Textbook Tradition in Natural Philosophy, 1600–1650," *Journal of the History of Ideas*, 30 (1969), 17–32. Many university manuals were modeled upon Benedict Pereira's *De communibus omnium rerum naturalium principiis et affectionibus* (1585), especially book 7, chapters 1 and 4 (pp. 262–64, on "nature" and "the natural," and pp. 266–68, analysis of Aristotle's definition of "nature"). On the seventeenth-century Dutch university developments in philosophy, see P. Dibon, *La Philosophie néerlandaise au siècle d'or*, vol. 1; E. J. Dijksterhuis and others, *Descartes et le cartésianisme hollandais;* and E. G. Ruestow, *Physics at 17th and 18th–Century Leiden*. By Spinoza's time, Heereboord and de Raey were working out a *via novantiqua*, a synthesis of the older Aristotelian textbooks and the newer Cartesian philosophy.

9. *PP* 1, Prolegomenon (G 1:141–49), *Principles*, 13–21. E. M. Curley, *Descartes Against the Skeptics*, sets forth the Cartesian strategy.

10. *PP* 1, Prolegomenon (G 1:144), *Principles*, 15.

11. *PP* 1, Prolegomenon (G 1:148–49), *Principles*, 20, 21.

12. *PP* 1, P7, S (G 1:160–64); *Principles*, 34–37. H. G. Hubbeling, *Spinoza's Methodology*, 23, 80, alerts us to an extentional and quantificational view of Spinoza's comparative terms.

13. *PP* 1, P5, S (G 1:159), *Principles*, 32. The term *beatitudo* (beatitude or blessedness) shows the radical presence of ethical considerations in Spinoza's treatment of method and metaphysics.

14. *PP* 1, P6, S (G 1:160), *Principles*, 33; italics added. The next quotation in the main body is from the same place.

15. *CM* 1:1 (G 1:235), *Thoughts on Metaphysics*, 109. The next quotation in the main body is from *CM* 1:3 (G 1:242), *Thoughts on Metaphysics*, 117.

16. *CM* 1:3 (G 1:240-44); *Thoughts on Metaphysics*, 115–19.

17. *CM* 1:3 (G 1:243), *Thoughts on Metaphysics*, 118. "From the eternal" is a concrete way of referring to God's necessary causal activity.

18. In their quoted order, these four texts are drawn from: (i) *CM* 2:9 (G 1:266), *Thoughts on Metaphysics*, 146; (ii) *CM* 2:7 (G 1:263–64), *Thoughts on Metaphysics*, 142; (iii) *CM* 2:12 (G 1:276, 277), *Thoughts on Metaphysics*, 156, 157; (iv) *CM* 2:9 (G 1:267), *Thoughts on Metaphysics*, 146. One can see here the need for the doctrine on naturing and natured nature formally worked out in *KV* and *E*.

19. Descartes, *Principles of Philosophy*, 1:28 (Miller, 14); Descartes, *Philosophical Letters*, trans A. Kenny, 54. Locke, too, is sensitive about this phrase's ambiguity. Although there are necessary human duties, "this is not because nature or God (as I should say more correctly) could not have created man differently." John Locke, *Essays on the Law of Nature*, trans. W. von Leyden, 199.

20. Descartes, *Principles of Philosophy*, 1:51 (Miller, 23): "a thing which exists in such a way that it needs no other thing in order to exist."

21. Descartes, *Meditations on First Philosophy*, 4, trans. D. A. Cress, 36. The next quotation is from Descartes, *Descartes' Conversation with Burman*, [29], trans. J. Cottingham, 20. See Descartes, *Principles of Philosophy*, 1:28 (Haldane and Ross, 1:230).

22. Descartes, *Le Monde ou Traité de la lumière* [*The World*], 7, bilingual edition, trans. M. S. Mahoney, 59–71; Descartes, *Meditations on First Philosophy*, 6 (Cress, 50–56). The meanings of nature in these texts are examined by James Collins, *Descartes' Philosophy of Nature*, 16–30, 80–87.

Chapter Two

1. For definition and deployment of the Dutch terms in these two paragraphs, see *KV* 1:2, 2:Pr, and 2:Ap (G 1:19–24, 51–52, 114–19), *Short Treatise*, 21–27, 63, 153–59. For the Latin terms, see *CM* 1:1 and 2 (G 1:237–39), *Thoughts on Metaphysics*, 111–15; *E*1D1, 3, 4, 8, and *E*2D2 and 5 (G 2:45, 46, 84, 85), *Ethics*, 45, 46, 82. There is a helpful Latin-Dutch glossary of Spinoza's terminology in *LS*, 1356–74. I translate *esse* as *actual to-be*, *actual-being*, or *active-being*. The advantage of the infinitive forms is their atemporality and hence their capacity to express the eternal order of nature. Cf. Spinoza's comparative linguistic remark: "The mode which the Latins call infinitive is among the Hebrews a pure unadulterated noun, and therefore an infinitive acknowledges neither present, nor past, nor any time whatsoever." *CG* 5 (G 1:303), *Grammar*, 29. Spinoza's actual usage is conveyed only approximately by the Elwes translation of *Ethics* and by Samuel Shirley's translation of Baruch Spinoza, *The Ethics and Selected Letters*.

2. Such a phrase as *de wezentlykheid van een ander zelfstandigheid* (*KV* 2:Ap [G 1:115], *Short Treatise*, 154) helps us to discern the meanings involved in *existentia substantiae* (*E*1P8S2 [G 2:50], *Ethics*, 49).

3. G. W. F. Hegel, *Lectures on the History of Philosophy*, trans. E. S. Haldane and F. H. Simson, 3:283. Hegel, *Science of Logic*, trans. A. V. Miller, 536–39, holds that only his speculative method and concept of spirit explain (rather than assume as a given) the procession of things from the absolute, as well as the basic terminology in philosophy. There are comparative studies by K. L. Schmitz, "Hegel's Assessment of Spinoza," in *The Philosophy of Baruch Spinoza*, ed. R. Kennington, 229–43; and by G. H. R. Parkinson, "Hegel, Pantheism, and Spinoza," *Journal of the History of Ideas*, 38 (1977), 449–59.

4. *KV* 2:Ap (G 1:114–21), *Short Treatise*, 153–62. G presents the appendix as a compound whole, having two internal components.

5. *KV* 1:1 and 2 (G 1:15–27), *Short Treatise*, 15–31.

6. *KV* 1:1 and 2 (G 1:17, 20), *Short Treatise*, 19, 22. Hence, the technical term *formalitas naturae*, used in *TIE* and in *E,* has a realistic and not just a formalistic significance. Cf. chapter 4, note 31, and chapter 5, note 6.

7. *KV* 1:2, and Appendix (G 1:19, 22, 116), *Short Treatise*, 21, 25, 156. The identification of God with naturing nature follows from regarding *"nature to be a being, of which all attributes are predicated." KV* 1:2 (G 1:27), *Short Treatise*, 30.

8. *KV* 1:2, and [First] Dialogue (G 1:24, 28), *Short Treatise*, 27, 32. P. Lachièze-Rey, *Les Origines cartésiennes du Dieu de Spinoza*, 5–46, regards *KV*'s First Dialogue as a sketch for considering total nature as the great healer and unifier of Cartesian dualisms. F. Kauz, *Substanz und Welt bei Spinoza und Leibniz*, 40–48, regards the necessary causal power of divine substance as the unifying principle uniting God and world in the Spinozan *alwezen.* For the comparison with Leibniz, see also G. Friedmann's classical study, *Leibniz et Spinoza.*

9. *KV* 1:7 (G 1:44), *Short Treatise*, 53. Spinoza makes some limited use of Descartes, *Reply to the First Set of Objections* (Haldane and Ross, 2:17–18).

10. *KV* 1:7 (G 1:46), *Short Treatise*, 54–55.

11. *KV* 1:8 and 9 (G 1:47-48), *Short Treatise*, 56–58; *E*1P29S and P31Dm (G 2:71, 72), *Ethics*, 68-69. In *Spinoza's Metaphysics: An Essay in Interpetation*, 50–77, E. M. Curley presents an analytically formulated metaphysical model of nomological and singular facts, covering the several meanings of nature.

12. *KV* 1:7 (G1;46:47), *Short Treatise*, 55.

13. For instances of the Latin terminology, see *TIE* 13 and 40 (G 2:8, 16), *Improvement*, 6, 15; *E*2P7S (G 2:90), *Ethics*, 87; and *Ep* 12 (G 4:54), *Correspondence*, 117. For instances of the Dutch terminology, see *KV* 1:8, 2:18, 19, and 20 (G 1:47, 86, 89, 90, 97), *Short Treatise*, 115, 119, 128.

14. *Ep* 64 (G 4:277-278), *Correspondence*, 306–8. The legitimate basis in reality for regarding God as a whole, and infinite understanding as a whole, lies in their respective activities of causal immanence in natured nature. *KV* 1:2 [First] Dialogue (G 1:30), *Short Treatise*, 34–35. G. L. Kline, "On the Infinity of Spinoza's Attributes," in *Speculum Spinozanum 1677–1977*, ed. S. Hessing, 333–52, distinguishes: (a) "Nature," in a systematic sense, as the whole universe or cosmos, both naturing and natured; (b) two idiomatic senses, "by nature, in character, in kind" and "its nature being preserved"; and (c) two nonidiomatic and nonsystematic senses, "kind" and "essence or character." One function of the surmodel is to interpret correctively (b) and (c) so that their emended meanings can be incorporated as then having a systematic significance. Although Spinoza and his copyists do not have a completely uniform policy on capitalization, they tend to capitalize *Natura* when it refers to: naturing nature, the whole of natured nature in one or more modal lines, or total nature as inclusive of the naturing and the natured.

15. On the medieval and Renaissance provenance of the terminology *naturing nature* and *natured nature*, consult: M. Gueroult, *Spinoza I; Dieu (Éthique, I)*, 564–68; H. Siebeck, "Über die Entstehung der Termini *natura naturans* und *natura naturata*," *Archiv für Geschichte der Philosophie*, 3 (1890), 370–78; H. A. Lucks, "*Natura Naturans—Natura Naturata*," *The New Scholasticism*, 9 (1935), 1–24; L. Ehrlich,

Karl Jaspers: Philosophy as Faith, 210; and S. H. Nasr, *An Introduction to Islamic Cosmological Doctrines*, 8–9, 61. More decisive for Spinoza than the historical tradition was the use of these terms in contemporary university textbooks. For instance, A. Heereboord's *Hermeneia Logica* (1657), II, 28, pp. 294–96, makes seven uses of *natura naturans* and *natura naturata* to designate the two aspects (God and world) of the order of nature, which a natural method serves to clarify.

16. *KV* 1:8 (G 1:47), *Short Treatise*, 56; *E*1P29S (G 2:71), *Ethics*, 68. See St. Thomas Aquinas, *Summa theologiae*, I–II, 85, 6,c.: "God is said by some to be *the Nature Who makes nature*," *Natura naturans*. *Basic Writings of Saint Thomas Aquinas*, ed. A. C. Pegis, 2:703.

17. The long-range consequences of this aspect of the naturing/natured distinction are worked out by J. G. Lennox, "The Causality of Finite Modes in Spinoza's *Ethics*," *Canadian Journal of Philosophy*, 6 (1976), 479–500.

Chapter Three

1. Descartes, *Treatise of Man*, trans. T. S. Hall. The other materials are collected in *Descartes: His Moral Philosophy and Psychology*, trans. J. J. Blom.

2. For instance *KV* 1:2 (G 1:23–27), *Short Treatise*, 27–31.

3. *KV* 1:2 (G 1:23), *Short Treatise*, 27. See Descartes, *Principles of Philosophy*, 4:188–98 (Miller, 275–82), for excerpts from a sketch of his projected mature treatise on man.

4. *KV* 2:Preface (G 1:51–53), *Short Treatise*, 63–66.

5. *KV* 1:9 (G 1:48), *Short Treatise*, 57–58.

6. A major purpose of the preface to *KV* 2 is to secure the control of the broader theory of nature over the analysis of particular things in natured nature, as expressed in typical differentiating statements: "This is such, and not such, this is this, and not that." *KV* 2:Preface (G 1:52), *Short Treatise*, 64.

7. *KV* 1:5 (G 1:40), *Short Treatise*, 47.

8. *KV* 2:1, 2, and 4 (G 1:54, 55, 59), *Short Treatise*, 67, 69, 74.

9. *KV* 2:1–4 (G 1:54–61), *Short Treatise*, 67–77. On Spinoza's several treatments of the kinds of human cognition, see G. H. R. Parkinson, *Spinoza's Theory of Knowledge*, 138–90; and M. Gueroult, *Spinoza II: L'Âme (Éthique, II)*, 381–90, 416–87 (on intuitive knowledge), 593–608. The important contribution of experience and imagination is shown by C. de Deugd, *The Significance of Spinoza's First Kind of Knowledge;* G. Fløistad, "Experiential Meaning in Spinoza," in *Spinoza on Knowing, Being and Freedom*, ed. J. G. van der Bend, 51–60; and E. M. Curley, "Experience in Spinoza's Theory of Knowledge," in *Spinoza: A Collection of Critical Essays*, ed. M. Grene, 25–59. L. C. Rice, "The Continuity of *Mens* in Spinoza," *The New Scholasticism*, 43 (1969–70), 75–103, adds that all these cognitive ways are continuous and integrated by our actively unifying mind.

10. *E*2P40S2 (G 2:122), *Ethics*, 113. The presential (*ut praesens*) and affective language of *E*, concerning intuitive knowledge and awareness of eternity, has its roots in the *KV* account. "In our emotions, particularly love, we sense and feel the characteristic existence of things, as expressions of God. When we come to understand clearly and adequately that which earlier we sensed and felt, Spinoza calls this *scientia intuitiva*."

D. Savan, "Spinoza on Man's Knowledge of God: Intuition, Reason, Revelation, and Love," in *Spinoza: A Tercentenary Perspective*, ed. B. S. Kogan, 97. On the ties between *KV* and *E*, see A. Pupi, "L' 'Etica' di Spinoza alla luce del 'Breve Trattato'," *Rivista di filosofia neo-scolastica*, 45 (1953), 229–52.

11. The lexical materials are supplied in *LS*, 928–51, 1162–66, 1340–43, and in *SE*, 289–98. P. Di Vona, "L'analogia del concetto di 'res' in Spinoza," *Rivista critica di storia della filosofia*, 16 (1961), 48–78. Spinoza seeks to detranscendentalize the transcendental notion "thing," which (at least for St. Thomas Aquinas) primarily signifies essence.

12. *KV* 1:10 (G 1:49), *Short Treatise*, 60.

13. *KV* 1:2, [First] Dialogue, and 8 (G 1:29, 46), *Short Treatise*, 34, 55. Italics added. The emendative plural also governs this text: "In order to be well conceived, natured nature has need of some substances." *KV* 1:8 (G 1:47), *Short Treatise*, 56. Gebhardt (G 1:470) accepts this plural form in Codex A, instead of the singular form ("some substance") in J. Monnikhoff's Codex B of *KV*. The sense of the plural reading is that we must view man and our modal world under two distinct attributes of naturing nature, not just under one attribute alone.

14. *KV* 1:2 [First] Dialogue, and 9 (G 1:28, 29, 48), *Short Treatise*, 32–34, 57. Here, as in the preface to *PP*, the target is Descartes' pluralization of substances.

15. *KV* 2:Preface (G 1:51), *Short Treatise*, 63. By way of contrast with this coming-to-be of particular modal things, the Dutch addition to *E*1P8S1 (G 2:49) reads "zelfstandigheit . . . wezentlijk te zijn/Existere/." It belongs to the nature of "substance . . . really to be, to exist" eternally, without coming into existence.

16. *KV* 2:16 (G 1:82, 83), *Short Treatise*, 107, 108. Two qualifications must be placed on these phrases: (a) Even a fancy belongs reductively to an operation of the human mind as a reality in nature, and (b) the contrast between a real being and a being of reason or imagination does not reinstate *ens* as a transcendental principle for dividing nature.

17. *KV* 2:22 and 24 (G 1:101, 104), *Short Treatise*, 134, 139.

18. For the criticism of Bacon see *Ep* 2 (G 4:8–9), *Correspondence*, 76–77. Bacon and Descartes are jointly criticized here for errors on God, the human mind, and free will. For the predication about God eminently but not formally, see *CM* 1:2 (G 1:237–38), *Thoughts on Metaphysics*, 112; *Ep* 73, 81, 83 (G 4:307, 332, 334), *Correspondence*, 343, 363, 365. Spinoza wants to assure that extension (but not quiescent mass or matter) is *formally* attributed to the divine essence.

19. *KV* 2:19 (G 1:90), *Short Treatise*, 119.

20. *KV* 1:7, and 2:Appendix, Proposition 4, Corollary (G 1:46, 116), *Short Treatise*, 119. The repeated expression *door zig zelfs*, "through itself," carries a joint ontological and epistemological meaning. It is most forcefully conveyed by translating the Latin *per se* literally as "through itself," instead of using a paraphrase. Also, this principle of nature's own manifestation or revelation keeps revelatory religions within total nature (Chapter Seven below).

21. *KV* 2:19 (G 1:89), *Short Treatise*, 119. This statement foreshadows the role of the lemmas on bodily individuation in *E II*.

22. *KV* 2:Preface (G 1:52), *Short Treatise*, 65.

23. *KV* 2:2 (G 1:55), *Short Treatise*, 69. This is the basis for Spinoza's naturizing of the language of mystical experience.

24. *KV* 2:16 and 18 (G 1:83, 86–87), *Short Treatise*, 108–9, 115. In text [2], the human understanding is a pure rather than enslaving passion, since it has the sense of exercizing a positive perception (*gewaarwordinge*) or *act of becoming aware* of some thing in nature.

25. *KV* 2:18 (G 1:87), *Short Treatise*, 115.

26. *KV* 2:15 (G 1:79), *Short Treatise*, 103.

27. *KV* 2:16 (G 1:84), *Short Treatise*, 110.

28. This text and the next one are from *KV* 2:18 (G 1:87, 88), *Short Treatise*, 115, 116. The words "welfare and happiness" (*heyl en gelukzaligheid*) point toward the culminating "salvation, or blessedness" of *E*5P36S (G 2:303), *Ethics*, 265. See below, Chapter Six, Note 41.

29. *KV* 2:18 (G 1:88), *Short Treatise*, 117.

30. *KV* 2:24 (G 1:104–6), *Short Treatise*, 139–41. G. Belaief, *Spinoza's Philosophy of Law*, gives a helpful conspectus.

31. *KV* 2:26 (G 1:112), *Short Treatise*, 148.

Chapter Four

1. Alexander Pope, *An Essay on Criticism*, lines 70–73, 88–91, in *The Poems of Alexander Pope*, ed. J. Butt, 146.

2. *TIE* 1–17 (G 2:5–9), *Improvement*, 3–7.

3. *TIE* 31 and 36 (G 2:14, 15), *Improvement*, 12, 14.

4. A. Heereboord, *Praxis Logica*, paragraphs 33–48, especially pp. 338–39. The hermeneutic importance of this source is suggested by James Collins, "Interpreting Spinoza: A Paradigm for Historical Work," in S. Hessing, ed., *Speculum Spinozanum 1677–1977*, 119–32. The various strains of Renaissance methodology are distinguished by N. W. Gilbert, *Renaissance Concepts of Method*.

5. ". . . cognitionem unionis, quam mens cum tota Natura habet." *TIE* 13 (G 2:8), *Improvement*, 6.

6. *TIE* 4, 7, 11 (G 2:6, 7, 8), *Improvement*, 5, 6, 41.

7. *TIE* 16 (G 2:9), *Improvement*, 7. Problems about Spinoza's title are discussed by P. D. Eisenberg, "How to Understand *De Intellectus Emendatione*," *Journal of the History of Philosophy*, 9 (1971), 171–91. Eisenberg has also made an excellently annotated translation of Spinoza, *"Treatise on the Improvement of the Understanding,"* *Philosophy Research Archives*, 3 (1977), #553.

8. *KV* 1:1 (G 1:16), *Short Treatise*, 17; *E*2P11–13 (G 2:94–96), *Ethics*, 90–92.

9. These nature-terms are clustered in *TIE* 12–14, 18 (G 2:8–10), *Improvement*, 6–8.

10. *TIE* 13 (G 2:8), *Improvement*, 6. Cf. *KV* 2:5 (G 1:62), *Short Treatise*, 79, on the weakness of our nature.

11. *TIE* 18–29 (G 2:10–13), *Improvement*, 8–11. These ways signify operational uses of our mind, not different faculties.

12. *TIE* 33 (G 2:14), *Improvement*, 12.

13. *Ep* 15 (G 4:72), *Correspondence*, 135.

14. *TIE* 18, 25 (G 2:10, 12), *Improvement*, 8, 10.

15. For the integral text, see *TIE* 38–42 (G 2:16–17), *Improvement*, 14–16. Taken

together, these precepts constitute what A. Darbon, *Études spinozistes*, 23–25, calls a *reflexive* method (not a purely formal-logical one) that positions us for grasping the source of nature as a whole.

16. *TIE* 18, 33–35, 41 (G 2:10, 14–16), *Improvement*, 8, 12–13, 15.

17. *TIE* 41 (G 2:16), *Improvement*, 15.

18. *TIE* 38 (G 2:16), *Improvement*, 14; *E2P7* (G 2:89), *Ethics*, 86. T. C. Mark, *Spinoza's Theory of Truth*, shows how the standard theories of truth as coherence and correspondence get transformed in relation to Spinoza's metaphysical and ethical content, which makes his own conception of truth distinctive.

19. *KV* 2:8 (G 1:70), *Short Treatise*, 88–89; *TIE* 44–48 (G 2:82–83), *Improvement*, 16–17; *E1Ap* (G 2:82–83), *Ethics*, 80; *Ep* 56 (G 4:260), *Correspondence*, 288–89. R. H. Popkin, *The History of Scepticism from Erasmus to Spinoza*, 229–48, concludes that Spinoza was dogmatic in his antiskepticism and skeptical in his treatment of religion. Spinoza's own stated intent, however, was to avoid the misconceptions of both dogmatists and skeptics. *TTP* 15 (G 3:180), Elwes, 190. See L. Strauss, *Spinoza's Critique of Religion*, 251–68; and W. Doney, "Spinoza on Philosophical Skepticism," in *Spinoza: Essays in Interpretation*, eds. M. Mandelbaum and E. Freeman, 139–57.

20. *TIE* 45 (G 2:17), *Improvement*, 16.

21. I use this term to unify Spinoza's remarks about the *modi expurgandi intellectum*. Each purifier serves as a *natura* or encouraging model for our speculative and practical growth beyond the dilemma of dogmatism versus skepticism.

22. *E1Ap* (G 2:79), *Ethics*, 77. Although mathematics uncovers a norm of truth purged of both sensuality and finalism, it does not itself constitute the ultimate standard for our conception of nature. Errors about there being many substances and actual infinities, as well as about equating mathematical-mechanical laws unconditionally with nature's causal laws, arise from "the common postulate that *number sovereignly governs Nature and our understanding. . . .* Number, and with it measure and time, are thrust upon most minds as being *the highest ideas of understanding and the fundamental laws of Nature.*" M. Gueroult, "Spinoza's Letter on the Infinite (Letter XII, to Louis Meyer)," in *Spinoza: A Collection of Critical Essays*, ed. M. Grene, 197. This happens when mathematics and mechanical philosophy are rendered absolute by being transformed from epistemological aids into ontological despots over our minds.

23. In *Ep* 56 (G 4:261), *Correspondence*, 290, Spinoza notes that the ancient atomists carry more weight with him than do Plato and Aristotle. *Ep* 13 (G 4:66–67), *Correspondence*, 126–27, affirms the constructive role of particular experiments in modern mechanical-corpuscular science and philosophy of nature which, however, still leaves a further cognitive range for Spinoza's surmodel and general theory of nature. Hubbeling, *Spinoza*, 65–72, summarizes previous research on Spinoza's view of the natural sciences. Recent information on his interest in probability theory, the rainbow, and other scientific issues is supplied by the editors of Spinoza, *Algebraische Berechnung des Regenbogens. Berechnung von Wahrscheinlichkeiten*, trans. and ed. H. -C. Lucas and M. J. Petry. The relation between science, metaphysics, and ethics is a major topic in Richard P. McKeon's *The Philosophy of Spinoza. The Unity of His Thought*.

24. This and next text in the main body are from *Ep* 6 (G 4:28, 33), *Correspondence*, 93, 96.

25. *TIE* 58 (G 2:22), *Improvement*, 21–22.

26. *TIE* 64 (G 2:24), *Improvement*, 24. On the use and abuse of fictions and doubts, hypotheses and probabilities, see *TIE* 52–65, 74–80 (G 2:19–25, 28–30), *Improvement*, 18–24, 28–31.

27. The purificatory influence of scriptural imagery upon our mind is practical, as distinct from the theoretical effects of mathematics and mechanical philosophy. *TTP* Pr and 5 (G 3:9–10, 77–79), Elwes, 7–9, and Wernham, 101–3.

28. *TIE* 47, 50 (G 2:18, 19), *Improvement*, 17, 18.

29. *TIE* 31 (G 2:14), *Improvement*, 12. Hence, the free man's method-regulated meditation on life *is* his wisdom. *E*4P67 and Dm (G 2:261), *Ethics*, 232. On the immediate background, see E. F. Rice, *The Renaissance Idea of Wisdom*.

30. Part One of *CM* (G 1:233-249), *Thoughts on Metaphysics*, 107–25, gives Spinoza's *phenomenology* of Cartesian and school-manual general metaphysics. The *pathology* of this reasoning is shown in his account of confusion and error about the order and means of philosophizing on nature: *TIE* 75–76 (G 2:28–29), *Improvement*, 28–29; *E*2P40S1 (G 2:120–21), *Ethics*, 111–13. As *therapy*, or methodological corrective and healing, Spinoza proposes an order of reasoning and definitions that are most appropriate for grasping the order of nature.

31. *TIE* 91 (G 2:34), *Improvement*, 34. On the ontological as well as logical significance of "formality of nature," cf. Chapter Two, Note 6 above. Concern for the reality and order of nature distinguishes Spinoza's genetic logic from that advocated in Hobbes's *Examinatio et emendatio mathematicae hodiernae* (1660). On the difference between these emendations, see F. Biasutti, *La dottrina della scienza in Spinoza*, 112–27, 228–33.

32. *TIE* 93 (G 2:34), *Improvement*, 34.

33. *TIE* 101 (G 2:36–37), *Improvement*, 37. The double advantage of regarding natured nature as a *codex* lies in suggesting that natured nature is a legible book, intelligible in some measure to our searching minds, and that it has an ordered meaning to which we can learn to give unified expression in a general theory of nature. S. Zac, "État et nature chez Spinoza," *Revue de métaphysique et de morale*, 69 (1964), 14–40. But see Chapter Six, Note 16, and Chapter Nine, Note 3, below.

34. This and the following text are from *TIE* 99 and 102 respectively (G 2:36, 37), *Improvement*, 36, 37. The human mode and conditions of our definitional reference to nature bring out the experiential aspect of the logic of discovery and order of inquiry in *TIE*. This affects the logic and order of demonstration in *E*, as noted by I. Franck, "Spinoza's Logic of Inquiry: Rationalist or Experientialist?" in *The Philosophy of Baruch Spinoza*, ed. R. Kennington, 247–72, weakening the assumption that Spinoza is a pure rationalist.

35. *TIE* 96–97 (G 2:35–36), *Improvement*, 35–36.

36. *TIE* 107–8 (G 2:38–39), *Improvement*, 39–40.

Chapter Five

1. Gustave Flaubert, *Bouvard and Pécuchet*, trans. T. W. Earp and G. W. Stonier, 244. Flaubert's *The Dictionary of Accepted Ideas*, trans. J. Barzun, 66, offers this satirical entry on bucolic Romanticism: "NATURE. How beautiful is Nature! Repeat every time you are in the country."

2. *E*1D1–8 (G 2:45–46), *Ethics*, 45–46.

3. *TIE* 97 (G 2:35), *Improvement*, 36.

4. *E*1A6 (G 2:47), *Ethics*, 46.

5. William James, *A Pluralistic Universe*, 27. *SE*, 429–30, lists instances of *quatenus*. S. von Dunin-Borkowski, *Spinoza*, maintains that the *quatenus*-theory is an intrinsic consequence of the doctrine on modes (2:227), and that it conveys the Spinozan version of analogy and God's immanent causality (4:280–82).

6. Since this concerns a human process of asking, we must here anticipate Spinoza's *Ethics II* view on the norm of adequacy for human cognition: (a) The problem is only being propounded in his definition of an adequate idea as one that has, in itself and not through any receptively extrinsic sort of reference to its object or ideatum, the intrinsic properties of a true idea. *E*2D4 (G 2:85), *Ethics*, 82. Does such an idea disrupt the interrelations in nature? (b) The interrelational, rather than disruptive, quality of an adequate idea depends on linking its adequacy with the truth it conveys about nature. In *KV* and *TIE*, a true idea in the strongest sense expresses the formality of nature, or the power and order of nature as a whole. Now in *Ethics II*, three sequenced waves of propositions lead to this same standard of human cognitional adequacy. (i) *E*2P24–31 (G 2:110–16), *Ethics*, 104–8. Our cognition is inadequate (confused and mutilated) when it isolates the human mind and takes only a contingent, durational view of things (the common order of nature). (ii) *E*2P36–40 (G 2:117–22), *Ethics*, 109–14. Ideas become adequate insofar as they clearly and distinctly refer to both the common properties of things and the constitutive idea of the human essence. Our cognition of man and other natured things becomes intrinsically adequate through active affirmation of their relationship to their immanent naturing cause. (iii) *E*2P41–47 (G 2:122–29), *Ethics*, 114–19. Cognitive adequacy of inquiry comes from emendating the first kind of perception by the other two, since reason and intuitive understanding know things precisely in their causal involvement in the eternal order of nature. To reason adequately is to relate ourselves and the whole modal world in a necessary reference to God's eternal causal essence. And to achieve adequate intuitive knowledge means to understand, in human measure, the modes of natured nature as unitedly proceeding from eternally naturing nature. (c) Hence, the intrinsicity of the Spinozan adequate, true idea excludes no reality but involves a view of each thing *ut actu existens*, as actually existing within that eternal order of nature whose immanently naturing principle is treated in *Ethics I*.

7. *E*1P11 (G 2:52), *Ethics*, 51. *SE* 130–31, 499–501, and *LS* 409–11, 583–84, 1289, link "to express" or *exprimere* with *explicare, involvere*, and *uytdrukken*. The noetic and ontic ramifications of "to express" are traced by G. Deleuze, *Spinoza et le problème de l'expression*, and by F. Kaufmann, "Spinoza's System as Theory of Expression," *Philosophy and Phenomenological Research*, 1 (1940–41), 83–97. A musical analogue is the "progressive tonality" employed by Carl Nielsen. The Danish composer often begins a piece in a remote key, working by gradual but inevitable tonal modulations *toward* the home key that gives directional order and unity to the entire work.

8. *E*1P29–31 (G 2:70–72), *Ethics*,106–8.

9. *E*P7 (G2:49), *Ethics*, 48. The next quotation is from *E*1P25 and S (G 2:67, 68), *Ethics*, 66.

10. *E*1P4Dm (G 2:47), *Ethics*, 47; *E*1P6Dm1C (G 2:48), *Ethics*, 48; *E*1P15Dm (G 2:56), *Ethics*, 55; *E*1P28Dm (G 2:69), *Ethics*, 67. On the singular and plural uses of "substance," see Chapter Three, Note 13. C. E. Jarrett, "The Concepts of Substance

and Mode in Spinoza," *Philosophia,* 7 (1977), 83–105, uses the distinction between naturing and natured nature to show that Spinozan substance is not a summation of modes and is not identical with the structural law of natured nature as a whole.

11. *E*1P21–29 (G 2:70–72), *Ethics,* 102–7.

12. *E*1P16 and Dm (G 2:60), *Ethics,* 59.

13. *E*1P30 (G 2:71), *Ethics,* 69; *E*1P31 and S (G 2:71, 72), *Ethics,* 69.

14. *E*1P29S (G 2:71), *Ethics,* 68–69. M. Gueroult, *Spinoza I: Dieu (Éthique, I),* 300–8, 342–45, comments on the systematic function of this text.

15. *E*1Ap (G 2:79), *Ethics,* 76. Similarly, Boyle criticizes eight received meanings and ten maxims concerning nature: *A Free Enquiry into the Vulgarly Received Notion of Nature,* in *Selected Philosophical Papers of Robert Boyle,* ed. M. A. Stewart, 176–91. A. J. Close, "Commonplace Theories of Art and Nature in Classical Antiquity and in the Renaissance," *Journal of the History of Ideas,* 30 (1969), 467–86, concludes from a study of eight maxims that there is neither an antithesis nor a discontinuity, but rather a continuity of human art with nature and a permeation of art by nature. Spinoza would specify that the art/nature distinction is drawn entirely within the totality of natured nature.

16. The phrase quoted in paragraph three is from *E*1P15S (G 2:57), *Ethics,* 55. Phrases quoted in the other numbered paragraphs are from *E*1Ap (G 2:79, 81, 80), *Ethics,* 76,78,77. Moses Maimonides, *The Guide of the Perplexed,* trans. S. Pines, 3:13 (pp. 448–56), offers a storehouse of arguments against seeking a final end or cause in natural things, including a relationship to man. There is an intended finality of nature, but it is determined by God's will or wisdom and for his glory. They remain hidden from us, as do the manner and reality of divine governance and providence (1:72, p. 193). Spinoza rejects divine volition and the appeal to mystery, whether in Maimonides or in Descartes. Comparative studies are L. Roth, *Spinoza, Descartes and Maimonides,* and P. Brunner, *Probleme der Teleologie bei Maimonides, Thomas von Aquin und Spinoza,* who suggests (88) that intellectual love of God is the Spinozan perfective purpose or fulfilling goal of all our striving.

17. *E*1P17C1 (G 2:61), *Ethics,* 60, italics added. On the *NS* version, see G 2:350.

18. *E*1Ap (G 2:79), *Ethics,* 77.

19. G. W. F. Hegel, *Lectures on the History of Philosophy,* 3:289. This criticism is continued by W. Cramer, *Spinozas Philosophie des Absoluten;* but R. Boehm, "Spinoza und die Metaphysik der Subjektivität," *Zeitschrift für philosophische Forschung,* 22 (1968), 165–86, argues that God as causal substance is a nonegoic subjectivity which interiorly expresses itself in our social life. The historical issue is reconsidered by D. Janicaud, "Dialectique et substantialité: Sur la réfutation hégélienne du Spinozisme," in *Hegel et la pensée moderne,* ed. J. d'Hondt, 161–92. Hegel's interpretation is partly affected by the image of Spinozism in German Romanticism, as delineated by H. Timm, *Gott und die Freiheit: Studien zur Religionsphilosophie der Goethezeit,* vol. 1, *Die Spinozarenaissance.*

20. *E*2 [Prologue] (G 2:84), *Ethics,* 82.

21. *E*2D1 (G 2:84), *Ethics,* 82.

22. The two definitions in this paragraph are: *E*2D3 and 4 (G 2:84–85), *Ethics,* 82. For comment on the definition of "adequate idea," see this Chapter, Note 6. G. H. R. Parkinson, " 'Truth Is Its Own Standard': Aspects of Spinoza's Theory of Truth," in *Spinoza: New Perspectives,* eds. R. W. Shahan and J. J. Biro, 35–55, stresses that true

ideas (such as those generating the surmodel of nature) are not entities but actions or ways of gaining the best cognitive relations with things. A. Naess, *Freedom, Emotion and Self-Subsistence: The Structure of a Central Part of Spinoza's Ethics*, translates *conceptus* as *conception*, not *concept*, in order to bring out the dynamism of *to conceive*. He proposes the neologism "lambanological" or "having to do with grasping" (12) as a way to contrast the cognitive acts of true conception with static results.

23. *E2D7* (G 2:85), *Ethics*, 83.

24. These three axioms are: *E2A1, 2,* and *5* (G 2:85, 86), *Ethics*, 83.

25. *E2P1* and *2* (G 2:86), *Ethics*, 83, 84. Spinoza had previously authorized the use of these terms in Meyer's preface to *PP*; cf. Chapter One, Note 6 above.

26. *E2P3Dm* (G 2:87), *Ethics*, 84.

27. *E2P3S* (G 2:87), *Ethics*, 84. The next quotation is from the same place, *Ethics*, 85. (a) In *L'Idée de vie dans la philosophie de Spinoza*, 17–56, S. Zac explains that God is life, in the sense of being *essentia actuosa*, whose naturing power is immanently working in natured nature. All natured things are vivified or *have* life through the causal presence of the divine actuous essence, but they remain distinct participants and cannot be said simply to *be* life. (b) Spinoza applies the "God-as-like-a-man" criticism not only to the crowd but also to those philosophers who adapt their treatment of God to the Mosaic law and parables about perdition and salvation. *Ep* 19 (G 4:93), Correspondence, 150. P. Siwek, *Spinoza et le panthéisme religieux*, 111–15, holds that Spinoza's abiding target is this anthropomorphism, resulting from an egoism of imagination. L. W. Beck, *Six Secular Philosophers*, 38, sees in the depersonalizing of God as naturing substance a countermeasure to an anthropomorphic type of religious view of God.

28. *E2P5P6C, P7C* and *S* (G 2:88–90), *Ethics*, 85–87.

29. *E2P7S* (G 2:90), *Ethics*, 86. One function of these expressions is to emphasize the irreducible distinction between the divine attributes of thought and extension, as well as between their respective modal manifestations. Yet just as the attributes truly constitute the essence of the same sole substance, so do particular proportioned finite modes (this mind and this body) constitute one singular thing (this human individual).

30. *E2P7S* (G 2:90), *Ethics*, 87.

31. Consult Spinoza's interchanges with G. H. Schuller and E. W. Tschirnhaus, *Ep* 63–66 (G 4:274–80), *Correspondence*, 304–10.

32. *E2D7; P8C* and *P9; E3P6Dm* (G 2:85, 91–92, 146); *Ethics*, 83, 87–88, 136.

33. *E2P11Dm* (G 2:94), *Ethics*, 91.

34. *E2P13* is followed by seven lemmas containing definition, axioms, demonstrations, corollary, and scholium. They lead directly into the six postulates of *Ethics II*. G 2:96–103, *Ethics*, 92–97. For D. R. Lachterman, "The Physics of Spinoza's *Ethics*," in *Spinoza: New Perspectives*, eds. R. W. Shahan and J. I. Biro, 71–111, the discussion of bodily structures is a new beginning and fulcrum of *E*, issuing in ethical consequences. For S. Umphrey, "*De Natura*," in *The Philosophy of Baruch Spinoza*, ed. R. Kennington, 273–91, *E* is a first physics, within which perhaps no ethical action is possible. Spinoza's theory of naturing nature and total nature is the indispensable interpretant of *how* we affirm singular bodies and the physical world, in a way that permits our mind to grow in activity and some moral freedom. The proportion between understanding nature as a whole and developing free activity is underlined by S. Hampshire, "Spinoza and the Idea of Freedom," in *Spinoza: A Collection of Critical Essays*, ed. M. Grene, 297–317.

35. *E*2P13L7S (G 2:102), *Ethics,* 96.
36. *E*2P14–31 and P32–49 (G 2:103–16, 116–36), *Ethics,* 97–108, 108–27.
37. *E*2P29C (G 2:114), *Ethics,* 106. Using idealistic language, H. H. Joachim, *A Study of the Ethics of Spinoza,* 80–81, 119–22, regards the common order of nature as the world of temporal presentation, as an inadequate and partial appearance of natured nature and, hence, as an illusion (or show) having some real basis in natured nature. In his commentary *Spinoza's Tractatus De Intellectus Emendatione,* 40–43, Joachim regards naturing nature as God's self-creating *essence,* and natured nature as God's self-created *existence* or self-actualization. But this view does not accord with Spinoza's own affirmation of the distinctive *esse* of naturing nature. In order to bring the common order of natured nature to an accommodation with reality without compromising the distinctive actuality of naturing nature's own essential and existential *esse,* A. J. Watt, "The Causality of God in Spinoza's Philosophy," *Canadian Journal of Philosophy,* 2 (1972–73), 171–89, stresses God's originative causation.
38. *E*2P29S (G 2:114), *Ethics,* 106–7.

Chapter Six

1. *E*3D3 (G 2:139), *Ethics,* 130.
2. *E*3D2 (G 2:139), *Ethics,* 129.
3. *TIE* 73–75 (G 2:28–29), *Improvement,* 27–28. The reformulation in terms of inadequate ideas, rather than Cartesian free will, comes in *E*2P35Dm and S, and P49S (G 2:116–17, 131–35), *Ethics,* 108–9, 121–26.
4. Spinoza makes this prolongation visible when he closes *Ethics II* with arguments for the *practical* benefit of denying a separate free will, and again when he begins *Ethics III* with *speculative* considerations on method, nature, and mind.
5. *E*4A (G 2:210), *Ethics,* 191. This thought is reiterated in the closing appendix of *Ethics IV;* see below, Note 27.
6. This and the next text are from *E*4P4 and Dm (G 2:212–13), *Ethics,* 193. E. Giancotti Boscherini, "Man as a Part of Nature," in *Spinoza's Philosophy of Man,* ed. J. Wetlesen, 85–96, examines the ensuing moral tension between impotence and power.
7. *E*3Pr (G 2:137), *Ethics,* 128. "The 'kingdom' which Spinoza denies man is not that of his occupying a special realm in nature, delimited by certain special properties he possesses in the universal order of things, but rather, as Spinoza explicitly states, that of his having 'an absolute power over his own actions' and of his being 'altogether self-determined' (*Ethics* III, Preface)." H. A. Wolfson, *Studies in the History of Philosophy and Religion,* 2:598.
8. *Ep* 32 (G 4:171–75), *Correspondence,* 210–12. This letter contains the words *arctiorem unionem,* expressing Spinoza's teleological ethical theme of seeking a "closer union" with total nature. For the suppositions about a thinking and speaking triangle, circle, and stone, see *Ep* 56 and 58 (G 4:260, 266), *Correspondence,* 288, 295. There is a commentary by W. Sacksteder, "Spinoza on Part and Whole: The Worm's Eye View," in R. W. Shahan and J. I. Biro, eds., *Spinoza: New Perspectives,* 139–59. T. Nagel, *Mortal Questions,* chapter 12: "What is it like to be a bat?" (165–80), uses the analogy, not based upon empathy, of conscious experience on the part of other organisms as a way to develop an objective phenomenology of mental experience.
9. These two terms and the next quoted long passage are from *E*3Pr (G 2:138), all italicized in G; *Ethics,* 225–26.

10. *E*4P57S (G 2:252–53), *Ethics*, 225–26. W. Z. Harvey, "A Portrait of Spinoza as a Mimonidean," *Journal of the History of Philosophy*, 19 (1981), 151–72, shows that, in both Maimonides and Spinoza, the appeal to a moral exemplar keeps good and evil relative to human purposes and thus is an antidote to the anthropocentric view of God's activity.

11. Their methodological usage in the *Ethics* is recorded in *SE*, 212 (*methodus*), 214–16 (*modus*), 242 (*ordo*), 281–84 (*ratio*), and 351–52 (*via*). Cf. *LS*, s.v., for Spinoza's other writings as well.

12. *E*4P17S and P18S (G 2:221, 222–23), *Ethics*, 200–2. Cf. *E*3P59S (G 2:189), *Ethics*, 172.

13. *E*4Ap[Pr] (G 2:266), *Ethics*, 236.

14. *E*5Pr (G 2:277), *Ethics*, 244. To signify that his ethical reform of method reaches just as far as his reform of ethical doctrine, Spinoza uses the term *via* again in the very last scholium of the *Ethics*: *E*5P42S (G 2:308), *Ethics*, 270.

15. *E*3P7Dm (G 2:146), *Ethics*, 136–37. To search for the modal *primum*, or conatus, is the finite analogue of the methodic precept to work from the *prima elementa*, or God as naturing nature: *TIE* 75 (G 2:28–29), *Improvement*, 28. Ontologically, the analogy is between the finite modal *essentia actualis*, or naturating essence, and the *essential actuosa* of God as naturing nature.

16. Spinoza executes his transformational project in *E*3P9S and P11S, *E*4Pr and D1, 2, 8 (G 2:147–49, 208–10), *Ethics*, 137–39, 189–91. Should language be regarded as an irremediable cause of error and as a ground for weakening all philosophical emendations? The drawbacks and capabilities of language are stressed respectively by D. Savan, "Spinoza on Language," and G. H. R. Parkinson, "Language and Knowledge in Spinoza." These essays are included in *Spinoza: A Collection of Critical Essays*, ed. M. Grene, 60–72, 73–100. Four Spinozan considerations suggest that language can aid our search for philosophical truth and happiness: (a) The first kind of knowledge through experience, imagination, and signs, can be emended and included in human wisdom. (b) Spinoza is sensitive to linguistic statement, which he tries to tune finely as an expression of his reflections and as a medium for their communication in discussion. (c) Thus language always remains improvable by the philosopher seeking to know and convey more about "oneself and nature." But Spinoza never shared in his century's pursuit after the phantom of either a formal or a natural language that would intrinsically and perfectly manifest the truth about nature, an ideal examined by R. Fraser, *The Language of Adam: On the Limits and Systems of Discourse*. (d) Spinoza would agree with Galileo that philosophy studies the book of nature to which, in matters of humanly knowable truth, Bible texts must defer. (M. De Grazia, "The Secularization of Language in the Seventeenth Century," *Journal of the History of Ideas*, 41 [1980], 319–29.) Yet Spinoza's naturization of language does not deverbalize the book of nature whose structure, laws, and causal origin cannot be totally rendered in mathematical form. A geometrical manner and order are instruments for the philosophical betterment of meanings, uses, and deployments of language stripped of mathematics.

17. *E*3DAf1 (G 2:190); cf. *E*3P56Dm (G 2:185), *Ethics*, 168.

18. *E*4D8 (G 2:210), *Ethics*, 191. There are four points to notice about this definition: (a) Human virtue belongs in the wider field of naturating *virtus* or power. (b) The methodically disciplined mind must "refer" the general theory of *virtus* to its human form. (c) In using *potestas*, Spinoza avoids *potentia*. (d) As in the definition of an adequate idea, so here a consideration of the laws alone of human nature is not isolative

but actively integrative of the virtuous man with the whole order of laws of natured nature, in its active or naturating response. Within these guidelines, Spinoza can safely reinterpret the language of perfection, good, and evil, without violating his theme of nature as a whole. See J. C. Campbell, "Spinoza's Theory of Perfection and Goodness," *The Southern Journal of Philosophy*, 18 (1980), 259–74; W. K. Frankena, "Spinoza on the Knowledge of Good and Evil," *Philosophia*, 7 (1977), 15–44.

19. *TIE* 13 (G 2:8), *Improvement*, 6.

20. *E*4Pr (G 2:208), *Ethics*, 198.

21. *Ep* 30 (G 4:166), *Correspondence*, 205.

22. *E*4P67–73 and Ap (G 2:261–76), *Ethics*, 232–43.

23. Honoré de Balzac, *Cousin Bette* (Part One of *Poor Relations*), trans. M. A. Crawford, 122.

24. *E*4P67 (G 2:261), *Ethics*, 232. That is why Spinozan morality seeks a right pattern of *living*, or right reason placed at the disposal of an enhanced life.

25. *E*4P68S (G 2:262), *Ethics*, 233. A. Matheron, *Le Christ et le salut des ignorants chez Spinoza*, studies Spinoza's view of Christ as reorienting simple believers toward faith and obedience, love and justice, thereby giving them a morally certain access to salvation and beatitude. See below, Chapter Seven, Notes 10 and 38.

26. *E*3P59S (G 2:188), *Ethics*, 171. H. A. Wolfson, *The Philosophy of Spinoza*, 2:218–20, 257, 328–29, gives the lineage of this doctrine in Aristotle and Seneca, Maimonides and Aquinas, and Descartes.

27. *E*4ApCh32 (G 2:276), *Ethics*, 242–43.

28. *E*5P10S (G 2:287), *Ethics*, 252–53. The next quotation is from *E*3P2S (G 2:143), *Ethics*, 134.

29. "I pass at last to the other part of ethic, which concerns the manner or way [*de modo, sive via*] that leads to freedom." *E*5Pr (G 2:277), *Ethics*, 244. Right to the end, Spinoza remains careful about his methodological language. The distinction between starting and continuing our moral effort rests on experience of the human conatus, and clarifies the real basis for the temporal and durational view of man in the common order of nature. The phrase quoted above can be taken even more broadly to announce that all previous parts of *E* are teleologically ordered toward the doctrine on human freedom and beatitude in *Ethics V.* On this internal finality of *E*, see B. Rousset, *La Perspective finale de "L'Éthique" et le problème de la cohérence du spinozisme*. R. McCall, "The Teleological Approach to Spinoza," *The New Scholasticism*, 17 (1943), 134–55, and L. C. Rice, "Emotion, Appetition, and Conatus," *Revue Internationale de Philosophie*, 31 (1977), 101–16, base their teleological interpretation upon the striving of our conatus toward fulfillment.

30. *E*5P1–20, P21–42 (G 2:281–94, 294–308), *Ethics*, 247–59, 259–71. Proposition 21 marks a turning point in the meaning of love. Up to this point, it signifies a perfective modal process that is inapplicable to God or naturing nature. Thereafter, its meaning is interpreted in a sense that is compatible with naturing nature's own activity.

31. *E*5P20S (G 2:293), *Ethics*, 257. On the human mind's active ordination of its affective life to love toward God, see *E*5P15–20 (G 2:290–94), *Ethics*, 255–59. The formulaic expression *love toward x* conforms with Spinoza's comparative linguistic remark that "the noun *love* requires the accusative, just as [does] its verb *to love*." *CG* 13 (G 1:346), *Grammar*, 81. The best annotated translation of *CG* is Spinoza, *Abrégé de Grammaire hébraïque*, trans. J. Askénazi and J. Askénazi-Gerson (see p. 136).

32. For instance, see *E*5P20S and P32C (G 2:294, 300), *Ethics*, 258, 263. *SE,*

272–73, gives many variants. K. L. Schmitz, "A Moment of Truth: Present Actuality," *The Review of Metaphysics*, 33 (1979–80), 673–88, regards metaphysics as a science of radical presence, a reflection upon the copresencing of knower and known in a living act.

33. These terms stud two sets of propositions: E5P22–23 and P29–31 (G 2:295, 296, 298–300), *Ethics*, 259–60, 261–63. It is only when the viewpoint of eternity becomes predominant that the human mind proportionately overcomes its initial lack of essential knowledge about itself, its own body, and other corporeal things.

34. E5P23S (G 2:296), *Ethics*, 260. The *Short Treatise*'s emphasis on experiential feeling is here reaffirmed and incorporated within a reasoned philosophical account of the human mind's liberation and blessedness. Demonstrations and experiential feelings are not opposed or kept separate, but are unified in the Spinozan theory of naturating nature. This illuminates two issues: (a) Spinozan reason and intuition constitute an interplay of ways of cognizing that can concern the *same reality*, including God. S. Carr, "Spinoza's Distinction between Rational and Intuitive Knowledge," *The Philosophical Review*, 87 (1978), 241–52. (b) The philosophical theory about naturing and natured nature as a whole evokes emotions of awe and joy, expressed in religious language. A. J. Watt, "Spinoza's Use of Religious Language," *The New Scholasticism*, 46 (1972), 286–307.

35. E5P23 and Dm, P38Dm, and P40C (G 2:295, 304, 306), *Ethics*, 259, 266, 268.

36. E5P24 (G 2:296), *Ethics*, 260. This proposition leads at once to further propositions intended to specify that "the more" consists of intuitive knowledge of God and other things, our highest satisfaction or peace of mind, the intellectual love of God, and, consequently, our most effective union with nature as a whole. E5P25–33 (G 2:296–301), *Ethics*, 260–64.

37. E5P31S (G 2:300), *Ethics*, 263.

38. E5P33S (G 2:301), *Ethics*, 264. The preceding proposition to which Spinoza refers is P31. S. Hampshire, *Spinoza*, 169, suggests that a different but more familiar association arises from substituting the phrase *intellectual love of Nature*, which characterizes the affective attitude of many scientists and artists.

39. E5P36S (G 2:303), *Ethics*, 265.

40. E5P36C (G 2:302), *Ethics*, 265. Spinoza uses the singular verb "is" with the plural subject in order to emphasize the expressive modal unity between the human mind and the infinite understanding, in respect to the act of intellectual love. P36 itself states that *"the mind's intellectual love toward God is part of the infinite love whereby God loves himself."* Our partitive participation in God's love of himself seals the union of our mind with naturing nature and is the foundation of our affective union with total nature. Although the resemblances with Spinoza cannot be pressed too far, see J. C. Nelson, *Renaissance Theory of Love*, 84–102, 163–256, for the love doctrines of Leone Ebreo and Bruno.

41. E5P36S (G 2:303), *Ethics*, 265. Spinoza's remark on "glory" (treated in the second subsequent paragraph of the main body) follows immediately upon the present text. His term for *salvation* is *salus*, or human welfare achieved through our growth in virtue and loving union with God. He avoids the term *salvatio* because of its theological connotations. *Salus* is registered in *LS*, 973–75, and in *SE*, 300. Neither work lists *salvatio*, although *salvator* is used once (*LS*, 975, from *TTP*). The topic is thematized by E. E. Harris, *Salvation from Despair: A Reappraisal of Spinoza's Philosophy*.

42. E5P40S (G 2:306), *Ethics*, 268.

43. These texts are from *E*5P39Dm (G 2:305), *Ethics,* 267. The tension between "the least part of the mind" and "the greatest part of the mind" arises from our unceasing endeavor to move from the common order of nature to the eternal order of nature.

44. *E*5P31S, and P36S (G 2:300, 303), *Ethics,* 263, 266. There are no entries for "person" or "personality" in *SE,* and only a few entries for them in *LS,* 828 (from *CM, TP,* and *TTP*). In the newly found Ep 12A cited in Chapter One, Note 3, Spinoza remarks that he understands the meaning of these terms as used by classical philologists, but not as used by Trinitarian theologians.

45. This term and the next quotation are from *E*5P42S (G 2:308), *Ethics,* 270.

46. *E*5P39S (G 2:305), *Ethics,* 267. The six adverbs quoted in the remainder of this paragraph in the main body are found in the same scholium and in P42S (G 2:308), *Ethics,* 270.

47. Sebastian Brant, *The Ship of Fools,* trans. E. H. Zeydel, 350; cf. 361. In *The Praise of Folly,* trans. C. H. Miller, 5, Desiderius Erasmus reminds us that "it is an honor to be insulted by Folly."

Chapter Seven

1. John Locke, *Two Tracts on Government,* ed. P. Abrams, 120; John Locke, *Epistola de Tolerantia: A Letter on Tolerance,* ed. R. Klibansky, trans. J. W. Gough, 61. Spinoza himself acknowledges the mixed prompting of his inquiry by "the age, philosophy, and finally the issue itself." *TTP* 2 (G 3:29), Elwes, 27. These considerations are reflected in the following sonnet:

Spinoza

"A feeble-witted schoolboy" said Spinoza
"Can realize that it must be illogical
To try to settle questions theological
By burning heretics. It's time we chose a
More rational solution. I propose a
Hypothesis: the meaning's analogical
(Forgive me if my manner's pedagogical)
For 'God' read 'Nature'; now we've solved the poser!
For there is nothing in the slightest odd
In saying now that all things move in God,
That God is both the Substance and the Cause,
That everything exemplifies His laws."
Since this is plain horse sense (a shade simplistic)
Spinoza naturally is called a mystic.

D. H. Monro, "The Sonneteer's History of Philosophy,"
Philosophy, 55 (1980), 368.

2. The historical evidence is marshalled by H. H. Rowen, *John de Witt, Grand Pensionary of Holland, 1625–1672,* 383, 391, 348–419.

3. *TTP,* Subtitle (G 3:3), Wernham, 49. S. Umphrey, "Spinoza's Defense of Human Freedom," in *Spinoza's Metaphysics,* ed. J. B. Wilbur, 44–65, notes that freedom of philosophizing underlies the Spinozan theory of religious and political freedoms.

4. L. Strauss, "How to Study Spinoza's *Theologico-Political Treatise,*" in his *Per-*

secution and the Art of Writing, 142–201. One must also consider the social turmoil caused by the messianic claims of Sabbatai Sevi. See G. Scholem, *Sabbatai Ṣevi: The Mystical Messiah, 1626–1676,* 518–45, for his impact on Amsterdam. The general influence of the Kabbalah is measured by H. W. Brann, "Spinoza and the Kabbalah," in *Speculum Spinozanum 1677–1977,* ed. S. Hessing, 108–18.

   5. *AT* 8 (G 3:253), Elwes, 271.
   6. *E2P49S* (G 2:135–36), *Ethics,* 126.
   7. *E5P41S* (G 2:307), *Ethics,* 268–70.
   8. *E4P50, 53,* and *54* (G 2:247, 249–50), *Ethics,* 221–24. In *An Enquiry concerning the Principles of Morals,* IX, i, Hume regards the "monkish virtues" of penance and humility as unredeemable by any personal or social value, and hence transfers them (more unqualifiedly than does Spinoza) to "the catalogue of vices." Hume, *Enquiries concerning Human Understanding and concerning the Principles of Morals,* ed. L. A. Selby-Bigge and P. H. Nidditch, 270. Although Spinoza criticizes humility and repentance in individual and social life, he is also careful to distinguish virtuous self-regard and self-satisfaction from excessive and foolish pride. *E4P55-57* (G 2:250–53), *Ethics,* 224–26.
   9. *E4P50S* (G 2:247), *Ethics,* 221–22.
   10. *E5P42* (G 2:307), *Ethics,* 270. The double negative is intended to purify the motivation of those religious believers who obtain salvation through obedient pursuit of justice and love, but without having Spinozan philosophical knowledge.
   11. *E5P41* (G 2:306), *Ethics,* 268–69.
   12. *Ep* 43 and 73 (G 4:219–26, 306–9), *Correspondence,* 254–59, 342–44. Here, Spinoza defends *TTP* against the charge of irreligion by noting three topics on which his philosophy and biblical religion have a similar practical significance: (a) God is the vivifying power in whom we live and move. (b) Our moral-religious aim is to love God for himself and as our highest good. (c) Divine wisdom manifests itself in the human mind and generates our religious response of seeking our eternal welfare.
   13. *Ep* 23 (G 4:146), *Correspondence,* 189. G prints both Spinoza's autograph Dutch and his Latin translation. The phrase *philosophically speaking* is used twice in this letter (G 4:147, 148, *Correspondence,* 191).
   14. *Ep* 19 and 21 (G 4:92, 133), *Correspondence,* 149, 180.
   15. These three texts are from *Ep* 19 and 23 (G 4:92, 93, 148), *Correspondence,* 149, 150, 190.
   16. *TTP* 3 (G 3:46), Wernham, 53. The philosophical truth about moral precepts and mechanical laws (the field of *secundum* statements) arises from their being rooted in divine causal power and intramodal causation (the field of *per* statements).
   17. *Ep* 21 (G 4:130), *Correspondence,* 177.
   18. *TTP* Pr (G 3:5), Elwes, 3, 4.
   19. *TTP* 6 (G 3:81–96), Elwes, 81–97.
   20. *TTP* 3 (G 3:46), Wernham, 53. All finite modal things and events come to be (*fieri*) in accordance with (*secundum*) natured nature's laws, but through (*per*) the active causal power of God or naturing nature.
   21. *TTP* 6 (G 3:83), Elwes, 83. Spinoza is careful to add in a note to the last sentence that "by 'nature' I do not here understand matter alone and its affections but, besides matter, infinite other" things or the entirety of natured nature. Hence, exceptions could not be localized without disrupting the whole order of natured nature.
   22. "I say that the method of interpreting Scripture scarcely differs from the method

of interpreting nature, but entirely agrees with it. For just as the method of interpreting nature consists chiefly in this, namely, in fitting together the history of nature from which, as from mixed data we infer the definitions of natural things: so also for interpreting Scripture it is necessary to furnish its genuine history and from that, as from fixed data and principles, to infer by legitimate arguments the intention [*mentem*] of the authors of Scripture." *TTP* 7 (G 3:98), Elwes, 99. Yet although the moral teaching of Scripture holds for all men, "its meaning must be determined from its history alone, and not from the universal history of nature that is the foundation of philosophy alone." *TTP* 15 (G 3:185), Elwes, 195. Three consequences follow: (a) Scriptural intents and precepts belong within a regional history having its own integrity, but not furnishing the philosophical foundations required by the theory of nature. (b) Hence, the authorial intents and imagery of Scripture cannot determine the philosophical definitions used to study natured nature as a whole. (c) The latter definitions are "universal" in the sense of fixing meanings and principles concerned with the causal order operative in all natural things, but these definitions are not composed of abstract "universals." J. C. Morrison, "Spinoza and History," in *The Philosophy of Baruch Spinoza*, ed. R. Kennington, 173–95, suggests that, just as Spinoza used human history to naturize Scripture, so today he might use philosophical knowledge to criticize historicism. In "Vico and Spinoza," *Journal of the History of Ideas*, 41 (1980), 49, Morrison states: "As Vico laid the basis for the modern *historization of philosophy*, so Spinoza laid the basis for the modern *historization of religion*." So far forth, this may be called a regional historization of natured nature. Spinoza does not advance the theme of a history of nature much beyond Bacon and Descartes. But in discussing the course or progress of nature (*progressus Naturae*), he does submit our descriptive and hypothesizing work to his theory on the aids to imagination and the common order of nature and experience. He also emendates any genetic inference from mathematical, mechanical, and metaphysical principles by his own analogical surmodel of the order of the whole of nature. *Ep* 12 (G 4:56–58), *Correspondence*, 118–19. For Buffon's subsequent development of a scientific and philosophical history of nature, see *From Natural History to the History of Nature*, eds. J. J. Lyon and P. R. Sloan.

23. *TTP* 7 (G 3:102), Elwes, 104.

24. *TTP* 1 (G 3:15), Elwes, 13.

25. To explain prophecy, Spinoza devotes two chapters to the particular imagery, dispositions, and opinions of the prophets and the Jewish people. *TTP* 2–3 (G 3:29–57); Elwes, 27–42, Wernham, 51–65.

26. *TTP* 2 (G 3:31), Elwes, 29.

27. *TTP* 2 and 4 (G 3:42–43, 66); Elwes, 41, Wernham, 85. Hence, Spinoza distinguishes between a *natura* or exemplary model of living based on philosophical knowledge and the religious models proposed by prophets and evangelists. The "sole exemplar of true life" furnished by the latter is the supremely just and merciful God, commending justice and charity among men, but in no way imparting metaphysical-ethical knowledge of God and man. *TTP* 13 (G 3:170–71), Elwes, 179–80.

28. *TTP* 4, 5, 12 (G 3:57–69, 158–66); Wernham, 67–89, Elwes, 165–74. S. Pines, "Spinoza's *Tractatus Theologico-Politicus*, Maimonides and Kant," *Scripta Hierosolymitana*, 20 (1968), 3–54, pinpoints Spinoza's break with Maimonides over the continued validity of Mosaic law, which is a restricted practical regimen.

29. *TTP* 4 (G 3:59), Wernham, 71.

30. *TTP* 7 (G 3:99), Elwes, 100. A Malet, *Le Traité théologico-politique de Spinoza*

et la pensée biblique, is informative about the Bible texts and commentaries used by Spinoza (13–17) and about the treatment of the Bible in works other than *TTP* (17–109) and in *TTP* (113–300). S. Zac, *Spinoza et l'interprétation de l'Écriture,* concludes that, as a philosopher, Spinoza does not merely interpret Scripture through itself but criticizes the "implicit philosophy" (229–31) in it or attributed to it.

31. *TTP* 14 (G 3:176), Wernham, 117.

32. *Ep* 67, 67A, 76 (G 4:280–98, 316–24), *Correspondence,* 310–34, 350–55.

33. *TTP* 15 (G 3:180–88), Elwes, 190–99. Consult B. Baudoux, "Philosophia 'Ancilla Theologiae'," *Antonianum,* 12 (1937), 293–326. In a private communication (September 21, 1979), V. J. Bourke remarked on the relative paucity of medieval uses of this metaphor, by comparison with its presence in modern and contemporary expositions of medieval sources. On Spinoza's opposition to speculative theology (whether biblically oriented or not), see M. Walther, *Metaphysik als Anti-Theologie: Die Philosopie Spinozas im Zusammenhang der religionsphilosophischen Problematik.*

34. *TTP* 5 and 14 (G 3:77, 177), Wernham, 101, 119.

35. *TTP* 15 (G 3:178), Wernham, 121.

36. *TTP* 14 (G 3:179), Wernham, 123. This thesis of disengagement permits Spinoza to philosophize about the human world in terms of nature rather than of the Bible. J. E. Force, "Spinoza's *Tractatus Theologico-Politicus:* A New Way of Looking at the World," *The Southern Journal of Philosophy,* 12 (1974), 343–55.

37. *TTP* 15 (G 3:182), Elwes, 192.

38. Thus in *Ep* 19 (G 4:93), *Correspondence,* 150, he refers jointly to "philosophers and, with them, all those who are above the law, that is, who follow virtue not as a law but out of love, because it is the best thing."

39. *AT* 3 (G 3:252), Elwes, 270.

40. *TTP* 15 (G 3:188), Elwes, 199.

41. *AT* 34 (G 3:264, 417), Wernham, 249. Here one should consult both the Latin *Adnotationes* and Gabriel de Saint Glain's 1678 French translation *Remarques.* Richard H. Popkin, "Cartesianism and Biblical Criticism," in *Problems in Cartesianism,* eds. T. M. Lennon, J. M. Nicholas, and J. W. Davis, 81, concludes that the principles of biblical criticism proposed by Spinoza and Richard Simon neither eliminate Jewish and Christian traditions of religiious belief nor leave Spinoza's theory of nature as the sole philosophical possibility.

Chapter Eight

1. *KV* 2:24 (G 1:106–7), *Short Treatise,* 141–42.

2. *KV* 2:24 (G 1:105, 106), *Short Treatise,* 140, 141. Two comments on the relation between individual integrity and community in natured nature are pertinent: (a) "By this community alone, *as an agent and no mere thing,* it [each mode] maintains, and not loses by mergence, its individual being." H. F. Hallett, *Benedict De Spinoza: The Elements of His Philosophy,* 38. (b) The individual organism has two traits: "its *autonomy* for itself, and its *openness* for the world: spontaneity paired with receptivity." H. Jonas, "Spinoza and the Theory of the Organism," in *Spinoza: A Collection of Critical Essays,* ed. M. Grene, 278.

3. "Nor may I separate God from nature in the way that all with whom I am acquainted have done." *Ep* 6 (G 4:36), *Correspondence,* 99. Cf. chapter 5, note 27, on

the "God as like a man" criticism. The community approach avoids the pitfalls of both separation and confusion.

4. *TIE* 16 (G 2:9), *Improvement*, 7.

5. *TIE* 13, 14 (G 2:8–9), *Improvement*, 6–7.

6. As socially constituted, these disciplines require not only a synchronic community of contemporary workers but also a diachronic community of historical learning to safeguard cultural achievements against "devouring time." *TTP* 7 (G 3:106), Elwes, 108.

7. Spinoza's account of the best philosophical method involves a transition from *my* to *our* perspective: *TIE* 25, 37, 42 (G 2:12, 15, 17), *Improvement*, 10, 14, 15. Similarly, his ethical inquiry culminates in an apprehension of *our* eternal being: *E*5P23S (G 2:296), *Ethics*, 260.

8. Common notions and true perceptions: *TIE* 75–76, 99–101 (G 2:28–29, 36–37), *Improvement*, 28–29, 36–37; *E*2P38, 39, 40S1 (G 2:118–20), *Ethics*, 109–11. Common order of nature: *E*2P29C and S, P30Dm (G 2:114–15), *Ethics*, 106–7. The theme of community requires us now to contrast common notions with the common order of nature (rather than, as previously, with universal and transcendental notions). This comparison brings out the foundation of common notions in the eternal order and community of total nature. One consequence is to recognize that "love of God arises from cognition of him; moreover, cognition of him must be derived from common notions [that are] fixed and known through themselves," that is, in virtue of naturing nature's self-imparting to us all. *TTP* 4 (G 3:61), Wernham, 75. On the meanings and cognitive roles of common notions, see M. Gueroult, *Spinoza II: L'Âme (Éthique, II)*, 326–62, 581–82; G. H. R. Parkinson, *Spinoza's Theory of Knowledge*, 127–28, 164–65; E. L. Schoen, "The Role of Common Notions in Spinoza's *Ethics*," *The Southern Journal of Philosophy*, 15 (1977), 537–50, who includes existence or thatness.

9. *E*4P35S (G 2:234), *Ethics*, 210. A. Matheron, *Individu et communauté chez Spinoza*, 377–81, 517–613, establishes that the societal reference humanizes the passions, encourages the contribution of their *quid positivum* to our well-being, and operates both in the life of reason (*Ethics IV*) and in our love for the eternal (*Ethics V*).

10. *E*4ApCh7 (G 2:268), *Ethics*, 237. Hence, in political theory, Spinoza argues that the right and power of nature are shared by both the wise man and the ignorant one. "For a man, be he either wise or ignorant, is a part of nature." *TP* 2:5 (G 3:277), Wernham, 269.

11. *E*4P35 (G 2:232), *Ethics*, 209.

12. *E*4P70S (G 2:263), *Ethics*, 234, italics added.

13. *E*4P40 (G 2:241), *Ethics*, 216–17.

14. This and the next quotation are from *E*4P37S1 (G 2:237), *Ethics*, 213. E. M. Curley, "Man and Nature in Spinoza" in *Spinoza's Philosophy of Man*, ed. J. Wetlesen, 19–26, differentiates between the intrinsic significance and conatus of animals and other nonhuman things and the instrumental moral rules toward them which are generated by the human community.

15. For "in the natural condition" and "in the civil condition," see *E*4P37S2 (G 2:237–38), *Ethics*, 213–15. References in the next paragraph to "from common consent" and "from the consent of all" are from the same place. For *status naturalis*, see *LS* 1026–27, and *SE* 310–11.

16. *TTP* 16 (G 3:189–91), Wernham, 125–29; *TP* 2:2–3 (G 3:276–77), *Treatise on Politics*, 267, 269. V. J. Bourke, "Is Thomas Aquinas a Natural Law Ethicist?" *The*

Monist, 58 (1974), 52–66, notes that Aquinas relates *jus naturae* and *recta ratio* in a way that leads to an orthological ethics, based upon right reason. Spinoza is also an orthological ethicist, in the sense that our moral life is to be guided by right reason as a human modal expression of God or naturing nature.

17. *TP* 2:4 (G 3:277), *Treatise on Politics*, 269.

18. *TP* 2:3–4 (G 3:276–77), *Treatise on Politics*, 267.

19. *E* P37S2, P73 and Dm (G 2:237–39, 264–65), *Ethics*, 213–15, 235; *TP* 2:5–17 (G 3:277–82), *Treatise on Politics*, 268–79. The development of civil society and its laws is never divorced from the context of nature, where man is subject "to infinite other laws that have regard for the eternal order of the whole of nature, of which man is a small part." *TP* 2:8 (G 3:279), *Treatise on Politics*, 273.

20. *TP* 2:6 (G 3:277), *Treatise on Politics*, 269. Political philosophy seeks to overcome this alienating heteronomy between human ends and nature's order. J. Préposiet, *Spinoza et la liberté des hommes*, 119–21.

21. *TP* 2:7 and 11 (G 3:279, 280), *Treatise on Politics*, 273, 275. Both *TP* and the political portion of *TTP* are bonded with *E* through the latter's model of the wise and free man, who unites a knowledge and love of God with an appreciation of political existence and brotherhood. See L. Mugnier-Pollet, *La Philosophie politique de Spinoza*, 255–65 (on politics and soteriology); S. Breton, *Spinoza: Théologie et politique;* and R. J. McShea, *The Political Philosophy of Spinoza*, 155, 204.

22. *TTP* 20 (G 3:241), Wernham, 231. The state can help us from degenerating into "brutes or robots," only because it enlists the reflective power, self-modificational activity, and liberational endeavor of each human agent considered as some *automa spirituale*. *TIE* 85 (G 2:32) *Improvement*, 32. S. Cremaschi, *L'automa spirituale: La teoria della mente et della passioni in Spinoza*, identified "spiritual" with the human mind's capacity for improving its ideas and reorienting its affects. Gerald M. Mara, "Liberal Politics and Moral Excellence in Spinoza's Philosophy," *Journal of the History of Philosophy*, 20 (1982), 129–50, wonders how Spinoza's individualism and denial of final causes permit him to reach a liberal political ideal. The Spinozan theory of political community rests, however, precisely on an analogous meaning of "individual" and an intrahuman teleology or social purposefulness.

Chapter Nine

1. Immanuel Kant, *Gesammelte Schriften*, Academy Edition, vol. 16: *Reflexionen zur Logik*, Reflection no. 2566, pp. 419–20.

2. A. R. Hall and M. B. Hall, "Philosophy and Natural Philosophy: Boyle and Spinoza," in *Mélanges Alexandre Koyré*, 2:241–56, approach the Spinoza-Oldenburg correspondence from a Boylean view of natural philosophy.

3. Two instances where Spinoza's thought functions as a cognitive model in historical comparisons are E. E. Harris, *Nature, Mind and Modern Science*, 208–18, and J. Collins, "Inquiry-Model on Philosophical Advancement," *The Modern Schoolman*, 52 (1974–75), 3–25 (Spinoza and Locke). For analytic, scientific, and phenomenological accounts of model theory respectively, see M. Black, *Models and Metaphors;* M. Hesse, *Models and Analogies in Science;* and P. Ricoeur, *The Rule of Metaphor*. Spinoza's cautionary remarks on language are meant to acknowledge the valuable

presence of metaphor and yet to prevent its dominion over his philosophy. The seventeenth-century view of nature as a book, codex, or text (whether written in mathematical equations or in imagery) has to be rectified and fundamentally rethought in accord with his surmodel conception of naturing and natured nature. The grammar and linguistic presuppositions of nature viewed through the text-metaphor are being explored by M. Foucault, *The Order of Things: Archeology of the Human Sciences;* J. Derrida, "White Mythology: Metaphor in the Text of Philosophy," *New Literary History,* 6 (1974–75), 5–74; and T. J. Wilson, *Sein als Text: Vom Textmodell als Martin Heideggers Denkmodell.*

4. N. D. Belnap and T. Steel, *The Logic of Questions and Answers.*

5. Anthony Ashley Cooper, third Earl of Shaftesbury, *Characteristics of Men, Manners, Opinions, Times,* 1:189. Despite its popularity in Spinoza's time, the term *systema* is not listed in *LS.* To avoid ungrounded formalisms and fantastic schemas, he hews closely to the philosophical study of nature. Hence, I employ the Spinozan surmodel of nature as an analogous general-system model to bring out indirectly his contributions to, and strictures upon, a theory of system.

6. For a historical, a theoretical, and a metaphilosophical approach respectively, see. J. E. Van Hook, *Systematic Philosophy,* N. Rescher, *Cognitive Systematization,* and E. Laszlo, *Introduction to Systems Philosophy.* Unfortunately, P. Wienpahl, *The Radical Spinoza,* 137, regards Spinoza as a mystic rather than as a systematic philosopher. But the Spinozan system tries to naturize and thus incorporates mystical experience and language, as suggested by H. G. Hubbeling, "Logic and Experience in Spinoza's Mysticism," in *Spinoza on Knowing, Being and Freedom,* ed. J. G. van der Bend, 126–43.

7. *E*4P22C and P26Dm (G 2:225, 227), *Ethics,* 203–4, 205.

8. See above, Chapter Four, Note 18, and T. C. Mark's afterthoughts, "Truth and Adequacy in Spinozistic Ideas," in *Spinoza: New Perspectives,* eds. R. W. Shahan and J. I. Biro, 11–34. A coherentist synthesis of pragmatic, correspondence, and intuitionist views of truth is made by N. Rescher, *The Coherence Theory of Truth.* Because of the open and dynamic quality of Spinoza's view of truth and concept, there is no need to withhold from his philosophy the humanistic values espoused by M. Weitz, *The Opening Mind.*

9. L. C. Rice, "Methodology and Modality in the First Part of Spinoza's *Ethics,*" in J. G. van der Bend, ed., *Spinoza on Knowing, Being and Freedom,* 144–55, points out that Spinoza's contribution to modal logic concerns, not the concept of necessary being, but the efficacious necessary causality of God, the several sorts of necessary connections among modes, and our several ways of knowing.

10. D. K. Lewis, *Counterfactuals,* maintains that possible worlds have ontological reality and existence, but that they do not exist in our actual world. But in criticizing the univocal application of counterfactual modal logic to God, M. D. Wilson, "Possible Gods," *The Review of Metaphysics,* 32 (1978–79), 729, remarks that "a different world-choice would imply a different God." That is why Spinoza denies that things could be produced by God in another way or with another structure than they do have. Hence, Spinoza uses and interprets counterfactuals as tools solely of human imagination, inquiry, and practical advantage. He recognizes our capacity for making many worlds of discourse, action, and value appreciation, such as outlined in N. Goodman's *Ways of Worldmaking.*

11. Reconsiderations are given expression by E. Nagel, *Teleology Revisited and Other Essays in the Philosophy and History of Science*, A. Woodfield, *Teleology*, and L. Wright, *Teleological Explanations*. On the distinction between teleology A, *telos/tele*, and teleology B, see James Collins, "A Telos Approach to Leibniz," *The Review of Metaphysics*, 33 (1979–80), 347–69.

12. The teleology of human action is a focus for S. P. Kashap, "Thought and Action in Spinoza," in *Studies in Spinoza*, ed. S. P. Kashap, 332–50; and J. Neu, *Emotion, Thought and Therapy. A Study of Hume and Spinoza*.

13. *Ep* 30 (G 4:166), *Correspondence*, 206; *E*4P37S1 (G 2:236), *Ethics*, 212. M. W. Wartofsky, *Models: Representation and Scientific Understanding*, 255–77, is so impressed with the inner teleology of *E* that he proposes a transcendental deduction. What method and doctrinal path should be followed in *Ethics I–IV*, in order to achieve *Ethics V?*

14. K. Hecker, *Spinozas allgemeine Ontologie*, 108–21, interprets Spinoza's speculative system as a clarification of and response to "common praxis" in individual and social life. Y. Yovel, "Bible Interpretation as Philosophical Praxis: A Study of Spinoza and Kant," *Journal of the History of Philosophy*, 11 (1973), 189–212, adds that Spinoza's moral treatment of biblical religion exhibits the praxic intent of his whole philosophy. On the history and present status of praxiology, consult N. Lobkowics, *Theory and Practice: History of a Concept from Aristotle to Marx*, and R. J. Bernstein, *Praxis and Action: Contemporary Philosophies of Human Activity*.

15. That Spinoza's exemplar of human praxis combines sageliness, fortitude, and communion with others is the theme of J. Wetlesen's *The Sage and the Way: Spinoza's Ethics of Freedom*. A comparative approach to human models is taken by R. C. Neville, *Soldier, Saint, Sage*.

16. *Ep* 30 (G 4:166), *Correspondence*, 205. Arne Naess, "Spinoza and Ecology," in *Speculum Spinozanum 1677–1977*, ed. S. Hessing, 418–25, enumerates sixteen points of agreement and convergence between Spinoza and today's ecologists. More generally, see John Passmore, *Men's Responsibility for Nature*. On the specific issue of man and animal rights (with some references to Spinoza's instrumentalism and egalitarianism), see above, Chapter Eight, Note 14; S. R. L. Clarke, *The Moral Status of Animals;* R. G. Frey, *Interests and Rights: The Case Against Animals;* and R. A. Watson, "Self-Consciousness and the Rights of Nonhuman Animals and Nature," *Environmental Ethics*, 1 (1979), 99–129, a cautious review of behavioral evidence for broadening moral agency.

17. The first three named paintings are analyzed by M. M. Kahr, *Dutch Painting in the Seventeenth Century*, 128, 217, 234. On the fourth one, see J. D. Burke, "Dutch Paintings," *Bulletin* (Saint Louis Art Museum), new series, 15 (1980), 21. Over two centuries later, van Gogh sent his brother two open-air sketches and noted about the coloring: "You see how in the sketch of the beach there is a blond tender effect, and in the wood there is a more gloomy serious tone. I am glad both exist in nature." *The Letters of Vincent van Gogh*, ed. M. Roskill, 168–69.

18. William Wordsworth, *The Excursion*, book 1, lines 191–96, in William Wordsworth, *Poetical Works*, ed. Ernest de Selincourt, 593. N. P. Stallknecht, *Strange Seas of Thought: Studies in William Wordsworth's Philosophy of Man and Nature*, chapter 6, examines the Spinozistic influence on Coleridge and Wordsworth.

Bibliography

Works Cited in the Notes

1. BARUCH SPINOZA: WRITINGS AND TRANSLATIONS

Abrégé de Grammaire hébraique, trans. Joël Askénazi and Jocelyne Askénazi-Gerson. Paris: Vrin, 1968.

Algebraische Berechnung des Regenbogens. Berechnung von Wahrscheinlichkeiten, Dutch-German edition, trans. Hans-Christian Lucas and Michael J. Petry. Hamburg: Meiner, 1982.

Briefwisseling, trans. F. Akkerman, H. G. Hubbeling, and A. G. Westerbrink. Amsterdam: Wereldbibliotheek, 1977.

The Chief Works of Benedict De Spinoza, trans R. H. M. Elwes. 2 vols. New York: Dover, 1955.

The Correspondence of Spinoza, trans. A. Wolf. New York: Dial Press, 1928.

Earlier Philosophical Writings, trans. Frank A. Hayes. Indianapolis: Bobbs-Merrill, 1963.

The Ethics and Selected Letters, trans. Samuel Shirley, ed. Seymour Feldman. Indianapolis: Hackett, 1982.

Hebrew Grammar, trans. M. J. Bloom. New York: Philosophical Library, 1962.

De Nagelate Schriften. Amsterdam: Rieuwertsz, 1677.

Opera, ed. Carl Gebhardt. 4 vols. Heidelberg: Winter, 1924.

The Political Works, trans. A. G. Wernham. Oxford: Clarendon, 1958.

Short Treatise on God, Man, and His Well-Being, trans. A. Wolf. London: Black, 1910.

"*Treatise on the Improvement of the Understanding,*" trans. Paul D. Eisenberg, *Philosophy Research Archives,* 3 (1977), #553.

2. BOOKS

Allison, Henry E., *Benedict de Spinoza.* Boston: Twayne, 1975.

Balzac, Honoré de, *Cousin Bette* (Part One of *Poor Relations*), trans. Marion A. Crawford. Baltimore: Penguin, 1965.

Beck, Lewis W., *Six Secular Philosophers.* New York: Harper, 1960.

Belaief, Gail, *Spinoza's Philosophy of Law.* The Hague: Mouton, 1971.

Belnap, Nuel D., and Thomas Steel, *The Logic of Questions and Answers.* New Haven: Yale University Press, 1976.

Bend, J. G. van der, ed., *Spinoza on Knowing, Being and Freedom*. Assen: Van Gorcum, 1974.

Bernstein, Richard J., *Praxis and Action: Contemporary Philosophies of Human Activity*. Philadelphia: University of Pennsylvania Press, 1971.

Biasutti, Franco, *La Dottrina della scienza in Spinoza*. Bologna: Patron, 1979.

Black, Max, *Models and Metaphors*. Ithaca: Cornell University Press, 1962.

Boscherini, Emilia Giancotti, *Lexicon Spinozanum*. 2 vols. with continuous pagination. The Hague: Nijhoff, 1970.

Boyle, Robert, *Selected Philosophical Papers of Robert Boyle*, ed. M. A. Stewart. New York: Barnes and Noble, 1979.

Brant, Sebastian, *The Ship of Fools*, trans. Edwin H. Zeydel. New York: Dover, 1962.

Breton, Stanislas, *Spinoza: Théologie et politique*. Paris: Desclée, 1977.

Brunner, Peter, *Probleme der Teleologie bei Maimonides, Thomas von Aquin und Spinoza*. Heidelberg: Winter, 1928.

Clarke, Stephen R. L., *The Moral Status of Animals*. New York: Oxford University Press, 1977.

Collins, James, *Descartes' Philosophy of Nature*. Oxford: Blackwell, 1971.

Cramer, Wolfgang, *Spinozas Philosophie des Absoluten*. Frankfurt: Klostermann, 1966.

Cremaschi, Sergio, *L'automa spirituale: La teoria della mente e della passioni in Spinoza*. Milan: Vita e Pensiero, 1979.

Curley, Edwin M., *Descartes Against the Skeptics*. Cambridge: Harvard University Press, 1978.

————, *Spinoza's Metaphysics: An Essay in Interpretation*. Cambridge: Harvard University Press, 1969.

Darbon, André, *Études spinozistes*. Paris: Presses Universitaires, 1946.

Deleuze, Gilles, *Spinoza et le problème de l'expression*. Paris: Éditions de Minuit, 1968.

Descartes, René, *Descartes' Conversation with Burman*, trans. John Cottingham. Oxford: Clarendon Press, 1976.

————, *Descartes: His Moral Philosophy and Psychology*, trans. John J. Blom. New York: New York University Press, 1978.

————, *Meditations on First Philosophy*, trans. Donald A. Cress. Indianapolis: Hackett, 1979.

————, *Le Monde, ou Traité de la lumière* [The World], bilingual ed., trans. Michael S. Mahoney. New York: Abaris Books, 1977.

————, *Philosophical Letters*, trans. Anthony Kenny. Oxford: Clarendon, 1970.

————, *The Philosophical Works of Descartes*, trans. Elizabeth S. Haldane and G. R. T. Ross. Reprint, 2 vols. New York: Cambridge University Press, 1973.

————, *Principles of Philosophy*, trans. Valentine Rodger Miller and Reese P. Miller. Dordrecht and Boston: Reidel, 1983.

————, *Treatise of Man*, trans. Thomas S. Hall. Cambridge, Mass.: Harvard University Press, 1972.

Deugd, C. de, *The Significance of Spinoza's First Kind of Knowledge*. Assen: Van Gorcum, 1966.

Dibon, Paul, *La Philosophie néerlandaise au siècle d'or*. Vol. 1. Amsterdam: Elsevier, 1954.

Dijksterhuis, E. J., and others, *Descartes et le cartésianisme hollandais*. Paris: Presses Universitaires, 1960.

Dunin-Borkowski, Stanislaus von, *Spinoza*. 4 vols. Münster: Aschendorff, 1933–36.

Erasmus, Desiderius, *The Praise of Folly*, trans. Clarence H. Miller. New Haven: Yale University Press, 1979.

Ehrlich, Leonard, *Karl Jaspers: Philosophy as Faith*. Amherst: University of Massachusetts Press, 1975.

Flaubert, Gustave, *Bouvard and Pécuchet*, trans. T. W. Earp and G. W. Stonier. Norfolk, Conn.: New Directions, 1954.

————, *The Dictionary of Accepted Ideas*, trans. Jacques Barzun. Revised ed. New York: New Directions, 1977.

Foucault, Michel, *The Order of Things: Archeology of the Human Sciences*. New York: Pantheon, 1970.

Fraser, Russell, *The Language of Adam: On the Limits and Systems of Discourse*. New York: Columbia University Press, 1977.

Freudenthal, J., *Spinoza: Sein Leben und seine Lehre*. Vol. I: *Das Leben Spinozas*. Stuttgart: Frommann, 1904.

Frey, R. G., *Interests and Rights: The Case against Animals*. New York: Oxford University Press, 1980.

Friedmann, Georges, *Leibniz et Spinoza*. New ed. Paris: Gallimard, 1962.

Gilbert, Neal W., *Renaissance Concepts of Method*. New York: Columbia University Press, 1960.

Goodman, Nelson, *Ways of Worldmaking*. Indianapolis: Hackett, 1978.

Grene, Marjorie, ed., *Spinoza: A Collection of Critical Essays*. Garden City: Doubleday Anchor, 1973.

Gueret, Michel, André Robinet, and Paul Tombeur, *Spinoza Ethica. Concordances, Index, Listes de fréquences, Tables comparatives*. Louvain-la-Neuves: Publications de CETEDOC, Université Catholique de Louvain, 1977.

Gueroult, Martial, *Spinoza I: Dieu (Éthique, I)*. Paris: Aubier, 1968.

————, *Spinoza II: L'Âme (Éthique, II)*. Paris: Aubier, 1974.

Hallett, H. F., *Benedict De Spinoza: The Elements of His Philosophy*. London: Athlone Press, 1957.

Hampshire, Stuart, *Spinoza*. Baltimore: Penguin, 1951.

Harris, Errol E., *Nature, Mind and Modern Science*. New York: Macmillan, 1954.

————, *Salvation from Despair: A Reappraisal of Spinoza's Philosophy*. The Hague: Nijhoff, 1973.

Hecker, Konrad, *Spinozas allgemeine Ontologie*. Darmstadt: Wissenschaftliche Buchgesellschaft, 1978.
Heereboord, Adrian, *Hermeneia Logica* . . . [bound in continuous pagination with] *Praxis Logica*. Third ed. Leiden: Lodenstein, 1657.
Hegel, G. W. F., *Lectures on the History of Philosophy,* trans. E. S. Haldane and F. H. Simson. 3 vols. New York: Humanities Press, 1955.
————, *Science of Logic*, trans. A. V. Miller. New York: Humanities Press, 1969.
Hesse, Mary, *Models and Analogies in Science*. Notre Dame: University of Notre Dame Press, 1966.
Hessing, Siegfried, ed., *Speculum Spinozanum 1677–1977*. London: Routledge and Kegan Paul, 1977.
Hintikka, Jaakko, *Models for Modalities*. New York: Humanities Press, 1969.
Hobbes, Thomas, *Examinatio et emendatio mathematicae hodiernae,* in vol. 4 of *Opera Latina*, ed. W. Molesworth. 5 vols. London: Bohn and Longman, 1839–45.
Hondt, Jacques d', ed., *Hegel et la pensée moderne*. Paris: Presses Universitaires, 1970.
Hubbeling, Hubertus G., *Spinoza*. Frieburg and Munich: Alber, 1978.
————, *Spinoza's Methodology*. Second ed. Assen: Van Gorcum, 1967.
Huizinga, J. H., *Dutch Civilization in the Seventeenth Century.* New York: Ungar, 1968.
Hume, David, *Enquiries concerning Human Understanding and concerning the Principles of Morals,* eds. L. A. Selby-Bigge and P. H. Nidditch. Third ed. New York: Oxford University Press, 1975.
————, *A Treatise of Human Nature,* ed. L. A. Selby-Bigge. Second ed. revised by P. H. Nidditch. New York: Oxford University Press, 1978.
James, William, *A Pluralistic Universe.* Cambridge: Harvard University Press, 1977.
Joachim, Harold H., *Spinoza's Tractatus De Intellectus Emendatione*. Oxford: Clarendon, 1940.
————, *A Study of the Ethics of Spinoza*. Oxford: Clarendon, 1901.
Kahr, Madlyn M., *Dutch Painting in the Seventeenth Century*. New York: Harper and Row, 1978.
Kant, Immanuel, *Gesammelte Schriften,* Academy ed., vol. 16: *Reflexionen zur Logik,* ed. Erich Adickes. Berlin: Reimer, 1914.
Kashap, S. Paul, ed., *Studies in Spinoza: Critical and Interpretive Essays*. Berkeley and Los Angeles: University of California Press, 1972.
Kauz, Frank, *Substanz und Welt bei Spinoza und Leibniz*. Freiburg i. Br.: Alber, 1972.
Kennington, Richard, ed., *The Philosophy of Baruch Spinoza*. Washington: Catholic University of America Press, 1980.
Kogan, Barry S., ed., *Spinoza: A Tercentenary Perspective*. Cincinnati: Hebrew Union College–Jewish Institute of Religion, 1979.

Lachièze-Rey, Pierre, *Les Origines cartésiennes du Dieu de Spinoza.* Paris: Alcan, 1932.

Laszlo, Ervin, *Introduction to Systems Philosophy.* New York: Harper and Row, 1972.

Lennon, T. M., J. M. Nicholas, and J. W. Davis, eds. *Problems in Cartesianism.* Kingston and Montreal: McGill-Queens University Press.

Lewis, David K., *Counterfactuals.* Cambridge: Harvard University Press, 1973.

Lobkowics, Nicholas, *Theory and Practice: History of a Concept from Aristotle to Marx.* Notre Dame: University of Notre Dame Press, 1967.

Locke, John, *Epistola de Tolerantia: A Letter on Toleration,* ed. Raymond Klibansky, trans. J. W. Gough. Oxford: Clarendon, 1968.

———, *Essays on the Law of Nature,* ed. W. von Leyden. Oxford: Clarendon, 1954.

———, *Two Tracts on Government,* ed. Philip Abrams. New York: Cambridge University Press, 1967.

Lyon, John J., and Phillip R. Sloan, eds., *From Natural History to the History of Nature: Readings from Buffon and His Critics.* Notre Dame: University of Notre Dame Press, 1981.

Maimonides, Moses, *The Guide of the Perplexed,* trans. Shlomo Pines. Chicago: University of Chicago Press, 1963.

Malet, André, *Le Traité théologico-politique de Spinoza et la pensée biblique.* Paris: Les Belles Lettres, 1966.

Mandelbaum, Maurice, and Eugene Freeman, eds. *Spinoza: Essays in Interpretation.* LaSalle, Illinois: Open Court, 1975.

Mark, Thomas C., *Spinoza's Theory of Truth.* New York: Columbia University Press, 1972.

Matheron, Alexandre, *Le Christ et le salut des ignorants chez Spinoza.* Paris: Aubier, 1971.

———, *Individu et communauté chez Spinoza.* Paris: Éditions de Minuit, 1969.

McKeon, Richard P., *The Philosophy of Spinoza. The Unity of His Thought.* New York: Longmans, Green, 1928.

McShea, Robert J., *The Political Philosophy of Spinoza.* New York: Columbia University Press, 1968.

Mélanges Alexandre Koyré. 2 vols. Paris: Hermann, 1964.

Mugnier-Pollet, Lucien, *La Philosophie politique de Spinoza.* Paris: Vrin, 1976.

Naess, Arne, *Freedom, Emotion and Self-subsistence: The Structure of a Central Part of SPINOZA'S ETHICS.* Oslo: Universitetsforlaget, 1975.

Nagel, Ernest, *Teleology Revisited and Other Essays in the Philosophy and History of Science.* New York: Columbia University Press, 1979.

Nagel, Thomas, *Mortal Questions.* New York: Cambridge University Press, 1979.

Nasr, Seyyed H., *An Introduction to Islamic Cosmological Doctrines*. Revised ed. Boulder, Colorado: Shambhala Publications, 1978.

Nelson, John C., *Renaissance Theory of Love*. New York: Columbia University Press, 1958.

Neu, Jerome, *Emotion, Thought and Therapy. Study of Hume and Spinoza and the Relationship of Philosophical Theories of the Emotions to Psychological Theories of Therapy*. Berkeley and Los Angeles: University of California Press, 1977.

Neville, Robert C., *Soldier, Sage, Saint*. New York: Fordham University Press, 1978.

Niftrik, G. C. van, *Spinoza en de sectariërs van zijn tijd*. Leiden: Brill, 1963.

Parkinson, G. H. R., *Spinoza's Theory of Knowledge*. Oxford: Clarendon, 1954.

Passmore, John, *Man's Responsibility for Nature: Ecological Problems and Western Tradition*. New York: Scribners, 1974.

Pereira, Benedict, *De communibus omnium rerum naturalium principiis et affectionibus libri quindecem*. Rome: Tornerius and Biricchia, 1585.

Pope, Alexander, *The Poems of Alexander Pope*, ed. John Butt. New Haven: Yale University Press, 1963.

Popkin, Richard H., *The History of Scepticism from Erasmus to Spinoza*. Revised and expanded ed. Berkeley and Los Angeles: University of California Press, 1979.

Préposiet, Jean, *Spinoza et la liberté des hommes*. Paris: Gallimard, 1967.

Rescher, Nicholas, *Cognitive Systematization*. Totowa, N. J.: Rowman and Littlefield, 1979.

————, *The Coherence Theory of Truth*. Oxford: Clarendon, 1973.

Rice, Eugene F., *The Renaissance Idea of Wisdom*. Cambridge, Mass.: Harvard University Press, 1958.

Ricoeur, Paul, *The Rule of Metaphor*. Toronto: University of Toronto Press, 1977.

Roth, Leon, *Spinoza*. London: Allen and Unwin, 1954.

————, *Spinoza, Descartes and Maimonides*. Oxford: Clarendon, 1924.

Rousset, Bernard, *La Perspective finale de "L'Éthique" et le problème de la cohérence du spinozisme*. Paris: Vrin, 1968.

Rowen, Herbert H., *John de Witt, Grand Pensionary of Holland, 1625–1672*. Princeton: Princeton University Press, 1978.

Ruestow, Edward G., *Physics at 17th and 18th-Century Leiden*. The Hague: Nijhoff, 1973.

Scholem, Gershom, *Sabbatai Ṣevi: The Mystical Messiah, 1626–1676*. Princeton: Princeton University Press, 1973.

Shaftesbury, Anthony Ashley Cooper, third Earl of, *Characteristics of Men, Manners, Opinions, Times*, ed. John M. Robertson. 2 vols. in one. Indianapolis: Bobbs-Merrill, 1964.

Shahan, Robert W., and J. I. Biro, eds., *Spinoza: New Perspectives*. Norman: University of Oklahoma Press, 1978.

Siwek, Paul, *Spinoza et le panthéisme religieux*. New ed. Paris: Desclée, 1950.

Stallknecht, Newton P., *Strange Seas of Thought: Studies in William Wordsworth's Philosophy of Man and Nature*. Bloomington: Indiana University Press, 1958.

Strauss, Leo, *Persecution and the Art of Writing*. Glencoe, Illinois: Free Press, 1952.

————, *Spinoza's Critique of Religion*. New York: Schocken, 1965.

Thomas Aquinas, St., *Basic Writings of Saint Thomas Aquinas*, ed. Anton C. Pegis. 2 vols. New York: Random House, 1945.

Timm, Hermann, *Gott und die Freiheit: Studien zur Religionsphilosophie der Goethezeit*. Vol. 1: *Die Spinozarenaissance*. Frankfurt: Klostermann, 1974.

Van Gogh, Vincent, *The Letters of Vincent van Gogh*, ed. Mark Raskill. New York: Atheneum, 1974.

Van Hook, John E., *Systematic Philosophy*. Hicksville, N.Y.: Exposition, 1979.

Walther, Manfred, *Metaphysik als Anti-Theologie: Die Philosophie Spinozas im Zusammenhang der religionsphilosophischen Problematik*. Hamburg: Meiner, 1971.

Wartofsky, Marx W., *Models: Representation and Scientific Understanding*. Boston: Reidel, 1979.

Weitz, Morris, *The Opening Mind*. Chicago: University of Chicago Press, 1978.

Wetlesen, Jon, *The Sage and the Way: Spinoza's Ethics of Freedom*. Atlantic Highlands, N.J.: Humanities Press, 1979.

————, ed., *Spinoza's Philosophy of Man*. Oslo: Universitetsforlaget, 1978.

Wienpahl, Paul, *The Radical Spinoza*. New York: New York University Press, 1979.

Wilbur, James B., ed., *Spinoza's Metaphysics*. Assen: Van Gorcum, 1976.

Wilson, Thomas J., *Sein als Text: Vom Textmodell als Martin Heideggers Denkmodell*. Freiburg i. Br.: Alber, 1981.

Wolfson, Harry A., *The Philosophy of Spinoza*. 2 vols. Cambridge, Mass.: Harvard University Press, 1934.

————, *Studies in the History of Philosophy and Religion*, eds. Isadore Twersky and George H. Williams. 2 vols. Cambridge, Mass.: Harvard University Press, 1973–77.

Woodfield, Andrew, *Teleology*. New York: Cambridge University Press, 1976.

Wordsworth, William, *Poetical Works*, ed. Ernest de Selincourt. New York: Oxford University Press, 1967.

Wright, Larry, *Teleological Explanations*. Berkeley and Los Angeles: University of California Press, 1976.

Yerushalmi, Yosef H., *From Spanish Court to Italian Ghetto. Isaac Cordoso, A Study in Seventeenth Century Marranism and Jewish Apologetics*. New York: Columbia University Press, 1971.

Zac, Sylvain, *L'Idée de vie dans la philosophie de Spinoza*. Paris: Presses Universitaires, 1963.

————, *Spinoza et l'interprétation de l'Écriture*. Paris: Presses Universitaires, 1965.

3. ARTICLES

Baudoux, B., "Philosophia 'Ancilla Theologiae'," *Antonianum*, 12 (1937), 293–326.

Boehm, Rudolf, "Spinoza und die Metaphysik der Subjektivität," *Zeitschrift für philosophische Forschung*, 22 (1968), 165–86.

Bourke, Vernon J., "Is Thomas Aquinas a Natural Law Ethicist?" *The Monist*, 58 (1974), 52–66.

Burke, James D., "Dutch Paintings," *Bulletin* (Saint Louis Art Museum), new series, 15 (1980), 1–24.

Campbell, John, "Spinoza's Theory of Perfection and Goodness," *The Southern Journal of Philosophy*, 18 (1980), 259–74.

Carr, Spencer, "Spinoza's Distinction between Rational and Intuitive Knowledge," *The Philosophical Review*, 87 (1978), 241–52.

Close, Anthony J., "Commonplace Theories of Art and Nature in Classical Antiquity and in the Renaissance," *Journal of the History of Ideas*, 20 (1969), 467–86.

Collins, James, "Inquiry-Model on Philosophical Advancement," *The Modern Schoolman*, 52 (1974–75), 3–25.

————, "A Telos Approach to Leibniz," *The Review of Metaphysics*, 33 (1979–80), 347–69.

DeGrazia, Margreta, "The Secularization of Language in the Seventeenth Century," *Journal of the History of Ideas*, 41 (1980), 319–29.

Derrida, Jacques, "White Mythology: Metaphor in the Text of Philosophy," *New Literary History*, 6 (1974–75), 5–74.

Di Vona, Piero, "L'analogia del concetto di 'res' in Spinoza," *Rivista critica di storia della filosofia*, 16 (1961), 48–78.

Eisenberg, Paul D., "How to Understand *De Intellectus Emendatione*," *Journal of the History of Philosophy*, 9 (1971), 171–91.

Force, James E., "Spinoza's *Tractatus Theologico-Politicus*: A New Way of Looking at the World," *The Southern Journal of Philosophy*, 12 (1974), 343–55.

Frankena, William K., "Spinoza on the Knowledge of Good and Evil," *Philosophia*, 7 (1977), 15–44.

Harvey, W. Z., "A Portrait of Spinoza as a Maimonidean," *Journal of the History of Philosophy*, 19 (1981), 151–72.

Jarrett, Charles E., "The Concepts of Substance and Mode in Spinoza," *Philosophia,* 7 (1977), 83–105.

Kaufmann, Felix, "Spinoza's System as Theory of Expression," *Philosophy and Phenomenological Research,* 1 (1940–41), 83–97.

Kiwiet, John J., "The Rynsburg Collegiants," privately circulated paper, 1976.

Lennox, James G., "The Causality of Finite Modes in Spinoza's *Ethics,*" *Canadian Journal of Philosophy,* 6 (1976), 479–500.

Lucks, Henry A., "*Natura Naturans—Natura Naturata,*" *The New Scholasticisim,* 9 (1935), 1–24.

Mara, Gerald M., "Liberal Politics and Moral Excellence in Spinoza's Political Philosophy," *Journal of the History of Philosophy,* 20 (1982), 129–50.

McCall, Raymond, "The Teleological Approach to Spinoza," *The New Scholasticism,* 17 (1943), 134–55.

Monro, D. H., "The Sonneteer's History of Philosophy," *Philosophy,* 55 (1980), 363–75.

Morrison, James C., "Vico and Spinoza," *Journal of the History of Ideas,* 41 (1980), 49–68.

Parkinson, G. H. R., "Hegel, Pantheism, and Spinoza," *Journal of the History of Ideas,* 38 (1977), 449–59.

Pines, Shlomo, "Spinoza's *Tractatus Theologico-Politicus,* Maimonides and Kant," *Scripta Hierosolymitana,* 20 (1968), 3–54.

Pupi, Angelo, "L' 'Etica' di Spinoza alla luce del 'Breve Trattato'," *Rivista di filosofia neo-scolastica,* 45 (1953), 229–52.

Reif, Patricia, "The Textbook Tradition in Natural Philosophy, 1600–1650," *Journal of the History of Ideas,* 30 (1969), 17–32.

Rice, Lee C., "The Continuity of '*Mens*' in Spinoza," *The New Scholasticism,* 43 (1969), 75–103.

———, "Emotion, Appetition, and Conatus," *Revue Internationale de Philosophie,* 31 (1977), 101–16.

Schmitz, Kenneth L., "A Moment of Truth: Present Actuality," *The Review of Metaphysics,* 33 (1979–80), 673–88.

Schoen, Edward L., "The Role of Common Notions in Spinoza's *Ethics,*" *The Southern Journal of Philosophy,* 15 (1977), 537–50.

Siebeck, H., "Über die Entstehung der Termini *natura naturata* und *natura naturans,*" *Archiv für Geschichte der Philosophie,* 3 (1890), 370–78.

Watson, Richard A., "Self-Consciousness and the Rights of Nonhuman Animals and Nature," *Environmental Ethics,* 1 (1979), 99–129.

Watt, A. J., "The Causality of God in Spinoza's Philosophy," *Canadian Journal of Philosophy,* 2 (1972–73), 171–89.

———, "Spinoza's Use of Religious Language," *The New Scholasticism,* 46 (1972), 286–307.

Wilson, Margaret D., "Possible Gods," *The Review of Metaphysics,* 32 (1978–79), 717–33.

Yovel, Yirmiahu, "Bible Interpretation as Philosophical Praxis: A Study of Spinoza and Kant," *Journal of the History of Philosophy*, 11 (1973), 189–212.

Zac, Sylvain, "État et nature chez Spinoza," *Revue de Métaphysique et de Morale*, 69 (1964), 14–40.

Bibliographical Note. Edwin M. Curley's translation of *Spinoza: The Collected Works* (2 vols. Princeton: Princeton University Press) provides an excellent translated and annotated English edition of Spinoza's text.

Index

Abstractions, 125, 233. *See also* Transcendental and universal notions
Action, 92, 106, 112, 164, 173–74
Actional turn, 175–77, 179
Adequate knowing, 149, 158, 164, 300
Affect, 164, 172–73, 174–75, 182–84, 187–88, 305
Affections, 163–64, 188
Agreement in nature and in social activity, 246–50
Alienation, 108–9, 237
All-being (*alwezen*), 34–36, 37, 46–47, 284, 294
Analogy: within nature, 18, 63–64, 111–12, 236–37, 299; of things, 60–64, 112; eminent and formal, 64, 66, 236–37, 295; man as toolmaker, 98; conscious worm, 168–70; anthropological, 180; moral modeling, 180–81; causal primary analogate, 214; community differentiations, 236–37; fabular entities, 248
Animals and men, 247–49, 254, 311, 314
Anthropology as philosophical, 152–53, 159
Anthropomorphism, 52–53, 143–44, 153, 169–70, 180, 189, 195, 214–15, 237, 274, 302
Argument structure, 33, 99, 121, 181–86, 258–62, 266–67
Aristotle, 3, 79, 256, 298
Art, 105, 269, 282–83, 301, 314
Atheism, 14–15
Attribute: infinite, 34–35, 61; definition, 38–39, 123, 125; of substance, 42, 47, 86, 127, 137; and modes, 137; yields philosophical knowledge of God, 225–26; irreducible distinction, 302
Awareness, 69, 92, 108–9, 185, 188, 237. *See also* Self-realization
Axioms, 149–51, 166, 292

Bacon, Francis, 4, 76, 88, 103, 122, 236, 296, 309
Balzac, Honoré de, 181
Bartók, Béla, 60,
Bayle, Pierre, 27
Beatitude or blessedness, 25, 72, 99, 147–48, 187, 189–200, 208–11, 212, 229, 244, 273, 291, 304. *See also* Happiness
Beck, L. W., 302
Being: *Wezen*, 28–29; *esse* or act-of-being, 28–29, 124, 293; God's reality, 34–35, 47; real, 47, 62, 296; "is and is conceived to be," 130
Belief, 223, 224, 308. *See also* Faith
Better part of ourselves, 185, 273, 277, 306, 307. *See also* Eternity: our mind as eternal in part; Mind: eternal part
Bible and scriptural religion, 36, 71, 102, 107–9, 110, 182, 202, 211–15, 215–23, 224, 228, 242, 282–83, 299, 304, 308, 309, 310, 314
Blyenbergh, W. van, 212, 213, 215
Body: general theory of, 10; corporeal nature of, 42, 56; and human mind, 56, 65–66, 156–61, 172, 190; one's own, 109; and what we perceive or feel, 150; and free activity, 302
Boehm, R., 301
Bourke, V. J., 310, 312
Boyle, Robert, 104, 107, 150, 168, 201, 301, 312
Brann, H. W., 308
Brant, Sebastian, 199
Bruckner, Anton, 196
Bruder, C. H., 290
Brunner, P., 301
Bruno, Giordano, 76
Buffon, G.-L. L., Comte de, 309
Burgh, Albert, 223
Burman, Frans, 22

Index

327

Eisenberg, P. D., 297
Emendation of the Understanding: 75–118
passim; title, 81–82; community intent,
237–44, 311; Hobbes' use of "*Emen-
datio*," 299; mentioned, 23, 25, 29, 32,
119, 122, 123, 124, 125, 132, 144, 165, 170,
179, 185, 203, 254, 260, 274
Emotion. *See* Affect
Emotive talk, 71
Empire-within-an-empire, 167–68, 253, 303
Enclave ethics, 167–68, 253, 303
Entity of reason or imagination, 47, 62, 105,
111, 128, 144
Epicurus, 103
Epistemic factor, 52–53, 55–60, 256
Epistemology, 55, 105, 163–66, 211, 226,
258–59, 275–76
Equanimity, 185–86
Erasmus, Desiderius, 198
Erotetic logic, 259–62
Error, 21–22, 105, 113, 165–66, 241
Essence: as known, 17; *Wezentheid,* 28–29;
divine, 36; formal and objective, 93–94,
95–96, 97–99; as involving existence, 124
Eternal and common order of nature, 150,
160–61, 190, 243–44, 245, 277, 303, 311.
See also Order and connection
Eternity: eternal welfare and life, 71–72, 108;
eternal order, 85, 160–61; necessary existence, 106; definition, 123, 128; nondurational and nontemporal, 128, 131, 188, 189;
our mind as eternal in part, 191, 196, 306;
divine causality, 292
Ethical and moral intent, 85–86, 163, 170,
256, 258–59
Ethics: divisions, 23–24, 142; *Ethics I–II,*
119–61 passim; *Ethics III–IV,* 162–200
passim; doctrine on piety and religion,
204–11; societal motif, 244–50; continuity,
266; mentioned, 19, 29, 31, 41, 44, 47, 56,
58, 69, 82, 86, 89, 92, 95, 99, 110, 111,
112, 115, 116–17, 201, 203–4, 215, 240,
243, 252, 254, 258–59, 261–62, 264, 266,
270, 274, 277
Euclid, 102
Exemplar for moral man, 177–87
Exemplarity of ideas, 98–99
Existence: as known, 18, 65–66, 106, 124;
Wezentlykheid, 28–29, 293; eternal necessity, 106, 115–16, 296
Experience, 48, 73–74, 104–5, 106–7, 186,
190–91, 295, 306, 313

Experiment. *See* Hypothesis and experiment
Expression, 53, 95, 130, 153, 167, 300
Extension, 42, 45, 54, 61–62, 151–54

Facticity of man, 53, 150
Faculty theory, 8, 168, 297
Faith, 223–29
Feeling, 66–67, 191, 299
Feuerbach, Ludwig, 70
Fiction and feigning, 105–7. *See also*
Hypothesis and experiment; Possible
worlds
Fieri and *ordinari* (to come to be, and to be
ordered or ordained), 217
Finality: Cartesian antifinalism, 21–22;
mathematical purifier, 103; moral aim,
162–200 passim; no final cause for God,
21–22, 231, 238, 271. *See also* Purpose;
Teleology
Firmness or fortitude, 182–84, 210, 277
Flaubert, Gustave, 119, 299
Foolish crowd, 199
Foundations: Spinozan bases, 8, 11–18,
263–65; Cartesian, 10–19; theory of God
and basic definitions, 122–23; as community with God, 232; conatus, 316
Franck, J., 299
Freedom: in philosophizing, 4, 226–29,
307–8; of God, 18, 24, 48, 251–53, 267;
free thing, 123, 128; versus compulsion,
123, 129; acceptance of necessity of total
nature, 168, 267, 278; achieved through
endeavor, 182, 305; of philosophizing,
202–3; purpose of state, 254; active attitude toward bodies, 302
Free man as moral exemplar: 177–87, 246,
249, 253–54, 273; neither brute nor robot,
312
Friendship, 183, 207, 247–48

Galileo Galilei, 14, 48, 73, 104, 304
Gassendi, Pierre, 103
Gebhardt, C., 27, 28, 296
Generality: diremptive and interpretive,
112–14
Generosity, 182–84, 210
Genus and species, 40–41, 43
Geometrical order and manner, 121, 171,
174–75, 304. *See also* Mathematics
Giancotti Boscherini, E., 303
Glory, 304
God: active idea of, 12–15, 34–35, 48, 122,

textbook form, 78; personal pattern, 84; true fruitful idea, 116–17; geometrical order and manner, 121, 171; moral piety and religion, 206–7; cognitive model, 255–59; reciprocity, 276–78, 312–13

Modes, 39, 42, 54, 61–62, 83–84, 85–86, 123, 126–27, 134–38, 153–56, 174, 205, 232–37, 279

Monro, D. H., 307

Montaigne, Michel de, 109

Moral and ethical motif, 85–86, 89, 128, 163, 165–66, 170, 237–44, 244–50, 275–78

Morrison, J. C., 309

Motion-and-rest, 42, 48–49, 54–55, 104, 272

"My order," 88–89, 171, 174, 276, 292

"My philosophy," 77, 81, 89, 170, 274, 307. *See also* Philosophizing activity

Mysticism, 74, 296, 313

Naess, A., 302, 314

Nagel, T., 303

Natural philosophy, 10, 24, 48–49, 54, 256, 301, 309, 312

Natural things, 16–17, 91–92, 142–43, 146–61, 172–73, 251. *See also* Thing

Nature: as extended, 8–9, 42, 62, 95–96, 97, 104, 151, 155, 274; as thinking, 8–9, 42, 62, 95–96, 97, 151, 155, 274; all the phenomena, 9–10; as corporeal modes, 11, 42, 95–96, 104, 107; order of, 17–18, 45, 48, 84–85, 92, 104, 113, 143, 150, 253–54, 261; natured, 18–19, 42–43, 45, 62, 73–74, 94, 95, 98–99, 104, 116, 126–27, 133–39, 147, 150, 163–64, 204–5, 233, 294, 309; whole or entire, 18–19, 37–38, 42–43, 45–47, 58–59, 61, 63, 64–66, 68, 73–74, 80, 85–86, 90, 98–99, 111–12, 128–29, 140–41, 154–56, 158, 233–34, 251, 279–85, 294; Cartesian meanings, 22–23; unity, 23–25, 143, 154; consideration of, 33, 155–56; formality or formally in, 33, 95–96, 112, 257, 267, 293, 299; and definition of God, 34–35, 133–39, 294; as all-being, 37; surmodel divisions, 42–44, 233; naturing, 42–43, 45, 47–48, 62, 73–74, 94, 98–99, 112, 115–16, 126–27, 133–38, 204–5, 212, 233, 264–65, 294; usage of "nature", 44–50, 83–86, 89–90; outside of, 45, 64, 110–12, 179; theory or epistemic factor, 51–53, 232, 256–59; this and that sort, 55–56, 84, 97,

239, 294, 295; intradifferentiations, 59, 93, 110–12, 234–37, 260; manifestation through itself, 65, 231, 296, 311; and mind, 86–99; really or in nature, 93–94; all that exist in nature, 97, 143; exemplar pattern, 99; things and actions, 106, 112; "in the nature of things," 135–36, 242; divine nature, 136; naturating response, 175–77, 183–84, 209, 212, 276–78; living whole, 185; inclusive of religion, 227–29; "in the natural condition," 249; free power as divine right of nature, 251–53; substance and modes, 261; as nurturing and violent, 282, 314; manuscript capitalization of *"Natura,"* 294; as codex or book, 299, 304, 313; commonplace meanings, 301

"Nature-reading" procedure, 120

Necessity: in things, 16–18, 131, 160–61, 267; in God, 17–18, 160–61, 267; in system, 266–67

Negation, 159

Nelson, J. C., 306

Newton, Isaac, 256

Nielsen, Carl, 300–301

Nietzsche, Friedrich, 109, 207, 275

Nominalism and natural things, 16

Non-discreteness, 93–97. *See also* Connectivity; Interrelatedness; Order and connection

Notes to the Theological-Political Treatise, 30, 310

Notions, 104–5, 243–44

Objectively and really, 93–94, 117

Obligation, 19, 184–85

Oldenburg, Henry, 105, 168, 181, 201

Ontology, 85, 226, 258, 275–77

Opinion, 56

Order and connection, 85, 88, 92, 95, 98–99, 153–54, 160–61, 174–75, 212, 217, 260–62, 266–68

Orthological ethics, 312

"Our developed geometrical order," 174–75. *See also* Geometrical order and manner

Parable mentality, 214–15

Parkinson, G. H. R., 301–2, 304

Participants or sharers in divine nature, 205, 207, 251–53, 277–78

Particular or singular thing, 62, 146–61, 197

Partitiveness, 277–78

Pascal, Blaise, 277